Acquisitions, Mergers, Sales
and Takeovers:
A Handbook With Forms

Acquisitions, Mergers, Sales and Takeovers: A Handbook With Forms

CHARLES A. SCHARF

PRENTICE-HALL, INC.   Englewood Cliffs, N.J.

PRENTICE-HALL INTERNATIONAL, INC., *London*
PRENTICE-HALL OF AUSTRALIA, PTY. LTD., *Sydney*
PRENTICE-HALL OF CANADA, LTD., *Toronto*
PRENTICE-HALL OF INDIA PRIVATE LTD., *New Delhi*
PRENTICE-HALL OF JAPAN, INC., *Tokyo*

LIBRARY OF CONGRESS
CATALOG CARD NUMBER: 70-150711

Portions of this book first appeared in the author's work
Techniques for Buying, Selling and Merging Businesses,
published by Prentice-Hall, 1964.

Ninth Printing . . . . . July 1977

"This publication is designed to provide accurate
and authoritative information in regard to the subject matter covered. It is sold with the understanding that the publisher is not engaged in rendering
legal, accounting or other professional service. If
legal advice or other expert assistance is required,
the services of a competent professional person
should be sought.

*. . . From the Declaration of Principles jointly
adopted by a Committee of the American Bar
Association and a Committee of Publishers and
Associations.*"

PRINTED IN THE UNITED STATES OF AMERICA
ISBN-0-13-003053-8
B & P

To
RUTHIE

About the Author

Mr. Scharf is a practicing attorney, a member of the New York Bar. He has been involved for many years in all aspects of purchases, sales and mergers of businesses, and is a frequent speaker before business and professional organizations, including Corporate Seminars, Inc., Practicing Law Institute, and the American Management Association, on different phases of the acquisition process. He has also served as guest lecturer at the New York University School of Continuing Education.

He is the author of the book *"Techniques for Buying, Selling and Merging Businesses"* (1964) and a contributor to the *"Encyclopedia of Tax Procedures,"* both published by Prentice-Hall. His many articles include *"Tax Aspects"* in *"Trademark Problems in Acquisitions and Mergers,"* United States Trademark Association, Mellon Press, Inc., New York, 1968; *"Brokerage. Negotiation, and the Contract"* in the *"Business of Acquisition and Mergers,"* President's Publishing House, Inc., 1968; and *"Merging and Selling A Business to Complete an Estate Plan,"* in *"The Practical Lawyer,"* October 1966. Mr. Scharf has also assisted in the preparation of law tapes for the continuing education of the bar dealing with Securities and Exchange Commission problems involved in acquisitions.

Preface

This book describes how to acquire, sell, merge, and takeover businesses. In addition, it sets forth the rules governing the legal, tax, securities, and accounting aspects of acquisitions and takeovers.

It develops specific approaches to: (1) planning to buy or sell; (2) choosing a buyer or seller; (3) determining a price; (4) developing the strategy for takeovers—both tender offers and registered exchange offers; (5) developing the strategy to defend against takeovers; (6) negotiating the acquisition or sale, and drafting the detailed acquisition contract; (7) closing the transaction; and (8) generally avoiding or solving the numerous problems—business, legal, tax, or accounting which may arise at any and all phases of the acquisition process.

The book is written for all those who participate to any degree in business acquisitions or sales, or wish to learn about making such acquisitions or sales, and should be helpful to the reader regardless of his level of participation.

The businessman, from the chief executive officer responsible for acquisitions to the staff researcher, should find the forms of business forecasts, formulae for pricing acquisitions, suggestions with regard to brokerage arrangements, negotiating strategy, options, memoranda of intent, analyses of Securities and Exchange Commission problems, investment letters and forms of indemnity and escrow agreements of special value in making sound decisions in specific transactions.

Business brokers should find the forms of brokerage arrangements, suggestions for fee arrangements and handling brokerage problems, and general descriptions of the acquisition process helpful in their effort to close acquisitions and earn commissions.

Professionals, the lawyers and accountants, should find the pricing chapters, the numerous forms of agreement, analyses of tax, SEC, accounting and legal problems, and checklists of help in advising their clients.

The book is also a form book. It contains numerous samples including forms of business analyses of prospects, brokerage agreements, options, memoranda of intent, acquisition contracts, special acquisition contract clauses, business, financial, legal and closing checklists, and miscellaneous forms used in connection with acquisitions, such as investment letters and indemnity and escrow agreements. The forms should be of value to those both experienced and inexperienced in acquisitions.

A basic premise is stressed. *Coordinated effort between the businessman, the lawyer, and the accountant should be achieved in the attempt to buy or sell businesses successfully.* From this book, the businessman, the lawyer, and the accountant should have a better understanding of the problems faced by their collaborators, and each should improve his special expertise to contribute to successful solutions, not only of his own problems, but of the general problems which may arise in consummating acquisitions and takeovers. In this connection, the book explores the relationship of the businessman, the lawyer, and the accountant to each other and the interdependency of each upon the other two.

Essentially, the book's approach to the acquisition process is a chronological phase by phase approach. It starts with descriptions of types of acquisitions and definitions, then proceeds to initial planning and the choice and search for a particular buyer or seller, the formulation of strategy, the tactics for a takeover bid, (or, where both the buyer and seller are willing participants to the negotiation) negotiating techniques, pricing, preparation of the detailed contract, the closing, and finally, methods of integrating the buyer and seller.

Many a prospective acquisition or takeover presents serious problems which, however, the practitioner may solve—by applying imagination, experience, and knowledge.

CHARLES A. SCHARF

Contents

DEFINITIONS OF SOME GENERAL TERMS. *Buyer. Seller. Acquisition. Statutory Merger. Statutory Consolidation. Asset Acquisition. Stock Acquisition.* ADVANTAGES AND DISADVANTAGES OF FORMS OF TRANSACTIONS. *Statutory Merger—Advantages. Statutory Merger Disadvantages. Asset Acquisition—Advantages. Asset Acquisition—Disadvantages. Stock Acquisition—Advantages. Stock Acquisition—Disadvantages.* DEFINITIONS OF SOME TAX TERMS. *Tax-Free Acquisitions. Tax-Free Merger. Tax-Free Stock Acquisition. Tax-Free Asset Acquisition. Taxable Acquisition.* DEFINITIONS OF SOME SECURITIES TERMS. *Securities Act of 1933. Securities and Exchange Act of 1934. Takeover Bid. Tender Offer. Registered Exchange Offer. Aggressor Company. Target Company. Non-Public Corporation.*

CHAPTER 2. PLANNING AND CHOOSING THE BUSINESS
              TO BUY OR SELL 11

KNOWLEDGE OF OWN BUSINESS. *The Five-Year Forecast.* THE MAR-
KET. THE COMPETITION. THE COMPANY'S PERFORMANCE. THE
COMPANY'S FUTURE REQUIREMENTS. COMPANY'S OPERATIONS
SUMMARY. COMPANY CASH FLOW. PREPARATION OF LONG-
RANGE PLAN. *Internal Growth. Major Elements of the Plan. Initial Screen-
ing Criteria.* CHOOSING THE SPECIFIC COMPANY. *Sources of Recom-
mendations. Approaching the Seller.* CHOOSING A TARGET COMPANY.
Approach to a Takeover Candidate.

CHAPTER 3. BUSINESS FINDERS AND BROKERS 33

LEGAL PRINCIPLES. *Finder vs. Broker. Finder vs. Broker—Court Opin-
ions. Statute of Frauds. Requirement of Writing—Quantum Meruit Recovery.
Licensing Requirements. Business Opportunity Publishers. Conflict of Laws.
Contract of Employment. Contract—Express and Implied. Contract—Im-
plied. Contract—Ratification. Whose Agent Is the Broker? Time of Earning
Commission. Amount of Commissions or Fees. Duration of Contract. Revok-
ing the Contract.* AN APPROACH TO BROKERAGE. *Types of Brokerage
Agreements.*

CHAPTER 4. DETERMINING THE PURCHASE PRICE .. 49

VALUE VS. PRICE. SOME APPROACHES TO PRICE. *Book Value.
Appraisal. Comparison with Other Companies.* MARKET VALUE OF
LISTED STOCK. A PROPOSED PRICING FORMULA. PROJECTED
EARNINGS. *Isolating Seller's Projected Earnings. Seller's Past Earnings.
Past Earnings of Seller's Industry. Future Earnings.* PRICE/EARNINGS
RATIO. *Price/Earnings Ratio—Risk. Price/Earnings Ratio—Historical.
Price/Earnings Ratio—Current. Price/Earnings Ratio—Stock Market Value.*

CHAPTER 4.   DETERMINING THE PURCHASE PRICE
                                                    (*continued*)

High Stock Market P/E—Buyer Advantage. PRESENT VALUE OF FU-
TURE EARNINGS. ADDITIONAL NECESSARY PRICE CONSIDERA-
TIONS. EFFECT OF METHOD OF PAYMENT. *Stock vs. Cash. Stock vs.
Convertible Debentures. Inventory Purchase. Loans. Installment Payments.
Contingent Purchase Price.* POSSIBLE PRICE INCREASES. LIMITS ON
MAXIMUM PRICE. *Earnings Per Share. Return on Investment.*

CHAPTER 5.   CONDUCTING THE NEGOTIATION AND
                    COORDINATING THE INVESTIGATION   71

THE NEGOTIATION. *The Negotiating Team. Negotiating Objectives. The
Desire for Secrecy.* THE INVESTIGATION. *Coordination of Effort. Cor-
relating the Information. Nature of Business. The Investigation—Business.
The Investigation—Legal. The Investigation—Accounting.* THE ACQUISI-
TION TIMETABLE. THE BUSINESS INVESTIGATION CHECKLIST.
THE LEGAL INVESTIGATION CHECKLIST.

CHAPTER 6.   INITIAL LEGAL CONSIDERATIONS   115

Legal Problems—Buyer. Legal Problems—Seller. UNINTENDED ASSUMP-
TION OF SELLER'S LIABILITIES—A BUYER PROBLEM. *Trust Fund
Theory. Other Theories. Collective Bargaining Contracts.* ANTI-TRUST
PROBLEMS—A BUYER PROBLEM. *Anti-Trust Problems—General.
Clayton Act, Section 7. Clayton Act, Section 7—"Acquisition." Clayton Act,
Section 7—"Line of Commerce." Clayton Act, Section 7—"Section of the
Country." Clayton Act, Section 7—"Tendency to Lessen Competition." Fed-
eral Trade Commission Notification Requirements. Past Anti-Trust Viola-
tions. Future Anti-Trust Violations.* STOCK EXCHANGE REQUIRE-
MENTS—A BUYER PROBLEM. STATE "BLUE SKY" LAWS—A

CHAPTER 6. INITIAL LEGAL CONSIDERATIONS
(continued)

BUYER PROBLEM. *Uniform Securities Act. Effect of Non-Compliance.* INSIDERS AND INSIDE INFORMATION—A SELLER PROBLEM. SELLING CONTROL—A SELLER PROBLEM.

CHAPTER 7. GENERAL CONSIDERATIONS IN STRUCTURING ACQUISITIONS

POOLING OF INTERESTS. *"Purchase"—Goodwill. "Pooling of Interests" —No Goodwill. The "Purchase"—An Example. "Pooling of Interests"—the Same Example. Accounting Criteria of a "Pooling of Interests." "Pooling" Criteria—Historical Background. Pooling of Interests—Current General Conditions. Attributes of the Buyer and Seller—Two Conditions. Manner of Effecting the Acquisition—Eight Conditions. Absence of Planned Transactions—Three Conditions.* STATE CORPORATION LAWS. FAVORABLE OR UNFAVORABLE CHARTER. NUMBER OF SHAREHOLDERS. PENSION, PROFIT-SHARING AND STOCK OPTION PLANS. NON-ASSIGNABILITY OF CONTRACTS. BANK LOAN AGREEMENTS. BULK SALES LAWS. INVESTMENT LETTER. SALES AND USE TAXES.

CHAPTER 8. SECURITIES AND EXCHANGE COMMISSION PROBLEMS—ACQUISITIONS

THE LAW AND SEC RULES. *Registration Requirements. The Buyer— Issuer. The Seller's Stockholders—Underwriters. The Practical Problem. Non-Public Offering Exemption—the Buyer. Rule 133 Exemption—the Buyer and the Seller's Stockholders. Applicability of Rule 133. The Required*

CHAPTER 8.   SECURITIES AND EXCHANGE
COMMISSION PROBLEMS—ACQUISITIONS
(continued)

Stockholders' Vote. Selling Stockholders. Restrictions on Controlling Stock-holders. Limitations on Shares Sold. Additional Restrictions in Rule 133. Uncertainties Under Rule 133. Uncertainties Under Rule 133. Investment Stock Restrictions—Seller's Stockholders. PROPOSED SEC RULE CHANGES. *Proposed Rule 181—Non-Public Offering. Proposed "160 Series" Rules—Underwriter. Proposed Rule 144—Underwriter.* CONCLUSION.

CHAPTER 9.   SECURITIES AND EXCHANGE
COMMISSION PROBLEMS—TAKEOVER BIDS 159

THE TENDER OFFER. *Pre-Williams Bill Tender. The Williams Bill. Form of Tender. Substantive Safeguards—Withdrawal of Tendered Shares. Substantive Safeguards—Pro Rata Acceptance. Substantive Safeguards—Price Increase. Tender Offer—Open Period. Tender Offer—Tax Consequences. State Statutory Law. State Common Law—The Offeror. State Common Law —The Target Company. The Williams Bill—The Target Company. Stockholder Lists. Rule 10b-5. Open Market Purchases. Section 16(b).* REGISTERED EXCHANGE OFFER. *Registration Statement. Open Market Stock Purchases. Rule 135 Statement. Target Company Information. Percentage of Ownership. Advantage of Registered Exchange Offer. Disadvantages of Registered Exchange Offers.* DEFENDING AGAINST TAKEOVER BIDS. *Operating Performance. Nature of Assets. Preliminary Defensive Considerations. Procedural Safeguards. Stockholder Relations. Defensive Merger Candidate. Preliminary Defensive Steps—Corporate Structure. Charter and By-Laws. Authorized Stock. Pre-emptive Rights. By-Laws. Preliminary Defensive Steps—Business. Stock Purchases. Contracts, Defensive Maneuvers to an Actual Takeover Bid. Schedule 14D. Possible Litigation. Publicity and Communications. Defensive Merger. Counter-Takeover Bid.*

CHAPTER 10. TAX CONSIDERATIONS—TAX-FREE VS. TAXABLE ACQUISITIONS 175

Tax Objectives of Seller. Tax-Free Transaction—Seller's Objectives. Taxable Transaction—General Objectives of Seller. Taxable Transaction—Seller's Objectives in Allocating the Purchase Price. Taxable Transaction—Seller's Desire to Delay Tax. TAX OBJECTIVES OF BUYER. *"Tax-Free" and Taxable Transactions—Buyer's Objectives. Taxable Transaction—Buyer's Objectives in Allocating the Purchase Price.* "TAX-FREE" *vs.* "TAXABLE" ACQUISITION. THE "TAX-FREE" ACQUISITION. *General. Merger or Consolidation. Merger—Procedure. Merger—Controlled Corporation. Merger vs. Stock or Asset Acquisition. Stock-for-Stock Acquisitions. Stock Transaction—Solely Voting Stock. Control. Stock Acquisition —by Subsidiary. Stock-for-Assets Acquisitions. Asset Transaction—Solely Voting Stock. Substantially All of the Properties. Asset Acquisition—by Subsidiary. Effects on Stockholders. Receipt of Other Property. Amount of Gain. Effect on Corporations. Non-Statutory Problems in Tax-Free Acquisitions. Business Purpose. Step Transaction. Continuity of Interest.*

CHAPTER 11. TAX CONSIDERATIONS—ADDITIONAL TAX PROBLEMS IN ACQUISITIONS 193

INSTALLMENT SALES. *Installment Sale—Requirements. Installment Sale —Tax Treatment. Evidences of Indebtedness—Exceptions.* IMPUTED INTEREST. *Payments to which Section 483 Applies. Unstated Interest— Calculation. Imputed Interest—Some Examples.* TAXABLE SALE OF ASSETS—SECTION 337. *Section 337—Requirements. Section 337—Inventory. Section 337—Recognition of Loss. Section 337—Depreciation and Investment Credit Recapture.* PREFERRED STOCK—SECTION 306 STOCK. *Section 306 Stock—Definition. Substantially the Same as Stock Dividend. Sale of Section 306 Stock—Tax Effect. Some Exceptions to Ordinary Income Tax Treatment. Section 306 Stock—Seller's Approach.* FOREIGN CORPORATIONS. COLLAPSIBLE CORPORATION—SECTION 341. NET OPERATING LOSS CARRYOVERS. *Reduction in Loss Carryover. Amount of Reduction. Taxable Acquisitions—Net Operating*

CHAPTER 11. TAX CONSIDERATIONS—ADDITIONAL
TAX PROBLEMS IN ACQUISITIONS
(continued)

Loss Carryovers. Net Operating Loss Carryovers—Section 269 Disallowance. BUYING STOCK TO ACQUIRE ASSETS—SECTION 334(b)(2). INTEREST ON ACQUISITION INDEBTEDNESS. *Corporate Acquisition Indebtedness—Definition. Ratio of Debt to Equity—Explanation. Earnings Test—Explained.* DISSENTING STOCKHOLDERS. *Substantially All of Seller's Assets—Dissenting Stockholders. Solely Voting Stock Test—Dissenting Stockholders. 80% Control—Dissenting Stockholders.* DEPRECIATION AND INVESTMENT CREDIT RECAPTURE. *Taxable Transaction—Recapture Problems. Depreciation Recapture—Personal Property. Depreciation Recapture—Real Estate. Investment Credit Recapture.*

OPTIONS AND MEMORANDA OF INTENT. *The Option. Option—Acquisition Contract Attached. Conditional Option. Restrictive Letter. Memorandum or Letter of Intent. Oral Understanding. Conclusions. A Restrictive Letter—Form. Letter of Intent—Form.* THE CONTRACT. *Representations and Warranties. A Source of Information. Time Periods. Description of Transaction. Representations of Seller.*

GENERAL STATEMENT OF AGREEMENT. REPRESENTATIONS AND WARRANTIES OF SELLER. REPRESENTATIONS AND WARRANTIES OF BUYER. ASSETS ACQUIRED BY BUYER. PAYMENT OF PURCHASE PRICE. BUYER'S ASSUMPTION OF LIABILITIES. SELLER'S INDEMNIFICATION OF BUYER. CONDUCT OF BUSINESS PENDING CLOSING. CONDITIONS PRECEDENT TO THE CLOSING. PLAN OF REORGANIZATION. BROKERAGE. GENERAL PROVISIONS.

*Acquisitions, Mergers, Sales
and Takeovers:
A Handbook With Forms*

CHAPTER 1

Types of Acquisitions and Definitions

During the decade of the 1960's, and extending into the 1970's, acquisitions and mergers among American business corporations took place in numbers never before equaled in the history of the United States. During this period, in addition to the traditional merger or acquisition involving two willing parties, a second type of acquisition, the takeover, gained popularity. The traditional acquisition is the negotiated acquisition, in which a willing buyer and a willing seller negotiate the terms under which an acquisition or merger occurs. In the second type of acquisition, the takeover, a seller's management may oppose the acquisition or merger, but the buyer makes a direct bid to the seller's stockholders to acquire the seller's stock—and thus control of the seller.

Regardless of the method of acquisition, whether by traditional acquisition or by takeover, in many instances buyers make acquisitions to accomplish specific business objectives which may be comparatively limited in scope. These objectives of a buyer may relate to the solution of specific business problems which may arise in any business—such as the need for new products, plant facilities, patents, sales capability, or personnel. From a seller's point of view, objectives may also be as varied as the problems which may arise in a seller's business. A seller may wish to retire or obtain additional financing or plant facilities, or research assistance, or obtain marketable securities in exchange for closely held securities for which there is no market.

Contrary to acquisitions by which the buyer seeks to solve specific business problems, the 1960's also witnessed substantial growth in the number of acquisitions by corporations which became known as "conglomerates," because they brought under single control many different and often unrelated businesses. Acquisitions by conglomerates often appear to have no other

1

business purpose than to increase the size of the conglomerate and to increase the earnings reported to stockholders—thus, hopefully, to increase or maintain the price/earnings ratios of the stocks of the conglomerates in the marketplace.

As mentioned, acquisitions have traditionally been considered as a merger of two willing partners. In the second half of the 1960's the takeover bid, in the form of a tender offer or a registered exchange offer gained popularity. If management of a prospective selling company was unwilling to negotiate a transaction with a prospective buyer, the buyer attempted to accomplish the acquisition by a takeover bid—offering to buy the stock of the seller directly from the stockholders of the seller. The offer could be made either for cash, or for stock and other securities of the buyer, or any combination of cash and securities. During 1968 and 1969 it became an almost daily occurrence to see an advertisement in the daily newspapers by a buyer offering to buy the stock of stockholders of a prospective target company.

The technique of offering to buy stock directly from selling stockholders has always been available, but until the technique gained general acceptance, offers made directly to stockholders of a corporation over the objections of a corporation's management generally imposed upon the offeror the label of a "raider." By the mid-1960's, the takeover bid in the form of a tender offer or registered exchange offer became an accepted and respectable method to accomplish acquisitions, where a seller's management opposed the acquisition.

Toward the end of the 1960's, both the conglomerate corporation and the takeover bid came under attack from various sources, and were subjected to varying degrees of threatened regulation. The conglomerates came under attack in the marketplace because of the methods of accounting which they employed, as well as concern for their ability to manage the varied businesses which they had acquired. The Justice Department also expressed concern that their rapid growth might have detrimental effects upon competition. The takeover bid came under attack for less obvious reasons, and resulted in the passage of the so-called "Williams Bill" to regulate cash tender offers. This bill provides for the filing of specified information with the Securities and Exchange Commission by any person intending to offer cash for publicly held stock.

Acquisitions on the one hand, involving two willing partners, and takeover bids on the other, involving an unwilling seller, require the use of different techniques to be successful and are subject to different regulatory requirements. In subsequent chapters in this book, in describing different techniques and legal, accounting, and regulatory requirements which effect acquisitions, an effort is made to distinguish between acquisitions involving willing partners and takeovers.

Before proceeding to a discussion of techniques for accomplishing acquisitions and take-overs in the varied forms they may assume, a general attempt to define terms used in this book and their meaning *as used in this book* should help clarify and make more understandable the different techniques employed to accomplish acquisitions and takeovers. In addition, this chapter includes a general brief description of the basic forms of acquisitions, and their advantages and disadvantages to illustrate the possible alternatives available in choosing forms of acquisitions.

DEFINITIONS OF SOME GENERAL TERMS

Acquisitions may take a number of different forms. They may involve acquisitions of a going business, including all or a part of a corporation's assets, or they may involve acquisitions of stock from the stockholders of a corporation. In one acquisition a particular problem area involving either corporate law, tax law, or securities law, may be of greater importance or present more difficult problems than the same area in another acquisition. Areas of difficulty will vary with differing circumstances of different acquisitions. The first group of definitions set forth below involves terms used in discussing acquisitions generally, without any particular emphasis on any specific possible problem area.

Buyer. The term "buyer" is limited to a corporation. This book concerns itself with acquisitions and mergers between corporate entities, and transactions which involve other types of legal entities such as individual proprietorships and partnerships as buyers are not considered. Thus, a buyer is a corporation which acquires the assets or stock of a seller.

Seller. A "seller" is also generally a corporation. However, in some situations where the selling business is owned by comparatively few individuals, sometimes members of a single family, the ownership may take the form of a number of different legal entities including a private corporation, a partnership, an individual proprietorship, or a trust. Though the term "seller" generally will mean corporation, it may also include a partnership, individual proprietorship, or trust, or any combination of such entities where all or a portion of the business being acquired is owned in other than corporate form.

Acquisition. The term "acquisition" is used to describe any transaction in which a buyer acquires all or part of the assets and business of a seller, or all or part of the stock or other securities of the seller, where the transaction is closed between a willing buyer and a willing seller, i.e., a seller whose management agrees to the acquisition and helps negotiate its terms. The element of willingness on the part of both the buyer and seller distinguishes an acquisition from a takeover, in which the seller's management is an unwilling partner to the combination of corporate entities. Provided the element of willingness is present, the mechanics for accomplishing a transaction will not effect its status as an acquisition. Included within the general term "acquisition" are more specific forms of transactions such as (1) a merger, (2) a consolidation, (3) an asset acquisition, and (4) a stock acquisition.

Statutory Merger. A "statutory merger" is a combination of two corporations pursuant to the requirements and procedures set forth in the corporation laws of the states of incorporation. Generally, merger statutes require that both boards of directors of the corporations approve and recommend the merger to the stockholders, and that the stockholders of each corporation approve the merger by a required favorable vote—normally two-thirds. In a statutory merger, one of the two corporations is merged into the other corporation—the latter generally being referred to as the surviving corporation. Under state law, the surviving corporation becomes the owner of all of the assets, business, and liabilities of the merged corporation by operation of law, i.e., automatically, at the time the necessary statutory merger certificate is filed with the Secretary of State of the surviving corporation. Specific title transfer documents are not required to transfer title to the business to the surviving corporation. Upon completion of a statutory merger, one of the two corporations involved falls heir to the combined assets and business, as well as all of the liabilities of the two parties to the merger; the other corporation disappears, and the disappearing corporation's stockholders normally substitute an equity interest in the surviving corporation for their equity interest in the disappearing corporation. Since a statutory merger requires the approval of the boards of directors and stockholders of both corporations, the statutory merger is an acquisition as opposed to a takeover.

Statutory Consolidation. A "consolidation" is also an acquisition which involves a combination of two corporations pursuant to state corporation laws. However, contrary to a statutory merger, both of the merged corporations disappear in a consolidation. A third corporation is formed and both of the corporations to be consolidated are merged into the new corporation. The new corporation becomes the survivor corporation and the heir to the combined assets and business, as well as all of the liabilities, of the two corporations which are consolidated into it. The two corporations thereupon cease to exist. As in the case of a statutory merger, a consolidation requires the approval of the boards of directors and stockholders of both corporations.

Asset Acquisition. An "asset acquisition" is an acquisition in which the buyer acquires all or a part of the assets and business of the seller, pursuant to a contract entered into between the buyer and seller. The asset acquisition may require the approval of the seller's stockholders, but generally not the buyer's. It is distinguishable from a stock acquisition in that assets of a seller are acquired—not stock of a seller's stockholders. It is distinguished from a statutory merger and a consolidation in that the transfer of title to the seller's assets is not effected by operation of law, but specific instruments of title must be delivered from the seller to transfer legal title to the buyer. The consideration paid by the buyer may be in any form, including cash, property, common or preferred stock, or bonds or debentures or other securities; the corporate structure of the seller remains intact; and ownership of stock by the stockholders of the seller is not affected. However, the seller may subsequently be liquidated and the stockholders of the seller, upon such liquidation, will receive the cash and securities paid for the assets of the seller as well as any other assets of the seller which were not sold to the buyer. Generally, where substantially all of the assets and business of a seller are sold, the second step, i.e., a liquidation of the seller, follows.

Stock Acquisition. A "stock acquisition" is an acquisition is which all or a part of the outstanding stock of the seller is acquired from the stockholders of the seller. As in the case of an asset acquisition, the stock of the seller may be bought for any property, including cash, common or preferred stocks, or debt securities, or any combination of such property. A stock acquisition does not require the consent of the management of the seller, but involves a direct contractual relationship between the buyer and the stockholders of the seller. Management of the seller may be opposed to the offer to purchase the stock of the seller and in such instances, the offer to purchase the stock is a takeover bid.

ADVANTAGES AND DISADVANTAGES OF FORMS
OF TRANSACTIONS

Statutory Merger—Advantages. Some of the advantages of a statutory merger are the following:

(1) Simplicity of title transfers. In a statutory merger, transfers of title to the assets of the

seller take place by operation of law. The filing of the merger certificate with the Secretary of State of the state of incorporation of the continuing corporation effects an automatic transfer of title to the assets of the seller. The numerous documents transferring titles which are required in an asset acquisition, i.e., deeds to real estate, bills of sale, assignments of patents, assignments of leases, assignments of licenses, franchises and miscellaneous contracts, etc., need not be prepared and separately delivered.

(2) Flexibility in the type of securities issued. In a tax-free acquisition, a statutory merger permits the issuance of preferred stocks and even, under some circumstances, debt securities without effecting the tax-free nature of the transaction; whereas in both an asset transaction and a stock transaction, with minor exceptions, only voting stock may be issued if the transaction is to qualify as tax-free.

(3) Elimination of minority interests. Under merger statutes, minority stockholders who object to a transaction generally have a right to dissent and have their shares purchased for cash at fair value. The appraisal procedure eliminates minority stockholders who object to the transaction, and results in 100% ownership of the seller by the buyer.

(4) Opportunity for charter amendment. Since meetings of the stockholders of both corporations are generally required in a statutory merger, dual meetings provide an opportunity to amend the corporate charter and adapt it to the needs of the continuing enterprise.

(5) Reverse merger. In a statutory merger, if the seller has valuable assets, such as franchises, which are not transferable even by operation of law, a reverse merger procedure may be instituted in which the seller becomes the surviving corporation.

Statutory Merger—Disadvantages. Some of the disadvantages of a statutory merger are the following:

(1) Assumption of liabilities. The continuing corporation remains liable for all of the liabilities and obligations of the combined enterprise, including all of the liabilities and obligations of the selling corporation, whether disclosed, or undisclosed, known or unknown, contingent or otherwise. This assumption of obligations and liabilities occurs through operation of law.

(2) Stockholders' meetings. Two stockholders' meetings, of both the buyer and seller, are generally required to approve the transaction. Normally a two-thirds favorable vote of the stockholders of each corporation is required, and each corporation must go through the expense of preparation of proxy material and mailing of notices of meeting, etc.

(3) Dissenters' rights. Generally, stockholders of both corporations have the right to dissent from the transaction and be paid off in cash. A large number of dissents may result in a substantial cash drain on the combined entity.

(4) Timing. Notice requirements to stockholders with respect to stockholders' meetings may cause delay in consummating the statutory merger.

(5) State merger statutes. Peculiarities of state merger statutes may limit types of transactions which may qualify for statutory mergers. Some states permit a merger only between corporations engaged in substantially the same business, and some states prohibit mergers where a foreign corporation is to become the surviving corporation.

Asset Acquisition—Advantages. Some of the advantages of an asset acquisition are the following:

(1) Elimination of minority interests. A buyer may obtain 100% control of a seller's

business; as in a statutory merger, in an asset transaction, a minority stockholder generally has no rights beyond the right to dissent and be paid off in cash.

(2) One stockholders' meeting. Only one stockholders' meeting is normally required, namely the meeting of the stockholders of the seller, although circumstances may exist in which a meeting of the stockholders of the buyer may also be required.

(3) No right of appraisal. In some instances, a seller's stockholders may not have a right of appraisal in an asset transaction. Under Delaware law, the right of appraisal of a seller's stockholders is limited to a statutory merger transaction; a stockholder in a corporation which sells substantially all of its assets may vote against the transaction, but if the transaction is approved by a sufficient vote of stockholders, the stockholder opposing the transaction is bound by the vote of the approving stockholders.

(4) Limiting liabilities. The liabilities to be assumed by the buyer may be designated in the contact, and the buyer may, subject to exceptions under special circumstances, avoid the assumption of undisclosed liabilities.

(5) Allocation of purchase price. From an income tax point of view, the buyer and seller may allocate the purchase price to specific assets in the acquisition agreement where such allocation has significant tax consequences. In an arm's length transaction between a buyer and seller where the allocation is reasonable, the allocation should generally fix the tax consequences of the transaction.

Asset Acquisition—Disadvantages. Some of the disadvantages of an asset acquisition are the following:

(1) Complexity. Of the three basic types of acquisition, the asset acquisition is the most complex from the viewpoint of the preparation of documents for the transfer of titles to assets. In asset transactions, separate instruments of assignment must be prepared, and then executed and delivered at the closing to transfer title to real property, personal property, leases, contracts, franchises, and intangible assets, such as patents and copyrights. Preparation and filing of such title documents is time consuming and expensive.

(2) De facto merger. Asset acquisitions, where the consideration involves securities of a buyer, may be construed as de facto mergers by courts long after the transaction has closed. In such instances, the transaction may be voided due to failure of proper notice to stockholders, stockholders may have rights of appraisal not previously granted, or a buyer may have assumed undisclosed liabilities of a seller as though a statutory merger had actually occurred.

(3) Consents to transfers. Consents may be required with respect to nonassignable contracts such as real property leases, license agreements, and franchises. Often, consents of third parties may be difficult or expensive to obtain.

(4) Bulk sales laws. In order to avoid liability to creditors of the seller, it may be necessary to comply with the bulk sales laws of the jurisdictions in which the seller's assets are located. Such compliance may be disruptive of the seller's business or expensive.

(5) Loan agreement restrictions. Long-term debt obligations of the seller, as set forth in loan agreements, may contain restrictions against sale and be accelerated by the sale.

(6) As in the case of a statutory merger, a meeting of stockholders must often be held, with possible expense and delay.

Stock Acquisition—Advantages. Some of the advantages of a stock acquisition are the following:

(1) Simplicity. Where the seller is a non-public corporation with comparatively few stockholders, the stock acquisition may be the simplest form of acquisition to consummate. From the seller's point of view, the only documents required to be delivered to effectively transfer title are the certificates representing the outstanding shares of the seller's stock, properly endorsed.

(2) Non-assignability problems. Since in a stock transaction the corporate structure of the seller continues intact and the conduct of the seller's business is not affected by the transfer of stock ownership, no problems arise with respect to the assignability of leases or other contracts requiring the consents of third parties to their assignment.

(3) Speed. Because of the simplicity of the transfer of the certificates representing shares of the seller's stock, unless the stock acquisition is contingent upon the receipt of rulings from governmental agencies, it may be accomplished in a short period of time. Since normally there is no requirement for holding stockholders' meetings in a stock transaction, the delay involved in giving notices or having proxy material cleared by the Securities and Exchange Commission are avoided.

(4) Unwilling management. In a stock transaction no approval of the board of directors of the seller is required. As a consequence, in those instances where a seller's management is opposed to an acquisition, the buyer may complete the acquisition in the form of a takeover by acquiring a controlling stock interest directly from the seller's stockholders.

(5) Seller's liabilities. In a stock acquisition where the seller remains a separate corporate entity from the buyer, the seller's liabilities are not assumed directly by the buyer. The seller's corporate entity remains liable for such liabilities and obligations, and the buyer does not become directly obligated with respect to the liabilities of the seller.

Stock Acquisition—Disadvantages. Some of the disadvantages of a stock acquisition are the following:

(1) Liabilities. The business and assets of the seller remain subject to all liabilities including unknown liabilities, since the corporate structure and business of the seller are not affected by the transfer of stock ownership. A buyer may not, by contract, limit the assumption of seller's liabilities to those specified in the acquisition contract, although the buyer may remain insulated from direct responsibility for the seller's liabilities.

(2) Minority interests. If any of the stockholders of the seller refuse to sell their stock interests, they remain an outstanding minority with a continuing interest in the seller's business.

(3) Allocation of purchase price. Where stock is acquired, from an income tax point of view, a contract may not be negotiated on an arm's length basis which will permit the allocation of purchase price to specified assets. Appraisals of the assets may not be as effective to bind the Internal Revenue Service should the seller subsequently be liquidated into the buyer.

(4) Depreciation recapture. Where a buyer acquires a seller's stock, from an income tax point of view, any inchoate payment with respect to depreciation recapture or investment credit recapture on the seller's assets is shifted to the buyer. The buyer may become liable for the payment of such recapture items should the buyer liquidate the seller after having acquired the seller's stock.

(5) SEC registration requirements. If the seller has a substantial number of stockholders, the issuance or transfer of securities by the buyer in the stock acquisition will have to be registered with the Securities and Exchange Commission.

(6) Fiduciary obligations of controlling stockholders. The controlling stockholders of the seller may have a fiduciary obligation to the minority stockholders to see that the minority are offered the same price per share as the controlling stockholders.

DEFINITIONS OF SOME TAX TERMS

The group of definitions contained in the section below are definitions of income tax terms. Under the Internal Revenue Code, certain types of corporate "reorganizations" are permitted to be accomplished on a "tax-free" basis. Section 368(a)(1) of the Internal Revenue Code defines six different corporate reorganizations which may be accomplished on a tax-free basis; of these six, the first three types of tax-free reorganizations are those of basic importance to acquisitions.

Tax-Free Acquisitions. A "tax-free acquisition" is one in which the acquisition, generally speaking, does not involve a taxable event, i.e., a seller or a seller's stockholder is not required to report gain or loss as a result of the acquisition, in the tax return for the fiscal year in which the acquisition occurs. Because of carryovers of costs or tax bases of assets in a tax-free acquisition—because such costs or bases remain the same—gain or loss may be reportable for tax purposes when the assets or stock with a carryover tax basis are sold or transferred in a taxable transaction in the future. In this sense, a tax-free acquisition should be considered to involve a tax postponement rather than a tax forgiveness; where the consideration received tax-free at the time of the acquisition is subsequently sold in a taxable transaction the amount of taxable gain or recognizable loss is determined by the carryover tax basis of the assets or stock sold. To further complicate tax considerations, in certain types of tax-free acquisitions a portion of the consideration may be taxable to the seller or the seller's stockholders, and in such situations the entire transaction may not be tax-free. The three types of tax-free reorganizations most often utilized in acquisitions to achieve tax-free status are defined below. The detailed requirements and tax consequences of such tax-free acquisitions as well as taxable acquisitions are described in Chapters 10 and 11.

Tax-Free Merger. Generally, three definitions of corporate reorganizations contained in Section 368(a)(1) of the Internal Revenue Code of 1954, as amended, determine whether or not a particular acquisition is tax-free. The first of these definitions, contained in paragraph (A) of the Section, states that a corporation reorganization means "a statutory merger or consolidation." When we speak of a "tax-free merger" or a "tax-free consolidation," we mean a statutory merger or a statutory consolidation which qualifies as a "reorganization" under the definition contained in the Internal Revenue Code, as well as under court imposed tests. This type of tax-free merger is often referred to as an "A" reorganization.

Tax-Free Stock Acquisition. The second definition of a corporate "reorganization" is contained in paragraph (B) of Section 368(a)(1) of the Internal Revenue Code. This paragraph provides in part that the term "reorganization" means "the acquisition by one corporation, in exchange solely for all or a part of its voting stock . . . , of stock of another corporation, if, immediately after the acquisition, the acquiring corporation has control of such other corporation. . . ." When the term "tax-free stock acquisition" is used, it means an acquisition of *stock of a seller* in exchange for solely voting stock of a buyer which qualifies as a "reorganization" under the definition contained in the Internal Revenue Code as well as under court imposed tests. This type of tax-free stock acquisition is often referred to as "B" reorganization.

Tax-Free Asset Acquisition. The third definition of a corporate "reorganization" is contained in paragraph (C) of Section 368(a)(1) of the Internal Revenue Code. This paragraph provides in part that the term "reorganization" means "the acquisition by one corporation, in exchange solely for all or a part of its voting stock . . . , of substantially all of the properties of another corporation. . . ." When the term "tax-free asset acquisition" is used, it means an acquisition of substantially all of the *assets of a seller* in exchange for voting stock of a buyer which qualifies as a "reorganization" under the definition contained in the Internal Revenue Code, as well as under court imposed tests. This type of tax-free asset acquisition is often referred to as a "C" reorganization.

Taxable Acquisition. A "taxable acquisition" is one which does not meet any of the definitions of tax-free reorganizations contained in the Internal Revenue Code. In a taxable acquisition, the transfer by a buyer of cash or stock and other securities for assets or stock of a seller triggers a taxable event and results in income, or gain or loss, which is includable in the income tax return of the seller or its stockholders for the fiscal year in which the acquisition takes place.

DEFINITIONS OF SOME SECURITIES TERMS

The Securities Act of 1933 and the Securities and Exchange Act of 1934 set forth certain requirements to be met by a buyer which utilizes securities to make an acquisition or which makes a tender offer for the stock of a seller's stockholders.

Under the Securities Act of 1933, unless an exemption applies to an offering, any offering by an issuer of its own securities for the business or stock of a seller is unlawful unless a registration statement is in effect with respect to the offering of the securities. One statutory exemption often of importance to buyers and sellers in acquisitions is an offering of stock or securities by an issuer not involving any public offering.

Under the Securities and Exchange Act of 1934, as amended by the Williams Bill, tender offers which are made for cash also require specified information to be filed and specified procedures to be followed.

Securities Act of 1933. The Securities Act of 1933 is the act which generally sets forth the requirements for filling registration statements of securities used in making acquisitions, as well as the form and content of such registration statements.

Securities and Exchange Act of 1934. The Securities and Exchange Act of 1934 generally sets forth the requirements for proxy material which must be submitted to stockholders in connection with stockholders' meetings held for the purpose of approving statutory mergers, consolidations, or sales of assets in connection with acquisitions. It also contains the requirements which must be met by a buyer in connection with a tender offer.

Takeover Bid. A "takeover bid" means an offer by a buyer to purchase stock of a seller where the management of the seller objects to the offer. In a takeover bid, the offer to purchase stock is made to the stockholders of the seller, generally through newspaper advertisements, or by direct communication with the stockholders of the seller where they are known to the buyer. Takeover bids may differ in the type of consideration offered by the buyer. The buyer may offer to purchase the seller's stock for cash, on the one hand, or for stock or securities, on the other hand.

Tender Offer. A "tender offer" is a takeover bid in which the buyer offers to acquire stock for cash. The distinguishing feature of a tender offer is that the takeover bid made by the buyer is made for cash. Tender offers are subject to the requirements contained in the Securities and Exchange Act of 1934, as amended by the Williams Bill, which are treated in detail in Chapter 9.

Registered Exchange Offer. A "registered exchange offer" is a takeover bid in which the buyer offers to acquire the stock of the seller in exchange for stock or other securities of the buyer. The distinguishing feature of a registered exchange offer, as opposed to a tender offer, is that the offer of the buyer is made in the form of stock or securities of the buyer, rather than for cash. The registered exchange offer is not subject to the requirements of the Williams Bill, but is subject to the general registration requirements discussed in Chapter 8 and 9. Both the tender offer and the registered exchange offer may be takeover bids, where the buyer is seeking control of the seller over the objection of the seller's management. The distinction between the two, however, is that the tender offer is for cash, whereas the registered exchange offer is for stock or other securities of the buyer.

Aggressor Company. An "aggressor company" or "aggressor" is a buyer which attempts to gain control of a seller through a takeover bid, whether such bid involves a tender offer or a registered exchange offer.

Target Company. A "target company" or "target" is a seller which is the subject of a takeover bid, whether such bid is in the form of a tender offer or registered exchange offer.

Non-public Corporation. A "non-public corporation" involves a distinction between a closely held corporation and a public corporation. The dividing line between the two may be shadowy. Generally, a closely held corporation means that the stockholders of 100% of the stock are relatively few, for our purposes no more than twenty-five individuals, whereas the public corporation is a corporation whose shares are more widely held. The distinction between the two types of corporations will be alluded to from time to time and may be of significant importance in connection with Securities and Exchange Commission rules and regulations.

To summarize, purchases of businesses may be made with the approval of the management of the seller, or over the objections of the management of the seller. Where the seller's management approves of the transaction, it is generally referred to as an acquisition; where the management disapproves, as a takeover. Acquisitions may be divided into three basic types, mergers, stock acquisitions, and asset acquisitions. Takeovers may be divided into two types, tender offers and registered exchange offers. From an income tax point of view both acquisitions and takeovers may be classified as taxable or tax-free, and from a Securities and Exchange Commission view, both acquisitions and takeovers may require the filing of a registration statement or be exempt from such filing requirements.

CHAPTER 2

*Planning and Choosing the Business
to Buy or Sell*

Many large corporations actively engaged in growth through acquisitions make permanent committees responsible for recommendations of purchases or sales of business units. These committees often report directly to the chief executive officer, and once a recommendation has been approved, these committees have the responsibility of negotiating the details and closing the transaction. Although smaller corporations not actively engaged in making acquisitions may find it impractical to establish groups which are responsible for acquisitions on a permanent basis, such corporations may nevertheless benefit by utilizing techniques employed by permanent committees such as are discussed below.

This study of techniques employed to choose a particular business unit for purchase or sale, is based on the assumption that the purpose underlying the purchase or sale is the strengthening of the buying or selling company and its continuation in business. Situations in which the acquiring company buys a business in order to siphon off its cash and similar assets and then liquidate the acquired company, or situations in which the company selling a business unit wishes to go out of business are not treated in detail, but even in these instances, the techniques we will discuss will help decide the company to be bought or the company to which the seller may best sell.

Where the objectives of the buyer are orientated primarily to the financial marketplace, encompassing such goals as building a conglomerate, increasing the price/earnings ratio of the buyer's stock by acquiring "glamour" businesses, increasing the buyer's reported earnings per share by continued acquisitions on a "pooling of interests" accounting basis, and generally conducting an acquisition program to increase the price of the buyer's stock on a stock exchange, different criteria for choosing a company to buy or a division to sell may be relevant.

Such situations are discussed toward the end of this chapter under the heading "Choosing a Target Company."

How, then, would you as the buyer or seller decide upon the particular company to buy or business unit to sell where the purchase or sale is made to strengthen your business?

Planning should include (1) development of accurate knowledge of the buyer's or seller's own business, (2) development of specific goals for future growth, (3) knowledge of the industries in which growth is planned, (4) careful choice and investigation of the business to be acquired or sold, and (5) avoidance of the numerous pitfalls—legal, SEC, tax, and others —which may befall acquisitions. When a business faces a major problem, the purchase or sale of a business unit may solve that problem. But planning will give better assurance that the proper solution will be found.

Making the choice of the particular business to buy or sell involves three basic elements which we will elaborate upon in this chapter. You as the buyer or seller should (1) know your own business and prospects in detail, (2) prepare a long-range plan of objectives, and (3) choose the company or business unit for purchase or sale utilizing the knowledge of your business and the long-range plan.

KNOWLEDGE OF OWN BUSINESS

The starting point in establishing any long-range policy should be a thorough study by the buyer or seller of its own business. This study should attempt to determine the capabilities, attributes, and drawbacks which are unique to the business. The study should include manufacturing and engineering capabilities, personnel, product lines, profitability of product lines, cash requirements, and sales capability. After a thorough study of the elements indicated, the buyer or seller should attempt to determine the course of its business in the future—perhaps over the next five-year period. Will the market for its products expand? Are any of its products in danger of obsolescence? What will be the effect of competition? Will necessary cash be available? Will the distribution system be capable of satisfying conditions imposed by increased production? Will sufficient executive personnel be available in view of the projected growth of the business?

The purchaser's or seller's study of its own business will indicate to it the possible areas of its business which will need bolstering. Any indicated product obsolescence will indicate a need for new products. Any indicated weakness in the sales or distribution organization will indicate the need for a remedy. Any weakness in manufacturing or engineering skills will indicate the need for strengthening this aspect of the business. It is in the context of knowledge of present business activities projected into the future that the long-range plan should develop.

Knowledge of your own business, as we use the term, involves more than knowing its present status; such knowledge also involves an objective projection of the future of each business unit in your organization. Knowledge of present status will highlight present deficiencies in your business operations; whereas knowledge gained from a projection of results into the future will highlight possible future deficiencies and will afford an opportunity to plan for solutions before the problems arise. A long-range forecast which attempts to forecast a company's future five years in advance to determine its present and future status is reproduced below. Although this forecast may be simplified for a less complex business organization, consideration of its six fundamental elements is essential to objective knowledge of the present and future status of any business. We will follow the format of this long-range forecast not because we consider this format the only approach to gaining an insight into a business—other approaches may be utilized successfully—but this formula has proven itself. Each year the five-year, long-range forecast may be adjusted and advanced one additional year into the future and actual results for that year may be compared with the predicted results contained in the prior forecast.

The five-year forecast. The elements which should be contained in the five-year forecast and which we will discuss in greater detail are (1) The Market—present and future product lines, (2) The Competition—present and future product lines of major competitors and the competitors' past performance and estimated future strategy, (3) Performance of the buyer's or seller's business units—past and future product prices, costs and industry trends, (4) Business Unit Requirements—capital improvement, expense and personnel requirements, (5) Business Unit Operations Summary—a summary of past and estimated future income, break-even data, and return on assets, (6) Business Unit Cash Flow—past and projected after-tax profits plus depreciation and amortization less uses of cash for inventory increases, capital expenditures, dividends, and other cash needs.

This chapter discusses these six elements of the five-year forecast. The pages of the form of forecast reproduced in the chapter represent a complete form of forecast.

BUYER
(COMPANY NAME)

19__–19__ *Long Range Forecast*

I THE MARKET

Company's Product Lines

MAJOR PRODUCT LINES	INDUSTRY CLASSIFICATION*	
	SIC #	Description
Present Major Lines 19__		
1.		
2.		
3.		
4.		
5.		
6.		
New Major Lines (to be introduced in the period **19__–19__**		
1.		
2.		
3.		

*Use most restrictive industry classification as given in the U.S. Standard Industrial Classification or other appropriate industry breakdown.

BUYER
(COMPANY NAME)

I THE MARKET

19___–19___ *Long Range Forecast*

Total Industry Volume ($000)

PRODUCT LINE	5TH PRIOR YEAR	4TH PRIOR YEAR	3RD PRIOR YEAR	2ND PRIOR YEAR	1ST PRIOR YEAR	CURRENT FISCAL YEAR	1ST FUTURE YEAR	2ND FUTURE YEAR	3RD FUTURE YEAR	4TH FUTURE YEAR	5TH FUTURE YEAR
Present Major Lines											
1.											
2.											
3.											
4.											
5.											
6.											
Present Lines Total											
New Major Lines											
1.											
2.											
3.											
New Lines Total											
Total Market Volume											

Explanation: Total Industry Volume means sales of Industry Classification on first page of Forecast.

Data Sources:

THE MARKET

Analyzing the market as a whole involves first a breakdown of a company's business into its present major product lines and its proposed future additional product lines expected to be introduced in the next five years. In order to establish a basis for comparison of the company's business with that of the industry as a whole, the product lines should be described by using the most restrictive classification contained in the United States Standard Industrial Classification or other appropriate industry breakdown such as reports based upon surveys of trade associations.

Once the company has classified its own present and future product lines, it should turn to an analysis of the total industry volume in each of the product line classifications. Such analysis may be accomplished by setting down total industry dollar volume in each product line for the most recent full year and each of the five preceding years, and, finally, to establish a basis for a projection of the company's business into the future, a forecast should be made of expected total industry volume in each product line for the succeeding five years.

BUYER	II THE COMPETITION
(COMPANY NAME)	
19___–19___ Long Range Forecast	Competitors' Standing

MAJOR PRODUCT LINES	THE COMPETITORS—LATEST COMPLETED FISCAL YEAR RANK AND % MARKET SHARE				
	First	Second	Third	Fourth	Buyer
Present Major Lines					
1.					
2.					
3.					
4.					
5.					
6.					
New Major Lines					
1.					
2.					
3.					

THE COMPETITION

To analyze its competition, a company should attempt to obtain information about its competitors' past performances, and its competitors' future strategy and outlook. Although all this information about the competition may not be readily available, it is often surprising how much information may be developed through concentrated effort; furthermore, the effort to place this information on paper is in itself rewarding as an indicator of a company's knowledge of its industry.

The company's determination of its competitors' standing in the industry should include a ranking of the company's competitors in accordance with each competitor's percent of market share of the individual present and future product lines of the company; the determination of its competitors' performance should include an analysis of each major competitor's earnings for the most recent and the five preceding years on the basis of net revenue, pre-tax profit, net assets employed, profit margin (as a per cent of revenue), assets turnover, and return on assets; and the determination of the competitors' future strategy and outlook and weakness

BUYER						
(COMPANY NAME)				II THE COMPETITION		
19___–19___ Long Range Forecast				Competitors' Performance ($000)		

MAJOR COMPETITORS	5TH PRIOR YEAR	4TH PRIOR YEAR	3RD PRIOR YEAR	2ND PRIOR YEAR	1ST PRIOR YEAR	CURRENT FISCAL YEAR
First _____ Net Revenue						
Pre-Tax Profit						
Net Assets Employed						
Profit Margin (as a % of Revenue)						
Assets Turnover						
Return on Assets						
Second _____ Net Revenue						
Pre-Tax Profit						
Net Assets Employed						
Profit Margin (as a % of Revenue)						
Assets Turnover						
Return on Assets						
Third _____ Net Revenue						
Pre-Tax Profit						
Net Assets Employed						
Profit Margin (as a % of Revenue)						
Assets Turnover						
Return on Assets						
Fourth _____ Net Revenue						
Pre-Tax Profit						
Net Assets Employed						
Profit Margin (as a % of Revenue)						
Assets Turnover						
Return on Assets						

compared to the company, as well as an estimate of their future share of the market, new products, and general strategy.

THE COMPANY'S PERFORMANCE

An attempt by a company to evaluate its own performance involves an objective appraisal of its position in its industry and a projection of how that position may change in the future. Of the many elements involved in making the appraisal and projection, the broad categories of considerations we will discuss should act as effective guideposts to a thoughtful estimate of a company's future prospects.

First, the major factors affecting performance should be considered, and in the consideration of future changes in these factors, the company should attempt to create a timetable for the changes expected. Of these factors, five are generally of importance in most businesses and should be given careful attention in attempting to foresee future developments, but other considerations unique to the particular company's industry may be important and may distort

<u>**BUYER**</u>	**II THE COMPETITION**

(COMPANY NAME)

19___-19___ *Long Range Forecast*   *Competitors' Strategy and Outlook*

COMPETITIVE POSITION	19___-19___ OUTLOOK
(Discuss Their Strengths and Weaknesses vs. Buyer)	(Discuss Share of Market , New Products , Strategy , etc.)
First _____	
Second _____	
Third _____	
Fourth _____	

(Attach Additional Sheets if Needed)

the projection if overlooked. Therefore, thorough knowledge of the industry forms the cornerstone of a reliable projection, but at a minimum the company should address itself to these five major factors: (1) the future price structure for its products, (2) future direct and indirect labor costs, (3) the market strategy of the company and its competitors, (4) the trends within the industry, and (5) technological changes which might affect the cost and use of the company's products.

After consideration of the major factors and their projected effect on the future of the business, the company should address itself to the prediction of its share of the future market for its present and new product lines. As a starting point, the company should list its total dollar volume of sales of each of its product lines for its present year and the five preceding and five succeeding years (remembering to detail the assumptions and factors upon which the volume projections are based). This list of volume of sales when compared to the schedule of total industry volume in the product lines prepared in the form indicated under the first element of the five-year forecast, "The Market," will establish the company's past and projected percentage share of the total industry volume in each product line. After the com-

BUYER
(COMPANY NAME)

III BUSINESS UNIT PERFORMANCE

19___–19___ *Long Range Forecast*

Factors Affecting Performance

FACTORS AFFECTING PERFORMANCE

(Discuss and Identify the Timing of Future Developments)

A. Future Price Structure for Products:

B. Direct and Indirect Labor:

	1ST PRIOR YEAR	CURRENT FISCAL YEAR	1ST FUTURE YEAR	2ND FUTURE YEAR	3RD FUTURE YEAR	4TH FUTURE YEAR	5TH FUTURE YEAR
Avg. # of Employees — Direct							
Indirect							
Avg. Hourly Rate — Direct							
Indirect							

Comments:

C. Market Strategy — Buyer vs. Competition

parisons, the company should analyze any future increases or decreases in percentage of total industry volume and determine the specific reasons for the projected increase or decrease.

THE COMPANY'S FUTURE REQUIREMENTS

No forecast of a company's future would be complete without an analysis of its future requirements. Basically, these requirements fall into two general categories: (1) its anticipated financial requirements for major supporting capital and expense programs and (2) its anticipated personnel requirements.

Included in the anticipated financial requirements should be estimated annual expenditures for research and development expense, additional machinery and equipment capital investment, additional buildings investment, advertising expense, other market development expense, and other possible capital requirements. In each instance the purpose of the anticipated expenditures and the timing of each future development should be stated as explicitly as possible.

<u>_____ BUYER _____</u>
(COMPANY NAME)

III BUSINESS UNIT PERFORMANCE

19___–19___ *Long Range Forecast*

Factors Affecting Performance

FACTORS AFFECTING PERFORMANCE
(Discuss and Identify the Timing of Future Developments)

D. Trends Within the Industry

E. Technological Changes Affecting Product Cost and Use

F. Other Considerations

Once again enumerating specific needs and identifying timing of future developments, personnel requirements should be broken down into the major components consisting of (1) management, (2) sales, (3) accounting, (4) engineering, (5) production, (6) industrial relations, and (7) shop labor, both skilled and unskilled. Furthermore, the program for personnel development should be carefully reviewed including plans both for recruiting and training personnel.

COMPANY'S OPERATIONS SUMMARY

In order to form an opinion as to the trend of the company's operations, a forecast of projected operations for an adequate period into the future is a necessity. The format for the forecast includes the company's operations during its last six full years of operation and a projection of its operations for the next five years.

The income summary sets forth the company's pre-tax profit as well as its pre-tax profit margin, which is defined as the pre-tax profit divided by total net revenues. These items are

BUYER

(COMPANY NAME)

19__–19__ Long Range Forecast

III BUSINESS UNIT PERFORMANCE

Past and Projected Buyer $ Volume ($000)

PRODUCT LINE	5TH PRIOR YEAR	4TH PRIOR YEAR	3RD PRIOR YEAR	2ND PRIOR YEAR	1ST PRIOR YEAR	CURRENT FISCAL YEAR	1ST FUTURE YEAR	2ND FUTURE YEAR	3RD FUTURE YEAR	4TH FUTURE YEAR	5TH FUTURE YEAR
Present Major Lines											
1.											
2.											
3.											
4.											
5.											
6.											
Present Lines Total											
New Major Lines											
1.											
2.											
3.											
New Lines Total											
Total Buyer Volume											

determined by setting forth in tabular form the total net annual sales plus other business income as well as direct operating profit and non-operating income.

Break-even data is also set forth in the form of an annual tabulation which indicates the break-even sales volume and the revenue in excess of break-even. Figures for past years are based upon actual experience while figures for future years must of necessity be projections.

The annual return on assets is determined by annually totaling the cash, receivables, inventories, leased machines, net property, plant and equipment, and all other assets, to arrive at net assets employed; turnover on assets is determined by dividing net revenue by net assets employed; and finally, percentage return is determined by dividing direct operating profit by net assets employed.

COMPANY CASH FLOW

A determination of the company's cash flow is important primarily to determine the company's cash requirements in future years. As used, the term "cash flow" means net

BUYER
(COMPANY NAME)

III BUSINESS UNIT PERFORMANCE

19___–19___ *Long Range Forecast*

Basis of Volume Projections

ASSUMPTIONS AND FACTORS INFLUENCING FUTURE VOLUME

Present Major Lines:

New Major Lines:

profits after income tax payments plus depreciation and amortization, less all uses of cash. Thus, the term "cash flow" defines the amount of excess cash or deficiency in cash generated annually. Since the importance of determining cash flow concerns future cash requirements of the company, the analysis of cash flow need not be made through an extended historical period. The last current year and one year prior thereto are deemed sufficient for comparison purposes; however, future cash needs should be projected for an adequate period into the future. The tabulation makes provision for a five-year projection.

The projection of cash flow should take into consideration all future uses of cash. Any cash requirements for increase in inventories, receivables or prepaid expenses and for facilities and equipment, dividends, and debt repayments, should enter into the computation of the total cash drain. From the net cash generated and the total cash drain the excess or deficiency of cash generated in each year may then be projected. After such projection, the cash position may be summarized by showing the cash balance at the beginning of each year and at the end of each year.

Finally, the working capital requirements should be given careful consideration to determine what items are in excess and what items are in deficiency status.

BUYER
(COMPANY NAME)

19___–19___ *Long Range Forecast*

III BUSINESS UNIT PERFORMANCE

% Share of Industry Volume

PRODUCT LINE	5TH PRIOR YEAR	4TH PRIOR YEAR	3RD PRIOR YEAR	2ND PRIOR YEAR	1ST PRIOR YEAR	CURRENT FISCAL YEAR	1ST FUTURE YEAR	2ND FUTURE YEAR	3RD FUTURE YEAR	4TH FUTURE YEAR	5TH FUTURE YEAR
Present Major Lines											
1.											
2.											
3.											
4.											
5.											
6.											
Present Lines Total											
New Major Lines											
1.											
2.											
3.											
New Lines Total											
Total Buyer Market Share											

PREPARATION OF LONG-RANGE PLAN

Once the buyer or seller has made a detailed study of its own business, the areas of weakness should become evident and it may set about developing a long-range plan to bolster or dispose of the troublesome business units. Has the study revealed a need for a new product line or additional manufacturing facilities? Or a business unit which cannot be properly integrated into future expansion programs? Or a cyclical business which could be aided by diversification? The long-range plan should be developed to correct business defects of this or any other nature.

Internal growth. At the outset, in attempting to formulate the long-range plan, any business should first give serious consideration to the possibility of future growth through internal expansion of business rather than by acquiring other businesses. The serious element of the unknown, often present in an acquisition may thus be avoided, since in making an acquisition a buyer may investigate carefully, but can nevertheless not be certain that it is acquiring a successful business. The seller may have information unknown to the buyer of

BUYER _____	III BUSINESS UNIT PERFORMANCE
(COMPANY NAME)	
19___–19___ *Long Range Forecast*	*Future Share of Market*

PRIMARY REASON(S) FOR GAIN OR LOSS OF MARKET SHARE
Present Major Lines:
New Major Lines:

imminent product obsolescence, of loss of key personnel, of possible invalidity of key patents, or of some other of the many serious problems which may affect the seller's prospects. Furthermore, if a buyer is in a vulnerable position from an anti-trust viewpoint (discussed in Chapter 6) in that additional acquisitions may violate Section 7 of the Clayton Act, the buyer should give serious thought to internal growth as the basic objective of its long-range plan. But if, after careful consideration, a buyer determines that other businesses should be acquired to realize future goals, the long-range plan which is developed should incorporate criteria to limit possible acquisitions to those which will best fulfill the buyer's requirements.

Major elements of the plan. The long-range plan should contain answers to questions such as the following:

1. In what industry or industries should the buyer's future growth take place?

2. How does the industry or industries complement the buyer's business as projected into the future?

3. Will the same or similar manufacturing techniques be employed in the industry or industries?

BUYER

(COMPANY NAME)

19___–19___ _Long Range Forecast_

IV BUSINESS UNIT REQUIREMENTS

Major Supporting Capital and Expense Programs ($000)

ESTIMATED EXPENDITURE FOR	CURRENT FISCAL YEAR	1ST FUTURE YEAR	2ND FUTURE YEAR	3RD FUTURE YEAR	4TH FUTURE YEAR	5TH FUTURE YEAR
Research and Development Expense						
Additional Machinery and Equipment Capital Investment						
Additional Buildings Investment						
Advertising Expense						
Other Market Development Expense						
Other Capital Requirements						

PURPOSE OF ANTICIPATED EXPENDITURES

(Identify Timing of Future Developments)

Research and Development Program

4. Does the buyer intend to supply management, engineering or manufacturing know-how?

5. Will the distribution system of the buyer lend itself to the distribution of the products in the field of interest?

With the answers to these questions in mind, the buyer should develop a detailed definition of the industry in which the projected future growth is to take place. The more specific the definition the greater will be the probability that an acquisition in the industry will be successful. Too broad a definition may result in expensive loss of time and effort in investigating possibilities which ultimately prove unsatisfactory, or may even result in acquisitions which subsequently prove unprofitable. For example, a prospective buyer which decides that the company's future growth should be in industries which supply products to satisfy the increased leisure time of the public, should fix a specific area in the leisure time industries in which to concentrate future efforts. Among the many products which may be classified as leisure time products are boats, mobile homes, golf equipment, camping equipment, baseball bats, fishing gear, and general sporting goods such as inflated balls, skis, tennis racquets, aqua-lungs,

BUYER	IV BUSINESS UNIT REQUIREMENTS
(COMPANY NAME)	
19___ -19___ *Long Range Forecast*	*Major Supporting Capital and Expense Programs*

PURPOSE OF ANTICIPATED EXPENDITURES
(Identify Timing of Future Developments)

Machinery and Equipment Program

Buildings Program

etc. Although each of the products mentioned falls within the category of leisure time products, the manufacturing and distribution techniques with respect to many of the products are entirely different. If the prospective buyer wishes to grow in a familiar field, it should determine which of the products is most like its own products in manufacturing and distribution techniques. On the other hand, if the product line to be acquired is entirely dissimilar from products manufactured by the buyer, the buyer must understand that in acquiring a business in which it has no know-how it runs the added risk of entering into a comparatively unknown field.

Initial screening criteria. Once the industry in which acquisitions will be sought has been clearly defined, the next step for a prospective buyer is to define or lay down initial screening criteria for judging the suitability of individual companies in the industry. These criteria should be so clear that they enable an initial decision with regard to any proposed acquisition to be made as a routine or mechanical matter, and all proposed acquisitions should first be tested against these criteria. The initial criteria should clearly define what the buyer requires with respect to each of the following elements:

<table>
<tr><td colspan="2">BUYER
(COMPANY NAME)</td><td>IV BUSINESS UNIT REQUIREMENTS</td></tr>
<tr><td colspan="2">19___–19___   Long Range Forecast</td><td>Major Supporting Capital and Expense Programs</td></tr>
</table>

PURPOSE OF ANTICIPATED EXPENDITURES
(Identify Timing of Future Developments)

Advertising Program

Market Development Program

Other Capital Requirements

1. The minimum size of a company which will be considered for acquisition should be stated. To investigate and acquire a small company often requires as much effort and expense as that involved in acquiring a large business. The return may be too small for the investment and time involved unless some minimum standard is recognized.

2. A minimum required return on invested capital and earnings per share should be fixed. If the projected return on invested capital would be less than the return on the buyer's capital invested in its own business, the buyer should think in terms of utilizing its funds in some other manner. If the projected earnings acquired by the buyer in exchange for the buyer's stock would be less per share than the projected per share earnings of the buyer's own business, the buyer would be diluting earnings of its own shareholders.

3. An estimate should be made of the minimum potential growth rate for an acquired company. Even if the industry in which the buyer hopes to acquire businesses is considered a growth industry, nevertheless, the buyer should attempt to define the potential sales growth required of the products manufactured by any proposed seller.

4. Management and personnel requirements should be clearly defined. If the buyer does

BUYER	IV BUSINESS UNIT REQUIREMENTS

(COMPANY NAME)

19___–19___ Long Range Forecast   *Personnel*

PERSONNEL REQUIREMENTS

(Enumerate Specific Needs and Identify Timing of Future Developments)

A. Management   E. Production

B. Sales   F. Industrial Relations

C. Accounting   G. Shop
                                                    Skilled —

D. Engineering   Unskilled —

PERSONNEL DEVELOPMENT

(Identify Timing of Future Developments)

A. Recruiting

B. Training Programs

---

not intend to provide management for any acquisition, the criteria should require reasonable assurance that efficient management will remain with the business considered for acquisition. Separate criteria should be established as to whether the general executive management, manufacturing and engineering management and sales management will be required or supplied.

5. The sales area and the distribution method of any proposed acquisition should be defined. Must the products have national distribution? Must the products be distributed through wholesalers? Must the selling company have its own internal sales organization?

CHOOSING THE SPECIFIC COMPANY

Sources of recommendations. After the buyer has established the initial screening criteria, it is prepared to set about finding the specific company which will meet its requirements. Among the sources which may supply recommendations of specific companies which may be satisfactory prospects as buyers or sellers, four of the major sources are the following:

1. If the buyer proposes to make acquisitions in the same general industry as that in

| BUYER | | | | | | V BUSINESS UNIT OPERATIONS SUMMARY | | | | |

BUYER
(COMPANY NAME)

19___–19___ Long Range Forecast

Past and Projected ($000)

A. INCOME SUMMARY	5TH PRIOR YEAR	4TH PRIOR YEAR	3RD PRIOR YEAR	2ND PRIOR YEAR	1ST PRIOR YEAR	CURRENT FISCAL YEAR	1ST FUTURE YEAR	2ND FUTURE YEAR	3RD FUTURE YEAR	4TH FUTURE YEAR	5TH FUTURE YEAR
1. Total Net Sales											
2. Rentals and Commissions											
3. Total Net Revenue											
11. Direct Operating Profit											
14. Non-operating Income (Exp.)											
15. Pre-Tax Profit											
Pre-Tax Profit Margin (% Rev.)	%	%	%	%	%	%	%	%	%	%	%
B. BREAK-EVEN DATA											
5. Breakeven Sales Volume											
6. Revenue in Excess of Breakeven											
C. RETURN ON ASSETS											
1. Cash (6% of Revenue)											
2. Receivables											
3. Inventories											
6. Leased Machines											
7. Net Property, Plant, Equip.											
8. Other Assets											
9. Net Assets Employed											
Turnover (Net Rev./Assets)											
10. Direct Operating Profit											
11. % Return	%	%	%	%	%	%	%	%	%	%	%

which the buyer is already engaged, or in a closely related industry, the best source of information is often the buyer's own personnel. Employees who have worked in the industry over a period of time will generally have knowledge of other companies in the industry and related fields. Therefore, any buyer may first seek information as to prospects for acquisitions from its own employees. A recommendation from within also has advantages in that the buyer will be better assured of the interest of operating personnel in the proposed acquisition where such personnel has made the original recommendation, and the enthusiastic support and interest of operating personnel often makes the difference between a successful acquisition and a failure. A seller may also avail itself of recommendations of employees, but only to the extent that it is willing to reveal its plans to sell.

2. Members of the board of directors of the buyer or seller, as well as commercial and investment bankers, are another source of finding prospective buyers or sellers. Outside board members have knowledge of the internal business problems of the buyer or seller, and often because of their outside business connections gain knowledge of other businesses which may help solve these problems through the acquisition process. Bankers, because most business

BUYER
(COMPANY NAME)

VI BUSINESS UNIT CASH FLOW

19___-19___ Long Range Forecast

Projected ($000)

	1ST PRIOR YEAR	CURRENT FISCAL YEAR	1ST FUTURE YEAR	2ND FUTURE YEAR	3RD FUTURE YEAR	4TH FUTURE YEAR	5TH FUTURE YEAR	
Sources of Cash								
Pre-Tax Profit								
less Federal Income Tax Payments – During year								
Net Profit								
Depreciation and Amortization								
Net Cash Generated								
(Uses) of Cash								
Inventories (Increase) or Decrease								
Receivables (Increase) or Decrease								
Prepaid Expenses (Increase) or Decrease								
Accounts Payable Increase or (Decrease)								
Total Working Capital (Increase) or Decrease								
Facilities and Equipment (Expenditures)								
Leased Machine (Expenditures)								
Other (Expenditures)								
Total Capital Investment (Increase)								
Long-Term Debt (Repayments)								
Total Cash Drain								
Excess (or Deficiency) of Cash Generated								
Summary Cash Position								
Cash Balance — Beginning of Year (6% of previous year's revenues)								
Excess (or Deficiency) of Cash Generated								
Cash Balance — End of Year Total								
Cash Balance — End of Year (6% of revenues)								
Cash Transfers to or (from) Corporate Headquarters								

problems may ultimately be said to involve money, are often in a unique position to know of possible prospective buyers or sellers.

3. Generally, after it becomes public knowledge that a company is interested in acquiring additional businesses, offerings by brokers become more and more frequent. How such offerings should be treated is discussed in detail in the next chapter. But if a broker has the authority to offer a company for sale and is conscientious in his approach, he will have sufficient financial and other information concerning the prospective seller to make the task of initial screening comparatively simple.

4. By a concentrated program of research, the buyer may develop its own independent choices of specific companies it wishes to acquire. This approach may consume substantial time and effort of available planning manpower but underlies not only a sound choice of a specific acquisition but the entire concept of long-range planning. Tools for the research, consisting of financial publications of all sorts, exist in perplexing abundance and may be classified as general financial publications and specific publications concerned with the industry in which the buyer proposes to make acquisitions. General financial publications such as those

<table>
<tr><td colspan="2">

BUYER
(COMPANY NAME)

19___–19___ *Long Range Forecast*

</td><td colspan="2">

VI BUSINESS UNIT CASH FLOW

Projected ($000)

</td></tr>
<tr><td colspan="4" align="center">COMMENT ON WORKING CAPITAL REQUIREMENTS</td></tr>
<tr><td colspan="4" height="600"></td></tr>
</table>

printed by Moody's, Dun and Bradstreet, and Standard & Poor's and statistics provided by the United States Department of Commerce are helpful in narrowing down the choice of companies to be approached. Furthermore, the buyer will generally have available a number of trade publications specifically concerned with the industry in which it is buying.

Approaching the seller. Once the buyer has chosen the company it wishes to acquire, the problem of approaching the prospective seller arises. If the company has been offered for sale or if a broker is involved, the course of approach may usually be easily plotted. But if the company has not actually been offered for sale and an initial approach is necessary to determine whether or not the seller is interested in a possible merger or acquisition by the buyer, a direct personal approach by the officer of the buyer responsible for acquisitions to the chief executive officer of the proposed seller is recommended as a method which has often proved successful. Naturally, where executives of the buyer are personally acquainted with executives of the proposed seller the approach may be made through one of these executives—or an acquaintance of both parties, such as a banker, may arrange a meeting.

At the time of this initial approach, a well-reasoned, long-range plan of the buyer may be the persuasive factor in initiating satisfactory negotiations. With such a plan, the buyer will be able to tell the proposed seller what the advantages will be of joining the buyer's organization. The buyer should be prepared to point out clearly where the mutuality of interests between the seller and the buyer lies. Even where the selling company has been offered for sale, a buyer which is able to discuss the long-range combination of the two companies and the mutual advantages to both will have a better opportunity to convince the seller that the buyer is the right company to make the acquisition.

The general procedures for conducting the investigation and negotiating with the buyer are discussed in Chapter 5. But as a general rule, starting with the initial meeting and throughout the negotiation, the buyer should approach the seller with two questions in mind. Why is it choosing this particular seller over all other possible sellers? What is the seller's true reason for selling?

As the investigation and negotiations proceed, buyers sometimes tend to concentrate more and more on *how* to make the acquisition rather than on the problem of whether the acquisition *should* be made. Bearing the two questions (Why choose this particular seller? Why is it selling?) constantly in mind will serve a two-fold purpose. Over-enthusiasm may be curbed in that the buyer will be reminded of other companies which might suit its needs, and the seller's true reasons for selling may indicate a basic weakness in the seller's business which may make the acquisition undesirable to the buyer. Why this seller and why is it selling? The answers to these questions should be checked and rechecked as facts are developed, negotiations proceed, and a binding agreement approaches.

CHOOSING A TARGET COMPANY

Utilization by a buyer of the study of its own business and a long-range plan should help assure success of an acquisition, whether the acquisition is undertaken as a negotiated acquisition or a takeover bid. However, where a buyer has reason to believe that a seller's management will oppose a proposed acquisition, the buyer may be forced to approach the proposed transaction as a takeover bid. In such situations a buyer should consider additional criteria relating to the seller to assess the possibility of success of the buyer's proposed takeover bid.

Studies of takeover bids have indicated that certain sellers are more vulnerable to successful takeover bids than others. Elements which may be considered involve the performance of the prospective target company's business and effect of the performance upon the target company's stockholders. First, how has the target company's stock performed in relationship to the market as a whole? If the target company's stock has remained stable or has declined during a period of an enthusiastic and rising market, the poor performance of the stock may tend to cause stockholder dissatisfaction, and make the target company a likely prospect for a successful takeover bid. Secondly, has there been a decline or cessation of dividend payments? The effect of such a decline may, as in the case of a decline in the market price of the stock on the market, cause dissatisfaction among the target company's stockholders. Thirdly, does the prospective target company have an excess of liquid assets? Where a corporation has a high ratio of cash assets, inventory, and receivables in relation to its current liabilities, the liquidity of its assets may be an invitation to a prospective aggressor company.

Approach to a takeover candidate. Where a buyer is convinced that the management of a prospective seller will oppose a proposed acquisition, the buyer may decide to proceed by means of a takeover bid. In such an event, the basic strategy of a buyer should be to make the takeover bid to the seller's stockholders without prior warning to the management of the seller. Surprise may be the buyer's strongest ally. An unexpected takeover bid will limit the time available to the management of the target company to muster an effective defense.

Many different tactics and strategies are available to both the aggressor (to bring victory) and to the target company (to avoid takeover). The time to accept a tender offer may be short, perhaps ten days to three weeks. Since such a short time period may be involved, the aggressor company should have all of its tactics and strategems clearly blueprinted before the tender offer is actually made. Also, where it suspects that it may become a target for a takeover bid, the target company should make as many preliminary preparations for defense against such a bid as possible. These matters are discussed in greater detail in Chapter 9, which discusses takeover bids.

To summarize, planning and choosing the business to buy or sell involves (1) detailed knowledge of one's own business and its prospects, (2) preparation of a long-range plan and (3) choosing the specific company to buy or sell. Knowledge of one's own business involves knowledge of (a) existing and future product lines, (b) the competition, (c) product prices, costs and industry trends, (d) capital improvement, expense and personnel requirements, (e) past and estimated future income, and (f) estimated future cash requirements. Such knowledge may be developed in the form of a five-year forecast such as is printed in this chapter. Development of the long-range plan should depend upon the present and future weakness of the buyer's business as revealed in the study and projection and should give careful consideration to the possibility of internal growth to cure weakness before turning to the acquisition route. The choice of a specific company may come from major sources of recommendations such as (a) employees, (b) members of boards of directors and bankers, (c) brokers, or (d) a concentrated program of research in financial and trade publications.

CHAPTER 3

Business Finders and Brokers

Be alert to possible brokerage problems. The time for settling questions of finders' or brokers' fees is at the beginning of a negotiation, not after a price has been agreed upon when both buyer and seller will be reluctant to pay an unexpected commission.

Early in any meetings between a prospective buyer and seller, the parties should attempt to determine whether a finder's fee or broker's commission will be payable and to whom. If the seller has been offered through a broker, the buyer will know that a broker is in the picture. On the other hand, if the buyer has approached the seller directly without the intervention of any third party, he should find out from the seller whether or not the seller has entered into any arrangement with a broker or finder.

The possible existence of a brokerage arrangement should be investigated to determine (1) whether a broker may have been employed by the buyer or seller; (2) which party, the buyer or seller, may legally become responsible for the payment of the brokerage commission; (3) under what circumstances the commission will be payable; and (4) what the amount of the commission will be. If in their early discussions of brokerage the parties determine there may be a broker involved in the transaction and the terms of the foregoing elements of the arrangement with the broker have not been settled, the parties should take immediate steps to formalize the brokerage arrangement by a written agreement with the broker.

The answer to each of the four questions implied from the preceding paragraph, if not incorporated in a written agreement, may rest in the legal rules surrounding arrangements with brokers and finders as those rules have been developed in decided cases. Differences exist in the law of the 50 states of the United States, but certain principles of law may be generally applicable, and will serve as guides for developing an approach to and protection against brokerage problems. Although the general principles discussed below are helpful in

33

developing an approach to brokerage, in specific instances brokerage problems may require detailed research into the law of a specific state.

From the broker's viewpoint, knowledge of the general principles involved will help the broker collect a commission, and formalizing the contract will minimize the need for a lawsuit to bring about the collection. Certainly, the broker or finder is in a better position where a contract establishes which of the two (buyer or seller) will pay the commission, the circumstances under which it is payable, and the amount of the commission.

We will first discuss some legal principles applicable to business finders and brokers, and then offer a general approach and suggested methods for coping with brokerage problems, including suggested forms which may be utilized to meet the needs of specific situations.

LEGAL PRINCIPLES

Finder vs. Broker. A distinction is made in law between a business finder and a broker. A business finder is one who finds, interests, introduces, and brings parties together for a transaction which they themselves negotiate and consummate. A finder is an intermediary or middleman who is not involved in negotiating any of the terms of the transaction.

On the other hand, a broker, within the accepted meaning of the term, is an agent who has the duty of bringing the parties to agreement in accordance with the terms imposed upon him by his employer, his principal. Normally, in order to bring the parties to agreement on the terms set forth by his principal, the broker is required to take some part in the negotiations, even if the part is limited to a presentation of the terms upon which a particular sale or purchase of a business is offered.

The legal distinction between a business finder and a broker is generally not of importance in fixing the amount of fees and commissions agreed to be paid to the finder or broker. The distinction may have an effect, however, in determining whether a broker or finder may legally enforce a claim for a fee in a state which may require a written agreement of the brokerage agreement or even a real estate broker's license. Under some circumstances, a finder may recover a fee from both a buyer and seller, regardless of the fact that the parties do not know that a double fee is being paid. Generally, a broker may not recover a double fee without the knowledge of both parties because a broker has a fiduciary relationship to his principal. Some excerpts from opinions in decided legal cases may help highlight the distinctions made between business brokers and business finders.

Finder v. Broker—Court Opinions. In a law suit brought in the courts of the State of New York by a plaintiff to recover for services rendered in connection with the sale of the defendant's brewery (*Knauss* v. *Krueger Brewing Company*, 142 N.Y. 70), the court held that the plaintiff was not a broker "in the strict sense of the word." The court held that the plaintiff was a finder and not a broker, and stated as follows:

> The record shows there was evidence of the employment of the plaintiff for the mere purpose of bringing the possible buyer and seller together, and with the understanding that if a sale were to result the plaintiff was to have some compensation from the defendant for his services. The plaintiff testified that he was to have nothing to do with fixing the price or the terms of the sale; the principals were to

do that part of the business; all he had to do was bring them together, and if through their subsequent negotiations a sale should result, the plaintiff was to be entitled to some compensation.

In another case (*Seckendorff* v. *Halsey, Stuart & Co., Inc.*, 254 N.Y.Supp. 250), a "finder" was defined as follows:

> Plaintiff was in nowise a broker. He merely was a finder of this piece of business. He was to receive his compensation for finding the business and bringing the same to the attention of Rogers Caldwell & Company and its associates. He claimed his compensation solely upon the ground that he was the originator of the business and had disclosed to Rogers Caldwell & Company and its associates the opportunity to engage in this financing.

From the foregoing quotations, it is clear that if a business finder is employed, and if he introduces two parties who then negotiate a transaction which closes, (except where special statutory requirements are not met) the business finder is entitled to compensation, in spite of the fact that the finder takes no part in the negotiations nor assists in any other way in bringing about the transaction—other than making the introduction.

To summarize, in law a business finder is a person who introduces two parties who subsequently negotiate and close a transaction, whereas a business broker is a person who not only introduces the parties but also assists in the negotiations to bring the parties to agreement and close the transaction. A business finder is entitled to a commission if his introduction results in a transaction. A business broker is entitled to a commission only if a transaction is closed in accordance with the terms set forth by his employer. As mentioned in the introduction to this chapter, variations exist in the law of brokerage within the different states. Not all states will necessarily make a distinction between a business finder and a business broker. However, in those states in which a distinction in law is made between a finder and a broker, the distinction may have the effect of permitting the recovery of a claimed commission, or denying such recovery dependent upon whether a claimant is categorized as a business finder or a business broker. The effect of the distinction is further developed below.

Statute of Frauds. It is the law of some states that any contract to pay compensation for services rendered in negotiating the purchase or sale of any business or a majority of the stock in a corporation is *void,* unless the contract or a memorandum thereof is in writing and is signed by the party who is charged with the payment of the commission. Statutes of this nature are generally referred to as "statutes of frauds." The underlying purpose of such statutes is to minimize the risk of unfounded claims for finders' fees or brokerage commissions in connection with sales or acquisitions of businesses.

New York State, a leading state in developing the law of business finders and brokers, has seen fit to enact a statute of frauds [N.Y. General Obligations Law §5–701 (10)] which provides as follows:

> Every agreement, promise or undertaking is void, unless it or some note or memorandum thereof be in writing, and subscribed by the party to be charged therewith, or by his lawful agent, if such agreement, promise or undertaking . . .
> 10. Is a contract to pay compensation for services rendered in negotiating a

loan, or in negotiating the purchase, sale, exchange, renting, or leasing of any real estate or interest therein, or of a business opportunity, business, its good will, inventory, fixtures or an interest therein, including a majority of the voting stock interest in a corporation and including the creating of a partnership interest.

"Negotiating" includes procuring an introduction to a party to the transaction or assisting in the negotiation or consummation of the transaction. This provision shall apply to a contract implied in fact or in law to pay reasonable compensation but shall not apply to a contract to pay compensation to an auctioneer, an attorney at law, or a duly licensed real estate broker or real estate salesman.

Under the New York statute, then, the agreement to pay a finder's or broker's fee in connection with the sale of a business is void, unless there is a writing evidencing the agreement, which is subscribed by the party against whom the finder's fee or brokerage commission is claimed.

Requirement of Writing—Quantum Meruit Recovery. Generally, statutes of fraud will be satisfied by writings which establish the fact of the employment of a broker or finder by a buyer or seller to render the alleged services; however, the writing must be subscribed by the person to be charged with the payment of the commission or such person's lawful agent. The note or memorandum must be such that, standing alone, it completely represents an acknowledgement or admission on the part of the buyer or seller of the existence of a promise by the buyer or seller to pay the commission. In a New York case (*Morris Cohon & Company* v. *Russell*, 23 N.Y. 2d 569) an acquisition contract contained a representation by the sellers that they had not dealt with any person other than the broker named in the contract as well as an indemnification of the buyers by the sellers against any claim for brokerage or finder's fees by the plaintiff-broker. No other written memorandum of the brokerage arrangement, subscribed by the defendant, had ever been made. Although the acquisition contract clause did not contain a statement of the amount of the fee to be paid, the clause was held to be sufficient evidence of the fact of the plaintiff's employment by the defendant to render the alleged services, and a sufficient writing to meet the requirements of the statute of frauds. The writing was held to be sufficient to evidence the obligation of the defendant to pay *reasonable compensation* for the services rendered. In other words, the writing was sufficient to support an action on the part of the finder or broker in *quantum meruit*.

In such an action, an action in quantum meruit as opposed to a contract action, the court would have the obligation to determine the reasonable value of the brokerage services, since the value or fee had not been specified in the writing. The court pointed out that to support a contract action, a memorandum in writing must contain by reasonable implication all of the material terms of the agreement, including the rate of compensation if there has been agreement on that matter to be sufficient under the statute of frauds. In the particular case considered, the contract provision involved was the following:

> ... The sellers represent and warrant that they have dealt with no person or persons other than Morris Cohon & Company as broker or finder in connection with the transactions in this agreement, and that all negotiations relative to this agreement have been carried on by them without the intervention of any other broker or finder,

and the Sellers agree to indemnify Buyer and the Company and hold them harmless against and in respect of any claim for brokerage or finder's commission relative to this agreement whether by said Morris Cohon & Company or otherwise.

On the other hand, a letter written by a broker to a buyer or seller, purporting to confirm a telephone understanding with respect to the payment of a fee, is not a sufficient writing if the broker is the only person who signs the letter. In order for the writing to meet the requirements of the statute of frauds, it must be signed by the party to be charged, i.e., the buyer or seller against whom the claim for a commission or fee is made, *Ames* v. *Ideal Cement Company,* 235 N.Y. Supp. 2d 622 (1962). In addition, the writing upon which a broker or finder relies must describe the transaction which actually occurred, and not a different transaction involving different parties, *Intercontinental Planning Limited* v. *Daystrom,* 24 N.Y. 2d 372 (1969).

Licensing Requirements. Many jurisdictions require that real estate brokers be licensed. In such jurisdictions, where the assets of a business include real estate, a requirement may exist that a business broker or finder be licensed as a real estate broker. The terms of the particular statute as well as the interpretation of the particular statute by the courts, will determine whether or not the business broker or finder is required to be licensed as a real estate broker before he may legally recover his brokerage commission or finder's fee. In Pennsylvania, an unlicensed broker was prohibited from recovering a stipulated commission for the sale of a manufacturing plant with land valued at about $9,000 and buildings with a going business thereon valued at $355,000, *Schultz* v. *Palmer Welloct Tool Corporation,* 207 F. 2d 652. In New Jersey, a person employed to find a buyer for a milk company where about one-third of the company's assets consisted of real estate, was held to be a real estate broker requiring a real estate broker's license, *Kenney* v. *Paterson Milk & Cream Company,* 110 N.J. Law 141, 164 Atlantic 274. In the state of Washington (*Grammer* v. *Skagit Valley Lumber Company,* 162 Wash. 677) a person employed by a seller of a lumber company which owned real and personal property, although the contract of employment restricted employees to negotiating and obtaining offers, was also held to be a real estate broker. Therefore, in any situation in which a broker is requested to sell the assets of a business which include real estate, the broker should determine whether or not he will be required to have a real estate broker's license in the particular jurisdiction, to have a legally enforceable claim to his commission.

Business Opportunity Publishers. Other types of individual state statutes may affect the rights of business brokers and finders. In New York State, a person may not act as a publisher of business opportunity advertisements unless he has filed with the Secretary of State of New York, in the form of an affidavit, a detailed statement as required in the statute. If a person acts as a business opportunity publisher without filing the necessary statement, the person may be guilty of a misdemeanor, and all third parties who have paid the business publisher fees may sue for the return of such fees, or if the fees have not been paid, may refuse to pay.

Conflict of Laws. The foregoing sections have indicated that in some jurisdictions a business broker or finder may require a real estate broker's license as a condition to a valid claim to a commission or fee, and in some jurisdictions, a broker or finder may not recover a commission or fee unless the agreement to pay the fee is in writing, subscribed by the party to be charged. Where different state laws may affect the enforceability of a claim for a commission, it may become important to determine which state law governs a particular brokerage agreement.

Assume a seller is incorporated under the laws of the state of Delaware and has offices and factories in New Jersey; the buyer is incorporated under the laws of the state of California and has offices and properties scattered throughout many western states. The broker who has brought the parties together has an office in New York, and negotiations have taken place in New York, New Jersey, and California. Should the laws of New York, where the broker is located, the laws of New Jersey, where the seller has its factories, the laws of California, where the buyer has its main office, or the laws of Delaware where the seller is incorporated, determine the law which governs the transaction?

The answer to this question lies in the application of principles of law grouped under the topic "conflicts of laws." Generally speaking, the law of the state in which the brokerage arrangement was made or the state which has the most significant contracts with the brokerage arrangement will be applicable in construing the validity of the brokerage contract. The place where the acquisition contract is made or the location of the properties, business, or headquarters of either the buyer or the seller will not normally determine the state law which governs and determines the validity of the broker's or finder's contract.

Contract of Employment. The legal relationship between a buyer or seller and a broker or finder is founded in contract law. In order for a broker to earn a fee, a contract must exist under which the buyer or seller, acting as principal, has employed the broker or finder as an agent.

Contract—Express and Implied. The contract of employment necessary to establish the relationship of agency between a broker and his principal, as those terms are used above, is governed by the law applicable to ordinary contracts. The contract need not be a formal one; it may either be express or implied. A written agreement defining the brokerage or finder's arrangement between the parties is an express contract and its terms will, of course, govern the rights of the parties. However, since no particular form is required for the contract, it may arise through correspondence, oral communications, or conduct of the parties. In such situations the contract may be an implied one and the terms may be left to implication.

Contract—Implied. For an implied contract to exist, the broker or finder need only act with the consent of the principal, whether such consent is given in writing, orally, or by implication from the conduct of the parties. For example, assume a person known to you to be engaged in a general brokerage business approaches you and says he might have a buyer for your business "if you're interested." You need only tell him to bring the prospective buyer around because you "might sell if the price is right." An ultimate sale to the buyer as a result of the introduction furnished by the broker may entitle the broker to a commission on the theory that an implied contract of employment existed between you and the broker, although the contract may be void in a jurisdiction which requires that it be in writing.

The above example illustrates the implied brokerage contract in its simplest form. The principal (buyer or seller) gives its consent to a certain course of action to be taken by the finder or broker, knowing he is engaged in the brokerage business, and the broker acts upon such consent or agrees to act upon such consent. Under contract law an implied contract exists. The principal may be bound to pay the broker some compensation if the broker successfully completes the course of action undertaken.

Contract—Ratification. A contract of employment of a broker or finder may also arise where a finder has completely performed his services and the buyer or seller subsequently ratifies his actions. Legally, the ratification of the finder's acts has the same general effect as the buyer or seller initially employing the broker to perform the services, and upon ratification the buyer or seller, as the case may be, may become liable to pay a commission to the broker. To illustrate, assume a broker comes to you, an owner, and says that he has signed a contract as agent for an undisclosed principal (you) to sell your business to a buyer for $1,000,000. In spite of the fact that you never intended to sell your business and never employed the broker, if you ratify the broker's acts by selling your business to the buyer in accordance with the contract, you may owe the broker a commission.

Whose Agent Is the Broker? The principal may be either the buyer or seller, and the broker or finder may be an agent to sell or buy, or for both purposes. Stated differently, the broker may be the agent of either the buyer, the seller, or of both. Where no express contract exists and the circumstances, correspondence, or conduct of the parties does not clearly establish whose agent the broker is, he is generally considered the agent of the one who first contacted him.

A broker's or finder's voluntary offer to become the agent for a buyer or seller, without any consent on the buyer's or seller's part, will not create an implied contract. But, if as a result of prior dealings between the principal and a finder, a finder could reasonably believe that by his silence the principal consents to such employment, an implied contract could exist. Assume, for example, that a friend of yours who knows you have your business for sale asks you how much you want for it. If this is the only communication you have with your friend concerning the sale of the business, and he sends a buyer to you to whom you sell, you probably will not owe your friend a commission. He is a volunteer, and you did not hire him to sell your business. But if you and your friend have had past dealings in which he has attempted to sell your business for an agreed commission, then a sale to a buyer sent by your friend could result in a legal obligation to pay the commission. By course of past conduct, an implied brokerage contract may exist between you and your friend.

Time of Earning Commission. When has the broker earned his commission? The answer to this question again depends upon the terms of the agreement between the broker and the buyer or seller. If the agreement is an express contract, its terms will provide the answer. But if the agreement has risen as an implied contract, then the broker or finder earns his commission when he has done the work for which he was hired. Generally speaking, however, in a business brokerage or business finder situation, a commission is not earned until the transaction actually closes.

In real estate brokerage different rules may apply. In a real estate situation, an implied contract may take one of two forms: (1) Where the owner has given the broker full and complete terms upon which he is willing to sell his property; or (2) where the owner is willing to sell but has not fixed the terms of the sale, except perhaps, the sale price. In the first case, a broker is entitled to his commission when he produces a customer "ready, willing, and able" to fulfill all the terms fixed by the owner. In the second case, the broker does not earn his commission until the buyer and seller reach agreement upon the price and the terms upon which a sale may be made, or, as often stated, the broker does not earn his commission until he has brought about a "meeting of the minds" between the buyer and seller. These rules are succinctly stated in a leading New York State real estate brokerage case decided in 1911, *Arnold* v. *Schmeidler*, 144 App. Div. 420, 129 N.Y.Supp. 408 at page 413:

> In the absence of a special agreement, the services rendered by a broker to an owner of real estate generally fall into one of two categories:
>
> (1) Where the owner has given the broker the full and complete terms upon which he is willing to sell his property, and not merely the asking price thereof;
>
> (2) Where the owner has his property for sale, and may or may not have set an asking price thereon, but does not fix the terms of the transaction leaving them to be determined thereafter.
>
> In the first case the broker's duty is fulfilled, and his commissions are earned when he produces a customer ready, willing, and able to comply with all the terms fixed by the owner. Should the latter then desire to add to the terms already imposed, the additional conditions must be germane to the original ones, if they are to furnish a sufficient reason for the refusal to pay the broker in case of the customer's refusal to agree to any modification of the original terms. In the second case the broker's commissions are not earned until the customer produced by him reaches an agreement with the owner upon the price and terms upon which a sale can be made. This, of course, does not mean that a contract in writing must be signed by the parties, but that their minds must meet not only upon the price, but upon the essential terms of an agreement to purchase.

Amount of Commissions or Fees. The size of the commissions payable to a business broker or finder may vary greatly, depending upon the terms which have been negotiated with his principal. No two situations are alike. Fees have ranged from as much as 10% or more of the total value of a transaction to less than 1%. Sometimes, fees paid to brokers or business finders appear exorbitant and may lead to private litigation, or even investigation by administrative agencies. For example, during 1968, proposals by Glen Alden Corporation to pay $5,000,000 in finder's fees in connection with a takeover attempt of Schenley Industries Inc., caused private law suits against Glen Alden as well as Securities and Exchange Commission investigations. On other occasions, finders have accepted fees substantially below those which the transaction could have warranted.

Although the amount of broker's commissions or finder's fees may vary greatly from situation to situation, a formula has developed which is often suggested as the formula for determining brokerage and finder's fees in a transaction which closes. This formula is as follows:

If the Amount of Consideration Paid Is:

Over	But Not Over	Commission or Fee
$0	$1,000,000	5% of consideration
$1,000,000	$2,000,000	$50,000 plus 4% of excess over $1,000,000
$2,000,000	$3,000,000	$90,000 plus 3% of excess over $2,000,000
$3,000,000	$4,000,000	$120,000 plus 2% of evcess over $3,000,000
$4,000,000		$140,000 plus 1% of excess over $4,000,000

The formula set forth above may be mentioned in fixing brokerage commissions, but is not necessarily followed. Often, in sizable transactions, the amount of the brokerage commission or finder's fees may be stated as a flat percentage of between 1% and 2% of the consideration paid.

Since the rights of the buyer or seller and the broker are determined by the contract terms, after the broker has carried out his obligations, he will be entitled to whatever commission was agreed upon. But where the contract is an implied one, the amount of his fees may not have been fixed. The contract may nevertheless be valid, and where the parties have not fixed the amount of commission payable, reasonable compensation will be implied. So many factors may enter into a determination of reasonable compensation in any particular acquisition that no general rule can be stated to fix such compensation in all cases. But as an indication of how the implied commission may be fixed, the general principle is that the commission should be sufficient to pay the broker or finder a commission or fee which (1) is commensurate with standard fees for such brokers, fixed by custom or otherwise, (2) is stated in the statutes of the state whose law governs where such statutes fix the commission, or (3) is the broker's or finder's usual fee, if such usual fee is reasonable.

Duration of Contract. Once a contract between a buyer or seller and finder exists, the duration of the agreement depends upon the intention of the parties as expressed in the written contract or implied from the terms of the implied contract. Where the period of employment is not fixed by the terms of the contract, differing circumstances and a number of differing events can cause its legal termination. Thus, the contract will terminate after a reasonable time, or after the broker or finder accomplishes the purpose for which he was hired, or definitely and finally fails to accomplish such purpose, or if the contract is otherwise modified or revoked. As an example of termination of a brokerage contract, assume you, as a prospective buyer, have hired a broker to negotiate the purchase of the Split-Second Outboard Motor Company. If some time after the broker has been hired and begins his work, you learn from your morning newspaper that the Split-Second Outboard Motor Company was acquired by your competitor, at a much higher price than you were willing to pay, you may assume that your arrangement with your broker has terminated.

Revoking the Contract. Unless the contract has a fixed duration, generally a buyer or seller always has the power to revoke the agency at any time and for any reason. Whether this right to terminate relations with a broker may be exercised without liability on the part of the buyer or seller depends upon the contract and the good faith of the buyer and seller. Although a principal may have the power to revoke a broker's or finder's agency, he may not breach the contract; and if he breaches the contract by terminating the relationship, he may be liable to pay damages. If a buyer or seller acts in good faith, he has the right to terminate the agency at any time before the commission has been earned. Generally, he may not, however, revoke in bad faith in order to avoid payment of a commission where the broker or finder has substantially accomplished his mission. Where a buyer hires a finder to find a company for the buyer to acquire and the finder finds a company acceptable to the buyer, the buyer may not, without incurring liability to the finder, revoke the agency and then buy the company.

AN APPROACH TO BROKERAGE

How should you approach brokerage situations? In general, to avoid uncertainties, all brokerage arrangements should be reduced to writing and should contain details of the understanding between the principal and the broker or finder of each of the major terms of the contract. As already mentioned, implied contracts of brokerage may arise, leaving important terms unsettled. Such unwritten, implied contracts should be avoided.

To illustrate, assume that you are an officer of a corporation known to be interested in acquiring companies in the electronics field. A broker arrives at your office and says: "I know you people are interested in acquiring companies in the electronics field. I know that Dyne-O-Space Electronics Company is for sale. Are you interested?"

You have some familiarity with Dyne-O-Space and might be interested in buying the company. How do you answer the broker?

Your answer to the broker should first question whether or not the broker has authority to offer Dyne-O-Space for sale. Determining the broker's authority to act at the outset will avoid possible subsequent disagreement between you and the seller as to the employer of the broker. You might say to the broker: "Of course you have written authority to offer Dyne-O-Space for sale. May I see it?"

If the broker has such written authority, the written authority may contain an agreement on the part of the seller to pay the broker his commission upon the completion of the sale, or it may provide that the broker must collect his commission from the buyer. At least the written authority will give you a concrete starting point.

Even if the broker has no written evidence of authority to act, it may be that you will feel that the broker could be helpful and you would be willing to pay the broker a commission if he could bring about a purchase of Dyne-O-Space. You may feel he can put you in direct touch with the proper officials of Dyne-O-Space or that he has developed detailed financial information of the company and projections of earnings in its field which could be helpful. In any event, whether you will pay the commission or whether the seller will pay the commission, the terms of the brokerage arrangement should be fixed in advance, in detail, in a written contract for the protection of both the principal and the broker. Certain of the aspects of brokerage arrangements mentioned in this chapter should be discussed with the broker with particular emphasis on the major elements: (1) Whose agent is the broker, i.e., who pays him? (2) What are the terms and conditions to be fulfilled? (3) What will the amount of commission be? (4) When will the commission be earned? (5) How long will the brokerage contract remain in effect?

Before you agree to move forward with the broker the details of the arrangement should be reduced to writing and signed by the buyer and broker, or seller and broker, as the case may be. Written brokerage agreements often take the form of a letter signed by both the broker and the party who agrees to pay the commission. A more elaborate contract is not necessary, provided the letter agreement details the major understanding.

As an example of a general form of brokerage letter agreement, printed below is a form of agreement the broker showed you when you asked him whether he had the authority to represent Dyne-O-Space:

DYNE-O-SPACE ELECTRONICS COMPANY
(Seller Corporation)

June   , 19

Dear Mr. Broker:

   We are writing to confirm the brokerage agreement arrived at between us concerning the sale of our company, Dyne-O-Space Electronics Company. We hereby employ you as our broker to bring about the sale of our company in accordance with the terms and conditions expressed in this letter.

The purchase price for our company, must be satisfactory to us in amount and must be paid in the capital stock of a company listed on a National Stock Exchange; the sale must be made as a "tax-free" reorganization under the U.S. tax laws, and the buyer and the terms and conditions of the Agreement and Plan or Reorganization must be satisfactory to us.

Should you bring about the sale of our company, we will pay you a commission of $20,000. This commission will be payable to you only as, if, and when, the transfer of substantially all of the assets or the stock of the company has been completed and the stock of the buyer has been received by our company or its stockholders. If the transaction is not consummated, no commission will be payable to you regardless of whether the failure to close is due to any action or failure to act on our part, or due to any action or failure to act on the part of a prospective buyer.

You warrant to us that you have no arrangement or understanding of any kind with any other person or firm who may claim a commission from us as a result of such arrangement or understanding and you agree to hold us harmless against any such claims. You also agree that you will not seek any commission or remuneration of any kind from any buyer of our company, and that our payment of $20,000 to you upon fulfillment of the conditions contained in this letter will be in complete discharge of any and all obligations to you in connection with the sale of our company.

This agency will automatically terminate 180 days from the date you sign this agreement, unless our company terminates the agency sooner by 10 days written notice to you.

If this letter sets forth the understanding arrived at between us, will you please sign and date the carbon copy of this letter below under the word "Agreed" and return the signed carbon to us.

> *Very truly yours,*
> DYNE-O-SPACE ELECTRONICS COMPANY
>
> _____
> *John Jones*
> *Vice President*

Agreed:
Dated: ___ *June* ___ *, 19* _____

_____
Jack Smith
Broker

You will note that Dyne-O-Space Electronics Company proposes to pay the $20,000 commission. This means that the assets of the company will be reduced by that amount, and you, as the buyer should take this fact into account in negotiating the price you are willing to pay. Sometimes, where the seller is a closely held corporation a buyer will insist that any brokerage commissions or finder's fees be paid by the seller's shareholders individually. But under the circumstances, a buyer may expect that the seller's shareholders will, in turn, take their agreement to pay commissions into account in negotiating a sales price.

If when the broker approached you with Dyne-O-Space Electronics Company, you were employed by a company which had specified conditions under which it would accept offerings of companies, you might say to the broker: "Our company imposes strict conditions under which it will accept information concerning proposed acquisitions. Before I talk to you about Dyne-O-Space, I would like you to read these conditions and see if you agree." With that you might hand the broker a document which might read as follows:

Conditions for Submission of Companies to the Buyer for Consideration as Acquisitions.

Buyer is a company which has grown by combination of internal expansion and the acquisition of related businesses. While buyer is anxious to take every opportunity to add profitable related businesses to its current product lines, it has found that certain precautions are required to protect the interests of itself, prospective sellers and their designated intermediaries. This is particularly true since buyer solicits suggestions for potential acquisitions from many sources, its employees, bankers, outside directors and others, and actively pursues these prospects through various business contacts and direct overtures to principals. Buyer, therefore, will only accept submissions which conform to the following conditions:

(1) Buyer must see an executed copy and be provided with a copy of the agreement between the seller and the intermediary, which includes: (a) The amount of the fee; (b) Who is responsible for payment; (c) The conditions under which payment becomes due; (d) The period of the agreement's effectiveness; (e) A statement indicating whether this particular agreement is exclusive for the period indicated.

(2) Any submission made to the buyer must be with the understanding that the buyer assumes no obligation to do more than consider such submission to the extent, in the buyer's sole judgment, the submission merits consideration, and to indicate to the intermediary the buyer's interest or lack thereof.

(3) Unless specifically requested in writing and agreed to by the buyer in writing, the buyer will not ordinarily return financial or other data submitted to it for analysis of the proposed acquisition.

(4) Although the buyer will treat the submission with care and discretion, it will not, however, agree to hold a submission in confidence. In making its analysis, the buyer must reveal the information submitted to various employees. Although these employees have instructions to keep the information confidential, the buyer is unwilling to assume responsibility that no disclosure of information will be made. It is understood, therefore, that no confidential relationship or agreement to compensate is entered into by reason of buyer considering the submission.

(5) No submissions will be accepted without an asking price for the business in question. The asking price will enable the buyer to inform the intermediary more quickly of whether or not the buyer has any interest in the proposed acquisition.

(6) The buyer is to be provided with complete and detailed operating statements, balance sheets, records of ownership, sales and product data, reasons for selling, and other information which the buyer may reasonably request for initial analysis.

Having read and understood the foregoing conditions, I hereby agree to comply with them, and I herewith submit Dyne-O-Space Electronics Company for your consideration on the conditions set forth above.

Signed this_____day of_____, 19_____.

_____
Signature of Intermediary

_____
Signature of Buyer Executive

Types of Brokerage Agreements. Some broker's or finder's arrangements consist of concise one page letters, while others are more elaborate and detailed. Examples of both types actually used in successful transactions are reproduced below, with the parties names fictionalized.

BEST FINDERS COMPANY

CONFIDENTIAL

May   , 19

Seller Company
U.S. Route 1,000
Happy Rest, Ind.

Attention: Mr. John Smith, President

Gentlemen:

This confirms you authorize us non-exclusively to initiate negotiations with companies approved in advance by you for possible acquisition, merger, or sale of your company on such terms and conditions as may be acceptable to you, your Board of Directors, and your stockholders.

We agree to use our best efforts to produce the buyer most acceptable to you, and to assist you in negotiations if you so desire.

If we produce a buyer with whom within eighteen months you conclude such a transaction, you agree in consideration of our efforts to pay us a fee of one and three-fourths percent (1 3/4%) of the total proceeds received. This fee is contingent upon such a transaction having been concluded by exchange of shares or receipt of funds by you or your stockholders, and is payable when, as, and if received by you or your stockholders.

If you are in agreement, kindly indicate by signing and returning this letter, keeping the duplicate for your records.

Agreed: *Sincerely yours,*
SELLER COMPANY   *Richard Roe*

By /s/ John Smith   *BEST FINDERS COMPANY*
      President   *Corporate Planning and*
Date _____   *Development Department*

The form of brokerage arrangement printed below is illustrative of the more elaborate type of agreement. Among other terms, it provides for the payment of a commission to the broker if a transaction closes within 18 months after the termination of the brokerage agreement, with a buyer introduced by the broker.

November   , 19

Mr. Robert Searcher, President
Excellent Finders & Company, Inc.
100000 Broadway
New York, New York

Dear Mr. Searcher:

I am writing to confirm the understanding we have reached concerning the proposed sale of the business or stock of Seller Factories, Inc. ("Seller"). You are hereby employed as a broker to bring about the sale of the assets or stock of Seller, subject to the terms and conditions expressed in this letter.

This brokerage arrangement is non-exclusive.

We expressly reserve the right to reject any proposed purchaser you submit to us. On your part you agree that you will submit the name of any proposed purchaser to us in writing, and our written approval noted on each submission will be a prerequisite, before you may reveal our name to any prospective purchaser.

You will be entitled to the commission mentioned below only if a prospective purchaser has been submitted to us and approved by us in writing, and an acquisition by such purchaser is actually consummated, i.e., the acquisition has closed, and we have received the full consideration specified in the contract of sale.

Should the Seller's business or the stock of Seller be acquired by a purchaser introduced by you and approved by us in accordance with this agreement, on behalf of Seller and myself and the other stockholders of Seller, we agree to pay to you a commission of 5% of the sale price for the business or stock of Seller.

Should the sales transaction take the form of an exchange of stock then, in such event, Seller or its stockholders will deliver to you 5% of the stock received by Seller or its stockholders after delivery to us.

Should the transaction take the form of a sale of assets, the 5% commission will be based upon the total purchase price paid by the buyer plus any cash or other assets that might have been retained by the Seller in the transaction, minus any liabilities retained by the Seller (not including any income tax due solely as the result of the sale of assets).

If the entire consideration is received by the Seller in stock or cash at the closing, the entire commission will be payable at the closing. If the consideration for the acquisition of the business or stock is paid in installments, any commission payable hereunder shall also be payable in installments at the time the installments are received from the purchaser, and each installment payment of commission will be equal to 5% of each installment as received.

If the transaction is not actually closed with a purchaser submitted by you to us in writing and approved by us in writing, no commission will be payable to you regardless of whether the failure to close is due to any action or failure to act on Seller's part or on the part of Seller's stockholders, or due to any action or failure to act on the part of the prospective purchaser submitted by you.

You agree that no charge will be made to us for any expenses incurred by you in your efforts and activities to effect the sale of the Seller's business or the stock of the

Seller. You warrant that you do not have and will not enter into any arrangement of co-brokerage, and you agree to pay any third parties retained by you in connection with this agreement and to hold Seller and its stockholders harmless against any such claims. You also agree that you will not seek any commission or remuneration of any kind from any buyer of Seller's business or stock and that Seller's payment of the commission to you in accordance with the terms contained in this letter will be in complete discharge of any and all obligations to you in connection with the sale of Seller's business or stock.

This agency will automatically terminate 180 days from the date you sign this agreement.

It is hereby understood and agreed that, should you have introduced us to a prospective purchaser approved by us as herein provided and a transaction is not actually closed with such purchaser prior to the expiration of this agency, should we continue, resume, or reinstate negotiations with such purchaser which ripen into a transaction which is actually closed within 18 months after the date of termination of this agency, we will pay you a commission with respect to such transaction as herein provided.

If this letter sets forth the understanding arrived at between us will you please sign and date the carbon copy of this letter below under the word "Agreed" and return the signed copy to us.

SELLER FACTORIES, INC.

By /s/ Bill Greatfellow
President

AGREED:
DATED: _____

/s/ Robert Seacher
President
EXCELLENT FINDERS & COMPANY, INC.

In summary, where a broker or finder is involved in the transaction, the buyer and seller should establish the responsibility for payment of commission between each other and with the broker or finder as soon as possible. The terms of the arrangement should be set down in a written contract before the principals have progressed to a point in the negotiations where they may be in substantial agreement. Without a written brokerage contract, the vague principles of implied contract may lead to future disputes between the parties or with the broker or finder, which can hinder and even ruin negotiations which would otherwise mature smoothly into an acquisition satisfactory to both parties.

CHAPTER 4

Determining the Purchase Price

In acquisitions, as in most business transactions, the question of price is fundamental. The seller may or may not know what it wants for its business, but will under most
circumstances not enter into serious discussions concerning sale until the buyer is ready to
discuss the sale price. The buyer, therefore, should be prepared to give some indication of
purchase price should the need to do so become apparent during the early negotiating sessions. At that time the buyer may have only limited information of the seller's business,
consisting most probably of a number of past years' financial statements.

As a general comment, in these discussions of price, as indicated in Chapter 3, the buyer
and seller should bear in mind possible finders' fees, if any, and should also bear in mind other
incidental expenses such as legal and accounting fees and who should pay these expenses.
Difficulties may arise when the negotiation has reached the contract stage and these details
have not been settled, since both the buyer and seller may then have fixed upon a price which
does not allow for deducting the incidental expenses, often sizable in amount.

Although many more factors may come into play in fixing the price for a going business,
the technique of negotiating price is no different from the technique of negotiating the price of
a home or any other property. The buyer may argue that the earnings trends are down, plant
needs repairs, patents are expiring, substantial additional working capital is needed, product
lines are becoming obsolete, and any other circumstance which would indicate a lower price,
while the seller may point to all the circumstances which indicate increased future earnings
and present value of the business. Ultimately, however, the parties must agree on a price
acceptable to both or no deal will result. Although fixing the price basically involves bargaining—horsetrading—methods or yardsticks exist to help establish the maximum price a buyer
should pay and a minimum price a seller should accept.

In the initial negotiations to set a price, the seller may have an advantage, since it knows

49

its own business and may have a fixed idea of the desired price. Therefore, this chapter will concern itself primarily with methods and yardsticks helpful to the buyer, but with which the seller should also be familiar. The seller, moreover, may establish a minimum acceptable price by using certain obvious yardsticks. In the first place, the seller may know what other buyers are willing to pay, and secondly, the seller may judge purchase price, as a last resort, against the liquidating value of the business.

In determining price, you as the buyer should bear in mind that your reason for buying will affect the price. If your objective is to acquire a going business and continue to operate it, an acceptable purchase price will differ from an acceptable price if your objective is otherwise (either to liquidate a portion of the business or to buy only a product line). Furthermore, in certain specialized industries such as public utilities, insurance companies, and banks, a purchase price would be determined by different methods than employed for an industrial corporation. The general methods and yardsticks discussed below are based on the assumption that you are acquiring a going industrial business and that you intend to integrate this business with your own.

VALUE VS. PRICE

The *value* of a business to each party may be determined by each party independently. The buyer and seller may each use such methods and yardsticks to determine the *value* of the seller's business for its own purposes as it should choose. On the other hand, the *price* to be paid may be determined only by negotiation between the parties. If the *value* placed on its business by a seller is substantially higher than the *value* placed on the business by the buyer, and if each remains firm that its determination of value should fix the *price,* the negotiations will not result in a compromise *price* acceptable to both and the acquisition will not be consummated.

In the discussion below, the various methods and yardsticks set forth are intended to indicate how a buyer or seller may determine what an *acceptable price* should be. In this sense, the yardsticks may be considered to provide methods for determining value.

SOME APPROACHES TO PRICE

First consider three approaches to price which rarely would be satisfactory as final determinants of an acceptable price. Each approach has severe limitations, but may be helpful as an adjunct in refining or adjusting a price fixed under different methods of determining price more acceptable to experts or others experienced in acquisitions.

Book value. Book value of the seller's business, generally the net value as shown on the seller's balance sheet including the capital stock account, may be considered in setting price. But in most industrial enterprises, book value of a business may be understated in times of inflation or overstated in times of depression, and within the concept of "generally accepted accounting principles," accelerated depreciation, Lifo or Fifo inventory treatment, or methods of treating reserves may inflate or deflate book value. Furthermore, whether book value is high or low will often have little effect upon the earnings of an industrial corporation, and earning power should be the <u>major consideration in fixing a purchase price.</u> On the other hand, in an acquisition of a bank, or investment company or other business consisting primarily of liquid assets, book value may have great relevance to price. Book value may also have some relevance in acquiring a public utility, or railroad or other business which is subject to rate fixing by governmental agencies. Such agencies often fix their rates on the basis of invested capital, and therefore book value may be important in determining price because of its effect on earnings.

Appraisal. Appraisal of value of plant, equipment, inventories, and intangibles is always useful and under certain circumstances may play an important role in determining price. If the buyer is acquiring a highly completive business with uncertain future prospects, an accurate appraisal of physical assets of the seller will indicate how much may be realized by liquidation of the business, and as a consequence what the maximum loss of the buyer will be. Or, if excess assets are utilized in seller's business, appraisal will indicate to the buyer what it will realize on the sale of such assets to offset the purchase price.

Comparison with other companies. As another approach, the buyer may compare the seller's business with other businesses in the same industry. Such a comparison may reveal the price/earnings ratio placed upon the comparable business by its stockholders, and may give the buyer an opportunity to compare the seller's net return on investment, inventory turnover, plant, patents, and similar items with other companies in the same industry. The value of such comparisons is limited, however, since no two businesses are identical. Though the products may be similar—size, differences in management, plant, distribution systems, patent position, market areas, and other factors will always cause a difference in value between two companies.

MARKET VALUE OF LISTED STOCK

In determining purchase price involving two publicly held companies with actively traded stock listed on a national stock exchange or actively traded in the over-the-counter market, the respective market values of the stock of each company will play a major role—and probably the deciding role—in determining purchase price. Unless the stockholders of the selling company receive payment, whether in the form of stock, cash or other securities of greater value than the market value of their stock, it is highly unlikely that they will approve the sale of their company.

The dominant effect of the market value of actively traded stocks may be observed from the prices offered to stockholders in takeover bids. Takeover bids as a rule involve an offer of a premium to the stockholders of the seller above the quoted market price of their stock. Takeover bids often involve premiums which exceed twenty percent or more of market price of a seller's stock. In all of these instances of takeover bids, the buyer acts on the premise that, unless a substantial premium is offered, the stockholders of the seller will not accept the offer to buy their stock.

Where the goal is to acquire control of a publicly held company with marketable, actively traded stock, considerations of projected future earnings, price/earnings ratios and discounted present value of future earnings are essentially academic in *fixing* the price to be offered. Such considerations, of course, remain of importance to the buyer in determining what the value of a prospective seller should be to a prospective buyer. If, however, based upon the price of the seller's stock in the market, the earnings per share or return on invested capital of the seller are too low to meet the buyer's requirements, the buyer is not in a position to bargain for a lower price which will meet the buyer's acquisition requirements. If the public had placed too high a price on the seller's stock, the only alternative of the buyer to paying such price may be to walk away from the proposed acquisition or wait until the price of the seller's stock reaches a more realistic level.

The effect of the dominance of the market price of stock upon the price to be paid for the acquisition of a publicly held company, is seen from the numerous reports of proposed acquisitions abandoned because of fluctuations in the market prices of the stocks involved. To cite a few examples, some time ago the *Wall Street Journal* contained a report that the planned acquisition of Congoleum-Nairn, Inc. by National Gypsum Company for $73,000,000 in stock and cash was called off. Frederick H. Cook, Chairman of Congoleum-Nairn, Inc. stated that negotiations had terminated because a decline in the price of the National Gypsum stock "had made it an unworkable transaction." Similarly, when Occidental Petroleum Corporation and Signal Oil & Gas Company announced the termination of their merger discussions, the companies were quoted as stating: "the present conditions of the stock market have so changed since the initial discussions concerning the merger that it can't take place as scheduled without substantial renegotiation of the merger terms."

A general approach to determining purchase price of a business is developed below. It involves projected earnings and price/earnings ratios, and probably would have little significance in *fixing* the price to be paid for a seller with publicly held, actively traded securities. Therefore, in considering the suggested framework for setting a price for a going business, you should have due regard for the effect of market value of actively traded securities. On the other hand, even though stock is publicly held and traded in the market place, in some situations controlling stockholders may have such large blocks that any attempt to sell in the open market may either depress the stock value substantially or may require registration of the transaction with the Securities and Exchange Commission by such controlling shareholders. In such situations, even though the stock of the Seller may be publicly held and actively traded, the pricing framework developed below may still be important and help in fixing the price for the control of the business insofar as the controlling stockholders are concerned.

A PROPOSED PRICING FORMULA

Most authorities agree that projected earnings are the key factor in fixing price. The buyer should answer this question for itself: What will this business which is acquired earn during the next three, four, five or more years? Having estimated these earnings, under the proposed pricing formula the buyer must then decide what the price/earnings ratio should be, or stated differently, what multiple of average projected earnings should determine the price.

Therefore, the suggested approach to determining the purchase price for a going business contains two basic elements: (1) What are the projected future earnings of the business to be acquired? (2) By what number—price/earnings ratios—should these earnings be multiplied to determine the price? After these basics have been determined, other elements such as assumption of debt and additional capital required may cause adjustment to price, but the two basic elements are the foundation of determining an acceptable price.

A word of caution before proceeding to develop the methods and yardsticks for determining price, as they are detailed below. The price for any one business is unique to that business in the sense that no two businesses can ever be identical in all details. Since many elements such as plant condition, possible expiration of patents, merchantability of inventory, present value of real estate, and many other detailed aspects of a seller's business may affect price, the general methods and yardsticks developed below should not be considered as the only approach to determining price. They should rather be looked upon as a suggested framework within which an acceptable price for a going business may be developed, subject to any unique element in the business which may require a deviation from the accepted framework.

PROJECTED EARNINGS

Projected earnings are a matter of judgment, since no one can predict with certainty what the future holds for any particular business. Nevertheless, disciplined use of tried methods and yardsticks will lessen the likelihood that the buyer's judgment may be wrong.

Isolating seller's projected earnings. For the purpose only of the initial projection of the seller's future earnings, the buyer should assume that the seller will continue to operate as an isolated unit and not as an integrated part of buyer's business. In other words, in the initial determination of future earnings the buyer should take no account of increased earning power, if any, which the buyer may bring to the business. Such increased earning power may subsequently be taken into account by the buyer in fixing the ultimate price it is willing to pay, but should not initially be injected as an element to further complicate the difficult task of predicting the seller's future earnings.

The suggestion to treat the seller's business as an isolated unit in projecting seller's future earnings is made to counteract a buyer's natural enthusiasm for a business which complements its own and adds growth potential. This type of enthusiasm on a buyer's part is not unusual: "Boy! If I had that product line, I could double sales inside of a year with my distribution setup." Immediately accepting the premise that sales will double, may lead to grossly overstated earnings projections. In order to curb what may be over-enthusiasm, a buyer should first make projections of the seller's earnings as though the seller would continue as a separate entity. The buyer's estimate of additional earnings it may bring to seller's business is a legitimate element to consider in deciding how much to pay for a seller's business, but the buyer should make this addition to earnings only after it has realistically appraised the seller's own potential.

Seller's past earnings. The start for projecting earnings should be an analysis of past earning; an indication of what a business has done under known facts and the economic influences of prior years. In studying past earnings you, as the buyer, should analyze these earnings to determine what contribution was made by each product line and adjust the same for any known abnormal factors which affected earnings. For example, if a competitor's factory burned down and the seller obtained all of the competitor's business while the factory was rebuilt, earnings were presumably high as a result, and this factor should be given weight in the analysis. As a further example, where a closely held corporation is being acquired, adjustments should often be made for such items as the expenses of a yacht charged to the business, failure of the owners to take adequate salaries to avoid excessive tax payments and the expenses of Cadillacs on the company's books which are used by the owners' wives.

As a start, the buyer should obtain profit and loss statements of the seller for a reasonably long, past period. If figures are available, a ten-year history of earnings of the seller should be a good indication of past history, while earnings for a five- or even a three-year period are often sufficient. The history of earnings should be not only of total earnings but of earnings by product lines. If the buyer is buying a business on the basis of its projection of earnings, it should know in detail how similar earnings were realized in the past.

For example, if you, as the buyer, are buying a machine tool company, licensed to sell imported machine tools, you should know how much of the income of the seller is realized from sales commissions on imports and how much is realized from tools manufactured and sold. You may have as your objective the purchase of a business in which the income is realized from the manufacture and sale of products, not one in which a major portion of the income is realized from a franchise which may be cancelled in the future. If you find that 75 per cent of the seller's earnings are realized from commissions on the sales of imported machine tools, the seller's business is not what you are seeking, or the price should be fixed to include only the manufacturing business. In summary, you as the buyer should start with a historical breakdown of earnings by product line in developing a price for the seller's business.

The analysis of the past earnings statements of the seller should include year-by-year comparisons to determine what the past profit trend has been. In this connection annual comparisons of (1) gross sales will indicate volume trends; (2) cost relationship to gross sales will indicate cost trends; (3) cost of labor relationship to material cost will indicate wage and mechanization trends, and (4) advertising and research and development expenditures will indicate the extent to which such expenditures tend to increase or decrease with earnings.

If the earnings statements are those of a division or wholly owned subsidiary of a larger business, care should be taken to adjust the statements for all inter-company transactions which may distort earnings. For example, services of a central research and development division or home office executive supervision may not have been charged to a division, and earnings should be decreased accordingly. To reiterate, if the seller is a closely held corporation, the buyer should eliminate all items of income and expense from the past earnings statements which should be eliminated to clearly reflect past earnings. Such items might consist of expenses incurred in connection with a hunting lodge operated by the seller for business entertainment which the seller would retain, or of unreasonably low salaries paid by the seller to its principal officer-stockholders who are in very high income tax brackets, or any other of the numerous items which may require adjustment to place the financial statements of a closely held corporation on a comparable basis to the statements of a publicly held company subject to strict audit procedures.

Past earnings of seller's industry. After completion of the analysis of the seller's past earnings, it should be compared with the past earnings of the seller's industry as a whole. Figures on past industry earnings may often be obtained from trade associations or U.S. Department of Commerce figures. By comparing the seller with the industry as a whole on the basis of annual figures, a buyer may determine how well a seller has done in the past in relationship to the seller's industry. Product line comparisons of such categories as total net annual sales, pre-tax profits, pre-tax profit margins, percentage return on net assets employed, total direct labor and inventory turnover will indicate the seller's general financial record as compared with its industry as a whole. Such comparisons will highlight the areas in which the seller has surpassed or lagged behind its industry in the past, and will help to project the seller's earnings into the future by adjusting industry projections by the seller's past proven areas of special weakness or strength.

As an example, assume the seller is in a cyclical and highly competitive industry such as the manufacture of industrial cranes. If a study of the past earnings history of this industry as a whole shows peaks and valleys in earnings and no clearly defined growth trend, but the study of the seller shows annual earnings increases and a definite growth trend, the buyer may feel justified in projecting greater future earnings for the seller than the seller's industry as a whole. However, before making such an assumption, a buyer should analyze comparative figures to isolate the reasons underlying the seller's apparent past superiority, and then attempt to forecast whether the same reasons will continue to apply in the future.

Future earnings. After analyzing the past earnings of the seller and its industry, the buyer should attempt to project these earnings into the future, an area of speculation calling into play all the imagination, all the judgment, and all the ability of the business man.

As a start in determining future earnings the buyer may ask the seller what future earnings the seller anticipates for the next five years. In this connection, the buyer may ask the seller to complete a form of Long-Range Forecast, such as was discussed in Chapter 2, which involves a projection of the seller's earnings five years into the future.

Normally, if the parties have reached a stage in the negotiations where they have agreed in principal that a merger may be mutually desirable, the seller should be willing to provide the information requested. The seller should and often does welcome an opportunity to tell the buyer how good its business prospects are.

As discussed in greater detail in Chapter 2, the Long-Range Forecast, when completed by the seller, will indicate in detail the seller's knowledge and projections of six major aspects of its business: (1) The Market—the seller's present and projected product lines; (2) The Competition—competitor's present and projected product lines and outlook for the future; (3) The Seller's Past and Projected Performance—the seller's volume and percentage share of the industry volume; (4) Seller's Requirements—projected cash and personnel requirements; (5) Seller's Operations Summary—past and projected income and return on assets; and (6) Seller's Projected Cash Flow—projected net cash generated and uses of cash.

In its analysis the buyer should adjust the seller's projections in the Long-Range Forecast for any assumptions of the seller which appear unwarranted, such as annual projected increases in profit margins not justified by past history. In addition to analyzing the seller's Long-Range Forecast, the buyer should make its own independent estimate of the future of the seller's business by research in financial publications, and often, of course, the buyer will have researched the seller's industry prior to opening discussions of a possible merger. The buyer should have as its major objectives a prediction of the future sales volume of the seller's products, and the profit margin to be applied to the sales volume.

To summarize, in determining the price to be paid for a going business the buyer should attempt to project the future earnings of the business. This projection involves two elements.

First a history of past earnings. Second a projection of those earnings into the future based upon the buyer's best judgment of all the factors which may affect the earnings in the future economic environment.

PRICE/EARNINGS RATIO

After determining present and projected earnings, the buyer should attempt to fix a multiple of those earnings which should be utilized to arrive at the price. Normally, this multiple is referred to as the price/earnings ratio and may be defined as the result obtained by dividing the purchase price by one year's after-tax earnings. What should the price/earnings ratio be, or stated differently, how many years should elapse before the total of after-tax annual earnings will equal the purchase price? The price/earnings ratio may also be considered from the viewpoint of return on investment. For instance, a 10 per cent after-tax return on investment (purchase price) would mean that 10 years are expected to elapse before the initial investment (purchase price) is recouped. Such a return would be synonomous with a price/earnings ratio of 10. The search for the proper price/earnings ratio is a search for the number by which one year's after-tax earnings is to be multiplied to fix the purchase price.

Price/earnings ratio—risk. A basic consideration in establishing the price/earnings ratio should be the amount of risk involved in actually realizing the projected future earnings of the seller's business. Earnings or profits are a businessman's reward for taking risks. The higher the risks, the greater the rewards should be. If a businessman can realize a fixed per cent return on an investment in United States Government Bonds he should think carefully before acquiring a business with a projected similar percentage return on investment, and should make the purchase at such a price only where the most extraordinary circumstances exist. Thus, the higher the risk in conducting the seller's business, the lower the price/earnings ratio should be.

Much has been written regarding price/earnings ratios by security analysts, economists, and financial writers; furthermore, administrative agencies and courts have rendered many decisions in which return on invested capital or price/earnings ratios were considered. No fixed rules may be determined from all of this written material, since the price/earnings ratio is a matter of the buyer's individual judgment, but a review of these various approaches to the price/earnings ratio indicates that they all contain one common concept—the riskier the business the lower the price/earnings ratio.

Although decisions of administrative agencies and the courts recognize the general principle that a stable business should have a higher price/earnings ratio that a risky one, such decisions are generally of little value in determining a price a buyer should pay for a going business. The Internal Revenue Service must often make a determination of the value of the goodwill of a closely held business to establish the value of the business as a whole for estate tax purposes. The approach in such instances is primarily theoretical, and does not necessarily reflect what a buyer would be willing to pay for the same business. Other governmental determinations of business values have been made in public utility rate cases and in bankruptcy reorganizations, but because public utilities are government sanctioned monopolies and bankruptcy situations contain unique features not normally involved in valuing a going industrial business, such administrative decisions are of little value as guides to price/earnings ratios applicable to industry in general.

Price/earnings ratio—historical. One author, Arthur Stone Dewing, in *The Financial Policy of Corporations** has made an extensive study of price/earnings ratios and has concluded that the price/earnings ratios printed below should apply under the circumstances indicated.

Recognizing that the price is a matter of judgment and that during boom periods businesses may sell at inflated price/earnings ratios and at depressed price/earnings ratios during depression periods, the author presents the following conclusions as to what "normal" price/earnings ratios should be for industrial businesses:

		P/E Ratio
1.	Business with long existence and established goodwill among many customers—like a milk business with established routes	10
2.	Businesses established for some time with proven ability to survive or manufacturing companies with large capital investments	8–7
3.	A business established less than ten or twelve years or grown up around a single personality	6
4.	Industrial corporation requiring management skill but not unusually rare special knowledge, without particular patent or trademark protection where capital requirements are not great	5
5.	Small special character business—like local flour mills, shoe shops or bakeries	4
6.	Highly specialized businesses dependent on the skill of a small group, or seasonal, or dependent on weather	2–1
7.	Businesses of a personal service character or businesses dependent on the skill of a single person like an authors' agency or an animal hospital	1

Since so many factors may influence the choice of a proper price/earnings ratio, including market conditions and methods of payment which will be discussed later in this chapter, a list of price/earnings ratios such as the above cannot normally fix the price in a given transaction to the exclusion of other considerations. But the list does once more illustrate that the riskier the business, the lower the price/earnings ratio.

Price/earnings ratio—current. The effect of the status of the general economy as well as the amount of acquisition activity (or lack of it) upon price earnings ratios is illustrated by a survey reported in the *Arthur Young Journal,* Autumn 1968.** This survey of acquisitions which occurred during 1965, 1966, and 1967 indicated a significant change in the acquisition market during those years. A comparison of the aggregate price/earnings ratios of acquisitions made during those years with the highs and lows of Standard & Poor's 425 industrial averages indicates the following:

	Number of Acquisitions	*Aggregate P/E Ratio*	*Standard & Poor's Average*
1965	200	15.8	17.8—15.6
1966	326	16.3	17.1—13.3
1967	468	18.0	18.2—15.3

---

* Ronald Press, New York, N.Y.: 5th Edition, 1953.
** Richard A. Winfield, "The Rising Cost of Mergers," *The Arthur Young Journal,* Autumn 1968.

The foregoing table indicates that the price/earnings ratio paid for acquisitions increased from 15.8 during 1965, to 16.3 during 1966, and to 18.0 during 1967; also, that the price/earnings ratio for acquisitions moved from the low side of the range of stock market ratios to the high side during those years.

Price/earnings ratio—stock market value. Each time a share of stock is purchased, whether on a national or regional stock exchange or in the over-the-counter market or in a private transaction, the purchase price could be stated in terms of a multiple of earnings: a price/earnings ratio. With the exception of an acquisition involving publicly held companies where the price placed upon the stock by the trading public is usually the most important factor in establishing the exchange ratio for the stocks, purchase of a comparatively few shares of stock in the open market should not be a basis for establishing price/earnings ratios for an industry. Such a purchase, often only a minute portion of total outstanding shares, involves so many considerations differing from the purchase of an entire business that price/earnings ratios established by stock market purchases should receive only slight attention for our purposes. An owner of a few shares of stock cannot set corporate policy, cannot liquidate a portion of assets, cannot integrate or reduce product lines in number, and cannot limit research expenditures to increase earnings. Finally, stock market psychology is a valid consideration in the purchase of stock for purposes of gain while such psychology should not be a consideration in acquiring a closely held going business.

A comparison of historical and current price/earnings ratios of stock in different industries will indicate the different opinions of investors as to stability and growth possibilities of these industries in different economic periods. For example, in early 1961 the Value Line Investment Survey indicated that among the stocks reviewed in that survey the ten-year, average price/earnings ratio in the petroleum industry was 13 and the ratio at that time was 13.9; in the agricultural equipment industry the average was 8.7 and the ratio at that time was 9.5; in the banking industry the respective ratios were 13.7 and 15.6; in the life insurance industry the average ratio was 11.4 and the current ratio 14.6, and in the automotive industry the ratios were 10.4 and 12.4, respectively.

The price/earnings ratios mentioned are ratios established for stocks which have a ready market, and authorities agree in principle that a closely held business with little or no market for its stock should command a lower price/earnings ratio. Nevertheless, in a period such as early 1961 when the marketplace established high price/earnings ratios and when individual stocks sold at highly inflated ratios—Polaroid at 65 times earnings, IBM at 52, and Minnesota Mining and Manufacturing at 50, a seller will be influenced by such price/earnings ratios in determining the value of its business. For instance, a seller of a closely held company at a time when the market has established high price/earnings ratios may feel that it can realize more for its business by going public than by selling to another company which would attempt to set the price on the basis of an historical or more conservative price/earnings ratio. At such times a buyer may be forced to offer more for a business than it would under other circumstances, or not buy.

Statistics and studies similar to those mentioned have indicated that price/earnings ratios will be different for different industries, and that the current stock market industry price/earnings averages will influence prices paid in making acquisitions. The table below, taken from *The Arthur Young Journal,* Autumn 1968, mentioned above, makes a three-year comparison of acquisition price/earnings ratios by industry during the years 1965, 1966, and 1967:

THREE-YEAR COMPARISON OF
ACQUISITION PURCHASE PRICE/EARNINGS RATIOS
BY INDUSTRY*

(Includes only industries for which purchase price/earnings ratios were
determined for at least two years.)

INDUSTRY	1965 P/E RATIO	1966 P/E RATIO	1967 P/E RATIO
AEROSPACE		9.4	28.3
APPAREL & TEXTILE MFG.	12.4	11.0	14.3
AUTO PARTS & ACCESSORIES	11.9	12.8	14.8
BAKING & MILLING		11.7	14.5
BANKING & FINANCE	10.8	23.1	23.3
BUILDING PRODUCTS	15.1	10.8	15.0
CHEMICALS	22.2	17.2	16.9
CONFECTIONERY	14.4	18.7	
CONTAINERS	14.0	17.9	
DRUG	18.6	18.8	
ELECTRICAL EQUIPMENT	15.0	17.6	19.1
ELECTRONICS	19.8	37.5	21.5
FOODS—CANNED	12.8	7.9	
FOODS—PACKAGED	17.0	15.8	11.8
HOME FURNISHINGS	18.4		13.3
MACHINERY—CONSTRUCTION & MAT'L HANDLING	15.6		9.0
MACHINERY—INDUSTRIAL	11.6	11.9	12.9
MACHINERY—MACHINE TOOLS		13.1	14.5
MACHINERY—SPECIALTY MACHINERY		10.5	16.0
MEDICAL & DENTAL SUPPLIES		19.9	14.8
METAL FABRICATING	12.1	9.5	15.0
MOTION PICTURE & BROADCASTING		21.3	18.0
OFFICE EQUIPMENT		19.6	18.8
OIL	23.5	14.3	24.8
PAPER	19.2	17.2	16.0
PUBLISHING		28.0	31.9
RETAILING—DEPARTMENT STORES	15.7	10.7	13.6
RETAILING—FOOD CHAINS	15.5		15.5
RETAILING—MSC. WHOLESALE & RETAIL	14.0	11.3	26.7
SHOES & LEATHER		10.6	12.2
TELEPHONE		27.1	32.7
VENDING		10.8	33.8

The analysis of acquisitions during the year 1967 set forth in the table below, taken from *The Arthur Young Journal,* Autumn 1968, indicates that the average acquisition price/earnings ratio within the same industry has a close correlation to the stock market average price/earnings ratio for that industry:

---

* *The Arthur Young Journal*, Autumn 1968.

ACQUISITION PRICE

INDUSTRY	NUMBER OF ACQUISITIONS	TOTAL OF PRICES PAID (000)
AEROSPACE	6	$ 140,848[1]
AIR TRANSPORT	5	85,578
APPAREL MANUFACTURERS	7	129,029
AUTO PARTS & ACCESSORIES	8	1,045,331
AUTO TRUCKS & PARTS	4	17,552[1]
BAKING & MILLING	3	9,419
BANKING & FINANCE	4	8,220
BROADCASTING	3	11,759
BUILDING: CEMENT COMPANIES	6	100,225
HEATING & PLUMBING	7	66,241
CHEMICALS	28	489,053[1]
CONSULTING: COMPUTER-ORIENTED	5	47,579
NON-EDP	9	67,386
DISTRIBUTORS & RETAILERS (MISC.)	16	508,755
EDUCATIONAL	7	16,959[1]
ELECTRICAL EQUIPMENT	23	541,017
ELECTRICAL HOME APPLIANCES	5	106,376
ELECTRONICS	27	413,599[1]
FILM PROCESSING	4	5,623
FOODS—PACKAGED	6	164,368
HOME FURNISHINGS	5	101,930[1]
HOTELS & RESTAURANTS	5	191,458
MACHINERY: CONSTRUCTION & MAT'L HANDLING	8	37,845
INDUSTRIAL	10	63,175[1]
MACHINE TOOLS	8	46,733
SPECIALTY MACHINERY	11	153,191[1]
MEDICAL & DENTAL SUPPLIES	6	39,390
METAL FABRICATING	33	618,956
MOTION PICTURES	5	273,763
OFFICE EQUIPMENT	7	93,910[1]
OIL: CRUDE PRODUCERS	3	13,524
OIL-WELL SUPPLIERS	4	46,890[1]
PAPER	11	342,689[1]
PUBLISHING	14	478,831
RADIO & TV MANUFACTURERS	5	159,140
RETAILING: DEPARTMENT STORES	4	32,758
FOOD CHAINS	3	135,076
SHOES & LEATHER	4	12,589
SPORTING EQUIPMENT	6	43,037[1]
TELEPHONE UTILITIES	30	569,347
VENDING	14	197,132
ALL OTHERS	86	3,248,895[1]
TOTALS	468	$10,886,770

* *The Arthur Young Journal*, Autumn 1968.
[1] The net assets of one or more of the selling companies in this industry were not available. Before calculating the purchase-price-to-net-asset ratios, the purchase price of these companies was excluded from the industry total.

SURVEY—1967*

EARNINGS OF ACQUIRED COMPANIES (000)	ACQUISITIONS; PURCHASE-PRICE-TO-EARNINGS RATIOS	NET ASSETS OF ACQUIRED COMPANIES (000)	ACQUISITIONS: PURCHASE-PRICE-TO-NET-ASSETS RATIOS	STOCK MARKET:[2] MARKET-PRICE-TO-EARNINGS RATIOS		
				HIGH	1967	LOW
$ 4,982	28.3	$ 29,166	4.6	22.5	—	15.5
4,677	18.3	20,362	4.2	18.5	—	12.1
9,030	14.3	49,139	2.6	17.0	—	13.6
70,411	14.8	389,796	2.7	15.0	—	11.2
1,939	9.1	7,973	1.5	17.0	—	11.5
652	14.5	3,424	2.8	15.6	—	7.3
353	23.3	5,519	1.5	14.4	—	9.0
354	33.2	2,612	4.5	14.1	—	11.2
6,852	14.6	72,580	1.4	18.4	—	10.2
4,266	15.5	53,647	1.2	17.8	—	7.2
28,869	16.9	236,271	2.0	18.4	—	15.1
1,753	27.1	6,524	7.3			
4,289	15.7	26,563	2.5			
19,076	26.7	109,508	4.7			
875	19.4	2,361	3.8			
28,396	19.1	212,506	2.5	22.3	—	15.3
5,726	18.6	73,341	1.5	20.3	—	14.9
19,321	21.5	102,649	3.8	32.2	—	19.7
220	25.6	1,470	3.8			
13,921	11.8	132,443	1.2	18.4	—	16.0
7,645	13.3	63,526	1.6	17.2	—	10.8
8,068	23.7	43,914	4.4			
4,194	9.0	26,443	1.4	23.7	—	16.2
4,902	12.9	22,074	2.7	14.0	—	9.5
3,221	14.5	14,743	3.2	13.3	—	6.5
9,571	16.0	68,926	2.2	15.8	—	10.2
2,655	14.8	12,457	3.2			
41,272	15.0	232,818	2.5	17.4	—	11.5
15,480	17.7	81,661	3.4	15.4	—	12.1
5,006	18.8	41,159	2.1	53.6	—	31.7
886	15.3	5,789	2.3	19.8	—	16.3
1,549	30.3	7,226	5.4	15.4	—	9.6
21,401	16.0	161,843	2.1	16.2	—	13.3
15,025	31.9	72,565	6.6	32.4	—	23.7
6,793	23.4	23,548	6.8	33.4	—	25.0
2,417	13.6	16,256	2.0	17.5	—	12.7
8,742	15.5	97,806	1.4	13.8	—	11.7
1,030	12.2	12,641	1.0	15.7	—	8.5
3,593	12.0	16,702	2.4			
17,405	32.7	163,640	3.5	17.1	—	13.9
5,840	33.8	38,412	5.1			
190,492	17.1	1,575,505	2.0			
$603,820	18.0	$4,340,385	2.5	18.2	—	15.3

[2] From Standard & Poor's *Industry Surveys*.

High stock market P/E ratio—buyer advantage. A buyer should not be left with the impression, however, that high price/earnings ratio established by the market place will always work to its disadvantage. Where the buyer is a listed company or its stock is actively traded, at a time of high price/earnings ratios, the market place may have placed a high price/earnings ratio on the buyer's stock. Under these circumstances, if the buyer uses stock to buy the seller, the buyer can well afford to pay more in dollar value of its stock than it normally would.

To illustrate the foregoing principle, assume that the average price/earnings ratio of the buyer's stock over the past ten years has been 10. If the buyer has earned $2 per share after taxes during these years, the average selling price of the buyer's stock has been $20 per share (price/earnings ratio of 10 × after-tax per share earnings of $2). Now assume that during a period of high price/earnings ratios, such as the first half of 1963, the market places a price/earnings ratio of 20 on the buyer's stock. In other words, assuming the same $2 in earnings the buyer's stock is selling at $40 per share (P/E ratio of 20 × $2). If the buyer is guided by the principle that the earning he acquires in exchange for its stock should exceed its own earnings on a share for share basis (discussed below in the section entitled "Limits on Maximum Price"), the chart printed below indicates different prices expressed in dollars which a buyer may offer a seller and still upgrade the buyer's earnings per share.

Assuming that the buyer is earning $2 per share and that the total after-tax earnings of the seller are $500,000, some computations of total dollar value, based on different price/earnings ratios, which a buyer may offer and still upgrade earnings on shares exchanged by 20 per cent are printed below. To realize such a 20 per cent increase in its $2 per share earnings on the shares exchanged, the $500,000 of the seller's earnings when divided by the number of buyer's shares exchanged should indicate earnings of $2.40 per share exchanged ($2 × 120%). Expressed in round figures, the buyer should therefore not pay more than 208,000 shares of buyer's stock for the seller's business (208,000 shares divided into $500,000 of earnings). Notice how the price the buyer may offer varies from $4,160,000 to $8,320,000 in shares of stock without changing the $2.40 earnings per share exchanged as the price/earnings ratio varies from 10 to 20:

No. of Buyer's Shares Offered	Earnings Per Share Offered	Price/Earnings Ratio of Buyer's Shares Offered	Market Price Per Share Offered	Price Offered (Total Market Value of Shares Offered)
208,000	$2	10	$20	$4,160,000
208,000	$2	12	$24	4,992,000
208,000	$2	14	$28	5,824,000
208,000	$2	16	$32	6,656,000
208,000	$2	18	$36	7,488,000
208,000	$2	20	$40	8,320,000

Contrary to the above reasoning that a buyer may offer a greater dollar value in shares when the price/earnings ratio of the buyer's stock is high, a different buyer might reason that the seller's business should be valued objectively and "realistically" and then paid for in buyer's stock at that value, without regard to the buyer's price/earnings ratio. In the above example, assume that a "realistic" appraisal of the seller's business calls for a price/earnings ratio of 8. With net after-tax earnings of $500,000, such valuation of the seller's business would dictate a price of $4,000,000 (P/E ratio of 8 × 500,000 net after-tax earnings). When the buyer's stock commands a price/earnings ratio of 20 and a price of $40 per share, on the basis of buyer's $2 per share earnings, buyer would be required to pay 100,000 shares to meet the $4,000,000 price ($4,000,000 price ÷ $40 per share price). Paying 100,000 shares for after-tax earnings of $500,000 would mean that the buyer would acquire $5 in earnings for each share exchanged as opposed to $2 per share earned by the buyer.

As a practical matter, the price bargained out between the buyer and seller would probably fall somewhere between the extremes of $8,320,000 and $4,000,000. The buyer might reason that in spite of an inflated price/earnings ratio for its stock, it could issue 208,000 more shares to the public and realize cash in the amount of $8,320,000, which would be, in its judgment, too high a cash price to pay. The seller might reason that although $4,000,000 would be a fair value for its business, the stock of the buyer was overpriced in that the earnings on the 100,000 shares to be received by the seller would be less than half the earnings of the business it was selling—this would be particularly true where the seller would incur substantial taxes on the sale of the buyer's stock or was under a disability to sell due to an investment letter.

After review of this discussion of price/earnings ratios, a buyer may properly conclude that no settled formula exists for establishing the ratio for any particular acquisition. This is true, since each business enterprise has its own price/earnings ratio upon a sale—that established by the buyer and seller through the agreed purchase price. However, awareness of the elements that should be considered in establishing price/earnings ratios, of the history of such ratios in the particular industry and of current ratios should better enable the buyer and seller to attack the price problem realistically.

PRESENT VALUE OF FUTURE EARNINGS

Another approach to determine the price which should be paid for a going business, is to place a present value upon the aggregate future after-tax earnings of the business to be acquired. This approach to price requires a determination of such elements as a projection of future earnings, discount ratios, a period for future earn-out, and a residual value of a business after the earn-out period.

In this approach to price, the first determination which should be made is a year by year estimate of the future after-tax earnings of the seller. In some instances, such a determination is made for an indefinite period into the future. In other instances, the determination is made for a limited period, perhaps 10 years, and a residual value is placed upon the seller's business after the earn-out period. The projection of future earnings may be made in the manner indicated in the foregoing section of this chapter, "Projected Earnings."

The second step involves the computation of the present value of the projected future earnings of each of the years for which the projection is made, based upon a chosen discount rate which may be 10%, 15%, 20% or such other discount rate as is chosen. The discount rate will normally be based upon the amount of risk involved in realizing the projected earnings, when considered in relationship to the risk element in the type of business being acquired from the seller.

If a finite period of years is utilized to project after-tax future earnings, a residual value should be placed upon the seller's business, should be discounted to a present value, and should be added to the sum of the present values of the future projected earnings in computing the purchase price.

Finally, from the present value of the sum of the future projected after-tax earnings plus the present value of the residual value of the business, the buyer should subtract the amount of cash which the buyer will be required to advance to the business at the time of acquisition to pay off debt of the seller or for similar reasons. The resulting figure should then indicate what may be a fair price for the seller's business.

As an example, in a situation in which a ten year earn-out period is utilized, during which it is estimated (1) that total after-tax earnings of the seller's business for the ten year period will amount to $8,550,000, (2) that the business will have a residual value at the end of the ten years equal to $4,000,000, and (3) that the buyer must advance cash in the amount of $1,000,000 to satisfy debt, the total of the estimated earnings and residual value, less the cash advance, would amount to $11,550,000. The present value of such total estimated earnings and residual value discounted at 10%, 15%, or 20%, respectively would result in fixing a purchase price of the seller amounting to $5,462,000, $3,927,000, or $2,885,000, depending upon the discount ratio which is chosen as indicated in the table below:

Ten Future Years	Estimated Earnings (After Tax)	Present Value at Discount		
		10%	15%	20%
1st	$ 680	$ 618	$ 592	$ 566
2nd	720	595	544	500
3rd	750	563	494	434
4th	790	540	452	381
5th	830	515	413	334
6th	870	491	376	291
7th	910	467	342	254
8th	950	444	311	221
9th	1,000	424	284	194
10th	1,050	405	259	170
Subtotal	$ 8,550	$ 5,062	$ 4,067	$ 3,345
Plus assumed residual value	$ 4,000	$ 1,400	$ 860	$ 540
Subtotal	$12,550	$ 6,462	$ 4,927	$ 3,885
Less cash advance	$ 1,000	$ 1,000	$ 1,000	$ 1,000
Total	$11,550	$ 5,462	$ 3,927	$ 2,885

ADDITIONAL NECESSARY PRICE CONSIDERATIONS

Once the buyer has fixed a price based upon earnings, or otherwise, it should be mindful that the price may require adjustments for any additional investment in the seller's business which will be necessary after the acquisition. For example, should there be outstanding indebtedness of the seller which the buyer must satisfy or should need for additional working capital exist, the buyer should consider this indebtedness or required capital as part payment of purchase price. In other words, after the buyer has determined a price based on earnings multiplied by its chosen price/earnings ratio, it should adjust the price and should subtract any additional investments it must make as a result of additional working capital required or necessary payment of indebtedness after the acquisition. Conversely, if there is an excess of cash, inventories, or other assets which may be liquidated, the buyer should consider any amounts realized from cash withdrawals or inventory or other asset liquidation as possible reductions of the price based on earnings.

Arguments are made that the total additional investment required after purchase of the seller's business should not be considered an addition to purchase price, but rather only the cost of obtaining the additional investment, i.e., the amount of interest, should be considered as additional purchase price. If this approach were carried to its logical conclusion, one could argue that the entire purchase price of the seller's business was not the amount paid to the seller but only the cost of borrowing that amount. The sounder course would appear to be to consider the entire necessary additional investment as part of the purchase price.

EFFECT OF METHOD OF PAYMENT

Different possible media and methods of payment of the purchase price may also permit adjustment in the initially conceived price, and since available media and methods of payment are as many and varied as the imagination of the parties and the circumstances of the transaction will permit, parties unable to agree on price should consider changes in how payment is to be made to arrive at a mutually satisfactory solution. Two extremes in the media of payment are (1) an acquisition solely for stock and (2) an acquisition solely for cash. Between these extremes innumerable combinations and methods for paying a purchase price are available.

Stock vs. cash. Assume, as is often the case, that a stockholder of a closely held business has a low tax basis for his stock; he would presumably wish to sell the business in a tax-free transaction to avoid payment of a substantial capital gains tax at the time of sale. As is explained in Chapter 10, a tax-free transaction will require payment in stock. Assuming the selling stockholder has indicated he is willing to accept $1,000,000 for the business without immediately incurring liability for payment of income taxes, $1,000,000 in the stock of the buyer, received tax-free, would satisfy the stockholder. However, if the buyer for reasons of its own wants to pay in cash, the cash payment would be taxable to the selling stockholder. Assume the seller's stock had a tax cost to him of $100,000. If the stock were bought for $1,000,000 in cash, the stockholder would realize a taxable capital gain of $900,000 and would be liable to pay capital gains tax, or a tax exceeding $225,000. Therefore, if the buyer insists on paying cash, the seller may insist upon an upward adjustment in price to compensate for payment of taxes.

Stock vs. convertible debentures. In a transaction between listed companies, originally conceived as an acquisition for stock, a substantial discrepancy exists between dividends paid on the buyer's and seller's stock. The seller's stock had over the years consistently maintained a trading price of $50 per share, and the seller had consistently paid a $2.50 dividend to its shareholders. As a consequence, the seller's stockholders had gradually, as a group, become older investors in the nature of retired individuals interested primarily in price stability and income realized on the shares. Furthermore, the price of the seller's stock had consistently remained at approximately $50 per share for many years. A study of the stock ledger revealed that by far the greatest portion of the shares had exchanged hands during these years, and presumably would have a tax cost in that area, thus minimizing the effect of a taxable transaction where the purchase price would be in the $50 per share range.

At the time of the negotiations the buyer's stock also sold at approximately $50 a share, but the buyer was paying a dividend of only $1.25 per share. The parties reasoned that the seller's stockholders would not approve the transaction on a share-for-share basis because of the resultant substantial loss in dividend income. The buyer therefore offered to give convertible debentures for the seller's business, offering for each two shares of the seller one $100 5½ per cent debenture, convertible into two shares of the buyer's stock at a price somewhat above the market price of the buyer's shares. As a net result, a selling stockholder's income from each $100 5½ per cent convertible debenture would be $5.50 annually as opposed to the $5 annual dividend the stockholder would receive on his two shares given in exchange; furthermore, through the conversion feature in the debentures, the selling stockholders would have an opportunity to share in the prospective growth of the buyer.

Inventory purchase. In one situation a buyer wished to acquire the seller's machinery and equipment which the buyer intended to dismantle and reassemble in the buyer's own factory in a distant city. Since the machinery and equipment were massive, the buyer estimated that it would take three months to complete the dismantling, shipping, and reassembling. Therefore, to supply customers during the three-month period and as a part of the purchase price, the buyer ordered a three month's estimated inventory from the seller for delivery at the closing of the transaction. This order for inventory and the profit the seller would realize from the order was taken into consideration as part of the payment of the purchase price for the machinery and equipment.

Loans. Situations arise in which a seller is in financial difficulties, and a buyer, not prepared to buy immediately, may lend the seller working capital in return for an option to buy and the temporary right to place someone on the seller's management team. From the seller's point of view two things are accomplished. The seller's immediate financial difficulties are solved, and if the option price is right, the seller may in the future be able to sell a business which, because of financial difficulties, could not be sold for a reasonable price at the time of the transaction. From the buyer's point of view, it gains an opportunity to study and perhaps acquire a business it desires, risking as its total possible loss the funds loaned to the seller. Each of the varying elements in such a transaction will affect ultimate price.

Installment payments. Installment payments should normally result in an increase in purchase price. Obviously, except for unique income tax situations, an immediate payment of the full purchase price to the seller is worth more to it than a promise to pay in future installments. Installment payments may be made either in stock or cash or other assets.

Contingent purchase price. Where a buyer and seller are unable to agree upon a purchase price because of different projections of estimated future earnings, a contingent price determined under a formula which fixes the price, payable in contingent future installments, as a function of the earnings actually realized in future years may bring the parties to agreement. Such arrangements for contingent price payments may also be effective where a buyer wishes to retain a seller's management and give the management an incentive to maximize future earnings.

In arrangements involving a contingent purchase price based upon future earnings, three basic elements should be considered:

(1) What portion of the purchase price should be contingent upon future earnings? Most generally the contingent portion of the price may range between 20% and 60%, although lower percentages and also higher percentages up to 100% of the price have been utilized;

(2) Over what period should the contingent price payments be determined?—Most generally this period will range between 1 and 5 years;

(3) On what basis should the amount of contingent payments be determined?—Most often the payments are determined by earnings of the seller's business above a specified level of base earnings, sometimes combined with a minimum market value for the buyer's stock to determine the number of the buyer's shares to be delivered.

The contingent price based upon future earnings is an appropriate tool when the buyer and seller are far apart on price, because the seller projects future earnings increases which the buyer does not believe attainable. In such a situation the buyer may say, "All right, I'll pay you the additional $1,000,000 in installments provided the business earns $300,000 net after taxes the first year, $350,000 the next and $400,000 the third as you've said it will."

To meet the objectives of the parties, the purchase price of a business may be paid in an unlimited number of ways: common stock, preferred stock, convertible securities, warrants, notes, cash, property of all kinds, and varying combinations of all of the foregoing. The parties should be aware that the method of payment may affect the ultimate price, and may make possible agreement on price where initially it appears that no agreement can be reached.

POSSIBLE PRICE INCREASES

In order to develop a systematic, objective approach to price, the foregoing discussion has taken no account of increases in future earnings of the seller's business as a result of integration with the buyer's business. Needless to say, a seller's business may have more value to one buyer than to another. One may need what the seller has to offer more than another. Deliberately, the foregoing discussion of price is based upon a theory that the seller's business will be operated as an isolated unit. But if the acquisition is well conceived, the acquired business will often complement and be complemented by the buyer's business organization, and should earn more than if the seller continued operations on its own.

Once having determined a price for a seller's business, treating that business as an isolated unit, a buyer should determine what improvement in the seller's projected earnings may result from integration of the two businesses. If the integration will apparently increase expected future earnings, the buyer has the flexibility of offering a premium over the price based upon isolated projected earnings of the seller. In this connection, any and all of the possible objectives for acquiring a going business may give added value to the seller's business when operated by the buyer.

To state a few examples, the buyer may expect to increase earnings (1) through economies effected by combining sales organizations or manufacturing facilities, (2) by utilizing the seller's established sales outlet in a geographical area of the country in which the buyer has no outlets, or (3) by utilizing the seller's heavy equipment or seller's personnel. If the buyer is acquiring the seller solely to obtain a new product line in order to avoid the loss of time and expense required in tooling up for the line and putting the line in production, the buyer may wish to take into account the savings in time and money as possible "plus factors" to the purchase price. Since plus factors may be added, in essence, because of the added value brought to the business by the buyer's operation of that business, the added value of the business theoretically should not accrue to the seller's sole benefit. However, a buyer may wish to consider increasing the price in the course of negotiation because of the added value which the seller's business may have when operated by the buyer.

LIMITS ON MAXIMUM PRICE

We have indicated that the price of a going business is largely a matter of judgment of projected earnings. Projected earnings are obviously speculative in nature, and only future events will confirm or deny that the price paid was justified. But two fundamental tests exist by means of which a buyer may, at least theoretically, determine what the maximum price should be.

Earnings per share. First, if the acquisition is to be made for stock, the buyer should satisfy itself that the earnings acquired from the seller divided by the shares used to pay the price, result in per share earnings in excess of the per share earnings of the buyer, taking no account of the possible acquisition. In other words, the earnings per share of the buyer should be upgraded by the acquisition. The upgrading need not necessarily take place on the basis of earnings of the seller at the time of acquisition. But at some time in the reasonably predictable future, it should appear that the earnings per share from the acquired business on the purchase price shares should exceed the earnings per share of the remaining outstanding shares of the buyer, taking no account of the earnings acquired from the seller.

For example, assume that the seller's business will show earnings per share on the buyer's shares used to buy the business, and the buyer's other outstanding shares (without regard to the seller's business) will show earnings per share, as follows:

Future Years	Projected Earnings Per Buyer Share Exchanged From Seller's Business	Projected Earnings Per Buyer Share From Buyer's Other Business
1st year	$1.00	$1.20
2nd year	1.25	1.32
3rd year	1.50	1.46
4th year	1.80	1.60
5th year	2.16	1.78

In the foregoing example, the seller's earnings are expected to slightly upgrade earnings per share of the buyer's exchanged stock by the end of the third year and to upgrade by an amount in excess of 20 per cent in the fifth year. In view of the possible future upgrading, a buyer may decide that the price on which the forecast was based is acceptable. On the other hand, if the projected per share earnings of the seller's business should indicate a continual downgrading of the buyer's future earnings per share, the price would appear excessive and the buyer should not agree to pay it without overriding considerations present in the situation. As a general rule, to justify the price in a stock transaction the earnings acquired per share of stock paid should be greater than the per share earnings of the buyer's outstanding stock—either at the time of the closing or within the reasonably foreseeable future.

Return on Investment. In a second basic type of transaction, a cash transaction, the buyer should determine what the after-tax return on its investment will be. As in the case of a stock transaction, this determination may be based upon earnings at the time of the negotiations as well as projected earnings. If the after-tax return on the buyer's own invested capital, realized from the conduct of the buyer's own business amounts to, let us say, 10 per cent, the buyer should think twice before investing in a seller's business in which the after-tax return is less than 10 per cent. Each acquisition should upgrade the buyer's earnings.

In summary of the price discussion, the negotiation of price entails bargaining between the buyer and seller in the same sense as in any commercial transaction. But the proposition has been advanced that the price should be based upon projected earnings—the earnings the business is expected to realize in the future. The multiple by which earnings should be multipled—the price/earnings ratio—is a variable, affected both by historical influences and market conditions at the time of sale. Also, additional investment required after purchase or realization of funds from excess liquid assets should be taken into consideration in fixing the price. And the media and method of payment, whether stock, cash, other securities or property, or immediate payment or an installment purchase, or a contingent price based upon earnings will affect the purchase price and may even bring about agreement on price where no agreement may initially appear possible. To set the price, a buyer may take into consideration the added value a seller's business will have when integrated with the buyer's business, but finally, a buyer should normally not pay a price which (1) decreases earnings per share on buyer's outstanding stock or (2) reduces the buyer's overall return on investment, after taking into consideration the relationship of the projected future earnings from the seller's business to the projected future earnings of the buyer's business.

CHAPTER 5

Conducting the Negotiation and Coordinating the Investigation

After the buyer and seller reach agreement in principle, they should next turn to the task of negotiating a detailed acquisition contract, during which the buyer may undertake a more detailed investigation of the seller's business. In practice, reaching agreement in principle, negotiating the detailed contract, and conducting the investigation cannot be approached as isolated functions; they are closely interrelated and dependent upon one another. For example, reaching agreement in principle will fix some of the major provisions of the detailed contract, and the investigation of the seller's business will uncover knowledge of additional facts and problems which will affect contract details.

Bearing in mind that these aspects of an acquisition are interrelated, discussing the conduct of the negotiation and coordination of the investigation as separate subjects, nevertheless, serves to highlight and clarify the major elements involved in each topic. Remember, however, that in the ordinary situation, the investigation of the seller's business by the buyer and the negotiation of the detailed contract proceed apace. As the contract is being negotiated, the seller ordinarily makes available to the buyer additional information about the seller's books of account, its tangible properties such as plant and equipment and its intangible properties such as contracts and patents, and often grants the buyer access to the seller's plant to observe the seller's business in operation.

Under those unusual circumstances where a seller has the bargaining power to insist that a detailed contract be signed prior to permitting the buyer to conduct its investigation, the buyer may still protect itself by exercising care to cover all imaginable contingencies in the contract as conditions precedent to the buyer's legal obligation to close, thus permitting buyer to refuse to make the purchase where subsequent investigation reveals a material defect in the seller's business.

71

THE NEGOTIATION

Negotiations are a personal matter conducted in accordance with the personalities of the individuals involved. Negotiations involve many instances where judgment is brought to bear to determine proper procedure and proper setting, under changing circumstances. Prior to each negotiating session, however, both the buyer and seller should consider carefully and decide who should be present—and who should be the major spokesman. Naturally, no fixed rule can be stated which will cover all circumstances, including who should participate and how the negotiation should be conducted, but general observations may be helpful.

The negotiating team. The first meeting, which may be called the "probing session," normally may not require attendance by the lawyer or accountant for either side. The person who has the responsibility for conducting the negotiation on behalf of the buyer (whether he be an officer of the buyer, a director of planning, or an acquisitions group executive) should meet with either the controlling stockholder or principal officer of the seller, as the case may be. If the initial meeting proves successful, and the buyer and seller feel there may be mutual advantages in consummating an acquisition, the parties should not delay in bringing in their respective lawyers. The lawyer should participate in the earlier stages of the negotiation to develop knowledge of the facts and problems to draft a satisfactory acquisition agreement. Some businessmen tend to delay too long in bringing lawyers into the negotiation sessions. Perhaps, the delay results from fear that the lawyer may adversely affect negotiations by raising unimportant technicalities. Such a fear is unfounded in the case of the great majority of lawyers practicing commercial law today. In fact, lawyers experienced in the acquisition field are often helpful in steering negotiations in the right direction and bringing negotiations to a satisfactory conclusion.

The negotiation should be conducted not only with a view to determine price and to decide whether or not the acquisition should be made but also to develop the acquisition contract. If a buyer buys or a seller sells, the contract fixes the deal for both. The sooner the lawyer is brought into the picture the sooner he may begin to outline the transaction and begin preparation of a draft of an acquisition contract. Such a draft will help point up areas still open for further negotiation between businessmen. Depending on the circumstances of each transaction, if the lawyer becomes involved in the negotiations at the earlier stages, he will also have an opportunity to cast the form of the transaction. Should the buyer acquire stock or assets? Should the seller sell stock or assets? Do SEC or tax considerations exist which may make one form of acquisition preferable to another? What is really being sold —a product line, people, patents? Many more considerations, discussed in Chapter 7, may have an affect on the form of the transaction.

The team, then, to negotiate an acquisition must, of course, include the businessmen responsible for recommending the purchase or sale and the price. And because of the intricacies involved, both of substance and form, the team should include the lawyer to help guide the transaction and put into words what the buyer and seller have agreed upon. Unless special circumstances exist, the accountant need not usually be a member of the negotiating team, but he should be given every opportunity to complete, in detail, the necessary investigation of the finances of the seller's business.

Negotiating objectives. Obviously, one of the basic negotiating objectives of both the buyer and seller is to fix a satisfactory price. However, both parties should bear in mind that normally they are not legally bound until the acquisition contract is signed, and the negotiating sessions give both parties an opportunity to test the general conclusion, previously reached, that the acquisition would be advantageous to each.

Obviously, from the buyer's point of view, its objective in conducting the negotiation should be to develop as many facts as possible about the operation of the seller's business and to ferret out trouble areas. In conducting the negotiation, the buyer should constantly strive to determine the actual reason motivating the seller to sell its business. When asked, the seller will give a plausible reason. The seller's principal stockholder may state that he faces possible estate tax problems, that the seller needs research facilities which the buyer may make available to it, that the rapid growth of seller's business has made financing difficult, or any one or more of the other numerous reasons for selling businesses. Although the reason given by the seller may be accurate, a study by Harvard Business School by interviewing executives engaged in acquisitions, indicated that in a great majority of instances, the seller did not reaveal its actual reason for selling—fear; fear that the competition was growing too strong; fear that a product was becoming obsolete; fear that substantial capital outlays would be required to remain competitive; fear that a basic patent might be proved invalid. In a very few of these instances did the seller tell the buyer the actual motivating force for selling its business.

The importance of determining the seller's true motive for selling cannot be stressed too strongly. Assume the buyer is negotiating to buy a business in which an engineer is an essential to the strength of the business. This engineer has invented all the new processes of the business and each advance of the business is largely the result of his genius, but the seller knows that this engineer intends to resign and compete with the seller. If, in the course of its investigation, the buyer does not uncover first, that this engineer is the mainstay of the business and, second, that he intends to resign, the buyer may pay a substantial amount for a business worth a great deal less.

Often the seller should also try to determine the buyer's reason for buying. In those instances where a seller is not just selling out for cash with the intent of retiring, the seller should also attempt to establish to its satisfaction the objectives motivating the buyer in making the purchase. For example, if some of the sellers, owners, or key executives expect to remain in the employ of the buyer and continue to conduct the seller's business, their objectives will not be met if it is the buyer's intention to liquidate the seller's business and utilize the quick assets for distributions to stockholders or strengthening of the buyer's business. Or, if the seller intends to retain the buyer's stock for retirement dividend income, the seller will have a rude awakening if the buyer cuts its dividend and needs the seller's assets to satisfy creditors.

The desire for secrecy. In an acquisition, a seller will often stress that it wishes to keep the negotiations secret. Generally, the seller will believe, and rightly, that rumors of an impending sale of the business may have adverse effects on employee morale or customer and supplier relationships. The buyer should also give consideration to the importance of continuing the smooth operation of the seller's business. Where secrecy is important, both parties should take all reasonable steps to satisfy that end. In this regard, negotiation meetings may generally be held away from the seller's and the buyer's places of business, in hotel rooms, or other neutral places. If the attorneys for buyer and seller maintain offices outside the parties' places of business, all correspondence may be addressed to the attorneys' offices. If the seller employs independent certified public accountants, the buyer's accountants may concentrate the major portion of the audit function in the offices of the seller's accountants. Any physical inspection of the seller's plant may be made after proper preparation of the seller's employees—the purpose of the inspection relates to fire insurance or some similar matter. The buyer and seller may cooperate in many ways to keep their negotiations from becoming public knowledge. But unfortunately, experience has shown that in spite of all precautions, rumors of negotiations for the sale of the seller's business often begin to circulate. In most instances, the buyer and seller should be prepared to accept this fact—should be prepared to take the steps dictated by the circumstances to cope with the situation, not permitting strong feelings on the part of either to cause a breakdown in negotiations.

People. No business is made up exclusively of plant and equipment, of inventory, of customers and suppliers. Every business includes as a major element the human beings who operate the business and cause it to function. And just this element, since it involves the uncertainties of human emotions, may become the biggest threat to the successful sale or purchase of a business. The seller's key executives, with big mortgages on their houses, may begin to worry about being replaced by the buyer's counterparts. The factory workers may begin to worry about their coffee break privilege gained under a boss they feel free to address by first name—a boss who started the business in a garage and gradually built his work force over the years. Both the buyer and seller should constantly be aware of the worries that an acquisition may spawn in the human beings involved and should be prepared to quickly dispel any unfounded fears.

Certainly, the negotiating teams for both parties should never fail to maintain their equilibrium. A show of sternness or even anger—if deliberately thought out—may be appropriate on occasion. But, rudeness never. If the accountants conducting the investigation of the seller's books decide they are messy, this fact should not be announced in the seller's bookkeeping department, unless to convey a predetermined effect. If the buyer's lawyer finds a lease that could have been drawn better by the youngest associate on his staff, let him keep this thought from the seller's attorney and make it known only to the buyer—if the thought is at all material to the negotiation. During negotiations emotions often becomes taxed, but should never be permitted to interfere with the fundamental objectives of the negotiation.

THE INVESTIGATION

Regardless of the specific tactics employed in the investigation, the buyer should observe the fundamental principle that the investigation of the seller's business be a team effort. The investigation should proceed in three separate areas. But the investigation of these areas should be coordinated. The seller's business should be investigated from (1) the business point of view; (2) the legal point of view; and (3) the accounting or financial point of view. Although the three areas of investigation are largely autonomous, the results should be coordinated. The tendency exists to conduct the investigation of the seller, in each of the areas mentioned, as isolated separate investigations. The businessman tends to forget the legal and accounting aspects; the lawyer tends to become engrossed in the legal problems; and the accountant tends to concentrate on an audit to the exclusion of the other aspects of the seller's business. For an investigation to be successful, this tendency should be overcome, and the investigators should coordinate their efforts. Why this is so is developed in greater detail in this and subsequent chapters.

Coordination of effort. Unification of the investigation of a seller's business involves a problem of communication. The problem arises from the lack of understanding by the businessman, the lawyer, or the accountant of the information which should be relayed to the other two investigating parties and from the natural tendency to concentrate in a known field of endeavor without consideration of the effect upon the other two related fields. Further, the lack of understanding of the businessman, the lawyer and the accountant of the information essential to the other two parties generally results from a failure to appreciate the roles of the others.

Each class of investigator should endeavor to keep the other classes of investigators informed as to problems which might arise in their area. For example, the businessman, in conducting an investigation of the customers of the seller may find unusual pricing structures or unusual arrangements with distributors. He should immediately bring such matters to the attention of the lawyer. The lawyer may then assess whether there has been a violation of the anti-trust laws and may be able to provide necessary indemnification or guard against liability for violations in the acquisition contract.

On the other hand, the lawyer in reviewing the seller's contracts may find Robinson-Patman Act pricing violations. Although the lawyer may guard the buyer against the assumption of liability for these violations in the contract, he should nevertheless call the violations to the attention of the businessman. The very profitability of the seller's business may depend upon the pricing violations. If the pricing structure must be amended to avoid violations of law, the businessman should have an opportunity to assess whether the required change in the pricing structure could be so detrimental to the seller's business that the businessman may not wish to make the acquisition.

The accountant, as he reviews the financial data, may uncover possible sizable income tax deficiencies of the seller for past years. The lawyer and businessman should be given immediate knowledge of this fact. The lawyer may protect the buyer by contract against the assumption of any obligations with regard to the taxes, by escrow or otherwise, and the businessman may assess the effect of the tax deficiencies on the going business.

Each of the investigators should keep sight of the objective that all collected information should be interchanged and correlated with the others.

Correlating the information. Businessmen and accountants are often of the opinion that an acquisition contract is a contract made up of "boiler plate" provisions. Their attitude is often: if they thoroughly perform their areas of the investigation, the acquisition contract is of little importance (except perhaps specific areas of specific personal interest). Nothing could be further from the truth.

The terms and all the conditions of the acquisition should ultimately be reflected in a basic document—the acquisition contract. This contract should be tailored to meet the facts and circumstances surrounding each transaction as they are developed. If, as stated above, a possible sizable tax deficiency for prior years is uncovered by the accountants, the lawyer should be made aware of this possible deficiency to protect the buyer by contract.

Since the contract embodies the transaction in its entirety, the clearing house for information developed in the course of the negotiation should be the lawyer's office. The safest procedure to follow is to have both the businessman and the accountant send to the lawyer all important information as developed, regardless of whether or not they believe the information will have any effect upon the contract. On his part, the lawyer should keep both the businessman and the accountant informed of information he develops independently.

Nature of business. The nature of the seller's business should also alert the buyer to the aspects of the business which should receive the most emphatic investigation. For example, if the buyer is acquiring a manufacturing business utilizing costly, heavy, or intricate manufacturing machinery and equipment, the buyer should obviously have its engineers make a careful evaluation of the condition of the machinery and equipment. Similarly, if a patent structure is the major asset of the business, the buyer's patent attorneys should make a careful search and evaluation of all patents to determine whether they might infringe on other patents or whether patent litigation involving the patents may exist. If a personal service business is being acquired, such as a consulting engineer's firm, the investigation should concentrate on the personnel and their willingness to remain with the business. Stated generally, the buyer should bear in mind the type of business it is acquiring to indicate where it should place the major emphasis in the investigation.

The investigation—business. If the planning for the proposed acquisition has been properly conducted, a general investigation of the seller's industry and the seller's business will have been completed prior to reaching agreement in principle with the seller. The buyer should have sufficient general knowledge of the seller and its industry to make the acquisition appear worthwhile on the surface. The further business investigation should be directed at developing specific facts of the seller's business and industry which the buyer may not normally develop from public knowledge and financial publications. Specifically, if the buyer is acquiring a manufacturing business, it should obtain access for its engineers to the factory buildings of the seller. On-the-spot observation of the seller's business operation will give the buyer's engineers an opportunity to assess whether the buildings, machinery, equipment, and processes are efficient, or whether they are in need of substantial overhaul. It is not extraordinary for a seller to request a buyer to make substantial capital outlays in the form of new factory buildings or expensive equipment—after an acquisition. Such capital outlays, if necessary, may convert an otherwise profitable acquisition into one of dwindling profits in the face of required additional cash investments on the part of the buyer.

Most investigations from a business viewpoint should also include field investigation of customers and distributors to determine product acceptance and pricing methods. Direct contact with customers and distributors may reveal weaknesses in the seller's business in the form of excessive product rejects or weaknesses in servicing customer complaints and problems.

An important aspect of the business investigation should be the employees and personnel of the seller. As indicated above, an important ingredient in every business is people. People constitute an intangible asset in the form of know-how, developed often over many years of experience, customer contact, and a general knowledge of the business which buyers cannot normally hope to develop successfully without the goodwill of the seller's employees.

Acquiring the employees of a business together with their goodwill is a delicate maneuver. When employees learn that a business is being sold, human nature comes into play and the employees worry about the effect the acquisition will have upon their personal lives. Worry is the general rule. If it is a buyer's intention to keep the personnel structure of the seller intact and keep the business intact, the buyer should take all reasonable steps to mollify any unfounded fears. Furthermore, where the buyer will be dependent upon the continued employment of key executives and employees of the seller to carry on the business, the buyer should obtain assurance that the key people will remain with the seller's organization and perhaps negotiate employment contracts with such personnel.

The investigation—legal. As stated above, the nature of the seller's business should have a major effect upon the buyer's choice of the areas of that business the buyer should emphasize in its investigation. The nature of the seller's business will have the same effect upon the lawyer's choice of the areas of investigation he should emphasize. However, in addition, the lawyer should give careful consideration to the mechanics of the acquisition (what is to be acquired and how the payment is to be made) in determining and advising on the direction of the investigation. These mechanics involve legal problems affecting the obligations of the buyer and seller discussed in part in Chapter 6. Will the buyer use stock or cash to make the acquisition? Will the seller sell stock or assets? The answers to these questions have a direct bearing on the areas of the investigation requiring major emphasis.

The business investigation should be made to determine the soundness of the seller's business as a going concern. The accounting investigation should seek to determine the correctness of income statements and balance sheets, as well as value of plant and inventory as reflected on the seller's books. In both instances, whether the acquisition is made for cash or stock, whether it is an acquisition of assets or stock, should have little effect on the basic investigation. However, from the lawyer's point of view, substantial differences in the areas emphasized in the investigation arise from the different form an acquisition may take. The lawyer must keep these differences in mind in his own investigation, but, of equal importance, he must call to the attention of the businessman and accountant the effect the form of the transaction has on their investigation.

For example, if an acquisition is one of assets for cash, the lawyer often need not concern himself with the assumption by the buyer of possible hidden liabilities of the seller's business, except perhaps for the effect of bulk sales law. On the other hand, if cash is utilized to acquire stock, a thorough investigation of all possible contingent liabilities must be made since, by acquiring stock, the seller's corporate entity and all its obligations, contingent or otherwise, continue to exist and indirectly become the obligations of the buyer. Furthermore, even if assets of the seller are acquired, if payment is made in the buyer's stock, the liabilities of the seller must often be carefully investigated. An indicated in Chapter 6, where the buyer utilizes stock it may assume unknown obligations through operation of law, and, as a practical matter, in approaching this problem may consider itself in the same position as a buyer of stock.

In general, where stock of the seller is being acquired, the lawyer should carefully check the minute books and stock books of the corporation. He should satisfy himself that the stock of the seller, when acquired, will be fully paid, non-assessable and not subject to any liens or encumbrances. The lawyer should be certain that the individual seller of the stock has good legal title to deliver.

For example, if the shares of stock have at any time passed through an estate, the lawyer should satisfy himself that the distribution of the stock from the estate has been made properly and is not subject to any outstanding estate tax liens or subject to possible invalidation of the transfer of the stock by disgruntled relatives of the decedent.

In every type of transaction, when real estate or other tangible assets are involved, the lawyer should satisfy himself as to the title to such assets. Title company policies and title abstracts should be brought down to date. Searches should be instituted to determine whether machinery and equipment are subject to chattel mortgages or conditional sales contracts.

A further necessary function of the lawyer is to review all major contracts, including leases to real property. These should be reviewed with the primary objective of determining whether any unusual terms exist which should be brought to the attention of the businessman or the accountant, and whether any arrangements might be illegal. Also, as part of this review, if assets are being acquired, the lawyer should be certain that all important contracts, license agreements, and franchises are assignable by the seller. If any are not assignable, provision should be made in the contract for the seller to obtain the consent to the assignment of the third party to the contract.

To obtain information about the real estate owned, the plant and equipment owned, the contracts in existence, the trademarks and patents and the employment contracts, representations and warranties made by the seller in the acquisition contract are helpful. In this sense the acquisition contract may be looked upon as one of the basic tools for developing the necessary information for a thorough investigation of the seller's business. Through representations and warranties made by the seller, the buyer develops the information required to investigate further each of these items. The importance of the acquisition contract is developed further in Chapter 12.

The investigation—accounting. The accounting investigation should be addressed to two fundamentals. First, do the profit and loss statements and the balance sheets supplied by the seller fairly present the income of the seller and fairly present the financial position of the seller? Second, and important, what differences exist between the seller's accounting methods and the buyer's accounting methods?

The second objective of the accounting investigation is an important factor in helping the businessman to determine the desirability of the acquisition and the price. Generally accepted accounting principles, because of the number of different principles applicable to each specific financial situation and the judgment factors involved in the ultimate selection of the principles, provide such a broad range of possible different profit and loss and balance sheet results, in the same business, that a change in the particular generally accepted accounting principles may, on paper, cause a low profit business to appear highly profitable.

For example, on pages 80–81 are imaginary Profit and Loss Statements of Company "A" and Company "B" first printed as pages 178 and 179 in the book *Management Problems of Corporate Acquisitions* published by the Harvard University Press, and reproduced here through the courtesy of the Harvard University Press and Leonard Spacek, managing partner of Arthur Anderson & Company, who prepared the statements. Company "A" and Company "B" do an identical amount of business. But note from these Profit and Loss Statements that the application of different accounting principles, all of which are generally accepted accounting principles, change the net profits reported by the same business from $1,076,000 to $480,000.

The profit and loss statements make it abundantly clear that the accountant, in his investigation, should note any differences in the seller's accounting methods from those of the buyer, and should reconstruct the seller's income by applying the buyer's accounting methods to the seller's business. The accountant should make certain that the businessman understands the accounting differences and the effect these differences may have on reported earnings. Assume the buyer finds out only after he acquired Company "B" that a change in Company B's accounting methods to conform them to the buyer's will reduce Company B's reported earnings from $1,076,000 to $480,000. The result is an unhappy buyer.

A specific accounting problem, the valuation of inventory, is often difficult to resolve. In many situations where inventory forms an important part of the seller's business, the problem of valuing inventory becomes a matter for detailed negotiation. If inventory constitutes an important part of the seller's business, the buyer should insist on the right to take a physical inventory as a condition to the acquisition. The buyer may not be willing to accept "obsolete" or "slow-moving" inventory as part of the acquired inventory. Under these circumstances, the buyer and seller may be faced with the difficult problem of defining what is meant by "obsolete" or "slow-moving" inventory. Where an attempt is made to define such inventory terms in the acquisition agreement, provisions relating to the definitions may run on for many pages.

In certain instances, the accounting investigation may be as thorough as a complete audit of the seller's business by certified public accountants. If a business is closely held and has not been audited regularly by certified public accountants, the accounting investigation should be much more thorough and perhaps consist of a complete audit. In other instances, and more generally the case, the investigation will not be quite as extensive. If the company being acquired has been regularly audited by independent certified public accountants and has certified annual financial statements, the investigation by the buyer's accountants may be limited to a verification of the financials from the work sheets of the certified public accounttants of the seller.

The procedure utilized in each investigation (that of the businessman, the lawyer, and the accountant) will differ under the varying circumstances of the acquisition, and no investigation should be conducted in a purely mechanical manner. As indicated above, different circumstances will vary the emphasis placed on investigating different areas of the seller's business. Judgment and thought should be the keynotes. However, checklists may help as final references to assure a buyer that no area of the investigation has been overlooked.

THE ACQUISITION TIMETABLE

After the buyer and seller have reached agreement in principle, and have commenced negotiations to agree upon a detailed acquisition agreement, the lawyers should begin preparation of a timetable for the transaction.

If the transaction involves approvals or rulings by administrative agencies, such as the Securities and Exchange Commission or the Internal Revenue Service, or involves meetings of stockholders of a publicly held buyer or seller, the timetable should take into consideration the time involved in dealing with such administrative agencies and notice requirements to shareholders with respect to meetings. The timetable should include a feasible closing date for the transaction, establish the order of priorities of the steps required to close the transaction and indicate the delegation of responsibility to the various parties involved for the preparation of the documents and fulfillment of the tasks required to close.

The tentative timetable set forth below was prepared in connection with the proposed acquisition of the assets of a seller, whose stock was traded in the over-the-counter market,

	Company A Col. 1	Use of Fifo in Pricing Inventory Col. 2	Use of Straight-line Depre-ciation Col. 3
Sales in units	100,000 units		
Sales in dollars	$100 each		
	$10,000,000		
Costs and expenses—			
Cost of goods sold	$ 6,000,000		
Selling, general and administra-tive	1,500,000		
LIFO inventory reserve	400,000	$(400,000)	
Depreciation	400,000		$(100,000)
Research costs	100,000		
Pension costs	200,000		
Officers' compensation:			
Base salaries	200,000		
Bonuses	200,000		
Total costs and expenses	$ 9,000,000	$(400,000)	$(100,000)
Profit before income taxes	$ 1,000,000	$ 400,000	$ 100,000
Income taxes	520,000	208,000	52,000
	$ 480,000	$ 192,000	$ 48,000
Gain on sale of property (net of income tax)	—	—	—
Net profit reported	$ 480,000	$ 192,000	$ 48,000
Per share on 600,000 shares	$ .80	$ .32	$ .08
Market value at:			
10 times earnings	$ 8.00	$3.20	$ .80
12 times earnings	9.60	3.84	.96
15 times earnings	12.00	4.80	1.20

( ) Denotes deduction.

Accounting Magic
Explanation of Columns 2 to 7, inclusive

Column	Company A	Company B
2.	Uses Lifo (last in, first out) for pricing inventory	Uses Fifo (first in, first out)
3.	Uses accelerated depreciation for book and tax purposes	Uses straight-line
4.	Charges research and develop-ment costs to expense cur-rently	Capitalizes and amortizes over five-year period

(If R & D costs remain at same level, the difference disappears after five years. The difference of $80,000 in the chart is in the first year, where A expenses $100,000, and B capitalizes the $100,000 but amortizes 1/5.)

Deferring Research Costs over Five Years Col. 4	Funding Only the Pensions Vested Col. 5	Use of Stock Options for Incentive Col. 6	Including Capital Gain in Income Col. 7	Company B Col. 8
				100,000 units
				$100 each
				$10,000,000
				$ 6,000,000
				1,500,000
				300,000
$(80,000)				20,000
	$(150,000)			50,000
				200,000
		$(200,000)		
$(80,000)	$(150,000)	$(200,000)	----	$ 8,070,000
$ 80,000	$ 150,000	$ 200,000	----	$ 1,930,000
42,000	78,000	104,000	----	$ 1,004,000
$ 38,000	$ 72,000	$ 96,000	----	$ 926,000
----	----	----	$150,000	150,000
$ 38,000	$ 72,000	$ 96,000	$150,000	$ 1,076,000
$ .06	$ .12	$ .16	$ .25	$ 1.79
$.60	$1.20	$1.60	$2.50	$17.90
.72	1.44	1.92	3.00	21.48
.90	1.80	2.40	3.75	26.85

Column	Company A	Company B
5.	Funds the current pension costs—i.e., current service plus amortization of past service	Funds only the present value of pensions vested

(Difference in pension charges might also arise where, as in the the case of U. S. Steel in 1958, management decides that current contributions can be reduced or omitted because of excess funding in prior years and/or increased earnings of the fund or the rise in market value of the investments.)

Column	Company A	Company B
6.	Pays incentive bonuses to officers in cash	Grants stock options instead of paying cash bonuses
7.	Credits gains (net of tax thereon) directly to earned surplus (or treats them as special credits below net income)	Includes such gains (net of income tax thereon) in income

in exchange for stock of a buyer, whose stock was listed on the New York Stock Exchange. This tentative time schedule illustrates in outline form the action which must normally be taken by a buyer and seller in a transaction of the nature indicated.

ACQUISITION OF ASSETS OF SELLER FOR STOCK OF BUYER

TENTATIVE TIME SCHEDULE

		Responsibility
June 28 (Friday)	*Meeting of board of directors of buyer to approve proposed acquisition of seller.*	*buyer*
July 1 (Monday)	*Meeting of board of directors of seller to approve acquisition by buyer.*	*seller*
	Press release.	*buyer and seller*
July 9 (Tuesday)	*Meeting of buyer and seller officers with counsel to review terms of acquisition and to assign drafting responsibility.*	*buyer and seller*
July 19 (Friday)	*First draft of agreement distributed.*	*buyer's counsel*
July 24 (Wednesday)	*Meeting of buyer and seller officers with counsel to review first draft of agreement.*	*buyer and seller*
July 25 (Thursday)	*Draft of proxy materials for special meeting of the stockholders of seller and revised draft of agreement distributed for review.*	*buyer's and seller's counsel*
	Buyer to commerce reviewing corporate records of seller.	*buyer's counsel*
	Draft of listing application for NYSE prepared.	*buyer's counsel*
July 29 (Monday)	*Meeting of buyer and seller officers with counsel to review agreement and draft of proxy materials.*	*buyer and seller*
July 30 (Tuesday)	*Special meeting of board of directors of seller for the for the purpose of:*	

(a) approving agreement.
(b) calling special meeting of stockholders to be held on September 25, to adopt the agreement, and setting record date therefor.

Responsibility

		Responsibility
	(c) approving proxy material and appointing proxies.	*seller*
	Special meeting of the board of directors of buyer for the purpose of:	
	(a) approving agreement.	
	(b) approving application for listing additional shares on the NYSE.	
	(c) extending authority of the transfer agent and registrar to cover shares issuable in connection with the acquisition.	*buyer*
July 31 (Wednesday)	*Execute agreement.*	*buyer and seller*
August 2 (Friday)	*File preliminary proxy materials with SEC.*	*seller's counsel*
	Mail joint letter from counsel for buyer and seller to the Commissioner of Internal Revenue requesting tax ruling with respect to tax aspects of the proposed acquisition.	*buyer's and seller's counsel*
August 23 (Friday)	*Obtain SEC comments on proxy material.*	*seller's counsel*
August 27 (Tuesday)	*Commence printing definitive copies of proxy material.*	*seller's counsel*
August 30 (Friday)	*Mail proxy material to:*	
	(a) all holders of record of seller.	
	(b) SEC.	*seller*
	File listing application and supporting documents with NYSE.	*buyer's counsel*
September 16 (Monday)	*Mail any follow-up letters deemed advisable in order to solicit further proxies of stockholders of seller.*	*seller's counsel*
September 25 (Wednesday)	*Special meeting of stockholders of seller at which the following action is to be taken:*	
	(a) approve and adopt the agreement.	
	(b) authorize such other matters as may be deemed advisable in connection with the acquisition.	*seller*
	Notify NYSE of stockholder approval.	*seller's counsel*
September 30 (Monday)	*Board of governors approves listing application pending notice of issuance.*	

Responsibility

| October 23 (Wednesday) | *Receive favorable tax ruling from IRS.* | *seller's counsel* |
| October 31 (Wednesday) | *Closing in New York, N.Y.* *Press release.* | *buyer and seller* |

Not only should the lawyers prepare a timetable similar to that printed above, but after the first draft of the acquisition agreement is prepared and the acquisition details begin to take shape, the lawyers should begin the preparation of a form of detailed closing memorandum such as is printed in Chapter 15 entitled Closing and Post-Closing. Preparing a draft of the closing memorandum will further highlight the documents required for the closing and and will provide added protection against overlooking any details or preparations required for the closing.

THE BUSINESS INVESTIGATION CHECKLIST

Printed below is a business investigation checklist. This checklist includes the major considerations in the financial area which should be checked by the accountants for the buyer. As indicated above, the accountant should not only investigate the financial aspects of the seller's business as set forth in the checklist, but should summarize for the buyer the differences in accounting principles utilized by the seller and the buyer, and should indicate to the buyer the significance and effect of these differences on future earnings of the seller's business.

The investigation of the seller's business should not be conducted solely through the use of the checklist printed below. However, a checklist of this nature is a handy tool for a buyer to assure itself that it has not overlooked some possible problem area involving the seller's business.

BUSINESS INVESTIGATION CHECK LIST

ITEM	ASSIGNED TO	COMMENTS
I. CORPORATE BACKGROUND		
A. Original name and purpose.		
B. Date of founding.		
C. Subsequent changes in corporate name or purpose.		
D. Brief description of present business.		

ITEM	ASSIGNED TO	COMMENTS
E. Classes of stocks or other securities.		
F. Concentration of ownership.		
G. Activity of shares and price ranges.		
H. Subsidiaries and operating investments.		
I. States in which qualified to do business.		
J. Legal location of all facilities and branches.		
K. Board Minute review.		
II. BASIS OF PROPOSED ACQUISITION		
A. Highlights of agreement		
B. Formula for evaluation of shares		
III. FINANCIAL		
A. General		
1. Source and authenticity of financial data.		
B. Financial Status		
1. Statement of condition (balance sheet).		
2. Analysis of assets. (a) Cash position (monthly for two years).		

ITEM	ASSIGNED TO	COMMENTS
(b) Projection of cash activity next six months.		
(c) Receivables (condition, turnover, bad debt experience and reserve).		
(d) Inventories (1) Amount and balance in raw materials and finished goods inventories in relation to production and sales requirements (turnover).		
(2) Policy and extent of forward commitments on raw materials.		
(3) Extent of vulnerability of business due to rapid price change of materials and time element in manufacture.		
(4) Condition and obsolescence.		
(e) Working capital position (monthly for 2 years).		
(f) Investments (kinds, condition and basis for evaluation).		

ITEM	ASSIGNED TO	COMMENTS
(g) Officers and employees loans (amounts and situations).		
(h) Analysis of prepaid expenses.		
(i) Analysis of deferred charges.		
(j) Properties (1) Operating and non-operating.		
(2) Extent depreciated and rates.		
(3) Net value related to sales volume.		
(4) Insurance coverage.		
(k) Goodwill (basis of valuation).		
3. Analysis of liabilities (a) Bank loans (amount, dates, sources and rates over past 2 years).		
(b) Accounts payable (policy on discounts).		
(c) Special reserves.		
(d) Contingent liabilities (1) Existing and threatened law suits.		

ITEM	*ASSIGNED TO*	*COMMENTS*
(2) *Notes and obligations guaranteed.*		
(3) *Liability under large purchase contracts.*		
(4) *Other commitments.*		
(e) *Status of income taxes (Federal, state & local).*		
(f) *Trend and status of real estate & personal property taxes.*		
C. *Financial Operations* 1. *Statement of operations (profit & loss statement).*		
2. *Analysis of sales & income*		
(a) *Sales by product by year over last 10 years.*		
(b) *Sales by product by month over last 2 years.*		
(c) *Present backlog by product.*		
(d) *Other income.*		
3. *Analysis of manufacturing costs and gross profits*		

ITEM	ASSIGNED TO	COMMENTS
(a) Amounts and relative proportion of labor, material and manufacturing overhead.		
(b) Important items & trends of raw material costs.		
(c) Important items & trends of labor costs.		
(d) Analysis of items & trends of manufacturing overhead costs.		
(e) Separation of fixed & variable manufacturing costs.		
(f) Factory profit & gross margins by product.		
(g) Factory profit & gross margins on popular and/or representative makes or models.		
(h) Possible economies.		
(i) Possible future cost increases.		
(j) Possible purchased material price increases.		
4. Analysis of expenses (amount, trends, & principal items). (a) Selling expenses.		

ITEM	ASSIGNED TO	COMMENTS
(b) Administrative expenses.		
(c) General expenses.		
(d) Possible economies in all expenses.		
(e) Royalties received & paid.		
5. Analysis of profit from operations. (a) Profits by branches, divisions, etc.		
(b) Profits by trade classes.		
(c) Deductions.		
(d) Final surplus net profit.		
6. Analysis of surplus net profit (a) Profits from operations.		
(b) Details of profits from other sources.		
(c) Deductions.		
(d) Final surplus net profit.		
7. Earning record for 10-year period (a) Cash gains or losses from operations.		

ITEM	ASSIGNED TO	COMMENTS
(b) Total gains or losses from operations.		
(c) Earnings in percent of sales.		
(d) Earnings in percent of invested capital.		
8. Dividend record for 10-year period (a) Kind & amount of dividends paid.		
(b) Percent of earnings paid out in dividends by years.		
(c) Dividends in arrears.		
IV. PRODUCTS		
A. Major Classifications & Relative Importance		
B. Analysis of Major Products 1. Catalogs & sales literature on products.		
2. Description & application of products.		
3. Competition (a) Names & grading of principal competitors.		
(b) Ranking in industry—past and present.		
(c) Relative qualities & prices of product.		

ITEM	ASSIGNED TO	COMMENTS
(d) Percent of national business obtained.		
4. Trend of market acceptance.		
5. Brand or trade name practices and value.		
6. Styling & packaging—status and importance.		
7. Completeness of lines.		
8. Seasonal sales patterns.		
C. Markets and Prices 1. Statistical. (a) Location.		
(b) Extent.		
(c) Trend.		
2. Characteristics. (a) Seasonal characteristics.		
(b) Economic factors influencing it.		
(c) Stability.		
(d) Susceptibility.		
3. Competitive practices. (a) Competitive and trade practices.		
(b) Extent of other co-operation.		

ITEM	ASSIGNED TO	COMMENTS
(c) Imports, tariffs and quotas.		
4. Price situation. (a) Fair trade policies.		
(b) Stability of price structure.		
(c) Factors influencing.		
(d) Trend of unit prices.		
(e) Future outlook.		
D. Government Business 1. Description of product.		
2. Status of supply contracts—prime and sub.		
3. Status of facilities contracts.		
4. Methods of pricing & payment.		
5. Present competitive situation.		
6. Future business outlook.		
7. Status of statutory renegotiation.		
8. Status of contract price redetermination.		
9. Security status.		

ITEM	ASSIGNED TO	COMMENTS
V. SALES		
A. Distribution		
1. Types of distribution used.		
2. Methods of securing and franchising distributors.		
3. Geographical distribution & coverage of market (domestic & foreign).		
4. Lists and ratings of principal customers.		
5. Present competitive situation.		
6. Extent of use of private brand.		
7. Distributor's or customer's attitude toward company.		
8. Trade class distribution.		
9. Concentration of sales among important accounts.		
B. Sales Organization		
1. Organization.		
2. Sales methods employed.		
3. Compensation of salesmen.		
4. Branch offices.		

ITEM	ASSIGNED TO	COMMENTS
C. Sales Policies 1. Prices.		
2. Discounts.		
3. Service and returns.		
D. Sales Planning 1. Objectives.		
2. Extent of sales forecasting.		
3. Extent of market research activities.		
E. Advertising & Promotion 1. Internal activities.		
2. Agency activities.		
3. Current program—costs, media.		
4. Advertising budgets.		
5. Public relations.		
VI. MANAGEMENT AND INDUSTRIAL RELATIONS A. General Organization 1. Organization chart.		
2. Number & type of employees by departments.		
3. Directors, officers, committees & their duties.		

ITEM	ASSIGNED TO	COMMENTS
4. Data on key employees.		
5. Balance & alignment of organization.		
6. Definiteness of duties & responsibilities.		
7. Employment contracts.		
8. Consultants & outside services used.		
B. Management & Office Personnel 1. Adequacy of leadership.		
2. Adequacy of office staff.		
3. Rating & evaluation of all people with managerial responsibility.		
4. Lines of succession—backing of key positions.		
5. Will management stay if merged?		
6. Methods & rates of compensation.		
7. Key employee insurance.		
8. Old age problems.		
9. Morale & points of friction, if any.		
10. Physical arrangement and adequacy of offices.		

ITEM	ASSIGNED TO	COMMENTS
C. Shop Labor		
1. Union contract status.		
2. Past difficulties.		
3. Present labor situation.		
4. Pending problems, if any.		
5. Methods of hiring and discharging.		
6. Job classification and rates.		
7. Methods of payment.		
8. Working conditions.		
9. Morale and productivity.		
D. Personnel Policies and Practices		
1. Personnel office and operating methods.		
2. Working rules and regulations.		
3. Stock option arrangements.		
4. Bonus arrangements.		
5. Profit sharing.		
6. Pension program.		
7. Medical plan.		
8. Other welfare programs.		

ITEM	ASSIGNED TO	COMMENTS
9. Vacation and holiday program.		
10. Employee purchases.		
VII. FACILITIES		
A. Land and Buildings		
1. Location, legal description, and ownership.		
2. Appraisals, if available.		
3. Plot plans and plant area layouts.		
4. Possibility of sale and leaseback		
5. Insurability—sprinklers, fire & police protection.		
6. Condition of buildings and repairs needed.		
7. Housekeeping.		
B. Equipment		
1. Description, age and value of major items of machinery.		
2. Special processing equipment—specifications.		
3. Flexibility and adaptability to other products.		
4. Condition and ownership of equipment.		

ITEM	*ASSIGNED TO*	*COMMENTS*
C. Services and Utilities 1. Transportation.		
2. Loading and unloading facilities.		
3. Electricity—capacity and ownership of transformers, etc.		
4. Lighting.		
5. Heat and air conditioning.		
6. Air, gas, water.		
7. Sanitary facilities.		
8. Maintenance.		
D. Adequacy and Future Needs 1. Location with respect to material, labor and markets.		
2. Present utilization of facilities.		
3. Expansion possibilities & plans.		
VIII. PRODUCTION METHODS AND PROCESSES A. Parts Fabrication Methods		
B. Assembly Methods		
C. Processing Operations 1. Heat treat and hardening.		

ITEM	ASSIGNED TO	COMMENTS
2. Applied finishes.		
3. Other.		
D. Quality Control and Inspection		
E. Salvage Control		
F. Material Handling 1. Conveyors.		
2. Trucking.		
G. Methods and Operation Sheets		
H. Tool Design, Procurement, and Repair		
I. Storage and Warehousing		
J. Safety		
K. Efficiency of Production Operations		
L. Adequacy of Facilities—Bottlenecks		
IX. ENGINEERING AND RESEARCH		
A. Engineering Personnel		
B. Facilities		
C. Importance to Product		
D. Adequacy of Product Engineering		

ITEM	ASSIGNED TO	COMMENTS
E. Research and Development		
F. Relations with Manufacturing and Sales		
G. Patents		
1. List of patents, trademarks, copyrights and applications.		
2. Importance to product.		
3. Patent policies, pools & licensing arrangements.		
4. Patent agreements with employees.		
X. CONTROLS		
A. Financial Controls		
1. Budgets of sales, production, costs, profits, cash requirements, etc.		
2. Kind of cost system employed.		
3. Method of sales, administrative and general.		
4. Method of controlling production costs.		
5. Status of operating procedures.		
6. Adequacy of internal checks.		
7. List of control reports issued.		

ITEM	ASSIGNED TO	COMMENTS
8. Methods of controlling capital expenditures.		
9. Accounting methods employed.		
10. Use of office machines.		
B. Production Planning & Controls		
1. Master schedules—how set.		
2. Coordination between sales and production.		
3. Adequacy of product specifications.		
4. Production scheduling and machine loads.		
5. Purchasing methods & lead times.		
6. Material and inventory control.		
7. Cost estimating procedure.		
8. Time study.		
9. Intra-plant coordination.		
XI. OUTLOOK FOR BUYER		
A. Earnings Prospects per Buyer Share		
B. Return on Capital Required to Buy and Operate Seller		

THE LEGAL INVESTIGATION CHECKLIST

Set forth below is a legal investigation checklist. Not every item appearing on the checklist must be checked out in each acquisition. Emphasis on the areas requiring thorough investigation will vary with the type of acquisition involved. For example, as mentioned above, greater emphasis may be placed upon investigating a seller's stock books and minute books in a stock transaction than in an asset transaction, whereas local bulk sales laws will be given greater consideration in asset transactions. As in the case of the business investigation checklist, the legal investigation checklist should help keep lawyer from overlooking possible legal complications which require solutions to close the particular acquisition.

LEGAL INVESTIGATION CHECK LIST

ITEM	ASSIGNED TO	COMMENTS
I. STATE LAWS		
A. State Corporation Statutes		
1. States of incorporation (seller and all subsidiaries).		
2. Preemptive rights of shareholders.		
3. Shareholder notice requirements.		
4. Vote of shares required to sell assets.		
5. Rights of dissenting shareholders.		
6. Statutory merger procedures.		
7. Restrictions on mergers with foreign corporations.		
8. Restrictions on mergers involving corporations in different businesses.		
9. Procedure of board of directors in either sale of assets or mergers.		

ITEM	ASSIGNED TO	COMMENTS

(I)

    10. States and countries in which qualified to do business (seller and all subsidiaries).

    11. Withdrawals or additional qualifications indicated (seller and all subsidiaries).

B. State "Blue Sky" Laws

    1. Permits required prior to negotiating agreement.

    2. Registration requirements and exemptions.

    3. Notice requirements and exemptions.

C. Bulk Sales Laws

    1. Requirements to comply.

    2. Effect of non-compliance.

    3. Possible escrow of portion of purchase price.

D. Assumption of Liabilities

    1. In an assets transaction, possible assumption of liabilities through operation of law.

II. SELLER'S CORPORATION ORGANIZATION, POWERS AND COMMITMENTS (SELLER AND ALL SUBSIDIARIES)

A. Corporate Charters

    1. Review all original charters and all amendments.

    2. Authorized capital structure, including description of classes of common, preferred, preemptive rights.

ITEM	ASSIGNED TO	COMMENTS

(II)

　　3. *Variance of stockholder vote requirements from statutory requirements.*

　　4. *Restrictions on sale of stock, and other restrictions.*

　　5. *If stock is being acquired, recommended amendments to charters.*

B. *By-Laws*

　　1. *Review for any unusual provisions, including powers of officers, notice provisions, etc.*

　　2. *If stock is being acquired, recommend amendments to by-laws.*

C. *Minute Books*

　　1. *Stock validly issued, fully paid and non-assessable.*

　　2. *Outstanding stock options.*

　　3. *Restrictions on transfers of shares.*

　　4. *Warrants or other rights to purchase stock.*

　　5. *Employment agreements.*

　　6. *Bonus plans.*

　　7. *Employee retirement payments.*

　　8. *Profit-sharing plans.*

　　9. *Pension plans, and other fringe benefit plans such as life insurance, Blue Cross, etc.*

ITEM	ASSIGNED TO	COMMENTS
(II)		
10. *Union contracts.*		
11. *Any major or long-term commitments.*		
12. *Any other operating details of importance such as the grant of exclusive licenses, franchises, state qualifications, etc.*		
D. *Stock Books*		
1. *Outstanding shares.*		
2. *Number of shareholders.*		
3. *Names and numbers of shares held by controlling shareholders.*		
4. *Shares held in the treasury.*		
5. *Payment of original issue and transfer taxes.*		
6. *Legality of any unusual transfers, such as transfers from estates and trusts.*		
III. *ASSETS (SELLER AND SUB-SIDIARIES)*		
A. *Real Properties*		
1. *Locations.*		
2. *Descriptions.*		
3. *Title abstracts.*		
4. *Title opinions.*		
5. *Title insurance.*		

ITEM	ASSIGNED TO	COMMENTS
(III)		
6. *Surveys*		
7. *Encumbrances, liens or charges, including tax liens, mortgages, rights of way and easements, restrictions, reversions, zoning laws and local ordinances.*		
B. *Real Property Leases*		
1. *Name of other party.*		
2. *Location, description and use.*		
3. *Date, term and termination rights.*		
4. *Rent per month.*		
5. *Net lease, or not.*		
6. *Guaranties.*		
7. *Defaults or breaches.*		
8. *Assignability.*		
C. *Personal Property*		
1. *Lists of machinery and equipment, and miscellaneous such as airplanes, trucks, cars, etc.*		
2. *Existence of any chattel mortgages, conditional sales contracts, or other liens.*		
3. *Where government contracts are involved are any assets the property of the U.S. Government?*		

ITEM	ASSIGNED TO	COMMENTS
(III)		
D. *Intangibles*		
1. Patents, inventions and knowhow.		
a. List patents.		
b. Patent search.		
c. Appraisal of strength of patent position.		
d. Review of patent license agreements.		
e. Determine approach to invention disclosures.		
f. Employee patent, trade secret and non-disclosure agreements.		
2. Review of trademarks, tradenames, and copyrights.		
IV. CONTRACTS		
A. *Contracts Should Be Listed in Categories such as:*		
1. Distributorship agreements.		
2. License agreements.		
3. Union contracts.		
4. Government contracts.		
5. Contracts with customers.		
6. Contracts with suppliers.		
7. Consulting contracts.		

ITEM	ASSIGNED TO	COMMENTS

(IV)

   B. All Major Contracts Should Reviewed to Check the Following:

     1. Assignability.

     2. Possible anti-trust violations.

       a. Relationship as customer or supplier of buyer.

       b. Requirement contracts.

       c. Robinson-Patman pricing problems—discounts, rebates, or allowances.

       d. Exclusive dealings, etc.

     3. Enforceability.

     4. Breaches or defaults.

     5. Redetermination clauses.

     6. Escalation clauses.

V. LIABILITIES

   A. Loan Agreements, Bonds and Debentures

     1. Check restrictive covenants to determine conflict with buyer's loan agreements, bonds and debentures, and limitation on buyer's conduct of business after acquisition.

ITEM	*ASSIGNED TO*	*COMMENTS*
VI. ANTI-TRUST CONSIDERATIONS		
A. Check for Existing Violations		
1. Sherman Act and Robinson-Patman violations, etc.		
2. Consent decrees.		
3. Federal Trade Commission proceedings and Justice Department complaints.		
4. Past and present anti-trust litigation and claims generally.		
B. Status of Acquisition Under §7 of Clayton Act and Sherman Act		
1. Are buyer and seller competitors?		
2. Are the buyer and seller related to each other as customers or suppliers?		
3. Study of the products, geographical areas of business, percentages of markets, etc.		
C. Conduct of Business After Acquisition		
1. How does buyer intend to integrate business?		
2. Will integration result in ultimate violations?		

ITEM	ASSIGNED TO	COMMENTS
VII. TAXES		
A. Income Taxes		
1. Tax-free acquisition.		
a. Are the requirements of Section 368(a) (1) (A) of the Internal Revenue Code met?		
b. Section 368(a) (1) (B)?		
c. Section 368(a) (1) (C)?		
d. Effect of basis, loss and all other carryover provisions on buyer and seller.		
e. Effect of depreciation and investment credit recapture provisions.		
2. Taxable acquisition.		
a. Allocation of purchase price.		
i. real estate.		
ii. buildings.		
iii. leasehold interests.		
iv. tools, dies and jigs.		
v. inventory.		
vi. patents.		
vii. customer contracts.		

ITEM	ASSIGNED TO	COMMENTS

(VII)

       viii. trademarks, tradenames.

       ix. goodwill.

    b. Effect of depreciation and investment credit recapture provisions.

    c. Will requirements of Section 337 or 334 of the Internal Revenue Code be met?

    d. Will appraisal of assets be obtained?

  3. Miscellaneous.

    a. Sales and use taxes.

    b. Have seller's past taxes been paid and reviewed by taxing authorities?

    c. Will buyer be subject to transferee liability?

    d. Social Security taxes —transfer of experience rating.

    e. Excise taxes.

    f. Real estate taxes.

VIII. BROKERAGE

  A. Is a Broker Involved?

    1. Name and proof of authority to act.

    2. Whose agent is the broker?

ITEM	ASSIGNED TO	COMMENTS

(VIII)

    3. *Who is to pay the commission—buyer, seller, or seller's stockholders?*

    4. *Has written brokerage agreement specifying all terms been signed with broker?*

    5. *Will the parties indemnify one another against brokerage claims?*

IX. *SECURITIES AND EX-CHANGE COMMISSION*

  A. *Registration of Buyers Stock*

    1. *Does non-public offering exemption apply?*

    2. *Investment letters.*

X. *STOCK EXCHANGE RE-QUIREMENTS*

  A. *Special Circumstances Requiring Special Action not Otherwise Required by Law or Charter*

    1. *Stockholder vote required if:*

      a. *Buyer's directors, or officers have an interest in seller.*

      b. *Stock to be issued by buyer represents an increase in outstanding shares of 20% or more.*

In summary, although the investigation of the seller's business should proceed in the three separate areas of (1) business, (2) law, and (3) accounting, the results of these investigations should be coordinated. The businessman, the lawyer and the accountant should each be kept abreast of the results of the investigation of the other two. Since the lawyer has the ultimate responsibility for incorporating in the acquisition contract all of the provisions necessitated by the facts and problems developed in the course of the investigation, the businessman and the accountant should transmit to the lawyer all information developed in their respective investigations. The procedure to be followed in a negotiation is dictated by the personalities involved, but, early in the negotiations, the lawyers should have an opportunity to consider possible initial legal problems and to shape the transaction. Basically the buyer and often the seller should, as a major objective, attempt to determine the *real* objective of the other party in buying or selling. Where deemed important, the parties should take all possible precautions to keep the negotiations secret. Finally, timetables and checklists similar to those printed in this chapter may be helpful to both the buyer and seller involved in an acquisition.

CHAPTER 6

Initial Legal Considerations

Once a buyer and seller begin to negotiate the details of a proposed acquisition, they should be alert to specific problems which may arise, in the legal, business, or accounting areas, and which may influence the substance, form, or mechanics of a proposed acquisition.

Some of these problems may be of such major importance to a transaction that the transaction may not be consummated unless the problems presented are first solved. Other problems may be secondary in nature and involve only mechanical considerations. However, the lawyer, businessman, and accountant should be aware of the possible problem areas, whether they be of substance or merely mechanical, and should be prepared to find solutions to the problems in the early negotiating sessions.

Two basic problem areas which may affect the substance of a transaction are the areas involving (1) Federal Securities Laws and (2) income tax considerations. In any particular acquisition, problems in these areas may be of such scope and involve such detailed considerations that they are discussed in separate chapters. Chapters 8 and 9 discuss problems involving the Securities Act of 1933 and the Securities and Exchange Act of 1934, particularly securities registration problems and regulation of takeover bids. Chapters 10 and 11 discuss the income tax problems most directly related to acquisitions.

In other problem areas, certain initial legal problems should be considered by the lawyers. Six of these are considered in this chapter. In Chapter 7 which follows, other general problems including problems involving accounting concepts and miscellaneous business problems are considered, as well as their relationship to structuring acquisitions.

As soon as the buyer and seller have reached an understanding that the proposed acquisition may be desirable and to the best interests of both parties, they should pause and consider what effect the transaction may have upon other possibly interested parties. For due to the nature of our society and legal institutions, other parties in addition to the buyer and the seller may have an important stake in the proposed acquisition. The public, the creditors of the seller and sometimes of the buyer, and the stockholders of both may have vested interests in the transaction which may not be violated.

The public's interest derives mainly from our laws against monopoly and unreasonable restraints of trade, as well as our laws regulating the sales of securities to protect the public's interests. Creditors may have advanced goods or funds to the buyer or seller and the rights of creditors to be repaid are protected by statutory law, common law, or private agreement. The stockholders of both the buyer and seller are part owners of the businesses and again their rights of ownership are protected by statutory law, common law, and sometimes private agreement. In any particular transaction, the determination of the nature and the effect of these rights—public, creditors, and stockholders—is a legal problem. Therefore, if the lawyers for the buyer and seller have not yet taken part in the discussions, they should certainly now be consulted.

At the outset, the lawyers should have an opportunity to consider possible legal problems which might arise affecting the public, the creditors and the stockholders, because prompt consideration of these problems will often save the expense of a detailed investigation and will help cast the ultimate form of the transaction. Initial consideration by the lawyers of the legal problems discussed below and in subsequent chapters, does not mean that all these problems will be present in every acquisition, a highly improbable situation. But the lawyers should have an immediate opportunity to consider which problems may exist and what to do about them. Other than Federal Securities Laws problems and income tax problems (discussed in Chapters 8–11), some initial legal problems are discussed below.

Legal problems—buyer. The initial legal problems will be discussed first from the viewpoint of the buyer and then from the viewpoint of the seller. As a start, four initial legal problems should be considered by the buyer's attorney:

1. Will the buyer assume liabilities of the seller and obligations of the seller to its creditors under applicable state law, without regard to the liabilities specifically assumed under the contract of sale?
2. Will the proposed transaction in any way violate anti-trust laws?
3. Are there any special stock exchange requirements which may have to be met due to the relationship of the parties or the nature of the transaction?
4. Are there any state securities law requirements (requirements for notification or registering securities with state authorities) which must be met in connection with the transaction?

Legal problems—seller. The lawyer for the seller should address himself initially to a minimum of two possible legal problems of a stockholder nature, which may affect the seller:

1. Are insiders, officers, directors, or controlling stockholders of the seller taking advantage of inside information for their own benefit?
2. Will there be any right of action on the part of minority stockholders where a sale of control of the seller will take place?

UNINTENDED ASSUMPTION OE SELLER'S
LIABILITIES—A BUYER PROBLEM

The acquisition of a seller may take the form of either a purchase of stock from stockholders or a purchase of the assets of the business. Where stock is bought, since the seller continues as a going business and the same corporate entity continues to exist, all liabilities of the seller will continue. A change in stock ownership will not have any effect on the outstanding liabilities of the seller. In other words, when one buys the stock of XYZ Corporation and it continues as a going concern without change, then the outstanding obligations and liabilities of XYZ Corporation will also continue without change. This is not the appropriate place, but we will discuss below how a buyer may obtain contract or other protection when it buys the seller's stock.

When the assets of a corporation are bought as a going business as opposed to buying stock, the buyer normally has greater protection against unwittingly assuming undisclosed liabilities of the seller. This is especially true where the buyer buys assets for cash in an arm's-length transaction.

With the exception of obligations specifically assumed by the buyer in the purchase contract, in a purchase of assets for cash the buyer normally assumes no obligations for undisclosed liabilities of the seller, and creditors must continue to look to the seller for payment. There are two major exceptions to this rule. (1) If the buyer acquires a going business for cash and pays the cash directly to the stockholders of the seller rather than to the corporation, the buyer may find itself liable to satisfy undisclosed creditors of the seller. (2) If the requirements of the applicable bulk sales law are not met, undisclosed creditors may be in a position to enforce their claims against the assets bought by the buyer. In a later chapter bulk sales requirements are discussed in greater detail.

Buying assets for cash, where the corporation receives payment and bulk sales law requirements are met, will generally eliminate assumption of undisclosed liabilities by the buyer, but buying assets of a going business for stock may result in the assumption of undisclosed liabilities by the buyer through operation of law. Where assets are bought for stock, a buyer may become liable to satisfy undisclosed liabilities of the seller even where the purchase contract specifically sets forth that the buyer does not assume any undisclosed liabilities. The courts invoke a number of theories to hold a buyer which pays with stock liable for obligations not assumed in the purchase contract.

Trust fund theory. One theory applied by the courts is that of the trust fund doctrine. Under this doctrine, some courts have held that where a buyer buys all of the assets of a selling corporation in exchange for the buyer's stock and the stock is then distributed to the selling corporation's stockholders, creditors of the seller may assert claims against the buyer. The courts have reasoned that the buyer knew at the time the transaction was consummated, by the nature of the purchase, that its stock was to be distributed among stockholders of the seller, and by permitting this stock, the last remaining asset of the seller, to be distributed the buyer should be liable to creditors of the seller. The buyer, these courts have held, received the assets of the seller in trust for the benefit of creditors of the seller. Under these circumstances, creditors of the seller may look to the buyer for payment of claims to the extent of the assets bought by the buyer. One judge has stated the trust doctrine as follows:

It follows that when this purchasing corporation took over in exchange for its own stock and bonds the assets of the other, and permitted these securities which it had substituted for the visible tangible property of the selling corporation to be distributed among the shareholders of the latter, without provision for the creditors of the latter, it thereby became a party, with full notice, to the diversion of a trust fund. As such, the purchasing corporation holds the property so acquired impressed with the same trust with which said property was originally charged, and the purchasing corporation is liable to the creditors of the selling corporation to the extent of the property thus obtained.

Other theories. A second theory under which unexpected liabilities are imposed on a buyer is that the purchase of assets for stock was in effect a merger or consolidation—sometimes referred to as a de facto merger. In this connection, courts have disregarded the actual transaction to which the parties have agreed and have treated the transaction as a merger or a consolidation under the state statutes. The usual effect of state merger or consolidation statutes is that the continuing company remains liable for all outstanding obligations of both of the corporations which were parties to the statutory merger or consolidation. By treating the transaction as a merger or consolidation, courts have concluded that the buyer assumed all of the obligations of the seller, regardless of the limitation of the assumption of obligations in the contract of sale.

A third theory under which a buyer of assets for stock is held liable for the obligations of the seller provides that a state should protect its creditors. Under this theory the courts reason that a seller which has sufficient tangible assets in the state to satisfy creditors before a sale may have no assets left after the seller distributes the buyer's stock to the seller's stockholders. The courts further reason that the creditors of the seller should not be forced to pursue the stock received by the seller's stockholders into foreign jurisdictions, but should rather be permitted to pursue the tangible assets left in the jurisdiction although owned by the buyer.

Under any of the theories mentioned, a buyer may find that he has taken the seller's property subject to unknown and unexpected rights of seller's creditors. If the lawyer for the buyer determines that applicable state law may result in assumption of obligations in addition to those assumed in the contract, he should take steps in the early stages of negotiation to protect his client. One method to obtain protection is an indemnification by the seller and a form of escrow agreement under which sufficient property or cash is pledged to protect the buyer against unassumed liabilities. The indemnity and escrow may be provided by all the seller's stockholders or the major stockholders involved in the transaction.

Collective bargaining contracts. Collective bargaining agreements may cause a buyer to assume obligations to a seller's employees which were not contemplated in the acquisition contract. In this connection, the National Labor Relations Board and the courts reason that the employees have a substantial interest in the continuation of their existing employee status, which they have a right to protect through bargaining. In at least one case, a court has gone as far as to hold that the entire collective bargaining agreement between a seller and its employees is binding upon a buyer, although the buyer did not assume the seller's obligations under the collective bargaining agreement in the acquisition contract. In one opinion, in holding that a buyer was required to bargain with the representative of the seller's employees, the National Labor Relations Board made the following statement:

. . . where, as here, the only substantial change wrought by the sale of a business enterprise is the transfer of ownership, the individuals employed by the seller of the enterprise must be regarded as "employees" of the purchaser as that term is used in the Act. Such individuals possess a substantial interest in the continuation of their existing employee status, and by virtue of this interest bear a much closer economic relationship to the employing enterprise than, for example, the mere applicant for employment. . . . The particular individuals involved here were unquestionably "employees" of the enterprise at the time of the transfer of plant ownership. The work they had been doing was to be continued without change. Clearly employees in such a situation are entitled to seek through bargaining to protect their economic relationship to the enterprise that employs them.

ANTI-TRUST PROBLEMS—A BUYER PROBLEM

Anti-trust problems—general. Three aspects of anti-trust problems should be considered in an acquisition. (1) Will the buyer inherit liability for any past violations of the anti-trust laws on the part of the seller? (2) Will the acquisition in and of itself constitute a violation of the anti-trust laws? And (3) will the intended future conduct of the business by the buyer result in any violations of the anti-trust laws?

Obviously, a complete discussion of the anti-trust laws is beyond the scope of this book. Volumes have been written concerning individual statutes which make up just a portion of the body of laws which are generally considered in their entirety as our anti-trust laws. This entire body of laws must be taken into consideration to determine whether any past violations by the seller exist and whether future conduct of the business will result in violations. This determination requires such a thorough knowledge of the seller's business methods, contracts, and relationship to his industry that the buyer's lawyers can only form an opinion of the broader anti-trust aspects as the investigation proceeds and knowledge is developed. But one anti-trust statute, Section 7 of the Clayton Act, specifically addresses itself to acquisitions. This is the section of the anti-trust laws which the lawyer must consider initially in any acquisition. And he must ascertain initially at least sufficient facts to make an educated guess concerning possible violation of Section 7 of the Clayton Act.

To place Section 7 of the Clayton Act in its proper context, briefly consider the broad scope of our anti-trust laws. There are three other Federal Acts which, read together with the Clayton Act, make up the major body of these laws. All of these are familiar by name.

The first is the Sherman Act, which provides that "every contract, combination in the form of trust or otherwise, or conspiracy, in restraint of trade or commerce . . . is declared to be illegal," and further that "every person who shall monopolize, or attempt to monopolize, or . . . conspire . . . to monopolize any part of . . . commerce" shall violate the Act. Note that the Sherman Act provides the contract or combination must *be* in restraint of trade, and further the monopoly or attempt to monopolize must actually be found. This Act, the first of the trust-busting statutes, prohibits among other things price-fixing, boycotts and allocations of territories through concert of action by competitors. It is also designed to curb the power and activities of corporations with monopoly or near-monopoly positions.

The second major act is the Federal Trade Commission Act, which provides that "unfair methods of competition in commerce, and unfair or deceptive acts or practices in commerce" are "declared unlawful." This Act prohibits, in addition to false advertising, unfair methods of competition which, if permitted to grow unchecked, might enable a company to achieve a monopolistic position.

The third act which is grouped among the anti-trust laws is the Robinson-Patman Act. Although this act is an amendment to the Clayton Act, it is generally referred to by its own name. This Act prohibits discriminations in prices where the probable consequences of such discriminations would be either a substantial lessening of competition or a tendency to create a monopoly or to injure competition between third parties and the person granting or receiving a discrimination.

Section 7 of the Clayton Act provides that the act is violated where a corporation acquires assets or stock in another corporation and the effect of the acquisition *may be* substantially to lessen competition, or to *tend* to create a monopoly. In other words it need not actually be demonstrated that the acquisition *has* or will definitely lessen competition. The statute by the use of the words "may be" only requires that there be a reasonable probability that the undesirable effects on competition will result.

Although very different in approach, and although very different in the practices at which they are aimed, these Acts have one fundamental objective common to all. That objective is to maintain a competitive business economy.

The Acts also have one important additional element in common. Each one affords wide discretion to the Department of Justice, Federal Trade Commission, and the courts to interpret their meaning. In this sense the Acts are like the Constitution of the United States—a document with broad general provisions, the meanings of which have developed with the years through interpretation by the courts of the general provisions as these provisions are applied to specific fact situations. In interpreting the anti-trust laws it is therefore not sufficient to refer only to the statutory language. One must try to determine the meaning given to the words of the statutes by government agencies and the Courts.

Clayton Act Section 7. With this background, consider pertinent language of Section 7 of the Clayton Act blocked out and enumerated to highlight its four basic elements:

> No corporation . . . shall
> [1] *acquire*, . . . the whole or any part of the stock, or . . . the whole or any part
> of the assets of another corporation . . . where in any
> [2] *line of commerce* in any
> [3] *section of the country*, the effect of such acquisition
> [4] MAY BE *substantially to lessen competition, or to* TEND *to create a monopoly.*

As indicated by the statutory language, four basic elements must be considered to determine whether a violation of Section 7 may occur, each of which is discussed below.

Clayton Act, Section 7—"acquisition." The presence of this element is obviously the easiest to establish. There must simply be an acquisition of all or a part of the assets or stock of another corporation. The acquisition may be made directly or indirectly by the acquiring company.

Clayton Act, Section 7—"line of commerce." The lessening of competition under the statute may take place in "any line of commerce." The statute does not refer to a lessening of competition in an *industry*. This language has given the enforcement agencies an opportunity to restrict and broaden relative product lines to attempt to prove possible lessening of competition. Generally, however, the courts and administrative agencies have now reached a conclusion that the line of commerce in each particular instance should be determined by means of the characteristics and end use of product. For example:

In ordering E. I. duPont to divest itself of its stock interest in General Motors, the Supreme Court held that the line of commerce was automotive finishes and fabrics, not paint and upholstery material in general. The Court felt that the invention of "DUCO" for use on automobiles in preference to varnish set the automotive finish market apart from the market for paints in general and that the pricing policies in the automotive fabrics market differentiated that market from the market for other fabrics where an established price prevailed. By restricting the line of commerce and thus reducing the size of the market under consideration, the Court laid the groundwork for finding the necessary tendency to the substantial lessening of competition or creation of a monopoly in the restricted line of commerce. To quote the language of the Court:

> However, within this broad market, well-defined submarkets may exist, which, in themselves, constitute product markets for antitrust purposes.

The Federal Trade Commission also narrowed the concept of a line of commerce when it ordered the Reynolds Metals Company to divest itself of Arrow Brands, Inc., a small manufacturer of aluminum foil. The Commission found that aluminum foil for sale to the florist trade was a separate line of commerce from aluminum foil for general household purposes. Foil for the florist trade was sold only to florists, was used only to decorate and wrap flowers, and its price fluctuated independently of the prices of household aluminum foil. Again, aluminum foil for the florist trade was not a large line of commerce, amounting to only 1½ to 2 million dollars annually, compared to many millions annually expended on aluminum foil for all purposes.

Clayton Act, Section 7—"section of the country." The tendency of lessening competition need occur only in "any section of the country," not the country as a whole. But the government agencies have the leeway of attempting to prove possible lessening of competition throughout the country or in localized sections, or both. In determining the area meant by "any section of the country" the courts have decided that there may be areas within areas. In other words, the area of competition may be the entire United States as one area. Within this area there may be localized areas of competition where smaller companies are engaged in localized activities, and such smaller companies may be less competitive where their competitor in the localized area is acquired by a larger corporation. For example:

In the Bethlehem Steel case involving Youngstown Tube, the Supreme Court found the section of the country within which competition had been lessened to be the United States, as a whole, because Bethlehem and Youngstown competed nationwide, and also found five separate regional areas, each of which was centered around a particular mill and was segregated from adjoining areas by the barrier of differing freight rates.

An extreme instance of a narrowing of the relevant geographic market to a small area occurred in a proceeding involving Erie Sand and Gravel Company where the Federal Trade Commission confined the section of the country within which competition between two gravel companies had been affected to the South Shore area of Lake Erie in the States of New York, Pennsylvania, and Ohio. This was the so-called "area of effective competition" since it was it was in this area that buyers from the merged companies were located.

Clayton Act, Section 7—"tendency to lessen competition." The acquisition must be one the effect of which *"may* be substantially to lessen competition, or to *tend* to create a monopoly." The effect on competition need therefore not be immediate. The words of the statute have been held by the courts to mean that a "reasonable probability" of a substantial lessening of competition is all that is required to violate the statute.

Decisions have also made it clear that a buyer does not have to buy a competitor to come within Section 7. Of course, buying a competitor will in and of itself lessen competition, and in such an acquisition the only remaining question relating to competition is whether the acquisition tends *substantially* to lessen competition or to create a monopoly. Where a buyer acquires a seller who is not a competitor, the courts have considered many factors to determine whether the competitive effect prohibited by the statute may occur. Among these are (1) the market shares of the companies, (2) the degree of concentration of business in a limited number of companies in the industry, (3) the ease of entry into the business from the standpoint of capital required, (4) the number of remaining competitors after the acquisition, (5) the industry trends and the number of previous mergers, (6) the anticipated or actual behavior of the merged company after the merger, and (7) the foreclosure of a potential market to others.

To quote the Court in the Bethlehem Steel case, the lessening of competition may occur when an acquisition "(1) substantially increases concentration, (2) eliminates a substantial factor in competition, (3) eliminates a substantial source of supply, or (4) results in the establishment of relationships between buyers and sellers which deprive their rivals of a fair opportunity to compete."

Each of the foregoing elements must be considered in the confines of the limited lines of commerce and geographical areas involved in the particular acquisition under consideration.

Federal Trade Commission Notification Requirements. Under a Federal Trade Commission requirement, the Commission requires a 60 day notice prior to the consummation of an acquisition by a buyer with assets of $250 million or more of a seller with assets of $10 million or more. The notice must be given within 10 days after agreement in principle has been reached. The same notification requirements apply to a buyer with less than $250 million in assets which proposes to acquire a seller with $10 million assets or more, and the resulting corporation would have assets exceeding $250 million.

The official instructions issued by the Federal Trade Commission with respect to the notice are as follows:

THIS REPORT IS REQUIRED BY LAW. It is mandatory under the authority of the Federal Trade Commission Act (15 U. S. C. 46). On or before the Reporting Date, complete and return one notarized copy of this Special Report to: Chief, Division of Mergers, Bureau of Restraint of Trade, Federal Trade Commission, Washington, D. C. 20580. Phone (202) 393–6800.

NOTICE OF DEFAULT. Failure to file this Special Report on or before the Reporting Date constitutes default and subjects the reporting company to penalties authorized by law.

REPORTING DATE. (1) The tenth (10th) day following the reporting company's entering into any agreement or understanding in principle to merge or to acquire assets of $10 million or more and no later than the sixtieth (60th) day prior to the consummation of the merger or acquisition. (2) The tenth (10th) day following the reporting company's amassing of 10 percent or more of the voting stock of another corporation with assets of $10 million or more.

(3) No later than the sixtieth (60th) day prior to the reporting company's effecting a stock acquisition which will result in the reporting company's holding 50 percent or more of the voting stock of another corporation with assets of $10 million or more.

The form of notice itself is as follows:

Merger Notification

FTC Form 6-21(4-69)   Budget Bureau No. 056-R-0026

Federal Trade Commission
Washington, D. C. 20580

SPECIAL REPORT

Approval expires April 15, 1972

MERGERS AND ACQUISITIONS

INSTRUCTIONS

For purposes of this Special Report, the "reporting company" includes your company and all companies in which your company has an ownership interest through either (1) holding a majority of the outstanding voting stock, or (2) holding the power to formulate, determine, or veto basic business decisions through the use of dominant minority stockholding rights, proxy voting, contractual arrangements, agents, or other means.

Each answer should identify the question to which it is addressed. If you are unable to answer any question fully, give such information as is available to you, explain why your answer is incomplete, and indicate the source from which a complete answer may be obtained. If books and records which provide accurate answers are not available, enter your best estimates and indicate the sources or bases of your estimates. Estimated data should be followed by the notation "est."

Except where stated otherwise, all inquiries refer to the reporting company's domestic operations. All references to "year" refer to calendar year. If the reporting company does not maintain its records on a calendar year basis, supply the requested data for the company's fiscal year reporting period which most nearly corresponds to the calendar year specified.

INFORMATION TO BE PROVIDED

1. State the correct corporate name, mailing address, and state and date of incorporation for (1) the reporting company, and (2) all active companies included within the reporting company.

2. Provide the following information on the (proposed) merger or acquisition:
   (a) the corporate names, mailing addresses, and principal business activities of the parties involved;
   (b) *if applicable*, the date on which the acquiring company had amassed 10 percent of the voting stock of the acquired company;
   (c) *if applicable*, the scheduled consummation date of the proposed merger or acquisition, description of the manner in which the transaction is to be carried out, a description of all stocks or assets to be transferred, and the consideration to be paid.

3. Furnish copies of all annual, quarterly, or other reports (including annual balance sheets and profit and loss statements) and proxy statements made by the reporting company to its stockholders during the most recent three-year period.

4. Submit a tabulation(s) which will provide the following information for the most recent calendar year:

(a) the reporting company's total domestic commercial sales in each of the following areas: manufacturing; mining; contract construction; wholesale and retail trade; finance, insurance, and real estate; agriculture, forestry, and fisheries; transportation, communication, electric, gas, and sanitary services; housing, repair and personal services; other industries (describe);

(b) the total sales of all foreign subsidiaries and divisions of the reporting company.

5. List and describe by its 4-digit SIC code and short title each industry listed in the 1967 *Standard Industrial Classification Manual* (Bureau of the Budget) in which the reporting company operated establishments in 1967 or currently operates establishments, and provide the following information for each such industry:

(a) the number of establishments operated by the reporting company in 1967;

(b) the number of establishments currently operated by the reporting company;

(c) the reporting company's 1967 value of shipments (sales, revenues received or other unit of value used in reports to the Bureau of the Census; for 4-digit industries in which value is not reported, show employment for payroll period which included March 12, 1967);

(d) for each merger or acquisition which the reporting company has made in the industry since January 1, 1961, indicate the name(s) of the merged or acquired company(s) and the date that the merger or acquisition was consummated. If the transaction represented the initiation of the reporting company's operation in the industry, so indicate.

6. Describe and list by its 7-digit Census product code each product produced in manufacturing establishments of the reporting company in 1967 and report value of shipments in calendar year 1967 for each such product. In addition, provide the following information:

(a) for each product manufactured in 1967 which has subsequently been dropped indicate the date upon which the product was dropped;

(b) for each product which was added in 1968 indicate the value of shipments in 1968 (give period covered by shipment figure);

(c) for each product which has been added since January 1, 1969, give the date upon which the product was added.

CERTIFICATION

This SPECIAL REPORT was prepared under my supervision and is true and correct to the best of my knowledge.

....
(Signature and title of company official)   (Date)

Subscribed and sworn to before me at the City of ...., State of .... this ..... day of ...., 19...... ....

Notary Public

My Commission Expires ....

Print or type the name, address, and telephone number of the person to contact regarding this SPECIAL REPORT

....
(Name)   (Business address)   (Business telephone no.)

Past anti-trust violations. As indicated, a discussion of the impact of the anti-trust laws in their broadest sense is beyond the scope of this book. Nevertheless, as the investigation proceeds, the lawyer for the buyer should be constantly vigilant to check all of the seller's contracts and pricing arrangements to uncover any possible past anti-trust violations. Of course, past violations may be eliminated by changing methods of doing business after the seller is acquired. Such a change in methods, however, may have considerable effect upon the profits of the seller's business. Contrary to the adage that "crime does not pay," undetected illegal activities carried on by sellers have on occasion produced substantial profits.

For example, assume that a major portion of a seller's business is done with one large customer under a contract which violates the Robinson-Patman Act. This contract may result in lower profits per unit sold to the major customer, rather than other customers, but may nevertheless be the basic reason for a major portion of the seller's profits. Should the price discrimination in favor of the major customer be corrected, this customer may seek a new supplier with a resultant loss of substantial profits in the seller's business.

Future anti-trust violations. The lawyer for the buyer should be alert not only to possible past anti-trust violations but should also consider the impact which the acquisition may have on future competition. The acquisition need not have an immediate effect upon competition to result in a violation of Section 7 of the Clayton Act. If the long-range effect of integrating the companies may be to substantially lessen competition a violation may occur. As indicated by the E. I. duPont case, where duPont was ordered to divest itself of its stock interest in General Motors more than a generation after its acquisition, an acquisition may not be illegal at the time of closing, but may become so because of the method of operating the acquired business.

As an example of circumstances a lawyer should consider in appraising the possible long-range effect of an acquisition on competition, assume that the buyer is a large distributor of household products who commands substantial shelf space in retail outlets. Should the buyer acquire a product completely unrelated to the buyer's own products, the acquisition at the time it is consummated may not be considered a violation of the Clayton Act. But if the buyer uses his powerful distribution system and shelf space to drive other manufacturers of the seller's product out of business, the buyer may be charged with violation of Section 7 of the Clayton Act as a result of his subsequent conduct of the acquired business.

STOCK EXCHANGE REQUIREMENTS—A BUYER PROBLEM

Where the stock of the buyer or seller is listed on a securities exchange, the rules of the exchange must be considered in all acquisitions. Even where cash is employed, a stock exchange rule may require the taking of action by the buyer or seller, which would not be necessary under the laws of the state of incorporation or under the provisions of the corporate charter. For example, companies listed on the New York Stock Exchange are required to keep studies of major acquisitions confidential when circumstances indicated in the Rule stated below exist. The New York Stock Exchange Company Manual contains the following provision relating to predisclosure handling of important corporate matters:

Internal Handling of Confidential Corporate Matters

Unusual market activity or a substantial price change has on occasion occurred in a company's securities shortly before the announcement of an important corporate action or development. Such incidents are extremely embarrassing and damaging to both the Company and the Exchange since the public may quickly conclude that someone acted on the basis of "inside" information.

Negotiations leading to acquisitions and mergers [emphasis supplied], stock splits, the making of arrangements preparatory to an exchange or tender offer, changes in dividend rates or earnings, calls for redemption, new contracts, products, or discoveries, are the type of developments where the risk of untimely and inadvertent disclosure of corporate plans is most likely to occur. Frequently, these matters require discussion and study by corporate officials before final decisions can be made. Accordingly, extreme care must be used in order to keep the information on a confidential basis.

WHERE IT IS POSSIBLE TO CONFINE FORMAL OR INFORMAL DISCUSSIONS TO A SMALL GROUP OF THE TOP MANAGEMENT OF THE COMPANY OR COMPANIES INVOLVED, AND THEIR INDIVIDUAL CONFIDENTIAL ADVISORS WHERE ADEQUATE SECURITY CAN BE MAINTAINED, PREMATURE PUBLIC ANNOUNCEMENT MAY PROPERLY BE AVOIDED. In this regard, the market action of a company's securities should be closely watched at a time when consideration is being given to important corporate matters. If unusual market activity should arise, the Company should be prepared to make an immediate public announcement of the matter.

At some point it usually becomes necessary to involve other persons to conduct preliminary studies or assist in other preparations for contemplated transactions, e.g., business appraisals, tentative financing arrangements, attitude of large outside holders, availability to major blocks of stock, engineering studies, market analyses and surveys, etc. Experience has shown that maintaining security at this point is virtually impossible. Accordingly, fairness requires that the Company make an immediate public announcement as soon as confidential disclosures relating to such important matters are made to "outsiders."

The extent of the disclosures will depend upon the stage of discussion, studies, or negotiations. So far as possible, public statements should be definite as to price, ratio, timing and/or any other pertinent information necessary to permit a reasonable evaluation of the matter. As a minimum, they should include those disclosures made to "outsiders." Where an initial announcement cannot be specific or complete, it will need to be supplemented from time to time as more definitive or different terms are discussed or determined.

Corporate employees, as well as directors and officers, should be regularly reminded as a matter of policy that they must not disclose confidential information they may receive in the course of their duties and must not attempt to take advantage of such information themselves.

In view of the importance of this matter and the potential difficulties involved, the Exchange suggests that a periodic review be made by each company of the manner in which confidential information is being handled within its own organization. A reminder notice of the Company's policy to those in sensitive areas might also be helpful from time to time.

The effective implementation of the foregoing is essential to the maintenance of a fair and orderly securities market for the benefit of a company and its shareholders. It should minimize the occasions where the Exchange finds it necessary to temporarily halt trading in a security due to information leaks or rumors in connection with significant corporate transactions.

While the procedures are directed primarily at situations involving two or more companies, they are equally applicable to major corporate developments involving a single company. Announcements of this type should usually be handled by telephone alert to the Department of Stock List.

The Manual also contains the following statement with regard to timely disclosures:

Timely and Adequate Disclosure of Corporate News

A corporation whose stock is listed on the New York Stock Exchange is expected to release quickly to the public any news or information which might reasonably be expected to materially affect the market for securities. This is one of the most important and fundamental purposes of the listing agreement which each corporation enters into with the Exchange. The agreement is discussed in greater detail in the latter part of this Section beginning on page A–27.

A corporation should also act promptly to dispel unfounded rumors which result in unusual market activity or price variations.

The discussion which follows will assist a listed corporation in making adequate and timely disclosure to its shareholders, the financial community, and the investing public and thus provide the basis for a market for its securities which will be fair to all participants.

Exchange Market Surveillance

For its part, the Exchange maintains a continuous market surveillance program through its Division of Stock Watch. The program is designed to closely review the markets in those securities in which unusual price and volume changes occur or where there is a large unexplained influx of buy or sell orders. Under such circumstances, the Company may be called by a member of the Department of Stock List to inquire about any company developments which have not been publicly announced but which could be responsible for unusual market activity. Where the market appears to be reflecting undisclosed information, the Corporation will normally be requested to make it public immediately. Occasionally it may be necessary to carry out a stock watch inquiry after the fact and the Exchange may request such information from the Company as may be necessary to complete such an inquiry.

The listing agreement provides that the Corporation will furnish to the Exchange on demand such information concerning the Corporation as the Exchange may reasonably require.

Listing Representative—Department of Stock List

Each listed company is assigned to a Listing Representative who is a member of the staff of the Department of Stock List. This representative serves as the liaison point for the Corporation and the Exchange. When the assigned representative is not available, another member of the staff will handle any inquiry, request, or report so that there will be no unnecessary delay in attending to listed company matters. The Secretary of the corporation is kept advised of the person serving in this capacity.

Preliminary discussions on important matters may be undertaken by listed company officials with the assurance that extreme security measures have been adopted by the Exchange to avoid revealing any confidential information which a listed company may disclose.

Furthermore, under state statute and corporate charter a buyer may generally acquire a seller in exchange for the buyer's stock without the need of obtaining approval of the buyer's stockholders. However, where the buyer is listed on a stock exchange, the stock exchange may require the buyer to seek approval of the acquisition by the buyer's stockholders—in spite of state corporation laws and the buyer's corporate charter. As a prerequisite for listing additional securities, a buyer listed on the New York Stock Exchange is required to obtain the approval of its stockholders of an acquisition where the directors, officers, or substantial security holders of the buyer have an interest in the seller, or where the relative size of the seller is substantial in relationship to the buyer. The rule as expressed in the New York Stock Exchange Company Manual is as follows:

Stockholder Approval—Exchange Policy

Stockholders' interest and participation in the corporate affairs of the companies which they own has greatly increased. This has been accompanied by a tremendous expansion in the number of shareowners. Management has responded by providing more extensive and frequent reports on matters of interest to investors. In addition, an increasing number of important corporate decisions are being referred to stockholders for their approval. This is especially true of transactions involving the issuance of additional securities.

Good business practice is frequently the controlling factor in the determination of management to submit a matter to stockholders for approval even though neither the law nor the company's charter makes such approval necessary. The Exchange encourages this growth in corporate democracy.

Stockholder approval is a prerequisite to listing securities to be issued for or in connection with the following:

1. Options granted to or special remuneration plans for directors, officers or employees. (See Sec. A–7)

2. Actions resulting in a change in the control of a company.

3. The acquisition*, direct or indirect, of a business, a company, tangible or intangible assets or property or securities representing any such interests:

   (a) From a director, officer or substantial security holder of the company (including its subsidiaries and affiliates) or from any company or party in which one of such persons has a direct or indirect interest;

   (b) Where the present or potential issuance of common stock or securities convertible into common stock could result in an increase in outstanding** common shares approximating 20% or more; or

   (c) Where the present or potential issuance of common stock and any other consideration has a combined fair value approximating 20% or more of the market value of the outstanding** common shares.

Companies are urged to discuss questions relating to this subject with the Department of Stock List sufficiently in advance of filing a listing application to allow time for the calling of a stockholders meeting and the solicitation of proxies where

---

* A series of closely related transactions may be regarded as one transaction for the purpose of this policy.

** Only those shares actually issued and outstanding (excluding treasury shares or shares held by a subsidiary) are to be used in making this calculation. Unissued shares reserved for issuance upon conversion of securities, exercise of options or warrants for any other purpose will not be regarded as outstanding.

this may be involved. All relevant factors will be taken into consideration in applying the above policy and the Department will be pleased to advise whether stockholder approval will be required in a particular case.

Listing Authorization Subject to Stockholder Action: Under certain circumstances, the Exchange will act upon a listing application, relating to a matter on which stockholders are to take action, prior to the time such action is taken. In such cases it is the practice of the Exchange to make its listing authorization subject to the action subsequently taken by stockholders on such matter, so that such authorization does not become final until stockholders have acted. Where this procedure is followed the application is not released for public distribution, nor is public announcement of the Exchange's action made, until advice of stockholder approval is received. By this procedure, early admission of the securities involved and, perhaps, early consummation of the transaction in which they are to be issued may be expedited, while there is avoided any possible influence which the prior announcement of the Exchange's listing authorization might have upon the outcome of stockholders' action.

STATE "BLUE SKY" LAWS—A BUYER PROBLEM

Although a buyer is not required to register its securities with the Securities and Exchange Commission, because the proposed acquisition falls within one of the exemptions, discussed in some detail in Chapter 8, below, state law may nevertheless require registration of the buyer's stock with a state securities commission or similar authority or at least notice to such an organization. Although many state laws have exemptions similar to the Federal exemptions, other states may require registration or notice despite a federal exemption being involved. To avoid violating state "blue sky" laws a buyer should therefore carefully check the blue sky laws of any states involved in an acquisition to determine the existence of any requirements for registration or giving notices.

Uniform Securities Act. The Uniform Securities Act, or portions of the Uniform Act are in effect as part of the blue sky law in a majority of the United States. Uniform forms for the registration of broker-dealers, investment advisors, and issuer-dealers, as well as for application for a salesman certificate, are in effect under the securities laws of many of the jurisdictions involved. In spite of the general acceptance of the Uniform Securities Act, many differences exist in the securities laws of the various states. For example, California has a comprehensive securities law which must be given careful consideration in any acquisition involving the issuance of stock to a California corporation or resident. As a result of differences in state law, each acquisition involving the issuance of securities in more than one jurisdiction, may involve consideration of the securities laws of each jurisdiction affected.

Effect of non-compliance. Although some states attempt to enforce their blue sky laws strictly, others lack necessary enforcement personnel, and therefore failure to comply with state blue sky laws often may not be serious from the point of view of action the state authorities may take. However, many state blue sky laws provide that a shareholder of a seller who receives securities of a buyer, which should have been registered with the state and were not, may void the transaction. He may sue to have the consideration paid returned by the buyer, often plus interest. Obviously, a selling shareholder who has received a buyer's stock will not sue if the buyer's stock increases in price. But if the buyer's stock declines in price, the selling shareholder may very likely be tempted to bring a law suit.

INSIDERS AND INSIDE INFORMATION—A SELLER PROBLEM

To what extent may insiders such as officers, directors or controlling shareholders of a seller take advantage of inside information for their own benefit in connection with an acquisition? Underlying this question is the problem of what fiduciary obligations, if any, the insiders have to minority shareholders. To explore this problem consider a typical acquisition situation.

A family corporation is operated and controlled by a father, John Jones, and two sons, Bill and Ed, who own in the aggregate 55% of the outstanding stock, and the remaining shares are held by approximately 200 outside shareholders. The stock is traded in the over-the-counter market, and in infrequent sales over the past year has commanded a price of $13 per share. In the course of negotiations with John, Bill and Ed, a prospective buyer has offered to buy all of the assets and business of the family corporation at a price equivalent to $20 per share. Armed with this knowledge, may the insiders solicit shares from minority shareholders at $13 per share, or do the insiders owe some fiduciary duty to the minority shareholders to disclose their inside information?

Under common law different jurisdictions came to different conclusions. At one extreme, courts held that insiders owed a fiduciary duty to disclose all information to minority shareholders. At the other extreme, they held that although an insider, such as an officer or director, owed a fiduciary duty to his corporation, he owed no such duty to outside shareholders and he could deal in the corporation's stock with such outsiders without disclosing important inside information. Other courts found a compromise solution, holding that an insider owed a duty to reveal unusual factors affecting the value of a stock in dealing in the corporation's stock with outside shareholders. Although common law remedies are still available, in a situation such as outlined above, regulations of the Securities and Exchange Commission provide outsiders with tailor-made remedies. Rule 10b-5 of the General Rules and Regulations under the Securities Exchange Act of 1934 is particularly applicable:

> It shall be unlawful for any person, directly or indirectly, by the use of any means or instrumentality of interstate commerce, or of the mails, or of any facility of any national securities exchange,
>
> 1. to employ any device, scheme, or artifice to defraud,
> 2. to make any untrue statement of a material fact or omit to state a material fact necessary in order to make the statements made, in the light of the circumstances under which they were made, not misleading, or
> 3. to engage in any act, practice, or course of business which operates or would operate as a fraud or deceit upon any person,
>
> in connection with the purchase or sale of any security.

Note that the rule makes it unlawful for *any person* to *omit to state* a material fact necessary in order to make statements made not misleading in connection with the purchase or sale of any security. If the rule is applicable, John and his sons Bill and Ed would be hard pressed to solicit stock at $13 a share and not violate the rule.

For federal jurisdiction to apply, a transaction must involve some element of interstate commerce or the use of the mails. But the deception itself need not be accomplished through the use of interstate facilities, as long as the facilities are incidentally used in connection with a transaction. For example, sending a confirmation slip through the mails is sufficient for federal jurisdiction to apply. Therefore, although no national securities exchange would be involved, let us assume that an attempt to solicit sales of stock from a substantial portion of the 200 outside shareholders would involve the use of the mails or some other instrumentality of interstate commerce. Therefore the rule would be applicable. In other words, John, Bill, or Ed need not buy the stock from a seller using a national securities exchange, or a recognized over-the-counter market. A private purchase is subject to the rule, provided some incidental use of interstate facilities is involved.

The rule applies to "any person." There is no doubt that insiders such as the Joneses are included. Court decisions have indicated that any person who has inside information may be covered by the rule, even if such a person is not an officer, director, or large stockholder. Thus the rule may apply to anyone who received inside information of an acquisition, such as a lawyer working on the matter or an employee doing research in a corporate planning division.

The person with the inside information must fail to state a "material" fact in order to violate the rule. The Joneses possess information that a buyer is willing to offer $20 a share for stock selling at $13 a share. This information is without question, material. Assume further that the buyer has offered John Jones a five year consulting contract at an annual fee of $100,000 if the acquisition is made—although, as the buyer understands, the main reason John Jones is considering selling is his wish to retire. The consultant arrangement could also be a "material" fact.

From the foregoing discussion, it is evident that if John, Bill, and Ed buy up stock from outsiders at $13 a share, they will in all likelihood be in violation of Rule 10 b-5 and subject to a suit for damages by selling shareholders to recover the illegal profits. Even if the Rule should not apply due to lack of federal jurisdiction, selling shareholders may have a right of action against the Joneses under common law.

SELLING CONTROL—A SELLER PROBLEM

Assume that the buyer who approached John Jones and his sons in the example discussed in the foregoing section offered to buy their 55 per cent controlling interest in the corporation for $20 a share, rather than all the assets and business of the corporation. The $7 a share premium over market price of $13 a share could look attractive to the Joneses. Could acceptance of the offer cause the Joneses legal difficulties or loss of the profits resulting from the sale? Although logic would dictate that a person may sell his own property for any price he is able to realize and that shares representing a controlling interest may have more value to a buyer than small minority blocks, the Joneses must give careful consideration to the legal consequences resulting from a sale of their controlling interest.

Although the courts generally state that a sale of a controlling block of shares will not in and of itself subject the sellers to legal liability for any premium received, courts often find that other circumstances are present in addition to the sale of control which may subject the sellers to liability. For example, where the sellers resign from management as a condition to the sale, the courts may find that some or all of the premium was paid for the corporation's offices. Such a sale of corporate offices would be a violation of fiduciary duty to the corporation. Or, if the sellers lie to minority holders by concealing a premium and stating that all of the stockholders are being offered the same price, or the corporation is looted after exchange of control, or the buyer uses corporate control to the buyer's own advantage rather than to the corporation's advantage, the sellers may be charged with legal liability for the premium they received for their controlling share interest.

An interesting case in this area of the law is *Perlman* v. *Feldmann* 219 F.2d 173. This case involved a steel company of which holders of a 37 per cent controlling block sold their shares at $20 a share when the stock was selling at $12 a share in the open market. At the time of the sale a severe shortage of steel existed. The buyer was a user of steel and obviously bought control of the seller to use the seller's steel in the buyer's business. Minority shareholders sued the sellers of the controlling interest, alleging that the sale of control would deprive the corporation of an opportunity to increase its goodwill by allocating steel to customers in a geographical area where the corporation could operate most profitably, and also of a further opportunity to expand the business by obtaining interest-free loans from other customers. The court held that the controlling shareholders would be required to account for the premium paid to them if the corporation ultimately was harmed as the minority shareholders alleged.

In the course of its opinion the court stated some of the applicable rules as follows:

> In Indiana, then, as elsewhere, the responsibility of the fiduciary is not limited to a proper regard for the tangible balance sheet assets of the corporation, but includes the dedication of his uncorrupted business judgment for the sole benefit of the corporation, in any dealings which may adversely affect it. . . . Although the Indiana case is particularly relevant to Feldmann as a director, the same rule should apply to his fiduciary duties as majority stockholder, for in that capacity he chooses and controls the directors, and thus is held to have assumed their liability. . . . This, therefore, is the standard to which Feldmann was by law required to conform in his activities here under scrutiny.
>
> It is true, as defendants have been at pains to point out, that this is not the ordinary case of breach of fiduciary duty. We have here no fraud, no misuse of confidential information, no outright looting of a helpless corporation. But on the other hand, we do not find compliance with that high standard which we have just stated and which we and other courts have come to expect and demand of corporate fiduciaries. In the often-quoted words of Judge Cardozo: "Many forms of conduct permissible in a workaday world for those acting at arm's length, are forbidden to those bound by fiduciary ties. A trustee is held to something stricter than the morals of the market place. Not honesty alone, but the punctilio of an honor the most sensitive, is then the standard of behavior. As to this there has developed a tradition that is unbending and inveterate. Uncompromising rigidity has been the attitude of courts of equity when petitioned to undermine the rule of undivided loyalty by the 'disintegrating erosion' of particular exceptions,". . . . The actions of defendants in siphoning off for personal gain corporate advantages to be derived from a favorable market situation do not betoken the necessary undivided loyalty owned by the fiduciary to his principal.
>
> The corporate opportunities of whose misappropriation the minority stock-

holders complain need not have been an absolute certainty in order to support this action against Feldmann.

In the light of the above discussion, John, Bill, and Ed Jones, should investigate before accepting the buyer's offer of $20 a share for their controlling block. Does the corporation have substantial liquid assets which may entice a buyer to undertake some gentle looting? Does the buyer have a reputation for acquiring corporations primarily for the purpose of syphoning off liquid assets for use in other ventures?

A lawyer advising the Joneses on the possible sale of their interest should consider all of the foregoing possibilities, and in advising the course of action to be followed may find that the only safe course for John, Bill, and Ed Jones to follow would be to insist that the buyer make the same $20 a share purchase offer to all of the corporation's shareholders.

To summarize, in addition to Federal Securities Laws and income tax problems, many other legal and technical problems may affect the substance, form, or mechanics of an acquisition. Initially, from a buyer's point of view, certain legal problems involving possible unintended assumption of a seller's liabilities, anti-trust laws, special stock exchange requirements, and state securities law must be considered. The seller and buyer should also consider legal problems with respect to the use of insider information by officers, directors, or others participating in an acquisition, as well as any rights of minority shareholders where a sale of control of the seller takes place.

CHAPTER 7

General Considerations in Structuring Acquisitions

In addition to the initial legal problems discussed earlier, the negotiators for both the buyer and seller should be aware of other problems which may affect not only the form but also the substance of an acquisition. Knowledge of the problems will help the negotiators develop a necessary ingredient to every acquisition—solutions to the problems which arise in the course of negotiations.

Not all the problems or considerations discussed below will be present in every acquisition, but, in an acquisition of any size, it would be most unusual if at least one of the problems or considerations discussed in this chapter were not present.

POOLING OF INTERESTS

For accounting purposes, an acquisition may be treated in only one of two ways: either as a "pooling of interests" or as a "purchase." The concepts of a "pooling of interests" and a "purchase" are purely accounting concepts which have no effect upon the actual cash position or cash earnings of the business a buyer has acquired from a seller. But whether or not an acquisition may be treated as a "pooling of interests" rather than a "purchase" may have a profound effect upon the future book earnings of a buyer and other aspects of a buyer's financial statements. From a buyer's viewpoint, the importance of the two different accounting treatments is that the treatment permitted may have a major effect on the per share earnings which a buyer reports to its stockholders in its annual report and other aspects of the buyer's financial statements.

"Purchase"—Goodwill. The concept of a "pooling of interests" generally assumes major importance only where a buyer pays more for a seller than the book value of the assets shown on the seller's books. In such a situation, where the price paid exceeds the book value of the seller's assets, if the transaction is a "purchase," generally accepted accounting principles will require that the excess which may not be allocated to specific tangible and intangible assets be set up on the buyer's books as an item of goodwill. In such a situation, where the price paid exceeds the book value of the seller's assets, if the transaction is a "purchase," the assets acquired by the buyer must be recorded at their cost upon the buyer's books. The cost is determined by the present value of the amounts paid consisting of cash, properties, and assumption of obligations. Assets acquired by issuing shares of stock of the buyer are recorded at the fair value of the assets received. The cost thus determined must be allocated to the individual assets which make up the seller's business. The total cost of the assets acquired is assigned to the individual assets on the basis of the fair market value of each. The difference between the sum of the fair values of the tangible and identifiable intangible assets acquired, less liabilities assumed, and the total costs of all assets acquired constitutes unspecified intangible values—normally referred to as goodwill. Goodwill should then be amortized and charged against income, based upon a reasonable estimate of the useful life of the goodwill. The period of amortization should not, however, exceed 40 years. Such amortization write-offs may substantially reduce reported book earnings, and since the write-off of goodwill is against after-tax earnings and is not deductible for income tax purposes, the reported earnings of the buyer are reduced and the buyer does not receive any offsetting tax benefit.

"Pooling of Interests"—No goodwill. Under the "pooling of interests" accounting treatment, the respective book values of the assets of the buyer and seller, the liabilities and the surpluses or deficits are added together (pooled) in the balance sheet of the successor business. Any excess par value or stated value of the capital stock account of the buyer, after the issuance of stock by the buyer and cancellation of the stock of the seller, over the sum of the individual capital stock accounts of the buyer and seller prior to the acquisition is charged to the combined capital surplus. If capital surplus is insufficient, earned surplus is charged to the extent necessary. Any reduction in the capital stock account resulting from the acquisition is credited to capital surplus. Since a "pooling of interests" essentially involves only an adding together of items on two separate balance sheets, no new item of goodwill is originated on the buyer's books, and no amortization or write-off need be made against the buyer's reported after-tax earnings. Although the difference in accounting treatment has other effects on the buyer's books, the effect on reported book earnings is most immediately of concern and will be discussed in the following examples.

The "purchase"—an example. Assume that the buyer pays $3,000,000 in market value of preferred stock and debentures for the seller, and the seller's assets have a book value of $500,000. The excess purchase price (excess market value of stock and debentures paid over the book value of the assets of the seller) is therefore $2,500,000 ($3,000,000 paid, less the net book value of assets, i.e., $500,000). If the acquisition is treated as a "purchase," generally accepted accounting principles require that if the excess purchase price may not be allocated to other identifiable assets, an additional asset of $2,500,000, usually designated as goodwill, be set up on the buyer's balance sheet. Accounting principles require that the $2,500,000 be amortized over a period of years, not exceeding 40 years, from after-tax earnings of the buyer. The amortization or write-off does not in any way affect actual net cash earnings, cash flow, or income taxes. But the effect that the amortization or write-off may have on the earnings the buyer reports to its shareholders in the buyer's annual report may be substantial.

Assume that the seller had annual after-tax earnings of $300,000 and that it is the buyer's accounting determination to write off goodwill over 10 years. As a result of the "purchase," the $2,500,000 written off over 10 years will cause an annual reduction of $250,000 for 10 years in the book earnings of the buyer—the earnings the buyer reports to its shareholders. The annual reduction of $250,000 must be made against after-tax income Therefore, if the seller's rate of after-tax annual income is maintained by the buyer at $300,000, the buyer may report an annual income of only $50,000 from the seller's business to the buyer's shareholders over the 10-year amortization period ($300,000 annual net after-tax income less $250,000 annual goodwill amortization).

Expressed in outline form, the effect of the "purchase" by the buyer of the seller's original $300,000 annual after-tax net income on the reported book earnings of the buyer is as follows:

(1) Purchase price paid in the buyer's stock: $3,000,000

(2) Book value of the seller's assets: $500,000

(3) Excess purchase price over the book value of the seller's assets: $2,500,000

(4) Goodwill in a "purchase": $2,500,000

(5) Annual amortization over a 10-year period: $250,000

(6) Annual after-tax net income from seller's business (before goodwill amortization): $300,000

(7) Annual book income reported by buyer from seller's business ($300,000 income less $250,000 goodwill amortization): $50,000

(8) Total book earnings from the seller's business reportable by buyer to its shareholders over 10 years: $500,000

As a result of treating the acquisition as a "purchase," the buyer must report to its shareholders total after-tax earnings of $500,000 over a 10-year period from a business which the buyer bought for $3,000,000. The actual after-tax net earnings realized by the buyer from the seller's business total $3,000,000, and the buyer has fully recovered its original investment in the seller's business over the 10-year period. But as a result of treating the transaction as a "purchase," the buyer, through its reported book earnings, has, in effect, reported to its shareholders that over the 10-year period it has recouped only 16.6 per cent of its original investment.

"Pooling of interests"—the same example. Assume that the same transaction reviewed in the preceding example as a "purchase" receives a "pooling of interests" accounting treatment. Stressing only the effect on reported earnings, if the same acquisition is treated as a "pooling of interests," the buyer may report earnings to its shareholders of $300,000 annually—500 per cent more than the $50,000, of annual earnings it may report under a "purchase" accounting treatment. Remember, if the acquisition is treated as a "pooling of interests," no goodwill need be placed upon the buyer's books. After-tax net earnings need not be reduced by goodwill amortization or write-off. Now note, by following the outline of the previous example of a "purchase" transaction, how a "pooling of interests" changes the reported book earnings realized by a buyer from the seller's business:

(1) Purchase price paid in the buyer's stock:	$3,000,000
(2) Book value of the seller's assets:	$500,000
(3) Excess of the purchase price over the book value of the seller's assets:	$2,500,000
(4) Goodwill in a "pooling of interests":	$000
(5) Annual amortization over a 10-year period:	$000
(6) Annual after-tax net income from the seller's business (without goodwill amortization):	$300,000
(7) Annual book income reported by the buyer from the seller's business ($300,000 net income, without amortization):	$300,000
(8) Total book earnings from the seller's business reportable by the buyer to its shareholders over 10 years:	$3,000,000

As a result of treating the acquisition as a "pooling of interests," the buyer reports to its shareholders total after-tax earnings of $3,000,000 over a 10-year period from a business which the buyer bought for $3,000,000. Thus, by treating the acquisition as a "pooling of interests" the buyer reports to its shareholders that the earnings from the seller's business over a 10-year period have fully paid the purchase price of the business.

Accounting criteria of a "pooling of interests." Since the difference between treating an acquisition as a "pooling of interests" or a "purchase" for accounting purposes may have such a profound effect upon a buyer's financial statements, it would appear that a buyer should choose the accounting treatment, in each acquisition, producing the best financial results to the buyer. However, certain arbitrary criteria must be met before an acquisition may be treated as a "pooling of interests." Furthermore, if an acquisition meets the accounting criteria for a "pooling of interests," it *must* so be treated for accounting purposes. All acquisitions not meeting the "pooling" criteria *must* be treated as "purchases."

"Pooling" criteria—historical background. In 1957 Accounting Research Bulletin No. 48 was issued by the Committee on Accounting Procedure of the American Institute of Certified Public Accountants. In this bulletin, the Committee set forth the criteria to determine whether an acquisition could be treated as a "pooling of interests" under generally accepted accounting principles. If an acquisition met the criteria set forth in the bulletin, the bulletin permitted, but did not require, that the acquisition be treated as a "pooling of interests" for accounting purposes. In other words, although an acquisition met the requirements for treatment as a "pooling of interests," the acquisition could, nevertheless, at the option of the buyer and its accountants, be treated as a "purchase."

Bulletin No. 48 set forth certain general criteria to qualify an acquisition for "pooling of interests" accounting treatment. The four basic criteria were (1) a continuity of equity ownership by the seller's stockholders in the buyer's business after the acquisition, (2) a continuation of the business of both the buyer and seller, (3) a continuity of management, and (4) the relative size of the buyer and seller. The first requirement contained in the bulletin, a continuity of equity ownership, contemplated that the basic consideration paid for a seller should consist of common stock of a buyer. Where cash or other property was paid for a seller, or a major portion of the price was paid in cash or other property, the bulletin contemplated that the "pooling of interests" accounting treatment would not be available. With the passage of time, the requirement of payment in common stock was eroded and transactions involving miscellaneous types of securities including preferred stocks and substantial amounts of cash were treated as qualifying for "pooling of interests" accounting treatment. In addition, concepts involving part "purchase" and part "pooling of interests" accounting treatment were applied.

The relative size between the buyer and seller required for the "pooling of interests" accounting treatment to be available was also stated in general terms in the bulletin. However, the bulletin contained a presumption that if the seller received only 10 per cent or less of the buyer's voting interest, the acquisition should be treated as a purchase. Again, however, with the passage of time, determinations made by accountants and the SEC permitted the test of the relative size between the buyer and seller to be eroded to a point of almost nonexistence. Poolings were approved where the size of the seller was less than 1 per cent of the buyer's size.

The relaxation of the basic conditions for treating an acquisition as a "pooling of interests" permitted the use of the "pooling of interests" accounting treatment to report the results of more and more acquisitions. During the 1960's, when the cost (based on the market value of securities issued) of the great majority of acquisitions was far in excess of the book value of the assets of the sellers, treatment of such acquisitions as "pooling of interests" permitted buyers to ignore the element of goodwill involved in the transactions in reporting the buyer's subsequent earnings. Frequent use was also made of other advantages of accounting for acquisitions as "pooling of interests," such as a subsequent sale of a seller's assets for a price substantially in excess of the seller's book value and the consequent increase in reported earnings of a buyer. Conglomerates, under constant pressure from the market place to report higher and higher earnings per share, made greater and greater use of the "pooling of interests" accounting treatment to continue reporting increases in earnings per share. Administrative agencies, financial writers, security analysts, and the accounting profession began to question the soundness of the "pooling of interests" accounting treatment as applied in many acquisitions. As a consequence, the entire area was reviewed by the Accounting Principles Board of the American Institute of Certified Public Accountants resulting in an exposure draft of a proposed Accounting Principles Board Opinion on Business Combinations and Intangible Assets, distributed under date of February 23, 1970. The result of the distribution of this exposure draft was the issuance of separate opinions, No. 16 "Business Combinations" and No. 17 "Intangible Assets," by the Accounting Principles Board setting forth new "pooling of interests" criteria, and rules for amortization of goodwill. The opinions were made to apply to all business combinations entered into after October 31, 1970.

Pooling of interests—current general conditions. Under present accounting criteria if an acquisition meets the conditions of a "pooling of interests," the buyer may no longer at its option determine whether it will treat the acquisition as a "pooling of interests" or a "purchase." If an acquisition meets the pooling conditions, accounting practice now *requires* that the buyer account for the acquisition as a "pooling of interests." The general conditions set forth in the accounting opinion of the Accounting Principles Board for a "pooling of interests" are classified by (1) attributes of the buyer and seller, (2) the manner of affecting the acquisition, and (3) the absence of certain planned transactions.

Attributes of the buyer and seller—two conditions. With respect to attributes of the buyer and seller, the following two conditions must be met:

(1) Each company, buyer and seller, must have been an active independent company for at least two years before the plan for the acquisition is initiated. This condition

requires that none of the corporations involved in the acquisition has been a subsidiary or division of another corporation within the preceding two years.

(2) The second condition requires that each of the combining companies be independent of the other combining companies. This condition means that, subject to certain exceptions, at the dates the plan of acquisition is initiated and consummated, the combining companies hold as intercorporate investments no more than 10 per cent in total of the outstanding voting common stock of any combining company.

It is interesting to note that any requirements with respect to the relative sizes of the buyer and seller were eliminated from the criteria with respect to a "pooling of interests."

Manner of effecting the acquisition—eight conditions. With respect to the manner of effecting the acquisition, the following eight conditions must be met:

(1) The acquisition should be effected in a single transaction or must be completed, pursuant to a plan, within one year after the acquisition is initiated.

(2) The buyer may issue only common stock with rights identical to those of the majority of the buyer's outstanding voting common stock, in exchange for substantially all of the voting common stock interest of the seller. Generally, the acquisition of substantially all of the voting common stock of the seller by the buyer means the acquisition of 90 per cent or more of the outstanding common stock of the seller. Also, generally, the stock to be issued by the buyer must be all common stock unless both preferred and common stocks of the seller are outstanding, in which case the buyer may issue common stock and preferred stock in the same proportions as the outstanding common and preferred stock of the seller.

(3) Neither the buyer nor the seller "changes" the equity interest of its voting common stock in contemplation of effecting the acquisition, either within two years before the plan of acquisition is initiated or between the dates the acquisition is initiated and closed. Distributions to stockholders which are no greater than normal dividends are not "changes" within the meaning of this condition.

(4) The buyer and seller reacquire shares of voting common stock only for purposes other than purposes related to the acquisition, and neither company may reacquire more than a "normal number" of its shares between the dates the plan of acquisition is initiated and consummated. Under this condition, treasury stock may be acquired for stock options and compensation plans and for recurring distributions, provided a systematic pattern of reacquisitions was established at least two years before the plan of acquisition was initiated.

(5) The relative interest of individual common stockholders in the buyer and seller may not be realigned by the exchange of securities in the acquisition. Under this condition each individual common stockholder of the buyer and seller must receive a voting common stock interest exactly in proportion to his relative common stock interest before the acquisition.

(6) The voting rights to which the common stock ownership interests of the stockholders in the continuing combined corporation are entitled must be exercisable by the stockholders; the stockholders may neither be deprived nor restricted in exercising these voting rights for a period of time. Under this condition, for example, shares of common stock issued to consummate the acquisition may not be transferred to a voting trust.

(7) The seller may distribute no more than normal dividends, and may not reacquire more than a normal number of shares of the seller's common stock after the plan for the acquisition is initiated.

(8) The acquisition must be completed at the time of closing, and no provisions in the plan of acquisition may relate to future issues of securities or other consideration. Under this condition, the continuing corporation may not agree to contingently issue additional shares of stock or distribute other consideration at a later date to former stockholders of the seller, nor may the buyer issue common stock to an escrow agent or issue other consideration to the escrow agent which is either to be transferred to the common stockholders of the seller or returned to the buyer, depending upon the resolution of contingencies.

Absence of planned transactions—three conditions. The following three conditions as to future transactions involving a buyer and seller must be met:

(1) The buyer may not agree, directly or indirectly, to retire or reacquire all or part of the common stock issued to consummate the acquisition.

(2) The buyer may not enter into other financial arrangements for the benefit of the seller's stockholders, such as a guarantee on loans secured by stock issued in the acquisition, which may have the effect of negating the exchange of equity securities.

(3) The buyer may not plan to dispose of a significant part of the combined assets of the buyer and seller within two years after the acquisition, except to eliminate duplicate facilities or excess capacity, as well as those assets which would have been disposed of in the ordinary course of business of the buyer.

STATE CORPORATION LAWS

In each acquisition, the corporation statutes of the states of incorporation of the buyer and seller must be studied to determine the effect they may have upon the proposed form of the transaction. Most states have fairly liberal corporation laws on their books. But some states still restrict certain types of acquisitions. For example, some statutes may provide that mergers between corporations may take place only if both corporations are engaged in "business of the same or similar nature." Therefore, in an acquisition involving a corporation incorporated under the laws of a state with such a statute, where the buyer and seller are in different businesses, a route other than statutory merger must be chosen, for example a stock-for-stock acquisition.

In addition, where a seller is selling assets, the laws of the seller's state of incorporation must be examined to determine the percentage of shareholders which must approve the sale and the rights of dissenting shareholders, if any. For example, in Delaware the vote of only a favorable majority of shareholders is required to sell assets and there are no dissenter's rights, whereas in many states a vote of at least two-thirds of the shareholders is required and dissenters may demand the fair value of their stock in cash. Further, under Delaware law, in a statutory merger rather than an acquisition of assets a favorable vote of a majority only of the shareholders is required, but dissenters may have a right to cash. In general, the laws of the states of incorporation must be studied to find any unusual provisions affecting the proposed acquisition.

FAVORABLE OR UNFAVORABLE CHARTER

In a merger, to determine which corporation should survive, the certificates of incorporation of both the buyer and seller should be studied to determine whether one certificate is more favorable than another. For example, if a New York corporation engaged in engineering is to be merged with another engineering firm, the corporate name provided in the certificate of incorporation may even determine which corporation should survive. Generally, since April 15, 1935, no corporation may be formed in New York with the word "Engineering" as part of its corporate title. Therefore, if one of the corporations has the word "Engineering" in its title, permissible because of its formation prior to April 15, 1935, this may be the corporation which should survive. One certificate of incorporation may have cumulative voting for directors and the other not. One may have unfavorable restrictions on the payment of dividends.

NUMBER OF SHAREHOLDERS

Often the number of shareholders involved will have an effect on the form of an acquisition. If a buyer wishes to gain 100 per cent control of a seller and leave no outstanding minority interest posing a threat of future stockholder's suits, where a seller has only relatively few stockholders, the buyer may obtain the required control by agreement of the shareholders in a stock-for-stock transaction. But if the seller's stock is widely held, an attempt to proceed on the basis of a tender of the buyer's stock to the seller's shareholders will not generally assure the buyer of 100 per cent control. In such an instance, the buyer may solve the problem by proposing to acquire the assets of the seller rather than the stock of the seller. In many states, the general rule is that sale of corporate assets by a corporation requires the affirmative vote of two-thirds of its shareholders. However, if the two-thirds favorable vote is obtained, any shareholders who do not wish to accept the buyer's offer are limited to a right to dissent. The right to dissent gives the dissenting shareholders a right to be paid off, but no right to continue as minority shareholders of the seller. As a protection against excessive cash drain due to dissenters, buyers often limit the amount of permissible dissents by the terms of the acquisition contract.

Where a buyer does not wish to undertake the expense or subject itself to other disadvantages of registering its securities under the Securities Act of 1933, the number of shareholders may again be of importance. As discussed in greater detail in Chapter 8, where the seller's stockholders are limited in number and take the buyer's securities as an investment, the transaction may exempt the buyer from filing a registration statement with the Securities and Exchange Commission with respect to the stock that the buyer uses to make the acquisition.

PENSION, PROFIT-SHARING, AND STOCK OPTION PLANS

As soon as possible in the process of negotiating a detailed acquisition contract, the relationship between pension, profit-sharing, stock option and other fringe benefit plans of the buyer and seller (if any) should be given careful consideration. Such plans involve not only possible grave business, legal and financial problems, but always involve human elements.

The seller's business consists not only of tangible and intangible assets but also of human beings who in some instances may cause the difference between a success and a failure of the seller's business.

From the business and financial viewpoint, the seller's pension plan may include such a large unfunded past service credit that the buyer must think in terms of discontinuing the plan, or negotiating into the price the obligation assumed by the buyer to fund the plan. Lawyers may be forced to consider the problem of whether or how the plan can be legally terminated. And never to be forgotten is the fear of the seller's employees that their pensions or fringe benefits may be lost or decreased. Nor will employees be happy if they are members of a non-contributory plan and are expected to become members of a contributory plan with similar benefits.

Two examples from an article entitled "Pension Pitfalls . . . in Company Mergers" by Geoffrey N. Calvert of Alexander & Alexander, Inc., highlight some of the serious problems pension plans may present in acquisitions:

EXAMPLE I.

Company A sold off a subsidiary as a going concern to Company B for $12 millions. The terms of the sale were agreed and a detailed contract was signed. No sooner had the actual transfer of the subsidiary been commenced, however, than it was realized with horror that nothing had been agreed about the pension rights of the employees in the subsidiary. Were they being terminated by Company A, which would benefit substantially from the release of their pension reserves? Should their accrued pension rights be vested, although many had not then qualified for vesting? Should the pension fund of Company A be segregated and a portion be transferred to Company B along with the pension credits of transferring employees? If so, how could the plan of Company B be adjusted without raising more problems with its own employees? Should the employees be given back service pension credits in the plan of Company B under its terms, and give up those in the plan of Company A? If the pension fund of Company A were segregated, how should this be done: (i) including previously-developed gains and surpluses, or (ii) excluding these items? How about past service benefits not yet funded? All of these questions were unanswered, and some extremely painful and difficult negotiations were necessary before the matter was finally straightened out, the solution being further complicated by the subsequent transfer of many employees from the sold-off subsidiary back into the service of Company A. Had this whole situation been foreseen and provided for in advance, much pain and embarrassment would have been avoided.

EXAMPLE II.

Company X with a pension plan in operation merged with Company Y which had no pension plan. After the merger, a new plan was developed to cover the employees of both companies, but on a future service basis only. Included in Company Y were some older employees with long years of service. Since their pensions were based on service after the merger only, the pensions of those retiring in the first few years were so small as to cause ridicule and resentment against the company. Further, employees having long prior service in Company Y found themselves working alongside those previously with Company X, and the differences in prior pension arrangements caused friction, bitterness, and unrest.

In establishing its new plan on a "future service only" basis, without any minimum benefit arrangements or partial, limited, recognition of prior service, the merged company acted against the advice of its consulting actuary. It was later forced, through pressure from its employees and its industrial relations department, to redesign the new plan and incur greater costs, much of which could have been avoided had a sound approach been used at the outset.*

Similar problems exist with respect to profit-sharing plans. If the seller does not have one, but the buyer does, the buyer should factor in the cost of including the seller's employees in the buyer's plan, a probable necessity, in negotiating the acquisition. Conversely, if the buyer does not have a profit-sharing plan it should consider the effect of terminating the seller's plan, if the buyer contemplates such action.

Employee stock options may cause similar problems. The mechanics of converting options held by the seller's employees to options on the buyer's stock are provided for in the Internal Revenue Code of 1954, as amended, and if the requirements of Section 425 of the Code are met (basically that the employee be in no better financial position as a result of the conversion), the conversion may be made without tax consequences to the employee. Where the buyer has no options outstanding, however, it must assess the effect upon its employees of substituting options on its stock for options held by the seller's employees.

Even where the buyer has options outstanding, it must consider the difference of relative prices between the seller's options and those of the buyer's employees. Relative differences between the stock option prices of the seller's and buyer's options may cause discontent in one or the other group of employees. Other fringe benefits such as group life insurance, hospitalization, and major medical plans may, to a lesser degree, cause difficulties.

In view of all of the problems which may arise from employee benefit plans, the directors of personnel, and the actuaries, where necessary, of both the buyer and seller should meet early in the negotiations to seek out possible problems and find solutions.

NONASSIGNABILITY OF CONTRACTS

If an investigation of the seller's contracts reveals that an important contract such as, perhaps, an exclusive license under a valuable patent or a contract to participate in a world's fair is nonassignable, an acquisition of the stock of the seller rather than assets would be indicated; unless, of course, the other party to the contract consents to its assignment.

BANK LOAN AGREEMENTS

If the seller has outstanding bank loan agreements containing restrictions which the buyer is unwilling to assume, the buyer may be required to make some provision to refinance outstanding loans. Conversely, the buyer's bank loan agreements may not permit the seller's loans to remain outstanding, and thus cause refinancing.

---

* Geoffrey N. Calvert, Alexander & Alexander, Inc.: "Pension Pitfalls in Company Mergers."

BULK SALES LAWS

Many states have so-called "bulk sales" laws on their books, intended to protect creditors against a seller selling his business and absconding with the proceeds. In general, these laws provide that a sale of assets of a business to a buyer is void or voidable insofar as the creditors of the seller are concerned, unless the requirements of the law have been met in connection with the sale. Bulk sales laws generally require proper notice to be given to creditors for compliance, which may often be done without too much difficulty. Where notice to creditors is not feasible, the buyer may protect itself by requiring an escrow from the seller in the acquisition contract. Where a buyer is buying assets and agrees to assume all liabilities of the seller, contingent or otherwise, the buyer may ignore the bulk sales law, since it must pay the seller's creditors in any event.

INVESTMENT LETTER

Where selling stockholders are expected to give investment letters in connection with an acquisition, they should be aware of the effect of signing such letters. The investment letter usually states that the stock is being taken for investment purposes only and that the stock-holders are not taking the stock with a view to distribution. A stockholder signing such a letter should be aware that there is no definite or fixed holding period after which he will be permitted to sell the stock without registering the shares with the Securities and Exchange Commission. Sometimes, it is stated that holding stock one or two years should conclusively indicate an investment intent. However, no such rule exists. Basically, the Securities and Exchange Commission takes the position that securities taken under an investment letter can only be sold where there is a "change of circumstances" on the part of the recipient. Such a change of circumstances does not mean a rise or fall in the market price of the stock. On the other hand, however, a drastic financial reversal incurred by the shareholders themselves, requiring the sale of the stock to obtain cash, would probably qualify as a change in circumstances.

In the Crowell-Collier Publishing Company case the Securities and Exchange Commission expressly stated the following with regard to the required holding period under an investment letter:

> An exemption under the provisions of Section 4(1) is available only when the transactions do not involve a public offering and is not gained by the formality of obtaining "investment representations." Holding for the six months' capital gains period of the tax statutes, holding in an "investment account" rather than a "trading account," holding for a deferred sale, holding for a market rise, holding for sale if the market does not rise, or holding for a year, does not afford a statutory basis for an exemption and therefore does not provide an adequate basis on which counsel may give opinions or businessmen rely in selling securities without registration.
>
> Purchasing for the purpose of future sale is nonetheless purchasing for sale and, if the transactions involve any public offering even at some future date, the registration provisions apply unless at the time of the public offering an exemption is available.

If a selling stockholder does not wish to hold a buyer's stock for investment purposes, he should not sign an investment letter. The parties should attempt to so cast the transaction that the signing of an investment letter is not required, and the selling stockholder is not subjected to the restrictions such a signing will impose.

SALES AND USE TAXES

In some jurisdictions sales and use taxes apply to the sale of tangible assets in connection with an acquisition of a business. In such jurisdictions, the tax may not be avoided by closing the transaction outside of the particular state or jurisdiction, since, at least in theory, the tangible assets transferred will be subject to the use tax since they are physically located in the taxing jurisdiction. In some instances where such a sales or use tax would be sizable in amount, the buyer and seller may consider an acquisition of stock rather than assets to avoid the imposition of the tax.

To summarize, whether an acquisition may be treated as a "pooling of interests" from an accounting point of view, may have a major effect on whether a buyer will be willing to make the acquisition. If the acquisition may not be treated as a "pooling of interests," the amount of goodwill which may result and which should be written off against after-tax earnings of the seller's business, may deter the buyer from making the acquisition. State corporation laws may make a statutory merger illegal while permitting an acquisition of assets, and a favorable or unfavorable corporate charter may dictate whether the buyer or seller should be the surviving corporation in a statutory merger. Where there are a large number of shareholders of the seller, and the buyer wishes to obtain 100 per cent control of the seller, the buyer may be forced to acquire assets rather than stock in order to be certain of obtaining such control. Pension, profit-sharing, and stock option plans may deter an acquisition where unfunded past service credits are sizable in amount, or where respective option prices for the stock of the buyer and seller subject to option are substantially different. In addition, nonassignability of contracts, bank loan agreements, bulk sales laws, requirements for investment letters, and sales and use taxes may have an effect on the form which an acquisition should take.

CHAPTER 8

Securities and Exchange Commission Problems—Acquisitions

THE LAW AND SEC RULES

Securities law problems in acquisitions may involve many areas of the law. For example, if a seller requires the approval of its stockholders to sell its business, the seller may be required to prepare and file with the Securities and Exchange Commission proxy material to hold its stockholders' meeting. The problems involved in the preparation of the proxy material for approval of the sale may be more involved than preparing such material for a regular annual meeting. Moreover, as a further example, some of the stockholders of a seller, because of their relationship to the seller, may become involved in problems of short-swing profits under Section 16(b) of the Securities Exchange Act of 1934. Securities law problems of this nature normally do not threaten the successful consummation of an acquisition.

On the other hand, where a buyer intends to buy a seller for stock or securities, a basic problem may arise under the Securities Act of 1933 which may cause collapse of negotiations and failure of the proposed acquisition, unless the buyer and seller find a solution satisfactory to each. This basic problem involves the registration requirements under the Securities Act of 1933, which, in turn, may involve the fundamental aims of the Act. These aims, as stated in the Act, are:

> to provide full and fair disclosure of the character of securities sold in interstate and foreign commerce and through the mails, and to prevent frauds in the sale thereof. . . .

Pursuant to these objectives, rules promulgated by the Securities and Exchange Commission under the Act seek (1) to inhibit the creation of public markets in securities of issuers which have not disclosed material information about themselves in appropriate filings with the SEC, and (2) to permit the sale in ordinary trading transactions of limited quantities of

147

the securities of issuers which are making such filings, where exemptions are not otherwise available.

Registration requirements. As stated, a basic Securities Law problem in the acquisition area involves registration requirements under the Securities Act of 1933 affecting stock or securities paid by a buyer to make an acquisition. Section 5 of the Securities Act of 1933 provides that *"unless a registration statement is in effect as to a security, it shall be unlawful for any person . . . to sell . . . or to offer to sell . . . such security . . . "*

Under the Act, the requirement that a registration statement be in effect to permit a lawful sale of a security, applies only to an *issuer, underwriter* or *dealer.* In this connection, Section 4(1) of the Act provides that Section 5 (the section which makes it unlawful to sell unregistered stock) *"shall not apply to transactions by any person other than an issuer, underwriter or dealer."* In acquisitions, the term "dealer," as used in the Act, does not normally present any special problems, nor is the term of any special significance. However, in acquisitions where a buyer pays its stock or securities for a seller, the acquisition involves an *"issuer"* and also will often involve an *"underwriter."*

The buyer—issuer. A buyer which utilizes its stock or securities to acquire either the assets or stock of a seller is an "issuer" within the meaning of the Act. The buyer is an issuer whether it transfers its treasury stock or transfers its authorized and newly issued stock to the seller or its stockholders. In addition, in a statutory merger where stock or securities of the continuing corporation are transferred to the stockholders of the disappearing corporation, the continuing corporation (the buyer) is also an "issuer" within the meaning of the Act. Since the buyer or the continuing corporation, as the case may be, is an "issuer" within the meaning of the Act, a transfer of its stock to the seller or the stockholders of the seller will be lawful only if a registration statement is in effect, or if an exemption to the registration requirements is available in the particular acquisition.

The seller's stockholders—underwriters. Under certain circumstances, a stockholder of a seller may be an "underwriter" and, therefore, may not lawfully sell securities of the buyer unless a registration statement is in effect with regard to the sales transaction. Under Section 2(11) of the Securities Act of 1933, "The term 'underwriter' means any person who has *purchased from an issuer with a view to,* or offers *or* sells for an issuer *in connection with, the distribution* of any security, or participates or has a direct or indirect participation in any such undertaking. . . ." Under the foregoing definition of an "underwriter" a seller's stockholders who receive stock of a buyer in connection with an acquisition and sell the stock, may be "underwriters" within the meaning of the Act. The stockholders may be "underwriters" if they are considered as links in a chain of transactions through which the stock moves from the buyer to the public. The sale of the buyer's stock by the seller's stockholder, where the stockholder is an underwriter, would be unlawful, unless a registration statement was in effect at the time of the sale, or if an exemption from registration existed with respect to the transaction.

The practical problem. The practical problem involving registration of securities under the Securities Act of 1933, arises where a buyer is unwilling to register the securities offered to make the acquisition, and the seller or its stockholders are unwilling to accept unregistered securities because such securities may not be saleable.

You may ask, why is the buyer not willing to register its stock? A buyer may be unwilling to register for numerous reasons, among which may be any one or more of the following:

(1) registration is expensive;

(2) registration is time consuming and disruptive of the conduct of the buyer's ordinary business, since the buyer's executives are required to devote substantial portions of their normal working time to the preparation of the registration statement;

(3) registration may impede the conduct of the buyer's business, since the buyer may be hindered from taking important action with regard to its business which could require an amendment to the registration statement and a delay in its effectiveness; and

(4) registration may be inconvenient at the time, because the buyer does not wish to reveal, either to the public or to a competitor, financial or other information which could at that time adversely affect the buyer's business.

Whatever the reason, if the buyer is unwilling to register, and yet wishes to acquire the seller's business for stock or other securities, a form of transaction should be negotiated which permits the buyer to pay with its stock or securities and does not require the filing of a registration statement.

From the seller's point of view, the stockholders of the seller should be willing to accept the buyer's stock or securities only if the stock or securities may be lawfully sold in the open market, or if the stockholders have reasonable assurance that the stock will be lawfully saleable at some definite time in the future. The assurance of saleability may be derived either under the Securities Act of 1933, regulations thereunder, or contractual obligations to register stock or repurchase the same assumed by the buyer. Certainly, any stock or securities of a buyer received by a seller's stockholders which are not saleable in the open market may have a substantially reduced value.

Therefore, in the negotiated stock acquisition, where a buyer is unwilling to register its stock, and where selling stockholders will accept stock in payment for their business only if the stock is saleable, the parties should seek to negotiate a form of acquisition which qualifies for an exemption under the Securities Act of 1933 to permit the transfer by the buyer of unregistered stock and the subsequent sale of such stock, or mutually satisfactory contract provisions respecting registration or sale. Failure to negotiate such terms may cause abandonment of the proposed acquisition.

Non-public offering exemption—the buyer. A buyer is normally an issuer when it pays for an acquisition in stock or securities. Therefore, such a buyer, as the issuer, falls directly within the prohibition contained in Section 5 of the Securities Act of 1933 and must seek an exemption to avoid registration. An exemption which may be available to a buyer where the seller's stockholders are comparatively few in number is the non-public offering exemption. This exemption, contained in Section 4(2) of the Securities Act of 1933, states that the "provisions of Section 5 shall not apply to . . . transactions by an issuer not involving any public offering." Therefore, under this exemption, where the transfer by the buyer of its stock or securities does not involve any public offering, the prohibition contained in Section 5 of the Act does not apply.

Whether a transfer of securities by a buyer qualifies as a transaction not involving any public offering, however, frequently may not be decided with certainty. Shortly after the effective date of the Securities Act of 1933, in Release No. 33–285, January 24, 1935, the General Counsel of the Commission stated:

the determination of what constitutes a public offering is essentially a question of fact, in which all surrounding circumstances are of moment. In no sense is the question to be determined exclusively by the number of prospective offerees.

Since that time, where the exemption is sought, issuers have been faced with the problem of determining whether, under the circumstances of each distribution of stock or securities, the particular distribution qualifies as a transaction not involving any public offering. Due to its factual nature, the question may often not be resolved with the degree of certainty desirable. Each transaction depends upon factors such as (1) the number of offerees, and their relationship to each other and to the issuer; (2) the number of units offered; (3) the size of the offering; and (4) the method or manner of making the offer.

Because of the doubt involved in determining what constitutes a public offering, attempts have been made by the Securities and Exchange Commission to promulgate rules which would add certainty to this area of the law. Some of such attempts are mentioned below, but the basic problem of what constitutes a transaction by an issuer "not involving any public offering" still remains a question of fact for determination under the differing facts and circumstances of each transaction, often leaving the answer doubtful.

Rule 133 exemption—the buyer and the seller's stockholders. Although the non-public offering exemption may protect a particular buyer in a qualifying acquisition, the exemption does not solve the problem of the seller's stockholders desiring to sell the stock received from the buyer. The Rules and Regulations under the 1933 Act contain an additional exemption from the requirements of registration available to both the buyer and the seller's stockholders to avoid the need for registration. The rule which provides this exemption is Rule 133, which is sometimes referred to as the "no sale" rule.

Applicability of Rule 133. Rule 133 only applies where the acquisition takes the form of a statutory merger or consolidation or where the buyer acquires the assets of the seller. In such situations the rule will come into play, provided the statutory provisions of the state of incorporation of the seller or the seller's certificate of incorporation requires a vote of a required favorable majority of the seller's outstanding shares of stock which will (1) authorize a proposed transaction and (2) bind all stockholders, except dissenters. Rule 133 states that under the circumstances indicated above there will be no "sale," "offer," "offer to sell," or "offer for sale" within the meaning of Section 5 of the Securities Act of 1933. Section 5 of the Securities Act, as mentioned above, makes a sale of securities unlawful under the Securities Act of 1933 unless a registration is in effect. The section applies only if a "sale" or "offer to sell" securities occurs. Since Rule 133 provides that an acquisition meeting its requirements does not involve a "sale," or "offer to sell," the shares of stock delivered by the buyer in a Rule 133 acquisition are not considered sold or offered for sale, and a registration statement need not be filed by the buyer. In addition, subject to certain exceptions, the seller's stockholders who receive the buyer's stock are free to sell this stock without the need of filing a registration statement.

The required stockholders' vote. State corporation statutes almost universally require a vote of at least a majority of the outstanding shares of stock of a seller to approve either a statutory merger, consolidation, or a sale of all of the assets of the seller. Therefore, in almost all instances where a statutory merger, consolidation, or acquisition of the assets of the seller takes place for the buyer's stock, Rule 133 will become applicable. In addition, corporation charters sometimes provide a specified percentage of favorable votes required to approve a merger, consolidation, or sale of the corporation's assets.

Selling stockholders. Where a transaction meets the requirements of Rule 133 and stock or securities of a buyer are received by a seller in exchange for its assets, the seller normally liquidates, and the stockholders of the seller receive the stock or securities of the buyer in the liquidation. Upon receiving the buyer's stock or securities, the seller's stockholders are free to sell such stock or securities on the open market, subject to the limitations imposed upon a special category of stockholders who are "affiliates," discussed below. In other words, a stockholder who is not an affiliate of the seller at the time of the transaction, is free to sell the stock or securities of the buyer on the open market when received. As a consequence, where the seller is a publicly held company, the great majority of stockholders are normally permitted to sell the stock of the buyer in the open market without a registration statement being in effect if the transaction qualifies under Rule 133.

Restrictions on controlling stockholders. Although the buyer need not register its securities if the provisions of Rule 133 are met, a certain limited category of the seller's stockholders may be limited in the number of shares of the buyer they may sell over specified periods of time. Restrictions on the right of any stockholder of the seller to sell the buyer's stock, generally affect only stockholders who are "affiliates" of the seller. An "affiliate" of a seller is a person who is in "control" of the seller as that term is understood for Securities Act purposes. The definition of control is inexact, as may be observed from the following quotations.

Commenting on the meaning of "control" a House of Representatives Committee report provides as follows:

> The concept of control herein involved is not a narrow one, depending upon a mathematical formula of 51% of voting power but is broadly defined to permit the provisions of the act to become effective wherever the fact of control actually exists.—House Committee Report No. 85—73rd Congress, 1st Session, p. 13.

Rule 405 of the General Rules and Regulations under the Securities Act of 1933 defines "control" in this manner:

> The term "control" (including the terms "controlling," "controlled by" and "under common control with") means the possession, direct or indirect, of the power to direct or cause the direction of the management and policies of a person, whether through the ownership of voting securities, by contract, or otherwise.

Under Rule 133, if the "affiliate" acquires the buyer's stock "with a view to distribution thereof," the sale of the buyer's stock by an affiliate (a controlling stockholder of the seller) at a time when a registration statement with respect to the stock is not effective, could place the controlling stockholder in violation of the Act. But such violation results only if the number of the buyer's shares sold by the controlling stockholder over a six month period exceeds the number of shares permitted to be sold under formulae contained in Rule 133, discussed below. In other words, under Rule 133 even if a selling stockholder is in control of the seller and acquires the stock of the buyer with a view to distribution of the stock, a registration statement need not be filed at the time the selling stockholder sells his stock of the buyer if the total number of shares of stock sold by the selling stockholder does not exceed the limitations established by the Rule, and the sale is made in "brokers' transactions," as mentioned below.

Limitations on shares sold. The limitation on the number of shares which may be sold by a controlling stockholder differs, under the Rule, where the buyer's stock (1) is not listed or (2) is listed on a securities exchange. If the stock is not listed, the selling stockholder may, within any period of six months, sell an aggregate number of shares of the buyer's stock equal to approximately 1 per cent of the number of outstanding shares of the buyer's stock at the time of the receipt by the broker of an order to execute the sale. If the stock of the buyer is listed on a securities exchange, the number of shares which may be sold in any period of six months is the *lesser* of two figures: (1) approximately 1 per cent of the buyer's shares outstanding at the time of receipt by the broker of the order to sell; or (2) the largest aggregate reported volume of trading on securities exchanges in the buyer's stock during any one week within four calendar weeks preceding the receipt by the broker of the order to sell the buyer's stock.

For example, assume that a buyer has 20,000,000 shares outstanding and is listed on the New York, Midwest and Pacific Coast stock exchanges. Assume the buyer acquires the assets of a seller in exchange for the buyer's stock under circumstances fulfilling the requirements of Rule 133, and that a controlling stockholder, upon liquidation of the seller, receives 180,000 shares of the buyer as a result of the acquisition. The first limitation applicable to the seller's controlling stockholder is that he may not dispose of more than 1 per cent of the outstanding shares of the buyer. Under the first limitation, the controlling stockholder may dispose of the total number of shares he received in the acquisition in any six month period. Since he received only 180,000 shares, he is within the limitation provided in the Rule which would permit him to sell 200,000 shares (20,000,000 shares outstanding × 1 per cent). However, the number of shares which may be sold is the *lesser* of the 200,000 shares and the figure represented by aggregate shares sold on exchanges. Under the Rule, the total number of shares of the buyer traded on securities exchanges during any one week within the four calendar weeks preceding the sale must be taken into account. Therefore, if during the four calendar weeks preceding the sale by the controlling stockholder the greatest aggregate number of shares of the buyer traded during any one week on the New York Stock Exchange, the Midwest Stock Exchange and the Pacific Coast Stock Exchange totalled 150,000 shares, the controlling stockholder of the seller would be limited to a sale of an aggregate of 150,000 shares of the buyer's stock. In other words, the controlling stockholder at the time of the sale would be limited to a sale of such number of shares which together with all other sales of the buyer's stock by the controlling stockholder within the preceding six months would not exceed 150,000 shares. This figure could increase, depending upon the amount of activity in the buyer's stock on securities exchanges.

Additional restrictions in Rule 133. In addition to the mathematical limitations imposed upon controlling stockholders to determine the number of shares they may sell under Rule 133, the controlling stockholders are also limited in the manner in which the securities may be sold. The securities may only be sold in "brokers' transactions." Under this limitation, the controlling stockholders may not, directly or indirectly, solicit orders to buy the stock and may make no payment in connection with the execution of the sale transaction to any person other than the broker. In addition, the broker is required to perform no more than the usual and customary brokers' functions, receiving no more than the customary commissions, and the broker may not solicit or arrange for the solicitation of orders to buy in connection with the transaction. Finally, the broker must not be aware of any circumstances which would indicate that the stockholder is making sales beyond the mathematical limits of sales permitted under the law.

Uncertainties under Rule 133. Although the language of Rule 133 appears to set forth the provisions of the rule with clarity, administrative interpretations by the Securities and Exchange Commission have led to uncertainties in determining whether the rule applies to specified transactions. Furthermore, even if Rule 133 is applicable, the number of shares which may be sold by a controlling stockholder in compliance with the formulae contained in the rule may be uncertain. In the area of the applicability of the rule, from time to time the Securities and Exchange Commission takes the position that if the number of stockholders of the seller is so limited that the stockholders' meeting held to approve the sale is a mere formality, Rule 133 should not apply. The Securities and Exchange Commission may reason that the transaction is a "negotiated" transaction, and since the stockholders' meeting is a mere formality, Rule 133 is inapplicable. The Securities and Exchange Commission may apply the negotiated transaction theory to a transaction in spite of the fact that either state corporate law or the corporate charter may require the holding of a stockholders' meeting to approve the sale by the seller. Where Rule 133 is applicable, administrative interpretations may require that a controlling stockholder who sells stock may be required to take into account sales of stock made by other controlling stockholders in determining whether the 1 per cent limitations are met. With respect to related stockholders, the Securities and Exchange Commission may take the position that the sales of all of the related stockholders must be totalled in order to determine whether the 1 per cent limitations under the rule have been met. Also, although Rule 133 by its terms permits the sale of the maximum number of shares under the 1 per cent rule to be made in *any* six month period, the Commission questions the number of consecutive six month periods during which such sales may be made. These uncertainties involving the applicability and interpretation of the Rule may make it difficult to determine when stock received by a seller's stockholder may be sold without penalty.

Investment stock restrictions—seller's stockholders. Where a buyer acquires a seller for stock in a transaction exempt from registration as a non-public offering pursuant to Section 4(2) of the Securities Act of 1933, the buyer often requires the seller's stockholders to sign so-called investment letters. In these letters the seller's stockholders agree that they are acquiring the stock of the buyer for investment purposes only without any intention of selling or otherwise disposing of the stock. A form of such letter is printed at page 290. Where the acquisition contract itself does not contain contractual undertakings on the part of the buyer to register its stock for the seller's stockholders, such provisions are sometimes inserted in the investment letter, and the buyer is made a party to the investment letter.

The execution and delivery of an investment letter by a seller's stockholders imposes severe limitations upon the seller's stockholders' right to sell the buyer's stock. Where the seller's stockholders take a buyer's stock under an investment letter, they may only be free to sell the buyer's stock at some indefinite future date—a date when the seller's stockholders have suffered a change in circumstances which would permit the sale. Absent such a change in circumstances, the seller's stockholders may be deemed to be underwriters, prohibited from selling the stock without a registration statement being in effect.

The question of whether a seller's stockholder has suffered a change of circumstances of such a nature as to permit the sale of the buyer's stock, is a question of fact which is difficult of determination. In this regard some pertinent extracts from Release No. 33–4552 of the Securities and Exchange Commission, November 6, 1962, provide the following:

> An important factor to be considered is whether the securities offered have come to rest in the hands of the initial informed group or whether the purchasers are merely conduits for a wider distribution. Persons who act in this capacity, whether or not engaged in the securities business, are deemed to be "underwriters" within the meaning of Section 2(11) of the Act. If the purchasers do in fact acquire the securities with a view to public distribution, the seller assumes the risk of possible violation of the registration requirements of the Act and consequent civil liabilities. This has led to the practice whereby the issuer secures from the initial purchasers representations that they have acquired the securities for investment.

> The view is occasionally expressed that, solely by reason of continued holding of a security for the six-month capital-gain period specified in the income-tax laws, or for a year from the date of purchase, the security may be sold without registration. There is no statutory basis for such assumption. Of course, the longer the period of retention, the more persuasive would be the argument that the resale is not at variance with an original investment intent, but the length of time between acquisition and resale is merely one evidentiary fact to be considered. The weight to be accorded this evidentiary fact must, of necessity, vary with the circumstances of each case.

> An unforeseen change of circumstances since the date of purchase may be a basis for an opinion that the proposed resale is not inconsistent with an investment representation. However, such claim must be considered in the light of all of the relevant facts. Thus, an advance or decline in market price or a change in the issuer's operating results are normal investment risks and do not usually provide an acceptable basis for such claim of changed circumstances. Possible inability of the purchaser to pay off loans incurred in connection with the purchase of the stock would ordinarily not be deemed an unforeseeable change of circumstances. Further, in the case of securities pledged for a loan, the pledgee should not assume that he is free to distribute without registration. The Congressional mandate of disclosure to investors is not to be avoided to permit a public distribution of unregistered securities because the pledgee took the securities from a purchaser, subsequently delinquent.

The foregoing excerpts indicate, among other matters, that the mere passage of time or advances or declines in market price of a buyer's stock do not constitute a change in circumstances within the meaning of the laws and the regulations.

Execution and delivery of an investment letter or a similar agreement by the seller's stockholders should be acceptable to the seller's stockholders only after careful consideration by their counsel and a clear understanding on their part of the obligations incurred.

PROPOSED SEC RULE CHANGES

Because of the uncertainties in determining whether an acquisition may involve other than a public offering, whether Rule 133 applies to a particular transaction, the number of shares a selling stockholder may sell in a Rule 133 transaction, and when stockholders who take stock for investment purposes only may lawfully sell such stock, the Securities and Exchange Commission has from time to time proposed rules to provide more definite solutions to these problems.

To highlight some of the difficulties in this area, in Release No. 4997 dated September 15, 1969, the Securities and Exchange Commission stated as follows:

> The absence of satisfactory objective tests for determining who is an underwriter under Section 2(11) of the Act both affects the ability of persons who acquire securities to realize on legitimate investments and burdens the staff of the Commission with a large number of requests for interpretations of the law and "no-action" letters. Moreover, the present rule permits sale of large quantities of securities without any of the disclosures provided by the Act or the Securities Exchange Act of 1934.

Some past proposals for making the rules more definite which have not been adopted by the Securities and Exchange Commission are discussed below.

Proposed Rule 181—non-public offering. Rule 181 of the General Rules and Regulations under the 1933 Act, proposed in Release No. 5012, October 9, 1969, would have defined the term "transaction not involving any public offering," as used in Section 4(2) of the Securities Act of 1933, in connection with the acquisition of a business by an issuer. This proposed rule would have provided that a transaction by an issuer would be deemed as "not involving any public offering" if it consisted of an offer and sale of securities:

(1) made solely in connection with the acquisition of a business by the issuer;

(2) to not more than 25 offerees who are holders of interests in such business.

A transaction meeting the above requirements would have been deemed to be one "not involving any public offering" whether it took the form of (1) a voluntary exchange of securities, i.e., a stock-for-stock transaction; (2) a statutory merger or consolidation; or (3) a purchase of the assets of the business.

Proposed "160 Series" rules—underwriter. Release No. 4997, September 15, 1969, included a series of proposed rules, Rules 160, 161, 162 and 163, which were intended to set forth objective tests for determining persons who should be considered "underwriters" within the meaning of Section 2(11) of the 1933 Act. Under this proposed series of rules, a seller's stockholder would have been deemed to be an underwriter with respect to the sale of stock of a buyer, only if the stockholder sold "restricted securities" in a "distribution" as those terms were defined in the proposed rules. Under Rule 161, a restricted security would have been any security acquired from a buyer (the issuer) in a transaction which was not a public offering. If the seller's stockholder received such a restricted security as a result of an acquisition by a buyer exempted from registration under the non-public offering exemption, the restricted security would have ceased to be a restricted security five years after it was acquired, provided, the buyer (the issuer) had at least $250,000 in gross revenues from operations in each of the five years in question.

A "distribution" was defined, under proposed Rule 162, as any public offering of a security, except certain limited sales in brokers' transactions of securities of a buyer (an issuer) which filed appropriate reports with the Securities and Exchange Commission under the Securities Exchange Act of 1934. The number of shares which could be sold in limited brokerage transactions under the proposed rule were essentially the same as the number of shares which could be sold by a controlling stockholder pursuant to the mathematical formulae contained in Rule 133 set forth at page 152, above. Proposed Rule 163 defined the "qualified issuers" with respect to whom the sale of shares in limited brokerage transactions would not amount to a distribution, generally, as issuers listed on a securities exchange or otherwise required to register under Section 12 of the Securities Exchange Act.

The release illustrated the operation of the proposed 160 series of rules as follows:

> To illustrate generally the operation of the proposed rules, assume that a person acquires securities in a private transaction from an issuer which is in active business but not required to file reports with the Commission under the Exchange Act. The purchaser of the securities would be required to hold those securities for five years before he could sell them without registration under the Act, unless in the interim the issuer became subject to the reporting requirements. On the other hand, assume a person acquires securities in a private transaction from an issuer required to file the appropriate reports with the Commission under the Exchange Act. The purchaser would, generally speaking, be able to sell specifically limited quantities of those securities in ordinary brokerage transactions after one year.

Proposed Rule 144—underwriter. In Release No. 5087, September 22, 1970, the Securities and Exchange Commission gave notice of a proposed Rule 144 to refine and make more definite the definition of persons presumed not to be underwriters. Proposed Rule 144 was intended to be adopted in lieu of the "160 series" of rules quoted above. In this connection the Securities and Exchange Commission release stated as follows:

> Proposed Rule 144 is being considered in lieu of a series of proposed rules (the "160 series") relating to underwriters, non-public offerings and brokers' transactions published for comment by the Commission on September 15, 1969 in Securities Act Release No. 4997. The Commission has carefully reviewed the many helpful comments received from interested persons in regard to those rules, has considered the proposed rules in the light of those comments and the staff's recommendation in regard thereto, and has determined, for the reasons set forth below, not to adopt those rules at this time.

Rule 144—As Adopted. On January 11, 1972, in Release No. 5223, the Securities and Exchange Commission announced the adoption of Rule 144 under the Securities Act of 1933. The new rule relates to the application of the registration provisions of the Act to the resale of securities acquired directly from an issuer in transactions not involving any public offering. The rule became effective on April 15, 1972.

Under Rule 144 a "restricted security" is a security acquired directly or indirectly from an issuer or from a person in a control relationship with the issuer in a transaction, or a chain of transactions, not involving any public offering.

A person may sell "restricted securities" in reliance upon Rule 144 and without a registration statement being in effect only if the person has held such securities for a period of at least two years prior to the sale. The aggregate amount of "restricted securities" which may be sold by a person is limited by a formula based upon the amounts of such securities sold during the preceding six month period. If the security is traded on a registered national securities exchange, the amount of such security which may be sold in any six month period may not exceed the lesser of (1) 1% of the amount of the class outstanding as shown in the most recent report or statement published by the issuer, or (2) the average weekly reported volume of trading on all such exchanges over the four week period prior to the date of a notice to sell which must be given to comply with the requirements of the rule. If the securities are not traded on an exchange, the amount which may be sold in any six month period may not exceed 1% of the amount of the class outstanding as shown in the most recent report or statement as published by the issuer.

A sale may be made under the rule only if there is available adequate current public information with respect to the issuer of the securities. This requirement is deemed to be satisfied if an issuer has been subject to the reporting requirements of Section 13 or 15(d) of the Securities and Exchange Act of 1934 for period of at least 90 days immediately preceding the sale of the securities, the issuer has filed all reports required by that Act and the rules and regulations thereunder, and in addition, has filed the most recent annual report required to be filed thereunder.

The manner of sale of the restricted security is limited under the rule to sales in "brokers' transactions" within the meaning of Section 4(4) of the Act. The person selling the securities may not solicit or arrange for the solicitation of buy orders or make any payment in connection with the sale other than to the broker who executes the order.

Finally, the rule requires that a person desiring to sell securities in reliance upon the rule must file with the Securities and Exchange Commission a notice to that effect. The notice must be sent to the Commission concurrently with the placing with a broker an order for the sale of the securities. If all of the securities mentioned in the notice are not sold within 90 days after the filing of the notice, an amended notice must be transmitted to the Commission concurrently with the commencement of any further sales of the securities. Transactions during any period of six months which do not involve more than 500 shares or $10,000, whichever is less, are exempted from the notice requirements.

CONCLUSION

The above rule changes proposed by the Securities and Exchange Commission indicate areas in which both the Commission and securities law practitioners believe objective standards are necessary. After extended consideration and comment by securities law practitioners upon the above proposals, Rule 144 was adopted. This rule establishes some objective standards to determine whether a particular transfer of stock or securities in an acquisition is an offering which does not constitute a public offering, or whether sales of stock or securities by seller's stockholders are sales by "underwriters" requiring registration of the shares sold. However, problems in these areas of the law still exist.

Whether an acquisition for stock or securities requires the filing of a registration statement may involve a fundamental question in a particular acquisition, the answer to which is subject to Commission rules, and the continued review and changing attitudes of the Commission. Because of the uncertainties involved in this area of the law, in an acquisition involving the use of stock or securities, where the question of registration is involved, both the buyer, as the issuer, and the stockholders of the seller, as possible underwriters, should obtain advice from a qualified source before attempting to negotiate the mechanics of the acquisition.

CHAPTER 9

Securities and Exchange Commission Problems—Takeover Bids

A takeover bid is an offer to buy securities of a corporation made directly to the shareholders of the corporation for the purpose of gaining control of the corporation. The offer may be for either cash or securities of the offeror, and it may be made with or without the approval of the management of the target company. Normally the target company is a publicly held company, since if the target company had absolute voting control concentrated in a few shareholders, the negotiations to acquire control would take place directly between the acquiring corporation and the controlling shareholders personally.

The takeover bid includes two fundamentally different types of offer.

If the offer to buy the stock is made for cash, the takeover bid is called a tender offer. If the offer to buy the stock is made for securities, the takeover bid is called a registered exchange offer. A tender offer is made for cash; a registered exchange offer is made for securities.

THE TENDER OFFER

The tender offer has long been available as a means of acquiring stock, or control, of a corporation in which the acquirer is interested. Since the enactment of the Williams Bill on July 29, 1968, the tender offer has been subject to regulation by the Securities and Exchange Commission, although it was free from such regulation prior to that time. The Securities Act of 1933 requires the registration of securities offered to the public; however, since the tender offer is an offer to buy for cash, it is not subject to the registration requirements of the Securities Act of 1933.

Pre-Williams Bill Tender. Prior to the enactment of the Williams Bill, the tender offer was often made in the following manner:

(1) The offeror made an offer to buy stock for cash to the shareholders of the target company either by newspaper advertisement, or, if the offeror had a stock list of the target company, by letter addressed to the individual shareholders of the target company.

(2) The offer was limited to a fixed period of time, perhaps thirty days, although the offeror often retained the right to extend the fixed period.

(3) The offer was for a fixed amount of cash, and generally included an agreement on the part of the offeror to pay all brokerage commissions.

(4) If the offer was not to acquire all the stock of the target company, the offeror often reserved the right not to buy shares tendered after the full number of shares offered to be purchased had been tendered.

(5) The offeror often reserved the right to withdraw the offer if any materially adverse change took place in the financial position of the target company, and the newspaper advertisement or letter to shareholders contained with it a letter of transmittal with additional terms of the agreement to be signed by the shareholder of the target company.

The Williams Bill. The Williams Bill codified the procedure to be followed in making a tender offer by requiring filing of certain information with the Securities and Exchange Commission prior to the time of making a tender offer. Under Section 14(d)(1) of the Securities Exchange Act of 1934, added to the Act by the Williams Bill, it is unlawful for a corporation to make a tender offer for any class of equity security which after consummation would make the corporation an owner of more than 5% of such class of security unless it has filed with the Securities and Exchange Commission in Washington a statement containing information specified in Section 13(d) of the Act.

Pursuant to Section 14(d)(1) and Regulation 240.14d–1 thereunder, the offeror is required to file with the Commission the information which is detailed in Schedule 13D printed below:

SCHEDULE 13D

Information to Be Included in Statements
Filed Pursuant to Rule 13d-1 or 14d-1

Notes. A. The item numbers and captions of the items shall be included but the text of the items are to be omitted. The answers to the items shall be so prepared as to indicate clearly the coverage of the items without referring to the text of the items. Answer every item. If an item is inapplicable or the answer is in the negative, so state.

B. If the statement is filed by a partnership, limited partnership, syndicate, or other group, the information called for by Items 2 to 6, inclusive, shall be given with respect to (1) each partner or any partnership or limited partnership, (2) each member of such syndicate or group, and (3) each person controlling such partner or member. If a person referred to in (1), (2), or (3) is a corporation or the statement is filed by a corporation, the information called for by the above-mentioned items shall be given with respect to each officer and director of such corporation and each person controlling such corporation.

Item 1. Security and Issuer.

State the title of the class of equity securities to which this statement relates and the name and address of the issuer of such securities.

Item 2. Identity and Background.

State the following with respect to the person filing this statement:

(a) Name and business address;

(b) Residence address;

(c) Present principal occupation or employment and the name, principal business and address of any corporation or other organization in which such employment is carried on;

(d) Material occupations, positions, officers, or employments during the last 10 years, giving the starting and ending dates of each and the name, principal business and address of any business corporation or other organization in which each such occupation, position, office or employment was carried on; and

(e) Whether or not, during the last 10 years, such person has been convicted in a criminal proceeding (excluding traffic violations or similar misdemeanors) and, if so, give the dates, nature of conviction, name and location of court, and penalty imposed, or other disposition of the case. A negative answer to this sub-item need not be furnished to security holders.

Item 3. Source and Amount of Funds or Other Consideration.

State the source and amount of funds or other consideration used or to be used in making the purchases, and if any part of the purchase price or proposed purchase price is represented or is to be represented by funds or other consideration borrowed or otherwise obtained for the purpose of acquiring, holding, or trading the securities, a description of the transaction and the names of the parties thereto.

Item 4. Purpose of Transaction.

State the purpose or purposes of the purchase or proposed purchase of securities of the issuer. If the purpose or one of the purposes of the purchase or proposed purchases is to acquire control of the business of the issuer, describe any plans or proposals which the purchasers may have to liquidate the issuer, to sell its assets or to merge it with any other persons, or to make any other major change in its business or corporate structure, including, if the issuer is a registered closed-end investment company, any plans or proposals to make any changes in its investment policy for which a vote would be required by Section 13 of the Investment Company Act of 1940 (15 U.S.C. 80a-13).

Item 5. Interest in Securities of the Issuer.

State the number of shares of the security which are beneficially owned, and the number of shares concerning which there is a right to acquire, directly or indirectly, by (i) such persons, and (ii) each associate of such person, giving the name and address of each such associate. Furnish information as to all transactions in the class of securities to which this statement relates which were effected during the past 60 days by the person filing this statement and by its subsidiaries and their officers, directors and affiliated persons.

Item 6. Contracts, Arrangements, or Understandings
With Respect to Securities of the Issuer.

Furnish information as to any contracts, arrangements, or understandings with any person with respect to any securities of the issuer, including but not limited to transfer of any of the securities, joint ventures, loan or option arrangements, puts or calls, guaranties of loans, guaranties against loss or guaranties of profits, division of losses or profits, or the giving or withholding of proxies, naming the persons with whom such contracts, arrangements, or understandings have been entered into, and giving the details thereof.

Item 7. Persons Retained, Employed or to be Compensated.

Where the Schedule 13D relates to a tender offer, or request or invitation for tenders, identify all persons and classes of persons employed, retained or to be compensated by the person filing this Schedule 13D, or by any person on his behalf, to make solicitations or recommendations to security holders and describe briefly the terms of such employment, retainer or arrangement for compensation.

Item 8. Material to be Filed as Exhibits.

Copies of all requests or invitations for tenders or advertisements making a tender offer or requesting or inviting tenders, additional material soliciting or requesting such tender offers, solicitations or recommendations to the holders of the security to accept or reject a tender offer or request or invitation for tenders shall be filed as an exhibit.

Signature

I certify that to the best of my knowledge and belief the information set forth in this statement is true, complete and correct.

_____   _____
            (Date)   (Signature)

If the statement is signed on behalf of a person by an authorized representative, evidence of the representative's authority to sign on behalf of such person shall be filed with the statement.

Form of Tender. In addition to filing Schedule 13D with the Securities and Exchange Commission, the corporation making the tender offer must also file the actual form of offer as well as all subsequent material by means of which it seeks to solicit the shares of the shareholders of the target company. Under the Regulations the tender offer must include the name of the person making the tender offer and the exact dates prior to which, and after which, security holders who deposit their securities will have a right to withdraw their securities as required by the Williams Bill. In addition, Regulations also require that the tender offer must contain the information required by Items 2(a), 2(c), 2(e), and 3, 4, 5, and 6 of Schedule 13D, quoted above, or a fair and adequate summary of these items.

Substantive Safeguards—Withdrawal of Tendered Shares. In addition to the mechanical requirements of filing the information required by Schedule 13D and the form which the tender offer must take, the Williams Bill provides certain substantive safeguards for the security holders of the target company. Section 14(d)(5) of the 1934 Act, added by the Williams Bill, provides that any security holder who tenders shares shall have the right to withdraw the shares at any time until the expiration of seven days from the date the tender offer is first published or given to security holders, and also after sixty days from the date of the original tender offer.

Substantive Safeguards—Pro Rata Acceptance. Section 14(d)(6) of the 1934 Act provides that if the person making the tender offer seeks less than all of the outstanding equity securities of a class, and if a greater number of shares than those sought or acceptable to the offeror are deposited within the first ten days after the offer has first been published, then the offeror must take the shares offered on a pro rata basis.

Substantive Safeguards—Price Increase. Finally, Section 14(d)(7) of the 1934 Act provides that any increase in the offering price prior to the expiration of the tender offer must also be paid to those security holders of the target company who have already tendered their securities. Any increase in price reinstates the ten day period during which the offeror must acquire excess shares tendered on a pro rata basis as mentioned in the preceding paragraph.

Tender Offer—Open Period. Although the law contains no requirement as to the length of time during which a tender offer must remain open, it would appear that the provisions of Section 14(d)(6) would require that the offer remain effective for at least ten days to give substance to the requirement that the offerer acquire shares on a pro rata basis where an excess of the number of shares sought to be purchased are tendered in the first ten days after the tender offer is first published or sent, or notice of an increase is given. In addition to the requirements of the Securities and Exchange Commission, the New York Stock Exchange has established a policy that all shareholders of a company be given an opportunity to participate on equal terms in any tender offer. Pursuant to Section A 10 of the New York Stock Exchange Company Manual, a tender offer should remain open for a minimum of ten days, but a longer period of thirty days is recommended. In addition, if a specified number of shares are to be purchased, the offer should be pro rata if more shares are tendered than purchased for the first ten days, after which it may be on a first come, first serve basis.

Tender Offer—Tax Consequences. A cash tender offer may effect adversely the possibilities of obtaining "tax-free" treatment for a subsequent reorganization involving the offeror and the target corporation. If the purchase of the securities of the target company for cash and the subsequent attempt to combine the offeror and the target company are treated as parts of an integrated plan, the tax-free nature of the subsequent reorganization may be destroyed because of the prior cash payment to the shareholders of the target company. In a subsequent statutory merger the requisite continuity of interest may not be present because of previous buy-out of certain of the target company's shareholders. A subsequent attempt to acquire the remaining outstanding stock of the target company in exchange for the offeror's stock, a "stock-for-stock" tax-free reorganization, or an attempt to acquire substantially all of the assets of the target company in exchange for the stock of the offerer, an "assets-for-stock" tax-free reorganization, may be taxable as not meeting the statutory requirement that the stock of the target company or the assets of the target company be acquired for "solely voting stock."

Under many circumstances, it should be noted, that the offeror may not be deterred from making the cash tender offer merely because a subsequent reorganization would not qualify as tax-free. When the offeror pays more for the stock which is tendered than the tax basis of the assets of the target company, as is often the case, a subsequent taxable rather than "tax-free" reorganization may be to the offeror's advantage. Upon the consummation of the taxable reorganization, the offeror may be in a position to write up the underlying assets for tax purposes and obtain substantial tax benefits in the form of increased depreciation or amortization deductions from such a write-up. These matters are dealt with in greater detail in Chapter 10 which deals with the "tax-free" aspects of acquisitions and mergers.

State Statutory Law. State corporation laws generally do not contain provisions regulating tender offers as was the situation with federal law prior to the enactment of the Williams Bill. After enactment of the Williams Bill some states took steps to enact similar legislation to protect local industry from the threat of tender offers. For example, Virginia enacted a statute which requires the filing of a Williams Bill type of statement as a part of its corporation law, and requires that the statement be delivered to a registered agent of the issuer twenty days prior to the making of the offer.

State Common Law—The Offeror. Common law rules as to the responsibilities of the directors of an aggressor and of a target company may pose problems. A board of directors of an offeror owes its shareholders the responsibility of taking due care in making an offer. Presumably, an exorbitant tender offer made without consideration of the value of the business of the target company could subject the directors of the offeror to liability. However, it is difficult to imagine circumstances under which the board of directors of an offeror would act so rashly as to lay a foundation for a shareholders' suit against them.

State Common Law—The Target Company. The directors of the target company are in a somewhat more difficult situation. Under common law, the directors of the target company have the right to remain silent and not recommend either acceptance or rejection of the offeror's offer. Such neutrality could be the safest course. However, if the directors have knowledge of non-public material information which could effect a shareholders decision concerning the offer, it is possible that such information would be required to be disclosed.

On the other hand, if the directors of the target company recommend acceptance of the offer, they must at the same time reveal any arrangements they may have with the offeror for continued employment or other rewards such as stock options. If management recommends rejection of the offer, it may find itself accused of attempting to perpetuate itself in office.

The Williams Bill—The Target Company. The Securities and Exchange Commission has adopted certain rules under the authority granted under the Williams Bill relating to the position of the management of the target company. Under Regulation §240.14d–4, management is prohibited from making any recommendation to its security holders either to accept or reject a tender offer unless, at the time the recommendation is made, management has filed with the Securities and Exchange Commission a statement containing the information specified by Schedule 14D. Schedule 14D is essentially a short form of Schedule 13D, in which the management must set forth its reasons for the recommendation to security holders to accept or reject the tender offer. Schedule 14D provides as follows:

SCHEDULE 14D

Item 1. Security and Issuer.

(a) State the title of the class of equity securities to which this statement relates and the name and address of the issuer of such securities.

(b) Identify the tender offer or request or invitation for tenders to which this statement relates and state the reasons for the solicitation or recommendation to security holders to accept or reject such tender offer, request, or invitation for tenders.

Item 2. Identity and Background.

(a) State the name and business address of the person filing this statement.

(b) Describe any arrangement or understanding in regard to the solicitation with (i) the issuer or the management of the issuer or (ii) the maker of the tender offer or request or invitation for tender of securities of the class to which this statement relates.

Item 3. Persons Retained, Employed or to be Compensated.

Identify any person or class of persons employed, retained or to be compensated, by the person filing this Schedule 14D, or by any person on his behalf, to make solicitations or recommendations to security holders and describe briefly the terms of such employment, retainer, or arrangement for compensation.

Item 4. Material to be filed as Exhibits.

Copies of all solicitations or recommendations to accept or to reject a tender offer or request or invitation for tenders of the securities specified in Item 1 shall be filed as an exhibit.

Signature

I certify that to the best of my knowledge and belief the information set forth in this statement is true, complete and correct.

_____   _____
            (Date)   (Signature)

If the statement is signed on behalf of a person by an authorized representative, evidence of the representative's authority to sign on behalf of such person shall be filed with the statement.

Under Regulation §240.14d–2(f) before filing Schedule 14D, a target company may send to its security holders a letter, which does no more than (1) identify the tender offer, (2) state that the management is studying the matter and will, on or before a specified date (not later than 10 days before the stated expiration of the tender date or such shorter period as the Commission authorizes) advise its security holders as to management's recommendation to accept or reject the offer, and (3) request the security holders to defer making a determination until they have received the management's recommendation. If such a letter is sent to security holders, management may not remain neutral, and must make a recommendation to the security holders.

Stockholder Lists. Under state law a stockholder of a corporation may generally examine a list of stockholders for any proper purpose. Whether the desire to make a cash tender offer is a proper purpose is open to question. In New York State it has been held that if the sole reason for requiring a stockholders list is the making of a tender offer, then the stockholder's purpose in requesting the stock list is not a proper purpose. Under the authority granted by the William Bill, the Securities and Exchange Commission is considering adopting a rule which would require the target company to provide a list of security holders or mail material directly to its security holders pursuant to a rule similar to rule 14a–7 of the proxy rules.

Rule 10b-5. Prior to the enactment of the Williams Bill, attacks upon cash tender offers under Rule 10b–5 (described in Chapter 6) of the General Rules and Regulations under the Securities Exchange Act of 1934, were generally unsuccessful. To cause the offeror's conduct to be unlawful, the rule required that the conduct "would operate as a fraud or deceit upon any person, in connection with the *purchase or sale* of any security." Since the plaintiff, who was attacking the tender offer would not make a purchase or sale of a security, the plaintiff normally had no standing under Rule 10b–5. Section 14(e) of the Securities Exchange Act of 1934, added by the Williams Bill, has eliminated this impediment to a non-tendering shareholder invoking his rights under Rule 10b–5. Under Section 14(e), the prohibited conduct is made unlawful if engaged in by any person making a tender offer, regardless of whether a purchase or sale of a security takes place.

In addition, prior to the Williams Bill the acquiring company was not an insider, and therefore was under no obligation to make disclosure of any pertinent facts in connection with the tender offer. Since the Williams Bill, of course, the acquiring corporation must file Schedule 13D, and has the obligation to make fair and truthful disclosures of the information required in the schedule. The requirement that the acquiring company make known its plans for future major changes in the business where control is being acquired, may present nontendering shareholders with opportunities to bring successful lawsuits, if the plans are not carried out in the future as set forth in Schedule 13D.

Open Market Purchases. If an offeror decides to make purchases of securities of the target company in the open market during the period that the tender offer remains effective, the offeror may be jeopardizing its legal position. If such open market purchases are not disclosed to the stockholders of the target company, such purchases could result in a breach of the contract made by the offeror with tendering shareholders, or could constitute a failure to reveal material information in connection with the tender offer in violation of Rule 10b–5. In this connection in Release No. 34–8712, Oct. 8, 1969, the Securities and Exchange Commission effected the adoption of Rule 10b–13 which prohibits any person who makes a tender offer from purchasing the same securities in the open market during the period that tendered securities may be accepted or rejected under the offer.

Section 16(b). Often it has appeared that the initial offeror making a cash tender offer could not lose. If after having acquired some of the stock of the target company as a result of the tender offer, the offeror is outbid by a third party's tender offer, the initial offeror will have a built-in profit in the stock of the target company, acquired prior to the defeat of its tender offer. Should the initial offeror be in a position to sell securities obtained in a tender offer, at a profit, the offeror should consider the effect of Section 16(b) of the Securities Exchange Act of 1934 before realizing the profit. This Section provides that the profits "from any purchase and sale, or any sale and purchase, of any equity security . . . within any period of less than six months," by a 10% shareholder inure to and are recoverable by the issuer. Therefore, if an offeror acquires more than 10% of the stock of a target company but is outbid by a second offeror, any profit realized by the first offeror from a sale within 6 months of the equity securities obtained in the tender offer, would be recoverable by the issuer. The first offeror should, therefore, avoid such a resale within the 6 month period. However, if the successful second offeror brings about a statutory merger between the issuer and the second offeror within the 6 month period, it may be beyond the control of the unsuccessful first offeror to avoid a sale within the 6 month period.

REGISTERED EXCHANGE OFFER

A registered exchange offer differs from a tender offer in that the consideration offered for the stock of the target corporation consists of securities of the offeror rather than cash. The offer to buy for securities is subject to different regulatory provisions than the cash offer, resulting in substantial differences in the time factors involved and in the mechanics for making the offer. Generally speaking, the registered exchange offer is a more cumbersome vehicle than the cash tender offer, and certainly, if the element of surprise or speed is considered important to success, should be employed only where overriding considerations dictate its use. For example, it may not be possible for the offeror to raise sufficient cash to make a cash tender offer, and under such circumstances a registered exchange offer may be required.

Registration Statement. A registered exchange offer, by definition, involves an offering of securities to the public. As such, prior to making the offering, a registration statement must be in effect with regard to the securities under the Securities Act of 1933. The preparation and filing of the registration statement, and the lapse of time until the registration statement is cleared by the Securities and Exchange Commission eliminate the surprise element, which an offeror could have achieved in a tender offer. Nevertheless, prior to the announcement of the registered exchange offer, the offeror's problem generally remains the maintenance of initial secrecy. The offeror will wish to achieve as much surprise as possible, in order to allow management of the target company as little time as possible to take defensive action. The difficulty in maintaining initial secrecy in a registered exchange offer, prior to the actual announcement of the offer, arises from the inescapable circumstance that the offeror must normally deal with many persons outside its own organization. Among such persons are investment bankers, brokers, banks, the SEC staff, lawyers and accountants, and public relations and proxy soliciting firms.

Open Market Stock Purchases. In addition, at the outset, the management of the offeror must determine whether or not it wishes to acquire stock of the target company in the open market, and if so, how many shares. A prior acquisition of stock, of course, gives an offeror a head start, and may provide an ultimate profit in the acquired stock if the offer fails due to a competing bid by a third party or defensive action taken by management. On the other hand, the prior acquisition of securities of the target company may lead to information leaks, may cause an increase in the cost of the offer, and may alert a watchful management of a target company that a takeover bid may be forthcoming.

Rule 135 Statement. Under Rule 135 of the General Rules and Regulations under the

Securities Act of 1933, a statement may be made in the form of a notice of the prospective registered exchange offer to security holders of the target company. The notice may contain only the information outlined in Rule 135. Rule 135 provides in part as follows:

> Reg. §230.135   (a) For the purpose only of Section 5 of the Act, a notice given by an issuer that it proposes to make a public offering of securities to be registered under the Act shall not be deemed to offer any securities for sale if such notice states that the offering will be made only by means of a prospectus and contains no more than the following additional information:

> (1) The name of the issuer;

> (2) The title, amount and basic terms of the securities proposed to be offered, the amount of the offering, if any, to be made by selling security holders, the anticipated time of the offering and a brief statement of the manner and purpose of the offering without naming the underwriters;

> *   *   *

> (4) In the case of an offering of securities in exchange for other securities of the issuer or of another issuer, the name of the issuer and the title of the securities to be surrendered in exchange for the securities to be offered, the basis upon which the exchange may be made, or any of the foregoing;

> *   *   *

> (6) Any statement or legend required by State law or administrative authority.

> (b) Any notice contemplated by this rule may take the form of a news release or a written communication directed to security holders or employees, as the case may be, or other published statement.

If a preliminary announcement is made containing the above information, it should be amended to include any material changes which may occur in the proposed offer during the pre-offering period.

Target Company Information. In addition to the normal problems encountered in preparation of a registration statement, namely the accurate presentation of information concerning the history, business, and finances of the offering company, the offeror is required to include in the registration statement information concerning the history, business, and financial information of the target company. A request for such information from the target company may result in a refusal, or, on the other hand, the submission of so much information to the offeror, that delay could be encountered in preparing the registration statement. One of the defensive measures which may be taken by a target company in connection with a registered exchange offer, is to deluge the offeror with information, making the preparation of the registration statement a difficult and time consuming task. On the other hand, where an offeror is unable to obtain information from the target company, the Securities and Exchange Commission permits the use of such available information as the offeror is able to obtain. Such information may include prior years' annual reports and registration statements of the target company, as well as proxy statement and various periodic forms under the Securities Exchange Act of 1934 such as Forms 10-Q, 8-K, 9-K, and 10-K.

Percentages of Ownership. Practical considerations, such as ownership of shares by unfriendly stockholders, may limit the percentage of the target company securities the offeror may be able to acquire. While on the other hand, corporate law, tax rules, or accounting rules may require acquisition of greater percentages of the stock to attain desired legal, tax, or accounting goals. From the viewpoint of corporate law, in many states to effect a statutory merger of two corporations, the merger agreement must be approved by a vote of at least two-thirds of the stockholders of each of the corporations. Therefore, under certain circumstances where the offeror plans a subsequent merger of the target company, the offeror may determine to seek to obtain at least 66 2/3% of the target company's stock. As discussed in greater detail in Chapter 10, tax rules provide that a stock-for-stock acquisition does not qualify as a "tax-free" reorganization, unless the acquiring company obtains at least 80% of the voting power and 80% of all other classes of stock of the target company. From an accounting point of view, to report the earnings of the two corporations on a consolidated basis, normally one corporation must own a specified percentage of the voting equity of the other. These factors may come into play in determining the number of shares of the target company which the offeror offers to purchase in connection with the registered exchange offer.

Advantage of Registered Exchange Offer. A basic advantage of the registered exchange offer is that an offeror, with limited cash resources may attempt a takeover bid with hope of success, since such exchange offers have been successful where the offeror was many times smaller than the target company and had minimum resources in comparison to the target company.

Disadvantages of Registered Exchange Offers. However, registered exchange offers involve disadvantages not present in cash tender offers. As mentioned above, a registration statement must be filed with the Securities and Exchange Commission with respect to the offeror's securities, since the exchange offer constitutes an "offer to sell" within the meaning of the Securities Act of 1933. The preparation of the registration statement and its clearance through the Securities and Exchange Commission causes delay before an exchange offer becomes effective. This delay, and the intricacy and detail of the information required to be included in a registration statement make the registered exchange offer vulnerable to attack by court action on the part of the target company.

DEFENDING AGAINST TAKEOVER BIDS

Theoretically, every publicly held company may be a prospective target for a takeover bid. If management has any cause to suspect that it may become such a target, it may decide to take defensive steps to make success of a takeover bid less likely. To determine whether a corporation is a likely candidate for a takeover bid, management should review the corporation's financial and business structure to lay bare any of a number of elements repeated with moderate frequency in companies which have become targets to takeover bids.

Operating Performance. Among the elements which may indicate candidacy for a takeover bid is a disappointing operating performance. If the financial records of a company indicate a decline in profits over a continued period of time, such a decline may be indicative to management that the company may become a target for a takeover bid. A continued decline in profits usually couples with it a decline in the price of the corporation's stock. If the market value of the stock has decreased over a period of time, or if the price of the stock has not risen in a period of general market extended buoyancy, a prospective offeror may conclude that stockholder unrest will make it likely that a takeover bid will succeed.

Nature of Assets. If the assets of a corporation consist to a large degree of liquid assets, i.e., that the cash, marketable securities and receivables are high in relationship to the total assets employed in the business, such a circumstance may increase the possibility that a third party may attempt a takeover bid for the corporation. On the other hand, a corporation may have hidden values in its assets which may appeal to a possible takeover bidder. Most often such values may be reflected in properties similar to real estate which have been held for a long period of time, and are largely depreciated on the books, or were bought at earlier bargain prices. A prospective takeover bidder, if successful, may plan to realize the value on such properties by liquidating them and utilizing the cash in other areas of the bidder's business.

Preliminary Defensive Considerations

Procedural Safeguards. Since any publicly held company may become the target of a takeover bid, management may wish to establish certain routine safeguards in an attempt to obtain information of a prospective takeover bid as early as possible. Certainly, if management has any reason to believe it likely that the corporation may become the target of a takeover bid, management should establish procedural safeguards to alert itself of any initial stirrings of a takeover bid as soon as possible. A daily check should be maintained on the volume of trading of the corporation's securities as well as on the list of security holders of the corporation to determine, if possible, the accumulation of any large blocks. Also, in connection with the trading of the stock of the corporation on a stock exchange, management should remain in close touch with the specialists handling the corporation's stock to keep abreast of any trading developments.

Stockholder Relations. If a takeover bid appears likely, management should consider taking action which may increase the market value of its outstanding stock. Such action could include (1) an increase in the dividend, (2) a stock split, or even (3) a change in accounting methods which may result in an increase in reported earnings per share. There should theoretically be some business justification for taking any of the suggested action, but if the justification exists, management should expedite taking the action rather than delaying. In general, every effort should be made to maintain good relationships with the corporation's stockholders. Where possible, communications should be sent to shareholders advising them of successes in the corporation's business.

Defensive Merger Candidate. Management should also consider the possibility of finding a friendly prospective merger candidate. An effective means of countering an unwelcomed takeover bid is to offer shareholders an opportunity to participate in a merger, or to have the corporation acquired by a friendly acquisition partner, whereupon a shareholder may receive greater after-tax market value of securities in a "tax-free" exchange than upon a sale of stock to the takeover bidder. An example of a transaction in which a tender offer was defeated by a merger with a friendly merger partner is the statutory merger of Harley-Davidson Corporation into American Machine & Foundry Company which occurred in 1969. In that transaction Bangor Punta Corporation made a registered exchange offer to the shareholders of Harley-Davidson, which was contested by management. The exchange offer was ultimately defeated when Harley-Davidson was merged into American Machine & Foundry Company.

Sometime prior to Bangor-Punta's registered exchange offer, American Machine & Foundry Company had approached Harley-Davidson concerning the possibility of acquiring Harley-Davidson and although the management of Harley-Davidson had not at that time opened serious acquisition discussions, such discussions opened quickly when the registered exchange offer of Bangor Punta was announced.

Preliminary Defensive Steps—Corporate Structure

Charter and By-Laws. Preliminary defensive steps may take the form of changes in the corporation's charter or by-laws to make it more difficult for an offeror to succeed in a takeover bid. Among the charter amendments which may be made is the inclusion of a requirement for approval by a greater percentage of stockholders to effect a statutory merger or sale of assets. In this connection, the New York Stock Exchange maintains a policy of careful scrutiny of any such charter amendments where the sole purpose appears to be a defense against takeover bid.

Authorized Stock. The charter may also be amended to increase the authorized stock of the corporation to make stock available for issuance to friendly parties as a defensive tactic. Or, provision may be made in a charter to authorize a class of preferred stock, if preferred stock is not already authorized, which may contain special voting privileges with respect to a proposed merger or acquisition.

Pre-emptive Rights. Also, if the corporation's charter grants the shareholders pre-emptive rights, consideration should be given to amending the charter to eliminate such rights. The elimination of pre-emptive rights will give management greater freedom in the issuance of stock to friendly shareholders who may support management and make it more difficult for any takeover bid to succeed.

By-Laws. In a similar manner the by-laws of a corporation may be amended to make it more difficult for an acquirer to succeed in a takeover bid. Management should consider staggering the terms of the board of directors, as well as providing cumulative voting for the board. Provisions permitting certain percentages of shareholders to call special meetings of the shareholders may be eliminated or the percentage requirement increased, if such provisions are included in the corporation's by-laws. Provisions permitting the removal of directors without cause may also be eliminated.

Preliminary Defensive Steps—Business

Stock Purchases. From a business point of view, management may help minimize the possibility of a successful takeover bid by the acquisition of stock of the corporation in the open market by interests friendly to management, as well as the acquisition of stock by the corporation itself. The Williams Bill, by adding Section 13(e)(1) to the Securities Exchange Act of 1934, granted to the Securities and Exchange Commission powers to regulate fraudulent, deceptive, or manipulative practices in connection with an issuer's purchase of its own securities. In this connection, the Commission has adopted Rule 13(e)–1 which requires disclosure when an issuer purchases its own securities during the period of a cash tender offer.

Contracts. Management may also review its contracts with substantial customers or suppliers, as well as loan agreements to determine whether amendments to these agreements restricting the rights of transfer of control could discourage a prospective takeover bidder.

Defensive Maneuvers to an Actual Takeover Bid

Schedule 14D. Management of the target company is prohibited from making any recommendation to its security holders either to accept or reject a tender offer unless management has previously filed with the Securities and Exchange Commission certain information specified under Schedule 14D. Therefore, the management of the target company should prepare and file with the Securities and Exchange Commission the form of Schedule 14D as promptly as possible. The information required to be filed pursuant to Schedule 14D is set forth in this chapter on page 165.

Possible defensive litigation. The target company should consider bringing litigation to prohibit or hinder the takeover. A number of areas of law may form the foundation of such litigation. Some of these areas are the following:

(1) If the proposed takeover has anti-trust overtones, the target company may bring an injunctive action against the aggressor;

(2) If the takeover bid is a registered exchange offer, the target company may bring an injunctive action, based upon the claim that the prospectus is faulty;

(3) If the takeover bid is a tender offer, the target company may claim that the tender offer violates the requirements of the Williams Bill, and base its injunctive action on such a claim;

(4) Additionally, the target company may claim that the margin requirements under Section 7 of the 1934 Securities and Exchange Act or Regulations T, U, and G promulgated by the Board of Governors of the Federal Reserve Board are being violated by the aggressor;

(5) If the aggressor requests a stockholder list from the target company, the target company may refuse to supply such a list and thereby put the issue into litigation;

(6) The target company may attempt to convince state securities authorities that state blue sky laws may be violated by the proposed takeover bid of the aggressor.

Publicity and communications. The target company should consider the advisability of communications with its stockholders, employees, and principal customers and suppliers, both through written communication and newspaper advertisements. In addition, the target company may communicate with investment bankers, brokers, and mutual funds which have a position or interest in the target company's securities to convince such institutions and funds that the takeover bid of the aggressor company will be unsuccessful. If the aggressor has conditioned its takeover bid upon obtaining a minimum percentage of the target company's securities, securities brokers and funds will not be willing to take positions in the target company's securities, unless such institutions are satisfied that the takeover bid will be successful. Should the bid be unsuccessful, the market price of the target company's stock would presumably recede to its price prior to the time of the takeover bid.

Defensive merger. If the target company has taken proper precautions to guard against a possible takeover bid, the target company may have had discussions with a prospective acceptable acquirer prior to the takeover bid. Under such circumstances, the target company may be in a position to consummate a merger or acquisition with a more friendly larger corporation and thus block the possible takeover bid. Even if discussions of a possible merger or acquisition have not been previously held, the target company may find a sympathetic hearing from a friendly buyer.

Counter-takeover bid. An interesting possibility involves a possible counter-takeover bid for the aggressor. If the aggressor's takeover bid is in the form of a registered exchange offer, presumably the target company will have substantially all of the information it would require in order to register its own registered exchange offer. If the counter-takeover bid should be made in the form of a tender offer, the target company need only meet the requirements set forth in the Williams Bill, which it would presumably be able to do in a relatively short period of time.

CHAPTER 10

Tax Considerations—
Tax-Free vs. Taxable Acquisitions

In determining the income tax effects of any proposed purchase or sale of a business, the buyer and seller are bound by the rules set down in our tax laws, those contained in the Internal Revenue Code of the United States. These rules dictate whether or not income taxes are payable upon a sale of a business and, if so, how much.

Any single acquisition of a business may involve many different provisions of the Internal Revenue Code, and the interpretations and refinements placed upon these provisions by court decisions and administrative rulings. To attempt to discuss the myriad of tax problems which could arise, which could run the gamut of the Code itself in any one acquisition, would be impractical here. Such a discussion could fill volumes. However, certain tax problems are present in most acquisitions and others arise with sufficient frequency in connection with acquisitions to deserve discussion and some attempt at elaboration of the tax rules providing possible solutions. In this chapter the overall problem of a tax-free acquisition as opposed to a taxable acquisition is discussed in some detail. Other tax problems which may arise in acquisitions are set forth and discussed in Chapter 11.

Bear in mind that an acquisition structured to achieve the best income tax results for a buyer may not achieve the best results for reporting earnings per share in the buyer's financial statements. A cash transaction which is treated as a "taxable" transaction for income tax purposes and a "purchase" for accounting purposes, may result in subtantial income tax savings from increased depreciation deductions flowing from the write-up of the tax cost of assets acquired from the seller. The "taxable" transaction may increase cash flow substantially. However, "purchase" accounting treatment may reduce reported earnings per share, due not only to increased depreciation deductions, but also to amortization of goodwill to which a portion of the price paid may have been allocated in a "purchase" accounting transaction. Management of the buyer may therefore insist that the form of transaction be recast in accordance with criteria set forth in Chapter 7 to achieve "pooling of interests" accounting treatment to avoid the increased depreciation and goodwill amortization deductions.

Not only may conflict exist between the best tax results from either a "taxable" or "nontaxable" transaction and the best accounting results from either a "purchase" or a "pooling of interests," but the criteria for determining whether an acquisition is "tax-free" from a tax viewpoint or a "pooling of interests" from an accounting viewpoint, although similar in some respects, differ in significant details. As a result of the differences in the tax and accounting criteria, it has been possible to treat an acquisition as "taxable," to obtain the benefits of increased depreciation deductions, and at the same time as a "pooling of interests" to avoid reduction in reported earnings per share due to amortization of goodwill.

This chapter and Chapter 11 limit discussion to the tax aspects of acquisitions, without regard to the accounting aspects discussed in Chapter 7.

Often the tax objectives of a buyer may be in conflict with the tax objectives of a seller. In this chapter let us first explore what these differing objectives may be.

TAX OBJECTIVES OF SELLER

The basic tax objectives of the seller will generally depend upon the relationship between the purchase price being offered and the tax cost of the stock or assets in the hands of the seller. Where the purchase price exceeds the tax cost, a tax-free transaction will generally be advantageous to the seller. Where the purchase price is less than the tax cost, a taxable transaction will generally be advantageous to the seller.

Tax-free transaction—seller's objectives. As indicated, a seller will often want a tax-free transaction if the purchase price exceeds the tax cost of the assets or stock in the hands of the seller. Consider a situation which occurs with relative frequency. The sellers started their closely held business a number of years ago with a minimum investment of $100,000 in capital. The sellers conducted the business sucessfully over the years, reinvesting earnings, and as a result sales have grown to $15,000,000 and a buyer is willing to pay $10,000,000 for the business. The average age of the sellers is now 66 and they wish to retire. Under these circumstances the sellers will generally seek a tax-free transaction.

In a taxable transaction, since the tax cost of the business in the hands of the sellers is only $100,000, the sellers would realize a taxable gain of $9,900,000 (the excess of the $10,000,000 price over the $100,000 tax cost). Even at capital gain rates the immediate tax could amount to in excess of $2,500,000. On the other hand, if the transaction is tax-free, no tax will be payable as a result of the receipt of the buyer's stock, and substantially the entire capital gains tax may be avoided if the sellers retain substantially all of the buyer's stock as an investment. At the time of the death of the sellers, the stock of the buyer in the hands of the estates will take a so-called "stepped up" tax basis consisting of the value included in the estate tax return, and the capital gain tax may be avoided. (The saving of the $2,500,000 capital gain tax may not continue to be possible, however, if the law is changed to tax the gain at the time of death as proposed to the Congress in the past.)

Taxable transaction—general objective of seller. A seller will often want a taxable transaction if the purchase price is less than the tax cost of the assets or stock in the hands of the seller. In such a situation, where a seller sells assets, a seller may realize a net operating loss for tax purposes which may be carried back and result in refund of income taxes. In addition, if the loss is sizable enough, a seller may attempt to utilize additional unused tax loss carry forwards by acquiring profitable businesses.

Taxable transaction—seller's objectives in allocating the purchase price. In a taxable transaction, the allocation of the purchase price among specified assets of the seller may lead to conflict in the objectives of the buyer and seller. The seller will generally want the purchase price allocated to assets on which the seller will realize capital gain. On the other hand, the buyer will generally prefer to have the price allocated to assets against which he may have an immediate or fast tax write-off—certainly to assets which will give the buyer some tax write-off. The two objectives are sometimes difficult to reconcile.

As indicated, in a taxable transaction where the price exceeds the seller's cost, the seller will normally wish to have the purchase price allocated to assets from which the seller will realize capital gain. Such assets consist generally of items such as (1) goodwill and trademarks, (2) land and buildings, (3) patents, and (4) leases. Of the above items, the one which would cause a buyer most difficulty would be the item of goodwill. From a tax point of view, a buyer will generally resist the allocation of any substantial part of purchase price to goodwill, because goodwill may not be amortized for tax purposes, and therefore no annual tax deduction is allowed against pre-tax earnings. Insofar as the machinery and equipment is concerned a seller may want an allocation of price which does not exceed the depreciated tax cost. Otherwise, under Code Section 1245 a seller may realize ordinary income to the extent the excess payment equals depreciation taken since December 31, 1961.

The allocation of price between land and buildings may also cause conflict in the tax objectives of a buyer and seller. Under Code Section 1250, a seller may realize ordinary income from the sale of a building to the extent of portions of depreciation in excess of straight-line depreciation taken or allowed after certain cut-off dates. Where the sale of a building may result in ordinary income, a seller may attempt to allocate more of the purchase price to land, rather than the building. The buyer may resist the allocation of price to land, because land is a non-depreciable asset for tax purposes.

The seller, on its part, may resist an attempt to allocate any of the purchase price to inventory to the extent the allocation exceeds the tax basis of the inventory. Unless the seller plans a liquidation within the provisions of Code Section 337, the seller could immediately realize ordinary income to the extent of the excess. Under Code Section 337, if the seller adopts a plan of complete liquidation and distributes its assets within the 12-month period beginning on the date of the adoption of the plan, then no gain or loss is recognized to the seller from the sale of property within the 12-month period. Inventory is included in property upon which no gain or loss is recognized, if substantially all the inventory is sold to one buyer in one transaction in a Section 337 liquidation.

Exceptions to the Section 337 rule, i.e., no gain or loss is recognized upon a sale of property in a Section 337 liquidation, result from the application of Code Sections 1245 and 1250, mentioned above, where a sale of assets is made. In spite of the non-recognition of gain under Code Section 337, if depreciable assets or buildings subject to Code Section 1245 or 1250 are sold, ordinary income taxes will be payable by the seller to the extent of certain depreciation taken or allowable on such assets during specified prior periods.

Where a buyer pays the seller for a covenant not to compete, the seller realizes capital gain or ordinary income depending upon the nature of the payment. For example, where the payment is for a covenant not to compete granted by an individual proprietor, the covenant may be ancillary to goodwill, and the seller may realize capital gain, and the buyer may not be permitted to amortize the payment. On the other hand an officer, who is not a stockholder of the corporation and gives a covenant not to compete, may realize ordinary income and the buyer may be in a position to amortize the payment over the life of the covenant for tax purposes.

Taxable transaction—seller's desire to delay tax. Where a transaction is taxable, the seller may wish to delay the payment of the tax. Under Section 453 of the Code a seller may report a sale on a so-called installment basis, which, in effect, spreads the taxable gain over the years in which payments are received. Basic rules are that property which qualifies must be sold for more than $1,000, the seller may not receive more than 30 per cent of the selling price in cash in the year of the sale, and the balance of the price may not be evidenced by demand notes or other defined types of negotiable bonds. The effect of treating the sale as an installment sale is to cause the seller to report as either capital gain or income that portion of the total gain which the payments received in any one year represent of the total purchase price. Refinements involved in the application of the installment sale rule are discussed in Chapter 11, but normally a seller wishing installment sales treatment will not meet any substantial resistance from the buyer.

TAX OBJECTIVES OF BUYER

As in the case of a seller, the basic tax objectives of a buyer will generally depend upon the relationship between the purchase price and the tax cost of the stock or assets being acquired from the seller. The general tax objective of a buyer is often the opposite of that of the seller. Where the purchase price exceeds the tax cost of the stock or property in the hands of the seller, a taxable transaction will generally be advantageous to the buyer. On the other hand, where the purchase price is less than the tax cost of these properties—the buyer will generally prefer a tax-free transaction to take advantage of the continued higher tax basis of the seller's properties in the hands of the buyer.

"Tax-free" and taxable transactions—buyer's objectives. As indicated, a buyer will often want a taxable transaction if the purchase price exceeds the tax cost of the assets or stock in the hands of the seller. Assume that the total tax cost of the assets of the seller's business amounts to $500,000. If the buyer is willing to pay $750,000 for the seller's business, the buyer may desire a taxable transaction in order to write the tax cost of the seller's assets up from $500,000 to $750,000. Assuming that the entire purchase price is allocable to depreciable assets, the buyer, after a taxable transaction, could write off against pre-tax earnings depreciation based on a cost of $750,000. On the other hand, in a tax-free transaction, the buyer would be able to depreciate only $500,000 against pre-tax earnings, because the seller's tax cost would carry over into the hands of the buyer in such a tax-free transaction.

In a taxable transaction, a buyer may accomplish its objective of raising the basis of the seller's assets to $750,000 whether the buyer buys assets directly, or buys stock from the seller's stockholders. If stock is acquired the buyer may raise the tax basis of the seller's assets in the buyer's hands by liquidating the seller after purchase of the stock in accordance with certain rules contained in Section 334 of the Code. However, where a buyer buys a seller's stock rather than assets, the buyer becomes liable for the ultimate payment of the ordinary income tax on depreciation under Sections 1245 and 1250 of the Code. On the other hand, if the buyer buys the assets, payment of any such tax becomes the seller's problem. Section 1245 and 1250 are considered in greater detail in the next chapter.

Taxable transaction—buyer's objectives in allocating the purchase price. As previously indicated, the allocation of purchase price to specific assets may also cause difficulties because of differing tax effects upon the buyer and seller. The seller's basic objectives, in a taxable transaction where gain is involved, will be to allocate as much of the price as possible to assets which result in capital gain. Therefore, a seller will attempt to allocate as much as possible of the purchase price to items such as goodwill and land and buildings not affected by accelerated depreciation.

A buyer will resist allocating purchase price to goodwill and land since such items may not be depreciated and deducted against pre-tax earnings for income tax purposes. A buyer will generally prefer to allocate purchase price to machinery and equipment, patents and leases and finally, buildings—since normally these items may be written off for tax purposes in the shortest possible time.

Prior to 1963, an allocation of purchase price to machinery and equipment and patents could meet the tax objectives of both the buyer and seller. Gain realized by the seller from the sale of such property could be treated as capital gain, and the buyer realized the tax advantage of a comparatively rapid depreciation of the machinery and equipment or patents against pre-tax earnings. But with the enactment of Section 1245 of the Internal Revenue Code in 1962, an allocation of purchase price to machinery and equipment and patents has again become a problem between a buyer and seller. Under Section 1245 of the Code, a seller will realize ordinary income on the sale of machinery and equipment or patents for more than their depreciated tax cost to the extent it has depreciated machinery and equipment and patents since December 31, 1961.

For example, assume a seller bought a machine for $1,000 and at the time of sale post-1961 depreciation amounted to $500 and depreciation during and prior to 1961 amounted to $250. The seller has a remaining tax cost or basis of $250 ($1,000 cost less $750 depreciation taken). If the seller sells the machine for $1,000 it will have a gain of $750 for tax purposes—the excess of the $1,000 price over the $250 remaining tax cost. This gain of $750 will be taxed as ordinary income to the extent of $500 (post-1961 depreciation) and, as capital gain to the extent of $250 (the gain in excess of post-1961 depreciation, actually the result of 1961 and prior years depreciation). Therefore, a seller may resist allocation of purchase price in excess of the depreciated tax cost to machinery and equipment or patents.

Real estate may also pose a depreciation recapture problem. Under Section 1250 of the 1954 Code certain "additional depreciation" may be subject to tax at ordinary income tax rates where a seller realizes a gain from the sale of real estate. "Additional depreciation" means depreciation with respect to real estate which exceeds depreciation which would normally be allowable on a straight-line basis. Generally speaking, certain percentages of "additional depreciation" allowable to a seller between December 31, 1963 and December 31, 1969 (based upon the period of ownership of the real estate) is subject to depreciation recapture, and all "additional depreciation" taken after December 31, 1969, is subject to depreciation recapture and the payment of ordinary income taxes by a seller. Sellers may, therefore, resist efforts by buyers to allocate extensive portions of purchase price to buildings, in a taxable acquisition.

The foregoing discussion of the general tax objectives of a buyer and a seller indicates that the first basic problem faced in an acquisition, from the income tax viewpoint, is whether the acquisition should be structured as a "tax-free" or "taxable" acquisition.

"TAX-FREE" VS. "TAXABLE" ACQUISITION

The broad, general tax problem involved in acquisitions of businesses is whether the acquisition is tax-free, or taxable. Although the term "tax-free" is somewhat misleading, the essential difference between the two types of acquisitions may be implied from the adjectives themselves. Subject to certain exceptions, a tax-free acquisition has no immediate tax effect and no income taxes are payable, whereas a taxable acquisition results in immediate tax consequences, and income taxes are payable with respect to any gains realized by the selling party.

Describing a tax-free acquisition as one which has "no immediate tax effect" is generally correct. A stockholder of a seller may receive a buyer's stock in exchange for the stockholder's shares of the seller, and need not pay income tax due to the receipt of the buyer's shares. This does not mean that the stockholder will never have to pay the tax. If the stockholder sells the buyer's stock for the same price as its fair market value when received, all of the gain will be taxed in the year of the sale. On sale, the full gain is taxed, because the original cost to the stockholder of his shares of the seller becomes the cost of the buyer's stock received in exchange. If the stockholder retains the buyer's stock until death, the full gain may escape taxation (as long as the tax law does not tax the gain at death, and continues to permit a write-up of tax basis to fair market value as a result of death). On the other hand, where a buyer's stock is ultimately sold by the seller's stockholder, a tax-free receipt of stock means a postponement of tax rather than escape from tax.

As an example, assume a stockholder of a seller paid $100 for his stock of the seller. In a tax-free exchange the stockholder receives stock of the buyer which has a value of $200. The $100 gain ($200 value received less $100 cost) is not taxed at the time the stockholder receives the buyer's stock. But the cost to the stockholder of the buyer's stock remains $100 —the same as the cost of the shares the seller originally held. Therefore $100 of gain will be recognized and taxed if the stockholder sells the buyer's stock for $200 ($200 cash from sale less the $100 carryover cost). Should the buyer's shares be valued in the stockholder's estate at $200, the tax may be avoided in its entirety. Proposals have been made to Congress that it tax the gain at time of death, and therefore this escape from the tax may be eliminated. But at the moment, the $200 value placed on the buyer's shares for estate tax purposes becomes the new tax cost of the shares. Therefore, if the shares are sold for $200 by the estate or a legatee no gain will result for income tax purposes ($200 received for stock with a new tax cost, or basis, of $200).

In the balance of this chapter, we will discuss the rules which make an acquisition tax-free or taxable, and some additional specific tax consequences of the each type of acquisition on the buyer and seller. Miscellaneous corollary tax problems which may arise from acquisitions and their possible effect upon the buyer and seller are discussed in Chapter 11.

THE "TAX-FREE" ACQUISITION

General. Every corporate acquisition involves a receipt or exchange of stock or other property, and the great majority of acquisitions also involve distributions by corporations to shareholders. Where a corporation buys a business for stock, the stock may be used to buy the assets of the business or the stock of the seller's business; where a corporation buys a business for cash, the cash also may be given for assets or stock, as may any combinations of stock, cash or other properties, such as notes. Furthermore, where assets are sold, the selling corporation frequently distributes the consideration, whether it be stock, cash, or other properties, to its stockholders. In these situations each acquisition involves a receipt or exchange and may involve a corporate distribution of property to shareholders.

Under our Internal Revenue Code the general rule is that each exchange of property and each receipt of property constitutes a taxable event, unless the transaction falls within one of the specific exemptions provided in the Code. Under the Internal Revenue Code gross income is defined as "all income from whatever source derived, including . . . gains derived from dealings in property." The law further provides that "on the sale or exchange of property the entire amount of the gain or loss . . . shall be recognized," which means that the gain or loss is taken into account in computing federal income taxes.

The foregoing general income tax rules are subject to exceptions which, under specific enumerated circumstances, permit a taxpayer to receive or exchange property without immediate tax consequences. As examples, the law excludes from gross income certain death benefits, gifts and inheritances, interest on state and municipal obligations, compensation for injuries or sickness, amounts received under accident and health plans, scholarship and fellowship grants, receipts of contributions to capital by corporations, and meals or lodging furnished for the convenience of an employer.

In addition to the enumerated receipts which are excluded from gross income, certain exchanges of property are treated as non-taxable. As examples, exchanges of property held for productive use or investment, with certain exceptions, are non-taxable; exchanges by a corporation of its stock for property is non-taxable to the corporation; the involuntary conversion of property as a result of destruction or similar event into similar property is a non-taxable exchange; the sale or exchange of a residence, where a new residence is bought, may be treated as non-taxable; and exchanges of certain types of insurance policies, stock for stock of the same corporation, and certain exchanges of United States obligations are also treated as non-taxable exchanges.

With this background, let us address ourselves to the specific provisions of the Internal Revenue Code which exempt exchanges and distributions of property and stock in acquisitions from immediate income tax consequences. In order to be tax-free, any exchanges or distributions in acquisitions must be exchanges or distributions made in connection with a "reorganization" as defined in our tax law. The tax law contains six definitions of such reorganizations. Since, however, only three of the definitions concern acquisition transactions, we will limit our discussion to these three—described generally as (1) a statutory merger or consolidation, (2) an acquisition of the *stock* of a corporation by another corporation for a part of its stock, and (3) an acquisition of the *assets* of a corporation by another corporation for a part of its stock.

Merger or consolidation. The first definition contained in the Internal Revenue Code of a reorganization which will qualify for tax-free treatment is "a statutory merger or consolidation." This type of reorganization is often referred to as an "A" reorganization, because it is defined in Section 368(a)(1)(A) of the 1954 Internal Revenue Code.

A technical distinction between a merger and consolidation, often made in print, is that a merger involves combining two or more corporations into one of the *former* independent corporations as the continuing entity, whereas a consolidation involves combining two or more corporations into a *new* corporation organized to conduct the combined former businesses. The distinction is largely technical, and since the merger route is the more customary of the two, this discussion speaks generally in terms of mergers. Most comments concerning statutory mergers would, however, apply to consolidations.

The essential element to qualify a merger or consolidation for tax-free treatment is that it be statutory, i.e., that it be accomplished in accordance with the procedures set forth in the corporation laws of the state or states of incorporation of the merging companies. The result of a merger or consolidation is the same as the acquisition of the assets of one corporation by another corporation, whether for stock or cash, in the sense that after the merger or consolidation or acquisition, two businesses, formerly conducted separately, are continued as an integral part of one corporate entity. In spite of this similarity, corporation laws of the various states relating to mergers and consolidations cause important procedural differences between a merger as a method of acquisition as opposed to an acquisition of a corporation's assets for stock or cash.

Merger—procedure. In most states the basic procedure prescribed for merger is that the boards of directors of the merging corporations must approve a plan or agreement of merger which sets forth the terms of the merger, and then submit the plan or agreement to the stockholders of each of the corporations for approval by the requisite statutory vote. For example, the New Jersey statutes provide that corporations may merge by having each board of directors adopt a plan of merger which must then be submitted to a vote of stockholders—a favorable vote of two-thirds of the stockholders may be required to effect the merger. In Delaware, an agreement of merger must be approved by the boards of directors of the merging corporations for submission to the stockholders for approval, but only a favorable vote of a majority of the stockholders, rather than a two-thirds vote is required to complete the merger.

Both the New York and Delaware corporation laws contain another attribute common to many state merger statututes, i.e., that stockholders of either corporation who oppose the merger may dissent. The dissent is a statutory method whereby a dissenting stockholder may have the value of his stock appraised by a disinterested referee or other official and be paid its fair value by the corporation.

Merger—controlled corporation. Under Section 368(a)(2)(D) of the Code, which applies to statutory mergers occurring after October 22, 1968, a merger of a seller into a subsidiary controlled by a buyer in exchange for stock of the buyer may qualify as an "A" type tax-free reorganization. Under this Section, a buyer may organize a new subsidiary into which a seller may be merged, and avoid the requirement for a meeting of the buyer's stockholders which would have been required if the seller were merged directly into the buyer. However, in order for this procedure to be available the state merger statutes must permit the issuance of stock of a third corporation (the buyer) where two other corporations, the buyer's controlled subsidiary and the seller are merged.

Merger vs. stock or asset acquisition. An acquisition by corporate statutory merger differs in an important fundamental from the acquisition of stock or assets of a seller in exchange for voting stock of a buyer. (Other types of tax-free acquisitions we will discuss below.)

Unless the merger is a Section 368(a)(2)(D) merger of a seller into a subsidiary of a buyer (where the buyer's directors may approve the merger), a statutory merger is generally subject to the approval of the stockholders of both the buyer and seller. In other words, the stockholders of the buyer desiring to make the acquisition through the merger have the right to vote upon the acquisition. Lacking exceptional circumstances, the stockholders of a buyer which acquires, in exchange for its voting stock, the stock or assets of a seller have no such right to vote upon the acquisition.

In one respect, however, an acquisition by statutory merger has a substantial advantage over the other two types of tax-free acquisitions which we will discuss below. You will notice when we discuss the acquisition of assets or stock in exchange for the stock of the buyer, the buyer is limited, with only a very limited exception, to the use of its *voting stock* to pay for the acquisition. The Internal Revenue Code imposes no such restriction upon a statutory merger to attain tax-free status. Therefore, in a tax-free statutory merger the consideration for the acquisition may include such securities as non-voting preferred stock, debentures, bonds and other classes of securities, limited only by the corporation statutes of the states involved. This flexibility from an income tax viewpoint in choosing the method of payment of the purchase price in an acquisition by merger may make possible a tax-free acquisition where circumstances require unique combinations of securities to satisfy the seller's stockholders or the buyer.

For example, assume a situation in which a buyer and seller, both listed companies, are traded at the same approximate price—$40 per share. The seller pays $2.00 in dividends annually and the buyer only pays $1.60 in dividends annually. The parties believe that the seller's shareholders would vote against a share for share exchange (in spite of the equal market values), because of the discrepancy in dividend payments. If the parties desire a tax-free transaction, and the buyer refuses to make up the dividend deficiency by offering more stock, the buyer could offer a package paying $2.10 for each share of seller's stock, consisting of ¾ of a buyer's share plus $15 principal amount of 6 per cent debentures ($1.20 in dividend income and $.90 in interest income). If the package is offered through the statutory merger route, the acquisition will be tax-free (except to the extent of the debentures), but if offered for seller's assets, the acquisition generally (subject to some exceptions) will be taxable in its entirety, and if offered for seller's stock, the acquisition will be taxable in its entirety. Subject to refinements discussed below, to be tax-free, an acquisition of assets or stock must be made solely for the buyer's voting stock, whereas if the merger route is followed, the buyer has flexibility in its method of paying the purchase price and still maintaining the tax-free status of the merger.

Another advantage, a non-tax advantage, of a statutory merger over an acquisition of assets, is that in a statutory merger, title to the seller's properties vests in the surviving corporation by operation of law. In other words, the numerous title documents involved in an asset acquisition are not required. The certificate of merger, filed with the proper authorities effects the transfer of title to all of the seller's assets in a merger. However, where assets are acquired, deeds to real property must be delivered and recorded separately, as well as assignments of leases, bills of sale of personalty, patent, trademark and contract assignments, and separate instruments must often be executed involving assumptions of obligations. If the seller owns a number of parcels of real estate, expenses involved in preparing, executing and recording just the real estate deeds may be sizable.

In summary, to qualify as a tax-free reorganization, a merger or a consolidation (subject to a continuity of interest test discussed below) must only meet the specific requirement under the Internal Revenue Code that the transaction involved meet the statutory requirements and follow the statutory procedures contained in the corporation laws of the states of incorporation. Although acquisition by merger may entail the complicating factor of requiring the approval of the acquiring company's stockholders, this type of tax-free acquisition has the tax advantage of substantial flexibility in the method of payment of purchase price and the non-tax advantage of transfer of title to assets by operation of law.

Stock-for-stock acquisitions. The second definition of a tax-free reorganization contained in the Internal Revenue Code relates to the acquisition by one corporation (in exchange for some or all of its voting stock) of stock of another corporation, often called a "B" reorganization since the definition is contained in Section 368(a)(1)(B) of the 1954 Internal Revenue Code. The statutory language is that a tax-free reorganization includes "the acquisition by one corporation, in exchange solely for all or a part of its voting stock . . . of stock of another corporation, if, immediately after the acquisition, the acquiring corporation has control of such other corporation (whether or not such acquiring corporation had control immediately before the acquisition)."

You will notice that the two major elements contained in the definition of a tax-free, stock-for-stock acquisition are that (1) the buyer must exchange solely its voting stock for the stock of the seller and (2) the buyer must have control of the seller immediately after the exchange.

Stock transaction—solely voting stock. The requirement that the acquisition be made for solely voting stock should be considered inflexible. Although on occasion a court decision may indicate that consideration other than voting stock may be given in a stock-for-stock reorganization, such decision should not be trusted and the words "solely voting stock" should be construed to mean that nothing other than voting stock may be given by the buyer in the exchange. In other words, if the buyer gives its common stock and other property, such as non-voting preferred stock or cash, in payment for the stock of the seller, the exchange will generally be taxable; the stockholders of the seller will be required to pay income taxes on any gain they may have realized in the exchange. Conversely, if a selling stockholder suffers a loss on the exchange, this loss may be taken into account in his income tax return.

Control. In a stock-for-stock tax-free reorganization, in addition to the requirement that the buyer give solely voting stock for the stock of the seller, the buyer must be in control of the seller after the transaction. The tax law defines the word "control" to mean "the ownership of stock possessing at least 80 per cent of the total combined voting power of all classes of stock entitled to vote and at least 80 per cent of the total number of shares of all other classes of stock" of the seller. To satisfy the requirements of this definition, the buyer must acquire at least 80 per cent of all classes of stock of the seller, or the transaction will not be tax-free. For example, if the buyer acquires 100 per cent of the voting common stock of the seller but acquires only 79 per cent of an issue of non-voting preferred stock of the seller, the exchange will not meet the definition of control and will be taxable.

One interesting aspect of the control definition is that a buyer may acquire a portion of the stock of a seller in a taxable transaction, such as a purchase for cash, but may at some later date, in a separate transaction, acquire additional stock of the seller in a tax-free manner. Such a result may be achieved only where the subsequent acquisition of the seller's stock not only meets the requirements of the stock-for-stock reorganization definition contained in the Code, but also is considered an entirely separate transaction from the first purchase of stock for cash. For example, assume that the seller is a publicly held company with only common stock outstanding, in which the buyer owns a 30 per cent stock interest which the buyer bought in the open market for cash. If the buyer subsequently acquires, in exchange solely for its voting stock, 50 per cent or more of the outstanding stock of the seller, in an entirely separate transaction, the second acquisition of the seller's stock will be tax-free, because, after this acquisition, the buyer will have the required 80 per cent control of the seller. In our example, the original purchase of a 30 per cent interest was taxable because the buyer paid cash for the stock, and the taxable nature of this purchase is not changed by the subsequent tax-free acquisition of the additional 50 per cent of the seller's stock.

Stock-For-Stock Reorganization: Diagram

The diagram below illustrates elements of a stock-for-stock, tax-free reorganization and will help differentiate this type of reorganization from a stock-for-assets reorganization discussed later. As the fundamental difference between these types, you will note that in the stock-for-stock transaction the agreement and exchange is not between the buyer and seller but between the *buyer* and the *stockholders* of the seller:

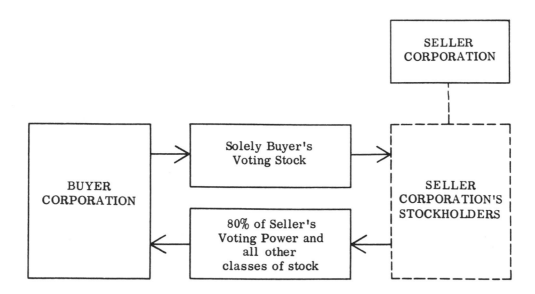

Stock acquisition—by subsidiary. The definition of a tax-free, stock-for-stock reorganization includes "the acquisition by one corporation, in exchange solely for all or a part of its voting stock (*or* in exchange solely for all or a part of *the voting stock of a corporation* which is *in control of the acquiring corporation*), of the stock of another corporation. . . ." Under this portion of the definition, a subsidiary may acquire the stock of the seller in exchange for voting stock of the subsidiary's parent, provided the parent controls the subsidiary and the subsidiary controls the seller after the completion of the acquisition. "Control" for each of these purposes means the 80% stock ownership as defined above.

Stock-for-Assets acquisitions. The third type of tax-free reorganization of importance in acquiring businesses involves the purchase of the assets of a seller for stock of a buyer.

The tax law defines this type of reorganization as "the acquisition by one corporation, in exchange solely for all or a part of its voting stock . . . of substantially all of the properties of another corporation, but in determining whether the exchange is solely for stock the assumption by the acquiring corporation of a liability of the other . . . shall be disregarded."

As in a stock-for-stock tax-free reorganization, the stock-for-assets reorganization involves two major requirements for tax-free treatment. First, subject to qualifications which we will discuss below, the medium of payment for the assets must be voting stock of the buyer. Second, the buyer must acquire substantially all of the assets of the seller.

Asset transaction—solely voting stock. The requirement that the assets of the seller be bought "in exchange solely for all or a part of [the] voting stock" of the buyer is expressed in language identical to that contained in the stock-for-stock, tax-free reorganization, but in an asset transaction, as opposed to a stock-for-stock transaction, the tax law contains exceptions to the requirement that the buyer pay for the assets in solely voting stock. The first exception, quoted above with the definition of a tax-free, stock-for-assets reorganization, provides that "in determining whether the exchange is solely for stock the assumption by the [buyer] of a liability of the [seller]" should be disregarded. To illustrate, assume that the seller's balance sheet is as follows:

SELLER CORPORATION

Balance Sheet at December 31, 19__

Assets		_Liabilities and Stockholders' Equity_	
Cash	$ 1,000	Accounts Payable	$ 2,000
Accounts Receivable	2,000	Mortgage on Plant	3,000
Inventory	7,000	Capital Stock	15,000
Plant & Equipment	15,000	Earned Surplus	5,000
Total Assets	$25,000	Total Liabilities and Equity	$25,000

If the buyer acquires the assets of the seller for voting stock, and the buyer agrees to assume the payment of both the accounts payable of $2,000 and the mortgage of $3,000, the additional payment made by the buyer in assuming the obligation to pay the seller's debts is ignored for tax purposes. The transaction is treated as though the buyer had bought the assets of the seller "solely" for voting stock of the buyer.

The second exception to the requirement that the buyer pay "solely" voting stock for the seller's assets flatly permits the buyer to make part of the payment in the form of money or other property. The law states that if an acquisition of assets for stock would qualify as a tax-free reorganization except that the buyer "exchanges money or other property in addition to voting stock," then if the buyer acquires "solely for voting stock," property of the seller "having a fair market value which is at least 80 per cent of the fair market value of all of the property" of the seller, the acquisition of assets will qualify as a tax-free reorganization. This exception, permitting a buyer to use cash or property in addition to voting stock, is subject to a refinement in determining whether the buyer has obtained 80 per cent of the seller's assets for solely voting stock of the buyer.

Under this refinement, if the buyer assumes any liabilities of the seller or takes property of the seller subject to liabilities in addition to paying the seller cash or other property, the buyer must treat the total of the liabilities "as money paid for the property" of the seller to determine whether the buyer acquired 80 per cent of the seller's property solely for the buyer's voting stock.

To illustrate the operation of this refinement, we will utilize the same balance sheet of a seller as appears on page 186. You will recall that if the buyer acquired the seller's assets for solely voting stock, then the assumption by the buyer of the $2,000 of the seller's accounts payable and the $3,000 mortgage did not affect the tax-free nature of the transaction. But under the refinement to the asset deal (assuming the fair market value of the seller's assets is equal to the balance sheet figures), if the buyer gives $1 in cash in addition to assuming the seller's accounts payable and taking the plant subject to a mortgage, the transaction will be disqualified as a tax-free transaction. Under our assumption the fair market value of all of the seller's property as reflected on the seller's balance sheet is $25,000. If the buyer gives $1 in cash in addition to stock for the seller's property, the assumption of $2,000 of seller's accounts payable and the $3,000 mortgage on the plant must be treated as money paid for the seller's property. Therefore, $5,001 is treated as paid in money for $25,000 of fair market value of the seller's assets. Since $5,001 paid in money exceeds 20 per cent of $25,000 (the fair market value of the seller's assets) less than 80 per cent of the property of the seller was acquired for solely voting stock of the buyer, and the transaction will not qualify as a tax-free reorganization.

As a final observation on the type of consideration a buyer may pay in an asset-type of tax-free reorganization, corporations generally have outstanding liabilities in excess of 20 per cent of the fair market value of their assets. Consequently, asset transactions in which a buyer assumes the seller's obligations and pays cash or other property in addition to the buyer's stock will, except in unique instances, be taxable rather than tax-free transactions.

Substantially all of the properties. These cond broad requirement for a tax-free assets transaction is that the buyer acquire "substantially all of the properties" of the seller. Generally, in determining whether substantially all of the seller's properties were acquired, you must distinguish current assets such as cash, accounts receivable and inventories and fixed assets such as plant and equipment. Limited amounts of cash, receivables, and even inventory may be retained by the seller and nevertheless the buyer may acquire "substantially all of the properties" of the seller. However, retention of similar percentages of plant and equipment by the seller may disqualify the reorganization. The definition of "substantially all of the properties" is generally fluid, but the Internal Revenue Service will probably not rule favorably where a buyer acquires less than 90 per cent of the seller's properties.

Stock-For-Assets Reorganization: Diagram

The diagram below illustrates the elements of a stock-for-assets, tax-free reorganization where the buyer gives nothing but voting stock for the seller's assets. In such a transaction, the buyer *may assume the liabilities* of the seller and the transaction will qualify as a tax-free deal. You will recall that in a stock-for-stock deal, diagrammed above, the buyer could give *only* voting stock and could not assume any obligations of the selling stockholders or give any other consideration. The diagram also indicates that in an asset deal the contract is between the buyer and the seller rather than between the buyer and the seller's stockholders as would be the case in a stock-for-stock, tax-free reorganization:

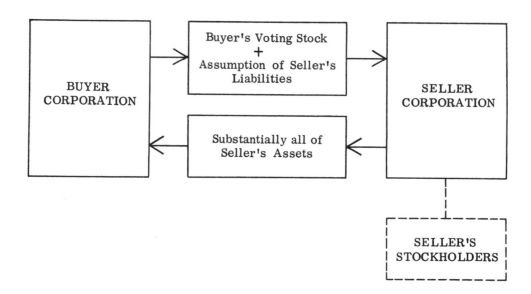

Of course, if the buyer in the above diagram gave money or other property as well as voting stock for the seller's assets, the liabilities assumed and to which the seller's property was subject would have to be treated as money to determine whether at least 80 per cent of the seller's property was bought solely for voting stock. If less than 80 per cent of the property was bought for solely voting stock, where the buyer gives money or other property in addition to voting stock, the transaction will not qualify as a tax-free, stock-for-assets reorganization.

Asset acquisition—by subsidiary. The definition of a tax-free stock-for-assets reorganization includes "the acquisition by one corporation, in exchange solely for all or a part of its voting stock (*or* in exchange solely for all or a part of *the voting stock of a corporation* which is *in control of the acquiring corporation*), of substantially all of the properties of another corporation. . . ." Under this portion of the definition, a subsidiary may acquire substantially all of the properties of the seller in exchange for voting stock of the subsidiary's parent, provided the parent controls the subsidiary within the meaning of the Code. "Control" for these purposes means the 80% stock ownership as defined above.

Effect on stockholders. Stated generally, and subject to the exceptions discussed below, stockholders who receive stock or securities in a statutory merger, stock-for-stock, or stock-for-assets tax-free reorganization neither realize taxable gain nor incur tax loss from the transaction. The law reads that "*no gain or loss* shall be recognized if stock or securities in a corporation a party to a reorganization are, in pursuance of the plan of reorganization, exchanged solely for stock or securities in such corporation or in another corporation a party to the reorganization." For our purposes the important part of the rule to remember is that "no gain or loss shall be recognized" when stock or securities are exchanged. In the usual statutory merger, stock-for-stock, or stock-for-assets transaction qualifying under a reorganization definition, the corporations involved will be parties to a reorganization, and generally the plan of reorganization will be provided in the acquisition agreement.

No gain or loss. What, then, do the words "no gain or loss shall be recognized" mean to the stockholders of a buyer or a seller exchanging stock in a tax-free reorganization? They do not mean that a tax will never be paid on gain. They do not mean that loss will never be deductible for income tax purposes. They mean that gain or loss will not be recognized from the exchange itself. But this non-recognition carries with it other tax effects which may subject gain to tax in the future or permit loss to be deducted in the future.

The basic tax effect of an exchange of stock by a stockholder of a buyer or seller in a tax-free reorganization is that the basis of the stock received "shall be the same" as the basis of the stock given up in the exchange. In other words, the cost for tax purposes of the stock received is the same as the cost for tax purposes of the stock given up in the exchange.

To illustrate this basic principle, assume a tax-free, assets transaction in which the buyer acquires all of the seller's assets in exchange for the buyer's stock, and the seller distributes one share of the buyer's stock to the seller's stockholders in exchange for each of their shares. Assume further that at the time of the exchange the buyer's stock had a fair market value of $50 per share.

Seller's stockholder A, who paid $30 a share for his 100 shares of Seller's stock—a total of $3,000 (100 shs × $30), receives 100 shares of Buyer's stock worth $5,000 (100 shs × $50). Stockholder A has no tax to pay on the $2,000 gain. But his basis (cost for tax purposes) of the $5,000 worth of buyer's stock which A receives remains the same as A's cost for the stock of Seller which he has given up in exchange, namely $3,000. If A should sell his 100 shares of buyer's stock he received for $5,000, $2,000 of gain would be recognized for tax purposes at the time of the sale. The gain arises because the $3,000 A paid for his 100 shares of the Seller carries over and becomes the cost, the tax basis, of the 100 shares of Buyer which A received in the reorganization.

On the other hand, consider the situation of Seller's stockholder B, who paid $70 a share for his 100 shares of Seller's stock—a total of $7,000 (100 shs × $70). Although he suffers a loss in the sense that he receives only $5,000 worth of buyer's stock for his seller's stock which cost him $7,000, the loss is not recognized for tax purposes. However, should B sell the buyer's shares he received and realize only $5,000, his $2,000 loss, the difference between his cost of $7,000 for his stock in the seller and the $5,000 proceeds from the sale of the buyer's stock, will be recognized for income tax purposes.

As a general observation applicable to both A and B, the holding period for tax purposes of the buyer's stock which they received in the reorganization will include the length of time they held the seller's stock at the time of the exchange. You simply add to the period the buyer's stock is held at the time of ultimate sale the length of time the seller's stock was held to the date of the reorganization exchange. If the total holding period to that time exceeds six months, A's gain or B's loss is treated as a long-term capital gain or loss for tax purposes. If held for less than six months, a short-term capital gain or loss results.

The carryover tax basis of A and B may be affected by an additional general tax rule. The tax basis of property forming the part of a decedent's estate is the fair market value of the property at the date of decedent's death or six months later. Thus, if A should die still holding Buyer's stock, the potential tax payable on the $2,000 inchoate gain resulting from the carryover of tax basis would be avoided. Since the stock has assumed a new tax basis from its inclusion in A's estate, the new tax cost will determine whether a sale of the stock after A's death will result in taxable gain or loss. For example, if the stock should have a value of $50 a share in A's estate and be sold for $50 a share soon after his death, no taxable gain would be realized. Eliminated from consideration is A's original cost of $3,000 for the Seller's stock carried over to the Buyer's stock; the $2,000 economic gain goes untaxed. B's estate, under the same circumstances as A's estate, would lose the right to deduct for tax purposes the economic loss it incurred.

Receipt of other property. The tax-free treatment of the recipient stockholders is subject to exceptions where other property or an excess amount of securities is received by the stockholder in addition to the stock which he is permitted to receive tax-free. In analyzing the treatment of stockholders who receive stock and securities in a tax-free acquisition the essential distinction between stock and securities in the tax law must be borne in mind. Stock under the tax law includes all types of stock, common—both voting and non-voting—and preferred stocks of all classes. Securities consist of debt instruments, obligations of the buyer or seller which establish a creditor relationship with the stockholder, such as debentures (including convertible debentures) or bonds.

You will recall that of the pertinent three types of tax-free reorganizations, (1) statutory mergers, (2) stock-for-stock, and (3) stock-for-assets, only the stock-for-stock transaction limited the buyer to the use of solely voting stock. On the other hand, in both statutory mergers and asset transactions other types of stock or securities as well as other property or cash may be used to pay a portion of the price, and the transaction may retain its fundamental characteristic as a tax-free reorganization. How, then, will receipt of securities or other property in addition to stock affect a stockholder of a corporation sold in an otherwise tax-free transaction? Let us consider each of the pertinent three types of reorganizations.

Amount of gain. Where a stockholder receives other property or money in addition to stock or securities which may be received tax-free in an otherwise tax-free transaction—gain, if any, is recognized to the stockholder but not in excess of the money plus the fair market value of the other property. Where securities (debt obligations) of the buyer are received, the securities are treated as other property unless an equal or greater amount of securities is given in exchange by the stockholder. To the extent that the principal amount of securities received exceeds the principal amount of securities surrendered, gain will be recognized but not in excess of the fair market value of the excess principal amount of securities.

To illustrate these general principles whereby a portion of a distribution results in recognized gain to stockholders in an otherwise tax-free acquisition, consider first a statutory merger and second a stock-for-assets transaction. Assume that the surviving corporation in a merger, i.e.—the buyer, distributes one share of its common stock, one share of preferred stock, one $10 debenture, and $10 in cash in exchange for each share of common stock of the merged company, i.e.—the seller. The table below illustrates the package received by the selling stockholder, together with assumed fair market values, in exchange for the one share of seller's stock:

STOCKHOLDER RECEIVES

Item	Fair Market Value
1. One Share Buyer's Common	$150
2. One Share Buyer's Preferred	10
3. One $10 Debenture	10
4. $10 in Cash	10
Total fair market value received	$180

If we assume that the selling stockholder paid $100 for the share of seller's stock which he gives up in the exchange, he will have realized an economic gain of $80 in the exchange ($180 received in exchange for $100 cost). But for income tax purposes only $20 of the gain is recognized. In this "tax-free" statutory merger, gain is recognized but not in excess of the fair market value of the excess amount of securities received (the $10 value of the $10 debenture) plus the $10 in cash.

If the selling stockholder should receive the same package as the result of a stock-for-assets transaction which qualifies as a "tax-free" reorganization, rather than a statutory merger, the income tax effect would be the same.

In connection with the receipt of property or money by a stockholder in addition to stock in an otherwise tax-free transaction, the tax law provides that no loss will be recognized for tax purposes. Although the receipt of property or money other than permissible stock or securities may subject a taxpayer to a taxable capital gain, receipt of the same property or money by the stockholder cannot result in a loss, deductible for income tax purposes. In other words receipt of property other than stock in a tax-free merger or assets transaction may result in taxable gain but not in deductible loss.

Finally, the law also provides that where the receipt of property or money results in recognized gain, the gain may be taxed as a dividend rather than a capital gain if the exchange "has the effect of a distribution of a dividend." Whether an exchange has the effect of a distribution of a dividend is often difficult to determine, but where the receipt of property or money in a "tax-free" exchange results in recognized gain, the parties should be aware that the gain may be taxed as a dividend and should investigate this possibility.

Effect on corporations. The general tax effect of a tax-free reorganization on a corporation is that no gain or loss will be recognized to the corporation from the exchange of property for stock or securities of the other corporate party to the reorganization. This additional rule for tax-free exchange of property is necessary to provide for the tax-free exchange of properties in exchange for stock in an assets transaction. As in the case of a stockholder receiving other property or money, tax gain but not tax loss, will be recognized to a corporation which receives such property or money and does not distribute it to its shareholders as part of the "tax-free" reorganization.

When a corporation receives other property or money in addition to stock or securities which may be received tax-free in an otherwise tax-free transaction, the corporation cannot deduct a loss incurred in the transaction. In this respect a corporation is placed in the same position as a stockholder. In each case, whether a corporation or a stockholder, when you receive other property or money in an otherwise tax-free transaction, gain may be recognized and taxed but loss will not be recognized and may not be deducted.

Another basic concept of the tax law is that the tax basis of the property transferred in a tax-free reorganization is the same in the hands of the transferee as it was in the hands of the transferor. In other words, where the buyer receives assets in a tax-free reorganization (in either a statutory merger or an assets transaction), the tax cost of the assets to the buyer remains the same as the depreciated tax cost of the assets to the seller, regardless of the value of the stock which the buyer may have given for the assets. This carryover of basis is often an important consideration in deciding whether the buyer should acquire assets in a tax-free or taxable transaction. In times of inflation and accelerated tax depreciation the fair market value of assets will often far exceed depreciated tax cost. For example, assume that a seller's depreciable assets have a fair market value of $1,000,000, but a depreciated tax basis of only

$500,000. If a buyer acquires the assets for $1,000,000 worth of stock in a tax-free acquisition, the tax cost of the assets to the buyer will remain its depreciated tax basis in the hands of the seller, i.e., $500,000. Assuming a 10-year life of the assets and straight-line depreciation, the buyer may deduct only $50,000 per annum in depreciation of the assets for tax purposes. On the other hand, assume the same asset values and depreciated tax basis; but the buyer acquires the assets for $1,000,000 in cash—a taxable transaction. Under these circumstances the $500,000 depreciated tax basis of the seller's assets does not carry over, but rather the tax basis to the buyer becomes the cost of the assets, $1,000,000. Now, if the buyer depreciates the assets on a straight-line basis over a 10-year period, it may take an annual $100,000 depreciation deduction for income tax purposes. At a 48 per cent corporate tax rate the $50,000 increase in depreciation deduction means a tax saving of $24,000 per year as a result of a taxable transaction rather than a tax-free transaction.

Non-statutory problems in tax-free acquisitions. The foregoing discussion of tax-free reorganizations was limited to the basic statutory provisions with little consideration of court-imposed refinements or more detailed problems which may arise. Some of these are considered in outline fashion in this section:

1. *Business purpose.* To be treated as a tax-free reorganization, courts have held that an acquisition must not only meet the statutory requirements discussed above, but must in addition meet a court-imposed test that it have a "business purpose." Acquisitions involving publicly held companies engaged in the active conduct of businesses will have no difficulty in meeting the business purpose test, but an acquisition and transfer solely for the purpose of distributing marketable securities to shareholders may not meet the "business purpose" test and may be taxable.

2. *Step transaction.* The Internal Revenue Service and the courts have applied a "step transaction" doctrine to determine whether an acquisition in the form of a reorganization which meets the technical statutory requirements is actually tax-free. For example, if a buyer wishes to acquire a division of a seller which forms only a small part of the seller's assets, the buyer could not directly acquire this division from the seller for solely voting stock in a tax-free reorganization because the buyer would not be acquiring "substantially all of the properties" of the seller as the Internal Revenue Code requires. If the seller organizes a subsidiary and transfers to it all the assets and business of the division (which the seller can do tax-free) and the buyer acquires all of the assets and business of the subsidiary for solely voting stock, the technical requirement of the law is met, since the buyer acquired not only "substantially all of the properties" of the seller (the subsidiary corporation) but all of these properties. However, the courts would, in all likelihood, tie the separate steps of the transaction together and hold that the net effect of the two steps was the acquisition by the buyer of a small portion of the properties of the seller, and thus hold the transaction to be taxable.

3. *Continuity of interest.* In addition, although the technical definition of a reorganization is met, an acquisition may still be taxable, where a so-called "continuity of interest" does not exist. Under this court-imposed concept the former stockholders of the seller must have an equity interest in the buyer after the acquisition. Obviously, if the selling stockholders received only bonds in exchange for their stock, they would become creditors, their equity interest would terminate and the transaction would be taxable.

CHAPTER 11

Tax Considerations—Additional
Tax Problems in Acquisitions

Chapter 10 explored the general tax objectives of the buyer and seller and indicated how these objectives could differ and conflict with one another. In addition, that chapter discussed the basic general tax problem involved in acquisitions—whether a particular acquisition is "tax-free" or taxable.

This chapter discusses some additional tax problems which may arise in acquisitions. The problems discussed arise with some frequency in the course of consummating acquisitions, and are considered in sufficient detail not only to present the problems but to offer solutions in the more usual situations, but discussion of the tax concepts is limited to the extent they may effect acquisitions without consideration of non-acquisition circumstances. No attempt is made, moreover, to present detailed explanations of the problem areas, and, therefore, in any situation involving unusual facts or circumstances, there is no substitute for careful thought and research into existing qualifications, exceptions and refinements to the general tax principles described.

Of the eleven general tax problems discussed in this chapter, the first six—Installment Sales, Imputed Interest, Section 337 Liquidations, Preferred Section 306 Stock, Foreign Corporations, and Collapsible Corporations—are primarily the concern of the seller; the next three problems—Net Operating Loss Carryovers, Buying Stock to Acquire Assets, and Interest on Acquisition Indebtedness—are primarily the concern of the buyer; and the final two problems—Depreciation and Investment Credit Recapture, and Dissenting Stockholders—are to a large extent the concern of both the buyer and seller.

As a practical matter, all tax problems and considerations, although theoretically the primary concern of one party, are often the concern of both the buyer and seller where one party refuses to proceed unless a satisfactory solution may be found to a particular burdensome tax problem.

193

INSTALLMENT SALES

In a proposed acquisition where the price is not to be paid in stock, a buyer may not be in a position to pay the entire purchase price in cash. To close a transaction, the seller may be required to accept a substantial portion of the purchase price in the form of promissory notes or other debt securities of the buyer. Under these circumstances, if the transaction is taxable, the seller may not realize sufficient cash to be willing to pay the entire income taxes owed as a result of the acquisition in one year. The solution is to cast the transaction in such a form that not all of the income taxes are payable for the year in which the transaction is closed. If the transaction is cast to qualify for installment sale treatment under the Internal Revenue Code, income taxes will be payable by the seller only as the proceeds of sale are actually realized in cash, i.e., as the evidences of indebtedness delivered by the buyer mature and are paid off. The seller will, therefore, have sufficient cash to pay taxes as the taxes fall due.

Installment sale—requirements. Under Section 453 of the Internal Revenue Code, to the extent applicable to acquisitions, for gain to be taxed under the installment method, the income must be realized from (1) a sale or other disposition of real property, or (2) a casual sale or other casual disposition of personal property (other than property of a kind which would properly be included in the inventory of the taxpayer if on hand at the close of the taxable year) for a price exceeding $1,000, and (3) in the taxable year of sale, the payments received by the seller (exclusive of evidence of indebtedness of the buyer) do not exceed 30% of the selling price.

Under the foregoing requirements, if a seller sells stock of a corporation for a consideration of $10,000 and if the consideration received consists of $3,000 in cash and $7,000 in evidences of indebtedness in the form of notes of the buyer, payable over a 7-year period, the transaction will qualify for installment sales treatment. As discussed below, the notes must qualify as evidences of indebtedness for the sale to be treated as an installment sale, and if the notes do not qualify, installment sales treatment will be denied in the transaction.

Installment sale—tax treatment. If a transaction qualifies as an installment sale under the Code, the seller may elect to report as gain or income in any taxable year only a portion of the installment payments actually received in that year. The taxable portion of the installment payments received in any particular taxable year is that portion of those payments which the gross profit, (the profit which will be realized when all payments are completed) bears to the total contract price of the acquisition. To illustrate, assume that selling stockholders sell 100% of the stock of the seller to a buyer in an acquisition that qualifies under the installment sales provisions, in accordance with the terms indicated in the following tabulation:

(1) Total contract price. $100,000

(2) Tax cost of selling stockholder's stock. . . . . $ 90,000

(3) Gross profit. . . . . $ 10,000

(4) Payment in year of closing. . . . . $ 30,000, cash

(5) Notes payable in years subsequent to closing $10,000 per taxable year in each of the 7 succeeding taxable years after the closing. . . . . $ 70,000

Under the foregoing example, the seller will receive a gross profit of $10,000 when all payments are completed. This gross profit represents 10% of the total contract price ($10,000 gross profit divided by $100,000 total contract price). Therefore, the seller must report 10% of the actual installment payment received in the taxable year in which the transaction closed as taxable gain, i.e., $3,000 (10% of the total installment payment of $30,000). In each of the subsequent seven years following the year of the closing, the seller will receive $10,000 of which 10% will represent the portion of the payment subject to tax. Therefore, in each of the seven subsequent taxable years after the taxable year in which the transaction is closed, the sellers will be required to report 10% of each $10,000 installment payment, i.e., $1,000 as taxable gain for income tax purposes.

Evidences of indebtedness—exceptions. As mentioned above, in determining whether the payments received in the taxable year of the sale do not exceed 30% of the selling price, evidences of indebtedness of the buyer received by the seller are excluded. Instruments on which the buyer is the payor providing for payments still to be made under an acquisition contract, including bonds, notes, and debentures qualify as evidences of indebtedness, with certain exceptions. Such evidences of indebtedness do not include bonds or other evidences of indebtedness which are payable on demand or which are issued by a corporation: (1) with interest coupons attached or in registered form (other than debt instruments in registered form which the taxpayer establishes will not be readily tradable in an established securities market), or (2) such bonds or other evidences of indebtedness in any form designed to render them readily tradable in an established securities market.

The provision of the code denying treatment of readily tradable securities as evidences of indebtedness under the installment sales provisions of the Code, were added to the Code in 1969 and became effective as of May 27, 1969. Prior to that time, an acquisition made by a buyer in exchange for solely debentures for which there was a ready market could qualify under the installment sales provisions, and in effect, give the seller tax-free treatment upon receipt of a readily tradable debt security.

IMPUTED INTEREST

Code Section 483 treats as taxable interest a portion of each deferred payment to which the section applies, received under a contract for a sale of property which does not provide for the payment of interest, or does not provide for the payment of sufficient interest under the Code. The effect of Section 483 is to convert some portion of each payment which could be a capital gain into ordinary income.

Payments to which Section 483 applies. The section applies to any payment on account of the sale of property which constitutes a part of the sales price and which is due more than six months after the date of the sale or exchange under a contract where (1) some or all of the payments under the contract are due more than one year after the date of the sale and (2) using a rate of 4% of simple interest provided by regulations, there is "total unstated interest."

Unstated interest—calculation. For the purposes of Section 483, the term "total unstated interest" with respect to a contract of sale, means an amount equal to the excess of (1) the sum of the payments to which Section 483 applies which are due under the contract over (2) the sum of the present values of such payments plus the present values of any interest payments under the contract. Present values are determined as of the date of the sale by discounting the deferred payments at the rate prescribed under tables contained in Regulation Section 1.483–1(g). The test interest rate used by the Internal Revenue Service in the regulations to determine whether an element of unstated interest is included in deferred payments is a 4% annual simple interest rate.

Imputed interest—some examples. Three examples taken from the regulations illustrate the operation of the imputed interest sections of the Code:

Example (1). On December 31, 1963, A sells property to B under a contract which provides that B is to make payments at the end of each of the next three years of $2,000 principal, plus 5 per cent per annum simple interest. Since the interest rate specified in the contract with respect to each payment is higher than the test rate (4 per cent per annum simple interest), it is not necessary to compute whether there is total unstated interest under subparagraph (1) of this paragraph, and Section 483 does not apply to any payments due under the contract.

Example (2). The facts are the same as in example (1), except that the interest rate provided in the contract is 2 per cent per annum simple interest. Since the interest rate specified in the contract is less than the test rate (4 per cent per annum simple interest), Section 483 applies to each of the payments of sales price due under the contract.

Example (3). On December 31, 1963, A sells property to B under a contract which provides that B is to make payments of $2,040 ($2,000 sales price plus $40 interest, $2,080 ($2,000 sales price plus $80 interest), and $2,120 ($2,000 sales price plus $120 interest), such payments being due, respectively, 1, 2 and 3 years from the date of sale. The determination of whether there is total unstated interest under the contract is made in the following manner:

(i) Sum of payment to which Section 483 applies. $6,000.00

(ii) Sum of:

Present value of $2,040 due 1 year from date of sale ($2,040 × .96154 (factor for 9 to 15 mos., col. (a), Table I)). $1,961.54

Present value of $2,080 due 2 years from date of sale ($2,080 × .92593 (factor for 21 to 27 mos., col. (a), Table I)). 1,925.93

Present value of $2,120 due 3 years from date of sale ($2,120 × .89286 (factor for 33 to 39 mos., col. (a), Table I)). 1,892.86 $5,780.33

Since the sum of the payments to which Section 483 applies ($6,000) exceeds the sum of the present values of such payments and the present values of the stated interest payments ($5,780.33), there is total unstated interest under the contract and the provisions of Section 483 apply to the payments of sales price due under the contract.

In the foregoing example, the computations of the present values of the payments and interest due under the contract were made in accordance with the tables set forth in Regulation Section 1.483–1(g), mentioned above.

TAXABLE SALE OF ASSETS—SECTION 337

Prior to the enactment of Section 337 of the Internal Revenue Code, a sale by a corporation of its assets and subsequent liquidation of the proceeds of the sale to its stockholders could result in two taxes. First, a tax on the corporation upon the sale by the corporation of its assets. Second, a tax on the stockholders upon the liquidation of the corporation and the receipt by its stockholders of the remaining sale proceeds. Under Section 337, if a corporation sells its assets in a taxable transaction and complies with the provisions of the section, double taxation may be avoided since no gain or loss is recognized to the corporation. (As noted below, the seller may be liable, however, for taxes resulting from depreciation recapture or investment credit reductions.)

Section 337—requirements. Section 337 provides that if a corporation adopts a plan of complete liquidation and distributes all of its assets within 12 months after the plan is adopted, then no gain or loss is recognized to the corporation from the sale of its property within the 12-month period. In other words, a seller selling its assets in a taxable transaction where it knows gain will be recognized may adopt a plan of liquidation and sell the assets and distribute the proceeds within 12 months and not be subject to a tax on the realized gain.

Section 337—inventory. Inventory may also be sold under a Section 337 liquidation without the recognition of gain or loss to the seller. However, to qualify, substantially all of the seller's inventory attributable to a trade or business of the seller must be sold to one person in one transaction. Therefore, if a seller sells one-half of its inventory to one buyer and the other half to a different buyer, gain on the sale will be taxed to the seller—presumably as ordinary income.

Section 337—recognition of loss. Where a seller is selling assets at a loss and would like the loss recognized for tax purposes, it should avoid the application of Section 337. Avoiding the application of the section is not always a simple matter. For example, the mere failure to adopt a plan of liquidation may not necessarily avoid the application of the section. In spite of the lack of a plan, the courts may imply the adoption of a plan even where none has been formally adopted. If Section 337 is to be avoided, a seller should not only fail to adopt a plan of liquidation, but for added safety, if circumstances permit, should also not liquidate completely until after 12 months from the date of sale.

Section 337—depreciation and investment credit recapture. Although no gain is recognized to a seller where a taxable transaction complies with Section 337, the seller must nevertheless pay the tax resulting from any recapture of depreciation or investment credit decrease for prior years. The recapture provisions are discussed in greater detail toward the end of this chapter as a tax problem affecting both the buyer and seller.

Two examples taken from the Regulations illustrate the operation of Section 337:

Example (1): Corporation A operates a grocery store at one location and a hardware store at another. Neither store handles items similar to those handled by the other. Both stores are served by a common warehouse. Pursuant to a plan of liquidation adopted by the corporation, the grocery store and all of its inventory, including that part of its inventory held in the warehouse, are sold to one person in one transaction. Thereafter, and within 12 months after the adoption of the plan of liquidation, all of the assets of the corporation are distributed to the shareholders. No gain or loss will be recognized upon the sale of all of the assets attributable to the grocery business, including the inventory items.

Example (2): Corporation B operates two department stores, one in the downtown business district and the other in a suburban shopping center. Both handle the same items and are served by a common warehouse which contains an amount of inventory items equal to the total of that in both stores. The part of the inventory in the warehouse which is attributable to each store cannot be clearly determined. Pursuant to a plan of liquidation adopted by the corporation, the assets of the suburban store, including the inventory held in such store, but not including any portion of the inventory held in the warehouse, are sold to one person in one transaction. Thereafter, and within 12 months after the adoption of the plan of liquidation, all of the assets of the corporation are distributed to the shareholders. No gain or loss will be recognized with respect to the sale of the property other than the inventory, but gain or loss will be recognized upon the sale of the inventory.

PREFERRED STOCK—SECTION 306 STOCK

Section 306 of the Code was enacted to prevent the so-called "preferred stock bail out." It was aimed at a situation where common stockholders of a corporation received preferred stock as a dividend on a tax-free basis. Subsequently, the preferred stock could be sold and the gain realized from the sale could be reported as capital gain. In effect, prior to Section 306, stockholders of a corporation could convert what would normally have been ordinary dividend income into capital gain through the device of the issuance of preferred stock dividends. Although the section was enacted to prohibit the use of the preferred stock dividend as a tax avoidance device, the application of the section is much more far-reaching. It may come into play in any tax-free acquisition in which preferred stock forms a part of the consideration paid to the seller by the buyer.

Section 306 stock—definition. For the purposes of considering tax problems involved in acquisitions, one definition of Section 306 stock is particularly applicable. Section 306 stock is stock received by a stockholder of a seller in pursuance of a plan of reorganization within the meaning of Section 368(a) of the Code, which is not common stock, but only to the extent that the effect of the transaction was substantially the same as the receipt of a stock dividend.

Under the above definition, Section 306 stock must be other than common stock. Therefore, the previsions of Section 306 will come into play in an acquisition only if preferred stock is utilized by the buyer to pay a portion of the price to the seller, or the seller's stockholders. Furthermore, the preferred stock must be received in connection with a tax-free reorganization within the meaning of Section 368(a) of the Internal Revenue Code, i.e., a tax-free statutory merger, stock-for-stock acquisition, or stock-for-assets acquisition described in Chapter 10. Finally, the effect of the receipt of such stock upon the seller's stockholders must be substantially the same as the receipt of a stock dividend.

Substantially the same as stock dividend. In some situations, the determination of whether or not the receipt of preferred stock is substantially the same as the receipt of a stock dividend, is simple. For example, if a seller' stockholders receive 95% of the consideration for the sale of their business in the form of a buyer's common stock and 5% in the form of a buyer's preferred stock, the receipt of the preferred stock would be "substantially the same as the receipt of a stock dividend," and the preferred stock would be Section 306 stock. On the other hand, where 100% of the consideration received by a seller's stockholders consists of preferred stock of a buyer, the receipt of the preferred stock would not be "substantially the same as the receipt of a stock dividend," and the preferred stock would not constitute Section 306 stock.

The regulations contain the following examples:

Example (1). Corporation A, having only common stock outstanding, is merged in a statutory merger (qualifying as a reorganization under Section 368(a)) with Corporation B. Pursuant to such merger, the shareholders of Corporation A received both common and preferred stock in Corporation B. The preferred stock received by such shareholders is Section 306 stock.

Example (2). X and Y each own one-half of the 2,000 outstanding shares of preferred stock and one-half of the 2,000 outstanding shares of common stock of Corporation C. Pursuant to a reorganization within the meaning of Section 368(a)(1)(E) (recapitalization) each shareholder exchanges his preferred stock for preferred stock of a new issue which is not substantially different from the preferred stock previously held. Unless the preferred stock exchanged was itself Section 306 stock, the preferred stock received is not Section 306 stock.

Sale of Section 306 stock—tax effect. Where a stockholder disposes of Section 306 stock the tax effect upon the stockholder may be the realization of ordinary income. If the Section 306 stock is sold, a portion or all of the proceeds of sale may be treated as if realized from the sale of a non-capital asset. If the issuing corporation redeems the Section 306 stock, a portion or all of the proceeds of redemption may be treated as if the stockholder has received a dividend.

Some exceptions to ordinary income tax treatment. The ordinary income tax treatment will not be applicable to a redemption of Section 306 stock which is a complete redemption of all of the stock of the corporation owned by the stockholder. Also such treatment does not apply to a disposition of Section 306 stock where (1) the disposition results in the termination of a stockholder's interest, (2) the disposition is in connection with a liquidation of the issuing corporation, (3) the disposition is one involved in a transaction in which no gain or loss is recognized to a stockholder with regard to the disposition of the Section 306 stock, and (4) if it is established to the satisfaction of the Internal Revenue Service that the distribution and the disposition or redemption of the Section 306 stock was not in pursuance of a plan having as one of its principal purposes the avoidance of federal income tax.

Section 306 stock—seller's approach. Because of the far-reaching effect of the Section 306 provisions, in any acquisition in which a seller's stockholders are to receive preferred stock, they should carefully investigate the question whether the preferred stock will be Section 306 stock, and if circumstances are appropriate, should apply for a tax ruling to the effect that disposition of the Section 306 stock will not result in ordinary income.

FOREIGN CORPORATIONS

Under Code Section 367, in the case of any exchange of securities in connection with a tax-free reorganization, a foreign corporation (one organized outside of the United States) is not considered as a corporation unless, before such exchange, it is established to the satisfaction of the Commissioner of Internal Revenue that the exchange is not in pursuance of a plan having as one of its principal purposes the avoidance of federal income taxes. Where a foreign corporation is involved in a reorganization, this section of the Code eliminates the tax-free treatment of exchanges of securities in connection with otherwise tax-free reorganizations, unless *prior to the exchange* a ruling is obtained from the Commissioner of Internal Revenue. Guidelines have been published by the Internal Revenue Service which set forth the circumstances and the extent to which favorable rulings will be granted under this section.

The guidelines indicate that a favorable ruling will, generally speaking, only be granted where in one manner or another taxes will be collected by the United States to the fullest extent possible in connection with the transaction. For example, if the assets of a domestic corporation are being acquired by a foreign corporation, a favorable ruling will normally be granted only if the domestic corporation agrees to include in its income any unrealized appreciation attributable to certain types of assets such as inventory, copyrights, accounts receivable, installment obligations, investment securities, etc. Furthermore, where a domestic corporation is acquiring the assets of a foreign corporation, a favorable ruling will be granted only if United States shareholders of the foreign corporation agree to report as ordinary income, upon the receipt of stock of the domestic corporation, an amount to reflect such shareholders' portion of the accumulated earnings of the foreign corporation.

COLLAPSIBLE CORPORATION—SECTION 341

Under Section 341 of the Internal Revenue Code a stockholder of a seller may find that gain from the sale of his stock will result in ordinary income instead of capital gain. If what the stockholder is selling is stock in a "collapsible corporation" (as that term is defined in the Code), a seller, in a taxable transaction, will realize ordinary income instead of capital gain. Speaking generally, the Code defines a "collapsible corporation" as a corporation formed or availed of principally for:

(1) the manufacture, construction, or production of property, or

(2) the purchase of inventory, unrealized receivables or similar assets, or

(3) the holding of stock in a corporation formed or availed of for such purposes,

with a view to the sale or exchange of the stock of the corporation, or the distribution of the corporation's assets to its stockholders *before* the corporation has realized a substantial part of the income from such manufacture, construction, production, or purchase of property.

To appreciate the underlying purpose of the collapsible corporation provision, consider a method of converting ordinary income to capital gain utilized in the film industry a number of years ago. Under this tax plan, a corporation would be formed to produce a film. After the film was produced and before any income was realized by the corporation from the film, the corporation was liquidated and its stockholders received the rights to any income to which the corporation would be entitled from film royalties. Since the stockholders received the film royalties as liquidating dividends they were subject to a maximum tax of 25 per cent under the capital gains tax rates. On the other hand, if the corporation had been permitted to receive the film royalties, the royalties would have been taxed an initial rate of 52 per cent on the corporation, and an additional tax would have been due from the stockholders upon distribution of the income from the corporation or upon liquidation of the corporation.

The collapsible corporation section of the Code may be broader in its ultimate application than may have been intended by the original draftsmen. The section is complicated with detailed presumptions as to when a corporation is a collapsible corporation as well as limitations and exceptions to the operation of its provisions. Where in a stock transaction, the prospective seller has substantial unrealized income, a review of Section 341 may be in order to determine its applicability.

NET OPERATING LOSS CARRYOVERS

Under Code Section 381, in a tax-free statutory merger or acquisition of assets, 22 specific statutory items involving tax determinations on future returns are carried over from the seller to the buyer. Of these 22 items, the one that has probably the most significance in acquisitions is the net operating loss carryover. Under Section 381, where a seller has a net operating loss, the loss carries over to a buyer who acquires the assets of the seller in a tax-free transaction. Generally, the type of transaction which will qualify for the carryover of a seller's net operating loss, will be a tax-free asset transaction under Section 368(a)(1)(C) or a tax-free statutory merger under Section 368(a)(1)(A).

Reduction in loss carryover. Although a net operating loss may be carried over from a seller to a buyer in a tax-free asset transaction, the amount of the loss which the buyer may utilize in the future may not equal the seller's total net operating loss. Under Code Section 382(b), the net operating loss of the seller which is carried over to the buyer, must be reduced if the stockholders of the seller (immediately before the sale) as a result of their prior ownership of seller's stock, own less than 20% of the fair market value of the outstanding stock of the buyer (immediately after the sale). The percentage of reduction in the net operating loss of the seller may be determined by subtracting from 100% 5 times the percentage of the fair market value of the outstanding stock of the buyer owner by the seller's stockholders (as a result of previously owning stock of the seller) immediately after the acquisition.

The regulations illustrate the operation of this reduction in the amount of net operating loss which may be carried over from a seller to a buyer:

Amount of reduction. (1) The amount of the reduction provided in Section 382(b)(1) shall be determined as follows:

(i) Determine the percentage of the fair market value of the outstanding stock of the acquiring corporation owned, immediately after the reorganization, by the stockholders (immediately before the reorganization) of the loss corporation, which is attributable to their ownership of stock in the loss corporation immediately before the reorganization.

(ii) If the percentage determined under subdivision (i) of this subparagraph is less than 20 per cent, compute the difference between such percentage and 20 per cent, and multiply such difference by five. The resulting product is the percentage by which the net operating loss carryovers are reduced.

(2) Subparagraph (1) of this paragraph may be illustrated by the following example:

Example. Assume that X Corporation acquires the assets of Y Corporation, a loss corporation, in a reorganization described in Section 381(a)(2), and that immediately after the reorganization the former stockholders of Y Corporation, as the result of owning stock of Y Corporation, own 8 per cent of the fair market value of X Corporation's outstanding stock. The difference between 8 per cent and 20 per cent is 12 per cent, which when multiplied by five produced 60 per cent. Therefore, the amount of the reduction is equal to 60 per cent of the net operating loss carryovers from the loss corporation, so that if the net operating loss carryovers from Y Corporation amounted to $100,000, the amount of the reduction would be $60,000.

The foregoing rules apply to net operating loss carryover problems in tax-free acquisitions of assets. In the normal tax-free acquisition of stock, namely a stock-for-stock tax-free acquisition pursuant to Section 368(a)(1)(B) of the Code (described in Chapter 10), the seller retains its corporate entity and its corporate tax attributes. Under these circumstances, if a seller has a net operating loss, the seller may normally continue to utilize this net operating loss against the seller's own future earnings.

Although the rules mentioned above normally apply to tax-free acquisitions, in any type of acquisition, including such tax-free acquisitions, *if the principal purpose* of the acquisition *is to obtain* the benefit of *the tax loss carryover*, the use of the carryover by the buyer may be denied. Section 269, discussed below, elaborates further on this concept.

Taxable acquisitions—net operating loss carryovers. In a taxable *asset* transaction, any net operating loss which the seller may have, remains with the seller and may be taken into account by the seller in determining the ultimate tax effects of the sale of assets to the buyer. No portion of a seller's net operating loss carries over to the buyer in such a taxable acquisition of assets by a buyer.

Moreover, in a taxable acquisition of the stock of a seller, the seller itself may not be able to continue to utilize its net operating loss against its own future earnings. Under Section 382(a) of the Code, where ownership, generally speaking at least 50% ownership of the stock of a seller, changes hands as a result of a taxable sale of stock, the net operating loss carryover of the seller is lost, if the seller does not continue to carry on a trade or business substantially the same as that conducted before the change in the ownership of the seller's stock. Therefore, where a buyer acquires 50% or more of the stock of a seller in a taxable transaction, and the seller has a net operating loss, the seller may carry over its net operating loss as a deduction against future earnings only if the seller continues to carry on a trade or business substantially the same as that carried on before the sale.

Net operating loss carryovers—Section 269 disallowance. Under Section 269 of the Code, in any acquisition of control of a corporation or acquisition of assets of a corporation where basis of assets carries over to the buyer (normally a tax-free merger or acquisition of assets), the carryover of a net operating loss may be denied. If the principal purpose for making such acquisition was evasion or avoidance of federal income tax by securing the benefit of such a net operating loss deduction, which the buyer would not otherwise enjoy, then such deduction may be disallowed. Under this section control is defined as ownership of stock possessing at least 50% of the total combined voting power of all classes of stock entitled to vote or at least 50% of the total value of shares of all classes of stock of the corporation.

The section applies to any acquisition of stock, taxable or tax-free, where such control is obtained. It also applies to all tax-free acquisitions of assets. Therefore, in any acquisition of control of a seller or assets of a seller, where the seller has a net operating loss, if the principal purpose of the acquisition is the evasion of avoidance of federal income tax, the deduction of the net operating loss in the future may be denied to either the seller or the buyer, as the case may be.

Even though a tax-free transaction appears to qualify for a net operating loss carryover under Section 382 described above, if the prohibition in Section 269 applies, the deduction of the net operating loss will be disallowed. The regulations set forth the following example of this principle:

Example (2). L Corporation has sustained heavy net operating losses for a number of years. In a merger under state law, P Corporation acquires all of the assets of L Corporation for the principal purpose of utilizing the net operating loss carryovers of L Corporation against the profits of P Corporation's business. As a result of the merger, the former stockholders of L Corporation own, immediately after the merger, 12 per cent of the fair market value of the outstanding stock of P Corporation. If the merger qualifies as a reorganization to which Section 381(a) applies, the entire net operating loss carryovers will be disallowed under the provisions of Section 269(a) without regard to the application of Section 382.

BUYING STOCK TO ACQUIRE ASSETS—SECTION 334(b)(2)

Where a purchase price exceeds the tax cost of assets in a seller's hands, a buyer may wish to acquire assets in a taxable transaction in order to obtain an increased tax basis for the assets. The seller may insist on selling stock. In such instances, a buyer may buy stock of a seller and still obtain an increased tax basis for the seller's assets, provided the buyer liquidates the seller in accordance with the rules contained in Section 334(b)(2) of the Code.

Generally, this section provides that the buyer may obtain a "stepped-up" tax basis provided the buyer receives the assets of the seller in a complete liquidation of the seller, pursuant to a Plan of Liquidation adopted not more than two years after the date on which the buyer acquires the seller's stock in a taxable transaction or transactions. To be applicable, Section 334(b)(2) provides that the buyer must have acquired, in taxable transactions and during a 12-month period, stock of the seller possessing at least 80 per cent of the total combined voting power and at least 80 per cent of the total number of shares of all other classes of stock.

This section of the Code is of importance because it offers a method for a buyer to obtain a stepped-up basis for a seller's assets even where a buyer is forced to buy stock. However, as indicated below, where a buyer buys stock to obtain the stepped-up tax basis, the buyer should consider the effect of the depreciation and investment credit recapture provisions of the Code, since the economic burden of the recapture falls upon the buyer at the time of liquidating of the seller.

INTEREST ON ACQUISITION INDEBTEDNESS

Under Code Section 279, no deduction is allowed for any interest paid or incurred by a corporation during a taxable year with respect to its "corporate acquisition indebtedness" to the extent that such interest exceeds a specified maximum amount. Under this rule, the maximum deduction permitted for interest paid or incurred during a taxable year with respect to "corporate acquisition indebtedness" is limited to $5,000,000. The $5,000,000 maximum allowable interest deduction must be reduced by interest paid or incurred on obligations issued after December 31, 1967, to provide consideration for the acquisition of (1) stock in another corporation or (2) assets of another corporation pursuant to a plan under which at least two-thirds in value of all of the assets used in the trades and businesses of the seller are acquired.

Corporate acquisition indebtedness—definition. The term "corporate acquisition indebtedness" means any obligation evidenced by a bond, debenture, note, or certificate or other evidence of indebtedness issued after October 9, 1969, by a corporation if such obligation is issued to provide consideration for the acquisition of (1) stock in another corporation, or (2) assets of another corporation pursuant to a plan under which at least two-thirds in value of all of the assets (excluding money) used in trades and businesses carried on by such corporation are acquired. To constitute "corporate acquisition indebtedness" the obligation must also fulfill each of the additional conditions mentioned below:

(1) *Subordination condition.* The obligation must be (a) subordinated to the claims of trade creditors of the issuing corporation generally, or (b) expressly subordinated in right of payment to the payment of any substantial amount of unsecured indebtedness of the issuing corporation.

(2) *Convertibility condition.* The bond or other evidence of indebtedness must either be (a) convertible directly or indirectly into stock of the issuing corporation, *or* (b) part of an investment unit or other arrangement which includes, in addition to such bond or other evidence of indebtedness, an option to acquire, directly or indirectly, stock of the issuing corporation.

(3) *Ratio of debt to equity or earnings condition.* As of the last day of the year in which the debt security was issued in connection with the acquisition, (a) the ratio of debt to equity of the buyer must exceed 2 to 1, *or* (b) the "projected earnings" of the buyer must not exceed 3 times the annual interest to be paid or incurred by the buyer.

Ratio of debt to equity—explanation. The ratio of the buyer's debt to the buyer's equity is determined by subtracting the buyer's total indebtedness from the aggregate net value of all of its assets to determine the amount of the buyer's equity. For these purposes, total indebtedness includes short-term liabilities such as notes and accounts payable, and the aggregate net value of all of the assets includes cash and the value of all other property equal to the adjusted basis of such property for tax purposes. The debt is compared to equity, and if the debt is more than twice the equity, the test is met.

To illustrate the computation of the foregoing ratio, assume that on January 1, 1971, buyer issued debentures to purchase all of the stock of the seller. On December 31, 1971, buyer had total assets of $200,000,000 and total indebtedness of $150,000,000. Buyer's equity is $50,000,000 ($200,000,000 assets less $150,000,000 indebtedness). Its ratio of debt to equity is therefore 3 to 1 ($150,000,000 indebtedness compared to $50,000,000 equity). Since the ratio exceeds the statutory 2 to 1 limit, the debentures issued to purchase the seller meet the statutory ratio of debt to equity test.

Earnings test—explained. Under the earnings test, the "projected earnings" of the buyer are compared with the "annual interest to be paid or accrued" on the buyer's total outstanding indebtedness. If the projected earnings do not exceed 3 times the annual interest cost, the earnings test is considered as having been met. Projected earnings for these purposes mean the "average annual earnings" for the three-year period ending on the last day of the year for which the determination is being made. For the purposes of the Code the buyer's earnings are computed without reduction for (1) any interest paid or incurred, (2) any depreciation or amortization deductions, (3) any federal tax liability, and (4) any dividends paid (dividends paid by the seller to the buyer are not included in the buyer's earnings and profits). The buyer's annual interest cost is the buyer's interest paid or accrued on its total outstanding indebtedness.

If a buyer which issues "corporate acquisition indebtedness" does not meet either the ratio of debt to equity test or the projected earnings test for each of 3 consecutive taxable years after issuing such corporate acquisition indebtedness, the interest deduction limit imposed on such obligations terminates, beginning with the first taxable year after the end of the three consecutive taxable years.

Section 279 of the Code contains many special rules in its treatment of acquisition indebtedness applicable to many different circumstances. Therefore, in any situation in which it appears that the section may apply to indebtedness incurred in making an acquisition, the buyer should carefully review the applicability of its detailed provisions to the proposed acquisition.

DISSENTING STOCKHOLDERS

Dissenting stockholders may cause peripheral tax problems. As discussed in Chapters 7 and 10, where a buyer acquires assets of a seller, in many jurisdictions, the seller's stockholders have a right to dissent to the transaction. By dissenting, the seller's stockholders may receive cash for their stockholdings. The receipt of such cash by the dissenting stockholders may cause tax problems to arise, particularly in connection with tax-free acquisitions.

Substantially all of seller's assets—dissenting stockholders. Since, in many jurisdictions, successful dissenting stockholders may be required to be paid the fair value of their stock by the seller, to the extent that the seller utilizes its cash to pay dissenting stockholders, the buyer will not be acquiring the cash thus eliminated from the seller's corporate assets. You will recall that to qualify as a tax-free reorganization under Section 368(a)(1)(C) of the Code, a buyer must acquire "substantially all" of the assets of the seller. If a large percentage of the seller's stockholders dissent and are paid off in cash, the cash drain could be so substantial that the buyer would not be acquiring "substantially all" of the assets of the seller. To protect against this possibility, acquisition contracts should be drafted to limit the percentage of dissenting stockholders, and provide a condition precedent to the buyer or seller's obligation to close the transaction that the percentage not be exceeded. If the limitation on the acceptable number of dissenting stockholders provided in the acquisition contract is sufficiently small, the problem of a buyer not acquiring "substantially all" of the assets of a seller may be avoided.

Solely voting stock test—dissenting stockholders. Generally, in both a tax-free acquisition of stock by a buyer and a tax-free acquisition of assets by a buyer, the consideration which a buyer may give to a seller is limited to "solely voting stock" of the buyer. In such tax-free acquisitions, where selling stockholders become entitled to be paid off in cash because of their dissent, the cash payments may not normally be made by the buyer or the buyer will not be acquiring the seller's stock or assets for "solely voting stock." To solve this tax problem, by the terms of the acquisition contract sellers are often permitted to retain sufficient cash to pay off dissenting stockholders. As a consequence, the seller, not the buyer, makes the cash payment to the dissenting stockholders.

80% control—dissenting stockholders. In order for a stock-for-stock acquisition to qualify as a tax-free reorganization under Section 368 of the Code, the buyer must acquire control of the seller. Control is defined as ownership of at least 80% of the total combined voting power of the seller as well as 80% of all other classes of stock. If, therefore, the parties desire a tax-free transaction, and question whether more than 20% of the seller's stockholders will refuse to sell their stock to the buyer, the acquisition contract may require, as a condition precedent to closing, that the buyer acquire at least 80% of the voting stock and all other classes of stock of the seller in the acquisition. Such a condition may also be provided in the offer to acquire stock in connection with a registered exchange offer, discussed in Chapter 9, where it is the intention to complete such a takeover as a tax-free reorganization. Where the buyer is unable to acquire a sufficient number of seller's shares to qualify under the control test, the parties may attempt to recast the acquisition as either a statutory merger or a stock-for-assets acquisition, if they intend to have the acquisition treated as tax-free.

DEPRECIATION AND INVESTMENT CREDIT RECAPTURE

The tax provisions providing for depreciation and investment credit recapture have little immediate significance in tax-free acquisitions discussed in Chapter 10. In tax-free transactions, the significance of the recapture provisions may be limited to an understanding by a buyer that upon disposition of the seller's assets in the future, the recapture provisions may come into play at that time if the future disposition involves a taxable transaction. The recapture provisions of the Code, however, may assume immediate importance to a buyer and seller in negotiating the terms of a taxable transaction.

Taxable transaction—recapture problems. As previously described in the chapter, by complying with the provisions of Code Section 334 or 337, in a taxable transaction, a buyer on the one hand, or a seller or its stockholders on the other, may normally accomplish the different tax aims of a buyer or seller, as the case may be, in a taxable transaction. Where a seller insists upon selling stock, a buyer may accomplish its goal of a write-up of the tax basis of the seller's assets to the purchase price for the acquisition, by fulfilling the requirements of Code Section 334. On the other hand, if a buyer insists upon acquiring assets, a seller may avoid the imposition of a corporate income tax upon the seller, by fulfilling the requirements of Code Section 337, leaving only a capital gains tax to be paid by the stockholders of the seller at the time of liquidation of the seller. Therefore, fundamental goals of both the buyer and seller may be realized in a taxable transaction, both where a buyer buys stock and where a buyer buys assets. However, depreciation or investment credit recapture may make a substantial difference in the tax bill payable by a buyer or seller, depending upon the form of transaction, sale of stock or sale of assets, ultimately agreed upon.

Where a buyer buys the assets of a seller, the seller becomes liable for the payment of depreciation and investment credit recapture. This liability must be satisfied out of the assets of the seller before these assets are distributed to the stockholders of the seller. Therefore, in an asset transaction, the burden of the depreciation and investment credit recapture falls upon the seller and, indirectly, upon the seller's stockholders. On the other hand, where a buyer buys stock from the stockholders of the seller, the tax burden with respect to depreciation and investment credit recapture falls upon the buyer, at such time as the buyer liquidates the seller to obtain the stepped-up tax basis of the seller's assets. At the time of liquidation, the tax is payable out of the assets of the seller. Since the buyer will have paid the consideration to the stockholders of the seller for the seller's stock, the burden of payment for depreciation and investment credit recapture falls upon the buyer due to the subsequent payment of the tax from the seller's assets.

In negotiating the form of any taxable transaction, a seller should be aware that the burden of the payment of depreciation and investment credit recapture falls upon the seller where the buyer acquires the assets; on its part, the buyer should be aware that the burden of such depreciation and investment credit recapture may fall upon the buyer where the buyer acquires the stock of the seller from the seller's stockholders.

Depreciation recapture—personal property. Under Code Section 1245, the sale of personal property, "Section 1245 property," generally property of a nature subject to the allowance for depreciation provided in Section 167 or to the allowance for amortization provided in Section 185, may result in ordinary income rather than capital gain to a seller. If gain is realized, the gain will be taxed to the seller as ordinary income to the extent of depreciation or amortization deducted after December 31, 1961 (or after June 30, 1963, with respect to elevators or escalators and December 31, 1969, with respect to livestock).

For example, assume a seller bought a color printing press at a cost of $150,000 on January 1, 1960, and the life of the press for depreciation purposes is 15 years, i.e. depreciation, taken on a straight-line basis, amounts to $10,000 per year. Assume further that the seller sells the equipment on December 31, 1972. Due to the scarcity of such equipment at the time, the seller is paid its full original purchase price of $150,000 for the equipment. In determining the depreciation recapture to be taxed at ordinary income tax rates to the seller, the seller may make the following computations:

(1)	Original cost of equipment	$150,000
(2)	Depreciation deducted from January 1, 1960 to and including December 31, 1972 at $10,000 per year	130,000
(3)	Tax basis ($150,000 minus $130,000)	20,000
(4)	Amount of taxable gain ($150,000 sale price less $20,000 adjusted tax cost)	130,000
(5)	Depreciation recaptured (depreciation deducted from January 1, 1962 to and including, December 31, 1972 at $10,000 per annum)	110,000

Of the total gain of $130,000 realized in the above example, $110,000 is therefore taxable as ordinary income in accordance with the depreciation recapture provisions of Section 1245 of the Code.

The effect of Section 1245 is to "recapture" depreciation subject to the section, by including as ordinary income proceeds of sale in excess of tax basis to the extent of the Section 1245 depreciation.

Depreciation recapture—real estate. Under Section 1250 of the Code, upon sales of real estate, differing portions of prior depreciation may be recaptured, depending upon the dates after which the depreciation was deducted, the method of depreciation, and the length of time during which the real estate was owned by the seller. As in the case of personal property, real estate depreciation recapture is limited to the amount of gain realized upon a sale.

Three basic rules apply in determining the amount of the depreciation recapture upon the sale of real estate (except with respect to residential rental property):

(1) Additional depreciation (depreciation taken in excess of straight-line depreciation) taken after December 31, 1969, is recaptured to the extent of 100% of such depreciation.

(2) Additional depreciation (depreciation taken in excess of straight-line depreciation) after December 31, 1963, to and including December 31, 1969, is recaptured to the extent of the full amount, or 100%, of additional depreciation if the real estate has been held for 20 months or less. If the real estate has been held for more than 20 months, the recapture percentage decreases by 1% for each full month the property was held over 20 months. In other words, there is no recapture of additional depreciation taken for the period from December 31, 1963, to and including December 31, 1969, where the real estate has been held by the seller for more than ten years.

(3) If real estate is held by a seller for 12 months or less, regardless of the date of sale, or the method of depreciation utilized, all depreciation (not only depreciation taken in excess of straight-line depreciation) is subject to recapture.

In applying the above rules, two separate computations may be required to determine the amount of depreciation recapture upon the sale of real estate held for more than 20 months but not more than ten years:

> *Computation (1).* Calculate the additional depreciation taken after December 31, 1969. If the total of this depreciation exceeds the amount of gain realized from the sale, the maximum depreciation recapture is limited to the amount of the gain.
>
> However, if the amount of the gain exceeds the additional depreciation taken after December 31, 1969–
>
> *Computation (2).* Calculate the additional depreciation taken between January 1, 1964, and December 31, 1969, and multiply this additional depreciation by the applicable recapture percentage in accordance with basic rule (2), above. The total of Computation (1) and Computation (2) is the amount of depreciation recapture under Section 1250, *unless* the total exceeds the gain—in which event the depreciation recapture is limited to the gain.

Investment credit recapture. Under Sections 38 and 46 of the Code, a taxpayer is allowed a credit against the income tax payable equal to 7% of certain qualified investments. The credit applies to certain investments in depreciable personal property prior to April 18, 1969. Under Section 46 of the Code, the amount of the credit depends upon the useful life of the property. An increasing percentage of the basis of the property is taken into account to determine the credit, as various properties have increased useful lives, in accordance with the following formula:

If the useful life is—	The applicable percentage is—
4 years or more but less than 6 years	33 1/3
6 years or more but less than 8 years	66 2/3
8 years or more	100

Investment credit recapture comes into play where a seller sells property (for which an investment credit has been taken) prior to the expiration of the useful life originally used in determining the amount of the investment credit. In such event, the original credit is reduced and recaptured by assuming that the original life utilized to determine the credit should be ended on the date of the sale of the property.

CHAPTER 12

The Acquisition Contract

The lawyers have the responsibility of preparing the acquisition contract. All parties involved in an acquisition should (but don't always) realize that the contract is the deal. Other aspects of the transaction such as requests for rulings from governmental agencies, securities registrations, stock listings, and closing documents involve mechanical considerations and are drafted in accordance with terms dictated by the acquisition contract. Once signed, the contract fixes all the terms of the deal—the rights and obligations of the parties, one to another. Once signed, neither party can unilaterally change the terms of the acquisition. For this reason, the lawyer should know as much as possible about the concrete details of the transaction before completing the draft of the contract. After the contract is signed, sudden knowledge of circumstances which could have been provided for but weren't may be costly.

The lawyer, although responsible for the preparation of the contract, is dependent upon information supplied by both the businessman and the accountant plus, of course, such information as he is given an opportunity to develop on his own. A successful acquisition generally evolves from a coordinated effort of the businessman, the lawyer, and the accountant. Because of the numerous possible pitfalls in buying another's business, the buyer should approach the acquisition as though the entire purchase price could be sacrificed as a result of some oversight and the effort in drafting the contract should be coordinated to guard against all pitfalls from the business, accounting and legal viewpoints.

Before proceeding to a discussion of the structure and details of the acquisition contract, first consider various possibilities for binding the transaction promptly or setting forth the basic terms of agreement reached by the buyer and seller. After businessmen have reached agreement in principle, they often wish to have a memorandum of understanding as soon as possible. The lawyers for both the buyer and seller should determine whether a memorandum of understanding, letter of intent, option, or detailed acquisition contract should be the first objective of the parties, and which would be most advantageous to either the buyer or seller —and acceptable to the other party.

211

OPTIONS AND MEMORANDA OF INTENT

After the buyer and seller have agreed upon a price, one or the other or both will often wish an immediate binding agreement. They may instruct their lawyers that a binding agreement should be signed that day. Any objection on the part of the lawyers on the grounds that an acquisition agreement should provide detailed coverage of many aspects of a going business, may be met with the argument that the details should be ignored and a short form of binding agreement should be entered into, detailing the major aspects of the transaction. The parties should avoid attempting to draw such a short form agreement, unless for a clear, limited purpose understood by both parties. Any such short agreement, if properly drawn, should contain conditions that the parties will not be legally bound to each other until such time as the detailed acquisition agreement has been signed. A number of different approaches to fulfilling the wish to "bind" the transaction promptly are feasible and sometimes helpful. One binding approach is the option. Other attempts to "bind" the transaction immediately range from the option to miscellaneous memoranda or letters of intent, to oral understandings that the seller won't seek or negotiate with another buyer while the present buyer is investigating the seller's business.

The option. In general, options are more more advantageous to the buyer than the seller. From the buyer's point of view, if it has bound the seller to an option contract, the buyer knows that should it, after investigation, decide to make the acquisition within the option period, the business will be available to the buyer. The buyer does not run the risk of losing an acquisition after an expensive investigation. On the other hand, from the seller's viewpoint an option has the disadvantage of prohibiting the seller from selling to a third party while the business is under option to the buyer, and the seller may lose an opportunity to sell its business to a third party for a higher price, because the buyer's option is outstanding.

Since an option is generally disadvantageous to the seller, under what circumstances should a seller grant an option? The answer to the question lies in the relative bargaining strength of the parties. An anxious buyer may offer a substantial price for the option. On the other hand, the seller may be in a position where it is most anxious to have the particular buyer make the acquisition. Many reasons could exist for this desire, such as the buyer's eminent position in the industry, excellent research facilities, promises of continued employment and pension coverage. The buyer wishes to make as thorough an investigation of the seller's business as is practicable, before making the acquisition. When a sizable business is investigated, the investigation, including attorney's and accountant's fees and time of the buyer's executives, can be quite expensive. Consequently, the buyer may refuse to proceed with negotiations and make its detailed investigation unless it has complete assurance, through an option, that the seller's business will be available should the buyer decide to buy. Under these or similar circumstances, a seller may be placed in a position where it grants an option.

Generally, for an option to be binding, consideration should pass from the buyer to the seller. In some instances, the sole consideration for an option has been a promise on the part of the buyer to supply the seller with a copy of the report of the seller's business prepared by those conducting the investigation for the buyer. In other instances, a cash payment to the seller, which may or may not be applied against the purchase price, is negotiated in return for the option.

The option is not necessarily a means of accelerating an agreement between the buyer and seller, and the buyer and seller should not mislead themselves into thinking it is. An option should not be unconditionally binding on either party unless it contains every term and condition of the acquisition or if a detailed acquisition agreement is attached to it. Otherwise the parties may have nothing more than an agreement to agree which may cause litigation.

Option—acquisition contract attached. To bind the parties, both legally and with the least possibility of future litigation due to failure to specify terms, the option should be drafted to provide that the buyer will buy in accordance with the terms of a complete acquisition agreement attached to the option. Such an agreement should contain not only the purchase price and the assets being acquired, but also all the miscellaneous terms involved in an acquisition agreement such as lists of real estate, lists of important contracts, lists of patents, treatment of pension plans, employment contracts, bulk sales law and the other numerous detailed questions which crop up in every acquisition. As a result of the need to attach an acquisition agreement to the option, the option agreement, as a practical matter, may not be executed in any shorter time that the execution of the acquisition agreement itself. Of course, once signed, the option agreement may give the buyer greater maneuverability, depending upon the conditions the buyer was able to negotiate permitting the buyer to refuse to exercise its option.

Conditional option. The buyer and seller may agree upon an option subject to the negotiation of a detailed acquisition agreement and the approval by the board of directors of each party and their counsel. From the buyer's point of view, the buyer is free to exercise or not to exercise its option, and has the assurance that, during the option period, the seller will not sell to a third party. However, if the detailed terms of acquisition have not been agreed upon, should the seller receive a better offer from a third party, the seller may negotiate such difficult terms with the buyer that the buyer must refuse to make the acquisition. Then, after the option period the seller will be free to sell to the third party. In essence, an option without agreement as to the details of acquisition is often, as a legal and practical matter, no more binding on the parties than a verbal agreement.

Restrictive letter. Occasionally, circumstances of a proposed acquisition are such that a seller will agree not to negotiate with third parties for a fixed period of time while the buyer investigates the seller's business. Such an undertaking on the part of the seller may take the form of a letter addressed to the buyer. And the consideration for such a letter is the buyer's undertaking to investigate the seller's business in good faith. Where the buyer and seller agree to such an arrangement, the restrictive letter will usually contain few, if any, of the terms of the acquisition and may even omit reference to the purchase price or a description of the business and assets to be acquired. The restrictive letter buys time for the buyer and limits the seller's rights to negotiate with others, but neither party has any assurance that the transaction will be closed if the buyer's investigation proves satisfactory to it.

Memorandum or letter of intent. The signed or initialed memorandum or letter of intent constitutes another approach to the problem of promptly "binding" the parties after they have reached agreement in principle. Such a document, often also referred to as a memorandum of understanding, generally should outline the major terms of the acquisition, such as price, a description of the business to be acquired and the major conditions to the acquisition—such as "tax-free" ruling, "pooling of interests" accounting treatment, and non-registration of stock with the SEC. The document should contain language to the effect that it is subject to the approval of the acquisition, and of a detailed agreement, by the boards of directors and counsel of both parties. In this sense the document has no binding legal significance. Nevertheless, the memorandum or letter of intent may be helpful as a ready reference to the major terms of the acquisition during the negotiation of the detailed contract.

Oral understanding. Experience indicates that in many acquisitions of businesses, after the parties have reached agreement in principle, the details of the acquisition are negotiated and the acquisition contract is drafted, without any prior written options or other written understandings. In many cases, the investigation of the seller's business by the buyer and the preparation of a detailed acquisition contract proceed concurrently. As the investigation proceeds and problems become apparent, the acquisition agreement is tailored to reflect the understanding or compromises of the buyer and seller. Often, by the time both parties approve the acquisition contract and are ready to sign, the buyer will have substantially or fully completed its investigation of the seller's business. The acquisition contract generally will provide for a "closing"—actual transfer of legal title to the business—some time after the contract has been signed to enable the buyer to complete its investigation and to enable both parties to satisfy the conditions precedent to the closing contained in the contract. However, it is not unusual, even in sizable transactions, for the detailed acquisition agreement to be signed and the transaction closed, i.e., legal title passed, on the same day.

Conclusions. In conclusion, attempts to bind a buyer and seller fully and legally as soon as agreement in principle has been reached are impractical. Theoretically, from the buyer's viewpoint, a binding option with a completely negotiated detailed acquisition contract attached is the most satisfactory approach to an acquisition; provided, of course, the price for the option is reasonable. From a practical point of view, since the detailed acquisition contract should be attached to such an option, the buyer often will have spent a good deal of money on the investigation before the option is signed, and a major portion of the advantage of the option to the buyer is thus lost before the option is signed. If the detailed option could be signed by the buyer without incurring any prior expense, the buyer would be in a position to investigate the seller during the option period and have a fixed transaction should it decide to buy.

Conditional options, restrictive letters, and memoranda or letters of intent do not accomplish the result desired by the parties—if the parties are to be fully and legally bound. But memoranda or letters of intent which contain the major terms of the deal may be helpful as reminders to the buyer and seller of the major terms of the acquisition, as the details are negotiated. Finally, experience has shown that the parties often obtain satisfactory results by conducting the investigation, and the negotiation of the detailed acquisition contract concurrently, without any prior written agreement of any sort. After all, one basic objective of both the investigation and the negotiation is to develop an acquisition contract satisfactory to both the buyer and seller. Why not look directly toward the realization of this basic objective, without adding the complication of negotiating options which may cause additional unnecessary peripheral negotiating difficulties?

A restrictive letter—form. Printed below is a restrictive letter, substantially in the form utilized by one of the better known conglomerates. The letter is restrictive in the sense that it prohibits the selling stockholders from negotiating for the sale of their stock pending execution of a formal acquisition agreement. The letter itself indicates many areas to be negotiated in detail in the formal agreement, and the selling stockholders could probably raise a number of additional conditions to be negotiated into the restrictive letter—particularly with regard to rulings by administrative agencies, such as tax rulings, which could be of importance to the selling stockholders.

B U Y E R
3000 Main St.
New York, N.Y.

Date

Selling Stockholders

Gentlemen:

We submit for your consideration a proposal relating to the transfer of all of the shares of capital stock of   a   corporation (hereinafter called the "Company") to B U Y E R ("Buyer") or to a wholly-owned subsidiary ("Subsidiary") of Buyer as Buyer may elect. This proposal is made upon the following terms and subject to the following conditions:

1. Upon transfer of such capital stock Buyer will issue and cause to be delivered to the stockholders of the Company

It is understood that if, prior to the date of such transfer, Buyer should

(A) declare any dividend payable in shares of its Common Stock, or

(B) split or combine its shares of Common Stock

appropriate adjustment will be made in the number of shares of Common Stock issuable.

2. As soon as reasonably practicable after acceptance of this proposal and not later than   , Buyer and the stockholders of the Company who shall have signed this letter ("Stockholders") shall enter into a formal agreement. Such formal agreement may require the approval of the Board of Directors of Buyer. Pending the execution of the formal agreement, the Stockholders will not discuss or negotiate with any other corporation, firm or other person, or entertain or consider any inquiries or proposals relating to the possible disposition of their shares of capital stock of the Company and will cause the Company to conduct its business only in the ordinary course.

3. The formal agreement referred to in paragraph 2 above will, among other things:

(a) set forth certain representations and warranties of the Company and its stockholders with respect to financial statements, litigation, tax and other liabilities, sources of supplies, collectibility of all receivables, titles to properties and compliance with applicable codes, material contracts, franchises, contracts with management, patents, trademarks, trade names and copyrights, absence of undisclosed or contingent liabilities, assignability of contracts, ownership and property of subsidiaries, such other items as may bear upon the value and acceptability to Buyer of the business and assets of the Company, and such further representations or warranties of Buyer or the Company and and its stockholders as either party may reasonably request, all representations and warranties to survive the closing for a period of 24 months;

(b) restrict the Company as to the incurring of indebtedness for borrowed money, issuing of additional stock, declaring of dividends, granting of stock options, entering into employment agreements with officers or directors, granting other than normal increases in compensation, and entering into material transactions otherwise than in the ordinary course of business;

*(c) provide that the effective date of the transaction shall be not later than
          ;*

(d) provide for the receipt by Buyer from the Stockholders of an undertaking satisfactory to Buyer that at least   % of the securities received by the Stockholders will be acquired for investment and not with a view to, or for sale in connection with, any distribution thereof;

(e) provide for an escrow fund of 10% of the securities to be delivered by Buyer to secure Buyer and Subsidiary against undisclosed liabilities, misrepresentations, and breaches of warranties;

(f) provide for the termination or abandonment of the transaction at any time prior to consummation thereof:

(i) by mutual consent of the parties;

(ii) by either Buyer or the stockholders of the Company, acting unanimously, if in the opinion of such party there has been a material misrepresentation or breach of warranty on the part of the other party in the representations and warranties set forth in the formal agreement referred to above;

(iii) by either Buyer or the stockholders of the Company, acting unanimously, if the transaction shall not have been consummated by   ;

(iv) by Buyer if the consolidated net worth of the Company, to be set forth in a balance sheet as of   certified by   as to fairness of presentation and compliance with generally accepted accounting principles, applied on a basis consistent with that of the preceding year, shall, in the unqualified opinion of the certified public accountants of buyer, be less than $;

(v) by Buyer if the consolidated net income of the Company for the   months' period ended   to be set forth in a statement of income, certified by   as to fairness of presentation and compliance with generally accepted accounting principles, applied on a basis consistent with that of the preceding year, shall, in the unqualified opinion of the certified public accountants of buyer, be less than $. For the purposes of giving such opinion, the certified public accountants of Buyer will rely on the certification of

as to the inventories of the Company as of   ;

(vi) by Buyer if it shall determine in its sole discretion that the transaction has become inadvisable or impracticable by reason of the institution or threat by state, local, or federal governmental authorities or by any other person of material litigation or proceedings against either or both of the parties (it being understood and agreed that a written request by governmental authorities for information with respect to the proposed transaction, which information could be used in connection with such litigation or proceedings, may be deemed by Buyer to be a threat of material litigation or proceedings regardless of whether such request is received before or after the signing of the formal agreement referred to above):

(vii) by Buyer if arrangements satisfactory to Buyer cannot be made for the assumption by Buyer or Subsidiary, or for the prepayment without premium, of all outstanding indebtedness of the Company for borrowed money;

(viii) by Buyer if the business or assets or financial condition of the Company

and its subsidiaries taken as a whole have been materially and adversely affected, whether by reason of changes or developments or operations in the ordinary course of business or otherwise;

    (ix) by Buyer if the Company shall not have received all consents and approvals of all governmental authorities having any jurisdiction over the business of the Company, or if such authorities shall withdraw any approvals, licenses, or permits given to the Company.

    (g) contain a representation that no broker or finder has been employed by the Company or its stockholders with respect to this transaction;

    (h) contain representations by the stockholders of the Company that the stock of the Company is validly issued, fully paid and non-assessable and owned by the stockholders free and clear of any liens, claims, options, or other encumbrances;

    (i) provide as a condition to closing, that Buyer, acting through its own management personnel, its counsel, its accountants or other representatives, designated by it, shall have full opportunity to examine the books and records of the Company and its subsidiaries to determine the acceptability to it of their titles and leases to properties, their patents and the condition of their plants and equipment, and to investigate all aspects of the business of the Company and each of its subsidiaries, and all of their assets and liabilities, and Buyer shall be satisfied to proceed with this transaction upon completion of such examination and investigation;

    (j) provide as a condition to closing that Buyer shall have received favorable opinions on such legal matters in connection with the transaction as it deems pertinent;

    (k) provide as a condition to closing that Buyer shall have satisfied itself that the business has been conducted in the ordinary course and that no withdrawals have been made by any shareholder since   ;

    If the foregoing proposal is agreeable to you, and you are prepared to accept it, would you please so indicate on the copy of this letter enclosed herewith in the space provided, and return the same to the undersigned as soon as you can conveniently do so.

                              Very truly yours,

                              B U Y E R

                              By _____
                                    Title:

Accepted this   day of
       , 19   .

_____

Letter of intent—form.   Printed below is a form of letter of intent which illustrates how such a document may set forth the major terms of a proposed acquisition. Note that the detailed terms of the proposed acquisition are subject to the approval of the boards of directors of both the buyer and the seller. In this sense the letter is not binding upon either party.

BUYER
3000 Main St.
New York, N.Y.

November 30, 197__

Mr. John Smith, President
SELLER
15 Green Street
Syracuse, New York

Dear Mr. Smith:

As a result of our discussions to date and a study of the information that you have furnished to us, it appears that it would be beneficial to both parties to consider an exchange of the common stock of Buyer for all of the outstanding and optioned capital stock of Seller on a "Pooling of Interests" basis, along the following lines:

1. Buyer will reserve 85,552 shares of its common stock out of the current authorized, but not issued, common stock for the sole purpose of exchange for Seller stock, as follows:

a) For the present 10,094
   shares of Seller stock
   outstanding   *80,725 shares*

b) For seller options not
   yet exercised   *4,800 shares*

                Total Reserved   *85,552 shares*

2. At the time of the Closing of such transaction (hereinafter called the Closing), Buyer will transfer to the then stockholders of Seller eight (8) shares of Buyer common stock for each outstanding share. Seller will not issue any additional shares except those that may result from exercise of options granted under the Seller Restricted Stock Option Plan.

3. Buyer, at the Closing, shall substitute for the stock options granted under the Seller's Restricted Stock Option Plan, to the extent that such options have not been exercised prior to the Closing, options to purchase shares of Buyer common stock in lieu of shares of Seller, on a basis which will comply with Section 425(g) of the Internal Revenue Code of 1954, as amended.

4. All shares of Buyer common stock issued under any of the conditions of this Agreement will be acquired for investment only, and not with a view to distribution, and your stockholders will be required to furnish Buyer with a Letter of Investment satisfactory to counsel.

5. It is Buyer's present intention that after the Closing the Seller's Profit Sharing Retirement Plan and Bonus Plan will be continued in full force and effect.

6. This Letter of Intent is subject to the owners of 100% of the outstanding shares of Seller agreeing to the sale.

7. Mr. John Smith and Mr. Robert Roe shall continue to be employed after the Closing to manage the affairs of Seller, subject to the discretion of the Board of Directors of Buyer.

8. This Letter of Intent is submitted subject to an independent audit and investigation, at Buyer's expense, by our accountants, market survey specialists, realty appraiser, and others, of your past and forecast future operations, and thereafter final approval by our Board of Directors. You agree to make available to our auditors, analysts, and others, such records and information as are needed for their independent investigation.

9. It is understood that this transaction was brought about by William W. Williams, and that no other agent or broker was authorized or instrumental in, or for, the negotiations of the transaction contemplated herein, and that Buyer will be solely responsible for any commissions due William W. Williams at the time of the Closing.

10. It is our understanding that you will warrant the Balance Sheet and the P&L Statement for the 9-month period ending September 30, 197_, and that you will further warrant that the business of Seller has been operated only in the ordinary course of business since that time, and that no dividends or unusual withdrawals or expenditures have been made.

11. You understand that the final Agreement and Plan of Reorganization will contain standard convenants, indemnities, conditions, and warranties required by Buyer, such as warranties as to litigation, inventories, receivables, real estate, trademarks, patents, tax liabilities, title to assets, and other related items.

12. This letter is not intended as a contract, but merely as a Statement of the present intentions and understandings of the parties. The transaction will be binding upon the parties only in accordance with the terms contained in the final Agreement and Plan of Reorganization, and if, as, and when such an Agreement has been executed by us and the Seller's stockholders.

13. If you are in agreement with the foregoing, please so indicate by having all of the stockholders of Seller sign and return the two copies of this letter which are enclosed herewith.

Very truly yours,

B U Y E R

D. W. Jones
Vice President and Secretary

Accepted by: *No. shs.*   *Date*

_____   _____   _____

_____   _____   _____

_____   _____   _____

_____   _____   _____

_____   _____   _____

THE CONTRACT

An acquisition contract performs the basic function of fixing the rights and obligations of the buyer and seller to each other. In addition, the contract may perform a second important substantial function of supplying a buyer with detailed information of a seller's business. From a structural point of view, acquisition contracts often are drafted to include three different time periods—first, the period ending with the date of the latest financial statements warranted by the seller to be accurate; second, the period from the date of the latest financials to the date of signing the contract; and third, the period from the date of signing of the contract to the date at which the transaction is closed. The contract may also be effective for a period of time after the closing, since the contract may provide for survival of representations after the closing and for escrow agreements. Additional general comments on the contract are made before a form of acquisition contract is discussed in detail.

Representations and warranties. From the buyer's point of view, the starting point in the contract is statements by the seller of the condition of the seller's business on a specified date. These statements by the seller, generally referred to as representations of the seller, fix the economic conditions under which the buyer believes it is buying the seller's business. For the lawyers to write the proper statements or representations of the seller into the acquisition contract, they must have detailed knowledge of the finances, physical plant, and intangible properties of the seller and the negotiations between the buyer and seller. As a simple example of how a lawyer may be misled, consider the basic representation of a seller that a balance sheet of the seller "fairly presents the financial position" of the seller as of the date of the balance sheet.

For instance, in the contract reproduced in this chapter, the seller represents that the balance sheet of the seller's business as of November 30, 1970, "has been prepared in accordance with generally accepted accounting principles consistently applied, and fairly presents the financial position of the seller as of the date of the balance sheet." Assume that in the proposed transaction a footnote to the seller's balance sheet indicates the strong possibility of an income tax deficiency of $2,000,000. If the buyer's lawyer is expected to draft a contract in a vacuum, without actual knowledge of what is contained in the balance sheet, he cannot guard against the possible tax deficiency. The balance sheet, when read with its footnotes, would actually fairly present the seller's financial position. But the balance sheet includes the possible tax deficiency. If the lawyer has had an opportunity to study the financial statements, he will be aware of the possible tax deficiency and may provide in the contract an escrow of a portion of the purchase price to protect the buyer against ultimate assessment of the tax deficiency.

A source of information. Aside from strictly legal considerations, from the buyer's point of view the contract should be a source of information about the seller's business. Generally, the seller is asked to represent the accuracy of the seller's financial statements. The buyer, therefore, obtains general information as to the purported financial condition of the seller. In addition, the seller is generally required to supply descriptions and representations as to real estate, plant and equipment, inventory, receivables, intangibles such as patents, trademarks, copyrights, and important contracts. By providing for descriptions and lists of these items, the buyer obtains detailed information which it may utilize in further investigating the seller's business.

From the seller's point of view, its prime objective should be that the price to be paid for the business is actually paid, and that to the extent possible, the seller be relieved of any future contingent liabilities which may arise after the business is sold. Depending on circumstances and the bargaining power of the seller, complete release from contingent future liabilities may, of course, not be feasible.

The contract should clearly describe the property to be sold and the price to be paid. This statement is axiomatic. But it is not unusual to encounter difficulties in defining even these two basics.

Time periods. In an acquisition contract, the representations of the seller generally are related to three different time periods. In the contract reproduced below the seller represents that the condition of its business is as indicated by the seller's latest certified balance sheet, dated November 30, 1970. Secondly, the seller represents that its business has not been adversely affected since the date of the balance sheet, November 30, 1970, to the date of signing the contract March 29, 1971. Thirdly, by conditions precedent to the closing, the seller represents that at the time of closing the condition of its business will still be sound. In other words, by the contract the seller states to the buyer: (1) "this was the condition of my business on November 30, 1970; (2) my business is still as good on this day we are signing this contract, March 31, 1971, and (3) my business will still be as good on the day we close the deal and you take legal title."

In addition, as will be noted, an acquisition contract generally contains representations and warranties of the buyer, miscellaneous covenants relating to the mechanics of reorganization, treatment of pension plans, employees, assumption of liabilities, and clauses relating to the date and mechanics of closing.

Whether stock is acquired or assets are acquired, the general substance of the acquisition contract is similar. In other words, regardless of the form of the acquisition the contract should contain clauses which define the property being acquired, the purchase price, the representations and warranties of the seller and the buyer, the liabilities, if any, to be assumed by the buyer, and the mechanics for closing the transactions. In spite of contract similarities, however, the nature of the transaction, whether assets or stock are acquired or a merger is contemplated, or whether cash or stock are used to pay the price, will cause certain differences in the form of contract which will be indicated below in the discussion of specific clauses.

The form of contract printed below is a simplified form involving a stock-for-stock acquisition. Since the contract sets forth a stock-for-stock acquisition, the parties to the contract are the buyer and the individual stockholders of the seller who are selling their shares. Sometimes, where a greater number of individual stockholders is involved, the agreement may be signed by a major shareholder acting as agent for all.

Description of transaction. The contract provisions are set forth in italics in loosely related groups. Where comment is considered helpful, comment is made respecting each related group of provisions.

This agreement and plan of reorganization made as of the 29th day of March, 1971, between XYZ Corporation, a corporation of New York (hereinafter called "buyer"), party of the first part, and John Jones, Joe Smith, Tom Brown, and Mary Black (here-inafter called "selling shareholders"), parties of the second part.

WITNESSETH:

The parties desire that buyer shall acquire all of the issued and outstanding shares of capital stock of ABC Corporation, a Delaware corporation (hereinafter called "seller"), by an exchange of all of said issued and outstanding shares of capital stock of seller solely for shares of the voting common stock of buyer, on the terms and conditions hereinafter set forth. Accordingly, the parties hereto covenant and agree as follows:

The above provisions serve to identify the parties and the transaction. In this stock-for-stock acquisition one group of the parties to the contract consists of seller's stockholders, because they own the property which is being bought, i.e., the stock of the seller, and should be legally bound. In the description of the transaction it is clear that the buyer intends to acquire all of the stock of the seller. This definition of the property to be acquired is simple, but in asset transactions (particularly where only a portion of the assets, such as assets of a division, of a seller are being acquired) the definition of the property to be sold is often difficult to draft. The following chapter contains clauses defining the assets to be acquired in assets transactions.

Representations of seller. The next broad group of provisions in the contract, all designated by the paragraph heading 1, followed by subparagraph letter designations, consists of representations of the seller's stockholders. It is basically through these representations that the buyer obtains (1) additional knowledge of the seller's business and (2) legal protection, should the represented facts subsequently prove to be false.

1. Selling shareholders represent that:

1(a) Seller is a corporation duly organized and existing under the laws of the state of Delaware, with authorized capital stock consisting of 20,000 shares of capital stock of the par value of $1 per share, all of which are duly issued and now outstanding, fully-paid and non-assessable; seller does not have authorized, issued or outstanding any other shares of stock or any subscription or other rights to the issuance or receipt of shares of its capital stock; all voting rights are vested exclusively in such capital stock; and seller does not have outstanding any evidences of indebtedness except as disclosed in its balance sheet as of November 30, 1970, and related notes thereto, referred to in paragraph 1(b) below;

1(b) The balance sheet of seller as of November 30, 1970, copies of which, including accompanying notes, have previously been delivered to buyer, has been prepared in accordance with generally accepted principles of accounting and fairly presents the financial position of seller at such date;

The above representations are representations as to the legal status of the stock and the condition of the business at the date of the balance sheet, November 30, 1970. In most acquisition contracts, the representations of a seller respecting its financial statements are broader than the above representation, in that the representations include the accuracy of profit and loss statements in addition to the balance sheet and may include financial statements for more than one year. You will note below that these representations are subsequently brought down to the date of the signing of the contract, March 29, 1971, and finally to the date of closing of the transaction.

1(c) All of the outstanding shares of capital stock of seller are owned beneficially and of record by the selling shareholders as follows:

Name	Number of Shares
John Jones	*10,000*
Joe Smith	*6,000*
Tom Brown	*3,000*
Mary Black	*1,000*

And each of the selling shareholders represent that he or she has full right and title, subject to no lien or encumbrance whatsoever, to the number of shares of capital stock of seller set opposite his or her name and full and unrestricted right and power to exchange and deliver the same pursuant to the provisions of this agreement and plan of reorganization.

By the above provisions the selling stockholders bind themselves legally that they own the stock and that the ownership of the stock is unfettered, subject to no liens or encumbrances. Since the buyer is buying stock and since stock forms the asset being acquired, these provisions are important in this stock-for-stock transaction but normally would not be included in a contract involving an asset transaction.

1(d) Seller is duly qualified and entitled to its respective properties and to carry on its business all as and in the places where such properties are now owned or such business is conducted.

Since, by state law, corporations are required to be licensed or "qualified" to do business where the business is conducted in states other than the state of incorporation, a provision relating to this subject matter is generally inserted in most acquisition contracts to assure that the seller has the proper licenses to conduct its business in foreign states. Often, as an aid to the investigation and as a means of information, the buyer will require the seller (or in this instance the selling stockholders) to expand the qualification clause to list all the states in which the seller is actually licensed to do business.

1(e) Seller has good and marketable title to all the property and assets (including title in fee simple to all real property) included in the balance sheet of seller as of November 30, 1970, referred to in paragraph 1(b) hereof, or purported to have been acquired by seller after said date, except, however, property and assets sold in the ordinary course of business subsequent to said date; the schedule of real property heretofore delivered to buyer, signed by the president of seller for identification, is a true and correct schedule and brief description of all real property owned or leased by seller, together with a brief description of all plants and structures thereon, which plants and structures and the equipment therein are in good operating condition and repair and conform with all applicable ordinances and regulations and building, zoning and other laws; all the properties and assets of seller are free from any liens or encumbrances not disclosed in said schedule of real property; seller occupies the land and building owned by it except such portion of the building as is leased to LMN Leasing Corporation from seller to LMN Leasing Corporation, under a lease heretofore submitted to buyer;

1(f) The schedule of patents and trademarks heretofore delivered to buyer, signed by the president of seller for identification, is a true and correct schedule and brief de-

scription of all patents, patent applications, trademarks, and trade names owned by or registered in the name of seller, and none thereof is being infringed or contested to the knowledge of selling shareholders; and seller possesses all necessary patents, patent rights to conduct its business as now operated, without known conflict with valid patents, trademarks, trade names, and copyrights of others;

The above representations concern the status of the ownership of tangible and intangible assets of the seller and also the physical condition of the tangible assets. Note that in this particular contract no reference is made to the condition of the inventory, presumably because the buyer was satisfied with the condition of the inventory or inventory did not form an important part of the seller's business.

Where, however, inventories are an important part of the seller's business, representations of the condition of the inventories often create difficult problems of substance between the buyer and seller and serious drafting problems. A buyer generally will not want to pay a seller for "slow moving" or "obsolete" inventory. The buyer will want contractual assurance that the inventory it purchases is "merchantable" or can be sold in the ordinary course of business and at a profit. Any attempt to define such terms as "slow-moving," "obsolete," or "merchantable," in relationship to the inventory of a particular business may be extremely difficult. For example, in the electronics industry where literally hundreds of categories of inventory may be involved, an attempt to define, for instance, "obsolete" or "slow-moving relays" may consume many contract pages and may often involve lengthy appendices to the contract. The inventory problem may be further complicated, because the seller may know that it has obsolete inventory on hand or that a substantial portion of its inventory is slow-moving. Nevertheless, the seller's accounting procedures may not be sufficiently accurate for the seller to estimate the amount of obsolescence with any assurance of the accuracy of the estimate. Under these circumstances, the seller will hesitate to bind itself to stringent inventory clauses. In the next chapter some forms which have been used to solve inventory problems are reprinted.

1(g) The schedule of contracts and suppliers heretofore delivered to buyer, signed by the president of seller for identification, is a true and correct schedule and brief description of:

(i) All patent license agreements, royalty contracts and research contracts to which seller is a party;

(ii) All employment agreements, agency agreements and territorial and franchise agreements which by their terms expire more than one year from the date thereof;

(iii) Each other contract or commitment of seller which expires more than one year from the date thereof or which involves an amount or value in excess of $10,000;

(iv) All railroad sidetrack agreements; and

(v) All principal suppliers of seller;

1(h) Seller is not a party to any pending or threatened litigation which might adversely affect the financial condition, business, or properties of seller, or interfere with the manufacture or sale of its products, nor to the knowledge of the selling shareholders, is there any threatened or pending governmental investigation involving seller or any of its products, including inquiries, citations, or complaints by the Federal Trade Commission, or any other federal, state or local administration; and there are no outstanding orders, decrees, or stipulations affecting seller or any of its products;

1(i) All returns for income taxes, surtaxes and excess profits taxes of seller for all prior periods up to and including November 30, 1970, have been duly prepared and filed in good faith and all taxes shown thereon have been paid or accrued on the seller's books; all franchise and real and personal property taxes for the year ended November 30, 1970, herein represented as having been accrued on the books, are reflected in the balance sheet of seller as of November 30, 1970, referred to in paragraph 1(b) hereof; and no proceeding or other action has been taken for the assessment or collection of additional taxes for any such periods;

1(j) All taxes and other assessments and levies which seller is required by law to withhold or to collect have been duly withheld and collected, and have been paid over to the proper governmental authorities or are held by seller in separate bank accounts for such payment and all such withholdings and collections and all other payments due in connection therewith as of November 30, 1970, are duly reflected in the balance sheet of seller as of November 30, 1970, referred to in paragraph 1(b) hereof;

The above representations relate to the general conduct of the seller's business. They are particularly important where a buyer buys the stock of the seller since the corporate life of the seller continues without interruption. Under these circumstances, all of the obligations, commitments, and liabilities of the seller continue after the buyer has acquired the selling stockholders' stock.

On the other hand, where the assets of a seller are bought for cash in an arm's-length transaction the contract may be so written that the buyer will assume only those obligations of the seller which are specifically enumerated in the contract. The problem of the carryover of the seller's commitments and obligations may be minimized. But even in an assets transaction, the requirement that the seller list its contracts, litigation, and tax situation is invaluable to the buyer in his general investigation of the seller's business. The representation of the seller concerning the status of litigation and action by governmental authorities, paragraph 1(h), provides the buyer with information which often could not be obtained in any other manner.

To provide further protection to the buyer and to aid in the investigation, the buyer often requests that the above representation of the seller relating to income taxes, paragraph 1(i), be expanded to include a representation as to the past years' income tax returns of the seller upon which tax audits have been completed by the Internal Revenue Service and the tax finally determined and paid.

1(k) Seller has not since November 30, 1970,

(i) Issued any additional shares of stock or other securities;

(ii) Made any distribution to its shareholders, as shareholders, of any assets by way of dividends, purchase of shares or otherwise;

(iii) Mortgaged, pledged or subjected to lien or encumbrance any of its properties or assets beyond that disclosed in the schedule delivered to buyer as provided in paragraph 1(e) hereof;

(iv) Sold or transferred any of its assets, tangible or intangible, except in each case in the ordinary and usual course of business; or

(v) Incurred any extraordinary losses or incurred or become liable for any obligations or liabilities except current liabilities incurred in the ordinary and

usual course of business, or made any extraordinary expenditures other than for additions and betterments to existing plant, equipment, and facilities;

(vi) Increased the rate of compensation of its officers;

1(l) The business, properties and assets of seller have not since November 30, 1970, been materially and adversely affected as the result of any fire, explosion, earthquake, flood, drought, windstorm, accident, strike, embargo, confiscation of vital equipment, materials or inventory, cancellation of contracts by any domestic or foreign government, or any agency thereof, riot, activities of armed forces, or acts of God or the public enemy;

1(m) Seller has no liabilities, contingent or otherwise, beyond those stated in the balance sheet of seller as of November 30, 1970, or described in the notes accompanying said balance sheet, referred to in paragraph 1(b) hereof, other than current liabilities incurred in the ordinary and usual course of business since November 30, 1970;

By the above clauses, the seller assures the buyer of the condition of the business on the date of the signing of the contract, March 29, 1971. In paragraph 1(b) of the contract, reproduced on page 222, the seller represented the condition of its business at the date of the seller's financial statement, November 30, 1970. To this point in the contract, the seller has made legally binding promises to the buyer of the condition of the seller's business on November 30, 1970, the date of the seller's financials, and on March 29, 1971, the date on which the contract is signed. Subsequent clauses in the contract bring the representations down to the moment of closing.

In paragraphs 3 and 4 of the contract, at pages 227 and 228, the selling stockholders promise not to permit prohibited acts and to conduct the business only in the ordinary course from the date of contract, March 29, 1971, to the closing date. In addition, by conditions precedent to the buyer's obligation to close, contained in paragraphs 7(a), 7(d) and 7(f) at pages 229 and 230, buyer need not purchase the selling stockholders' stock if the condition of the seller's business is not, at the time established for closing, as has been represented by the selling stockholders.

Thus, an acquisition contract generally is structured in three separate periods of time: (1) a period preceding the date of the latest financial statements of the seller incorporated in the contract; (2) the period of time from the date of the financials to the date of signing the contract; and (3) the period from the date of the signing of the contract to the date established for the closing, i.e., the date at which the purchase price is to be paid and the legal title to the stock or assets is to be transferred.

1(n) Selling shareholders, in acquiring shares of common stock of buyer as herein contemplated are acquiring the same for the purposes of investment only, with no present intention of selling or otherwise marketing or distributing such shares.

The foregoing representation has the two-fold purpose of (1) avoiding the need for registration of the buyer's stock under the Securities Act of 1933, since the selling shareholders agree to accept the buyer's stock for investment purposes only, and (2) providing further assurance of the continuity of the equity ownership in determining whether the transaction may be treated as a "pooling of interests" for accounting purposes. The securities registration and "pooling of interests" problems are discussed in Chapters 7 and 8.

1(o) No representation by selling shareholders made in this agreement and no statement made in any certificate or schedule furnished in connection with the transaction herein contemplated contains or will contain any knowingly untrue statement of a material fact or knowingly omits or will omit to state any material fact necessary to make any such representation or warranty or any such statement not misleading to a prospective purchaser of all of the stock of seller who is seeking full information as to seller and its affairs.

The foregoing is a catch-all representation modeled on language contained in Rule 10b–5 of the General Rules and Regulations under the Securities Exchange Act of 1934. Often the clause is strengthened by omitting the word "knowingly" in each place where it appears in the above example of this type of clause.

2. Buyer represents:

2(a) That it is a corporation duly organized and existing under the laws of the state of New York with an authorized capital stock consisting of 10,000,000 shares of common stock of the par value of $5 per share, all having full voting power of which at December 31, 1970, 8,768,000 shares (less 52,000 thereof held in treasury) have been duly issued and are outstanding, fully paid and non-assessable;

2(b) That the shares of buyer deliverable pursuant to this agreement will be shares of common stock, fully listed, or approved for listing on official notice of issuance, on the New York Stock Exchange of the same class of common stock presently issued and outstanding, which shares buyer shall have full and lawful authority to deliver, and when so delivered, will have full and equal voting rights and will be fully paid and non-assessable;

2(c) That in acquiring the shares of stock of seller hereunder, buyer is acquiring the same for purposes of investment only with no present intention of selling or otherwise marketing or distributing them.

Since the buyer will pay the purchase price in buyer's stock, the foregoing representations are intended to assure the selling stockholders of the validity of the issuance and transfer of the buyer's stock. Note that the buyer makes no representations as to the condition of the buyer's business. In some situations the seller may also require representations and proof as to the soundness of the buyer's business. This is particularly true where the seller signs investment letters with respect to the buyer's stock and must therefore retain the stock for some period of time.

Paragraph 2(b) requires that the stock of the buyer be listed or "approved for listing on official notice of issuance" on the New York Stock Exchange. This language is dictated by the mechanics of listing stock on the New York Stock Exchange. Stock is not fully listed on the Exchange until after official notice of issuance, which can only be given after the stock has been issued for delivery to the seller. Fully listed stock may be used as consideration for an acquisition, however, where the stock has been purchased in the open market, since such stock of a listed company would normally already have been fully listed. A form of listing application is reproduced in Chapter 15.

3. Selling shareholders shall not cause, suffer or permit seller, subsequent to the date hereof and prior to the delivery hereunder, to

(i) Issue any additional shares of stock or other securities;

(ii) Make any distribution to its shareholders, as shareholders, of any assets by way of dividends, purchase of shares or otherwise;

(iii) Mortgage, pledge or subject to lien or encumbrance, any of its properties or assets;

(iv) Sell or transfer any of its assets, tangible or intangible, except in each case in the ordinary and usual course of business;

(v) Incur or become liable for any obligations or liabilities except current liabilities in the ordinary and usual course of business, or make any unusual or extraordinary expenditures; or

(vi) Increase the rate of compensation of its officers.

4. During the period prior to the closing date hereunder selling shareholders shall cause seller to conduct its business in the usual and normal course.

5. Selling shareholders shall cause seller to grant to buyer the right and opportunity to make such examination and investigation of seller's business, properties and affairs as buyer may deem necessary or desirable for all purposes relating to this agreement and to that end to open its books of account and records for examination by buyer's representatives, accountants and counsel.

These three contract paragraphs contain covenants, affirmative undertakings on the part of the selling shareholders concerning the conduct of the business from the date of the contract, March 29, 1971, to the closing date. Note that in paragraph 3 above, the selling shareholders agree not to permit the seller to do certain things or incur certain obligations, identical to the occurrences which the selling shareholders represented in paragraph 1(k) of the contract had not happened since November 30, 1970, to the contract date, March 29, 1971.

The right of the buyer to make the investigation is almost universal in acquisition contracts. However, often a paragraph such as 5 contains an additional clause to the effect that, if the acquisition is not consummated, the buyer will return all material gathered from the seller and will keep confidential all trade secrets and similar information the buyer has gathered from the seller with respect to the seller's business.

6. Subject to the terms and conditions of this agreement, the parties have adopted and agreed to the following plan of reorganization to be performed on the closing date hereinafter provided for:

6(a) Selling shareholders shall transfer and deliver unto buyer all shares of capital stock of seller owned by them respectively, such shares and the certificates representing the same to be free and clear of all liens and encumbrances. The certificates representing such shares shall be duly endorsed in blank for transfer or accompanied by separate written instruments of assignment, with signatures guaranteed by a commercial bank or trust company having an office or correspondent in the City of New York, or by a member firm of the New York Stock Exchange, and shall be accompanied by such supporting documents as buyer or its counsel may reasonably require;

6(b) Subject to the provisions of this paragraph 6 and paragraphs 7 and 8 hereof, buyer shall deliver, in exchange for all of the shares of capital stock of seller, to selling shareholders, pro rata in accordance with their respective holdings of capital stock of seller, certificates representing 176,000 shares of common stock, $5 par value, of buyer, to the nearest full share;

6(c) If less than all of the shares of capital stock of seller are duly tendered for ex-

change, buyer shall have the right, at its option, either to withdraw from this agreement and plan of reorganization, or to deliver to the respective selling shareholders duly tendering their shares of exchange the same number of shares of buyer's common stock which they would otherwise have received, without thereby being deemed to have elected any remedy or to have waived any of its rights against any selling shareholder failing to duly tender all his or her shares;

6(d) All stamp taxes payable in connection with the transfer of shares of common stock of buyer to be delivered to selling shareholders pursuant to this agreement and plan of reorganization shall be paid by buyer, and all stamp taxes, including documentary and stock transfer taxes, payable on the transfer or delivery to buyer of shares of stock of seller shall be payable by selling shareholders.

As indicated in Chapter 10, for an acquisition to be tax-free the exchange must be pursuant to a Plan of Reorganization. A formal plan is not required under the tax laws. A plan is deemed sufficient even if the plan consists only of resolutions contained in the corporate minutes. The custom has grown, however, to outline the plan in the acquisition contract, when a tax-free transaction is contemplated.

Note that the number of shares of common stock to be paid by the buyer is fixed at 176,000 shares. Where a buyer is a publicly held listed company and a substantial period of time is expected to elapse between the signing of the contract and the closing, the number of shares is often not fixed in the acquisition contract. In such instances, to lessen the effect which market fluctuations in the buyer's stock may have on the purchase price, the parties often base the number of shares to be paid on a formula related to a fixed dollar price, with upper and lower limits on the number of shares the buyer will pay.

Some formula price clauses are printed in Chapter 13.

7. All obligations of buyer under this agreement are subject to the fulfillment, on or prior to the closing date, of each of the following conditions in addition to the conditions set forth in paragraph 6 hereof:

7(a) That the representations of selling shareholders shall be true at and as of the closing date as though such representations were made at and as of such time;

7(b) That buyer shall have received a written opinion, dated on the closing date, of counsel representing selling shareholders, to the effect that seller has been duly incorporated and is on the closing date validly existing as a corporation in good standing under the laws of the state of Delaware with a capitalization as represented in this agreement and plan of reorganization; that seller is duly qualified or licensed as a foreign corporation in the states of New York and New Jersey, the only states where in the opinion of such counsel, such qualification is required; that the shares of stock of seller delivered to buyer at the closing have been validly issued and are outstanding, fully paid and nonassessable, and constitute all of the issued and outstanding shares of capital stock of seller; that seller has good and marketable title in fee simple to all its real properties other than leasehold interests and good and marketable title to all its personal properties and assets and that the said real and personal properties and assets are free of any mortgages, pledges, liens, conditional sales agreements, encumbrances and charges other than as stated in the schedule referred to in paragraph 1(e) hereof; that such counsel knows of no litigation, proceeding or investigation pending or threatened, which might result in any material adverse change in the business, properties or financial condition of seller or in any liability on the part of seller, or which questions the validity of this agreement and plan of reorganization or of any action taken or to be taken pursuant to or in connection with the provisions of this agreement and plan of reorganization other than as set forth in such opinion; and that the assignment and delivery to buyer of the shares of capital stock of seller pursuant to this agreement and plan of reorganization will vest in buyer all right, title and interest in and to such shares, free and clear of all liens, encumbrances and equities;

The above provisions are conditions which must be met prior to the closing in order for the buyer to be obligated to deliver the buyer's shares to the selling shareholders. If the conditions are not met, the buyer may, without breach of contract, refuse to close the transaction.

The foregoing conditions precedent cover the entire transaction in a general manner. Often the lawyer for the seller is not in a position to render an opinion as broad as that required above in paragraph 7(b). In a large complex, nation-wide business, unless the lawyer for the seller is peculiarly conversant with the seller's business, he will only be able to represent the specific states within which the seller is qualified to do business. The lawyer generally would not give an opinion that the seller is qualified wherever necessary. Also the lawyer's opinion on items such as real estate titles often contains a statement that the lawyer may rely on opinions of local counsel, since the lawyer normally would not have knowledge of the real estate in foreign states, and the laws of such states as they affect the real estate titles. Furthermore, the lawyer may not be able to render an opinion that the personal property of seller and the seller's stock is not subject to any lien or encumbrance.

7(c) That buyer shall have received a certificate dated on the closing date, signed by the president of seller, that since the date of this agreement and plan of reorganization seller has not done or permitted to be done any of the acts or things forbidden in paragraph 3 of this agreement and plan of reorganization;

7(d) That the auditors and accountants for buyer appointed by buyer to examine the books of account and records of seller shall not have rendered a report to buyer stating that the financial condition of seller is not substantially as represented herein or that in their opinion seller has contingent liabilities material in amount beyond that described in its balance sheet as of November 30, 1970, or the notes thereto referred to in paragraph 1(b) hereof;

7(e) That no claim or liability not fully covered by insurance shall have been asserted against seller and that seller shall not have suffered any loss on account of fire, flood, accident or other calamity of such a character as to materially adversely affect its financial condition, regardless of whether or not such loss shall have been insured, and that buyer shall have received a certificate dated on the closing date and signed by the president of seller so stating;

7(f) That all covenants herein made by selling shareholders which are to be performed at or prior to the closing date hereunder shall have been duly performed;

7(g) That selling shareholders shall deliver to seller on the closing date written tenders of resignation by all directors and officers of seller, such resignations to be effective upon acceptance by buyer;

As mentioned previously in this chapter the above conditions precedent effectively bring the selling shareholders' representations of the condition of the business and the covenants in the contract down to the closing date. Similar provisions are found in virtually all acquisition agreements.

Paragraph 7(e) above is often expanded to protect the buyer from a possible adverse effect upon the ability to conduct the business, regardless of whether the calamity is fully covered by insurance.

The requirement in paragraph 7(g) that directors and officers tender resignations is often included in acquisition contracts and is generally written to cover officers and directors of subsidiaries of a seller, as well as the seller. The buyer and seller should, however, mutually have agreed before the closing date which resignations are to be accepted and which officers and directors of the seller will continue in office.

> *7(h) That seller shall have delivered to buyer all working formulae for all products and all ingredients of products manufactured by seller;*
> *7(i) That seller shall have, prior to the closing, entered into a sales agency agreement with Jack Salesman satisfactory to buyer and its counsel;*
> *7(j) That seller shall have, prior to the closing, entered into an employment agreement with Herbert President satisfactory to buyer and its counsel;*

The above conditions precedent, paragraphs 7(h), 7(i) and 7(j), are good general illustrations of the fact that each acquisition contract must be tailored to the particular transaction. Apparently, the buyer, in its investigation of the seller's business prior to the signing of the contract, determined that three aspects of the seller's business were important for its continued success. One was the working formulae for the products and ingredients in the products. Therefore, the buyer required that it receive all of such formulae from the seller as a condition to closing. In addition, the buyer apparently concluded that Jack Salesman and Herbert President were so important to the business that the buyer would not be willing to close the transaction unless both Jack and Herbert had entered into satisfactory agency and employment agreements with the seller.

This acquisition contract does not contain any conditions precedent to the obligation of the seller's stockholders to close the transaction. In some acquisitions, where a seller or its stockholders are applying to administrative authorities for rulings concerning the tax effects of the proposed transaction or concerning the applicability of a Securities Act exemption, the acquisition contract may contain conditions precedent to the seller's or the seller's stockholder's obligations to close, conditioned upon obtaining favorable rulings.

> *8. Under no circumstances shall buyer be required to register with the Securities and Exchange Commission pursuant to the provisions of the Securities Act of 1933, as amended, any shares of its common stock deliverable to selling shareholders hereunder.*

Registration of securities under the Securities Act of 1933 is often expensive. Furthermore, a registrant must be careful not to become involved in any major transactions material to its business after filing a registration statement and before its effective date, because any such transaction will require an amendment to the registration statement and cause the waiting period for the effective date to be extended. For these reasons, buyers are often reluctant to be required to register their securities. The delivery of shares by the buyer in a transaction such as is reviewed in this chapter, normally would be exempt from registration as "not involving any public offering" under Section 4(2) of the Securities Act of 1933, because of the limited number of selling stockholders and their investment undertakings pursuant to paragraph 1(n) of the contract. Often, where a buyer is not to register its stock, the buyer will imprint its stock certificates with a legend to this effect, or, on the other hand, where a buyer gives a seller's stockholders registration rights, the acquisition contract will set forth these rights. A form of such legend and stock registration clause is printed in the next chapter.

9. All transactions contemplated by this agreement and plan of reorganization as well as the form and substance of all legal proceedings and of all papers and documents used or deliverable hereunder, shall be subject to the approval of Messrs. Jones, Jones & Jones of Jersey City, N.J., as counsel for selling shareholders, and of Messrs. Roe, Roe & Roe of New York, N.Y., as counsel for buyer.

10. The closing under this agreement and plan of reorganization and all deliveries hereunder shall take place at the office of Roe, Roe & Roe, 14000 West 42nd Street, New York 200, N.Y., at 10:30 o'clock a.m. Eastern Standard Time, on the 30th day of May, 1971.

11. All notices under this agreement and plan of reorganization shall be in writing and any notice to buyer shall be considered delivered in all respects when it has been mailed, first class postage prepaid, addressed as follows:

> *Buyer*
> *20,000 East 42nd Street*
> *New York, N.Y.*

and any notice to selling shareholders shall be considered delivered in all respects when it has been mailed, first class postage prepaid, addressed as follows:

> *John Jones*
> *1100 Eastern Avenue*
> *Jersey City, N.J.*

12. This agreement and plan of reorganization shall bind and inure to the benefit of the parties hereto and their respective legal representatives, successors and assigns, provided, however, that this agreement and plan of reorganization cannot be assigned by any party except by or with the written consent of the others. Nothing herein expressed or implied is intended or shall be construed to confer upon or to give any person, firm or corporation other than the parties hereto and their respective legal representatives, successors and assigns any rights or benefits under or by reason of this agreement and plan of reorganization.

13. This agreement and plan of reorganization may be executed in any number of counterparts, each of which shall be deemed an original, but all of which together shall constitute one and the same instrument.

In witness whereof, the parties hereto have respectively executed this agreement and plan of reorganization as of the day and year first above written.

Date of Signature:	*XYZ Corporation*
March 29, 1971	By /s/ John Signatory *Vice President*
March 29, 1971	By /s/ John Jones *John Jones*
March 29, 1971	By /s/ Joe Smith *Joe Smith*
March 29, 1971	By /s/ Tom Brown *Tom Brown*
March 29, 1971	By /s/ Mary Black *Mary Black*

The foregoing provisions are the formal provisions found in most acquisition contracts relating to the approval of counsel, place and date of closing, notices, the fact that the contract is not assignable and, finally, the boilerplate requiring proof of only one contract in litigation. Often provisions relating to the place and date of closing will contain provisions for adjournment of the closing date, should circumstances warrant.

To summarize, the lawyers have the responsibility of drafting the acquisition contract. Since this contract, once signed, fixes the rights and obligations of the buyer and seller, the businessman and accountant should strive to supply the lawyer with all relevant information which the lawyer needs to protect either the buyer or seller, as the case may be.

Clauses contained in acquisition contracts, including the simplified stock-for-stock contract contained in this chapter, may be grouped in 12 categories for convenience in analysis:

1. General Statement of Agreement.
2. Representations and Warranties of Seller.
3. Representations and Warranties of Buyer.
4. Assets to Be Acquired by the Buyer.
5. Payment of Purchase Price.
6. Buyer's Assumption of Liabilities.
7. Seller's Indemnification of the Buyer.
8. Seller's Conduct of the Business Pending the Closing.
9. Conditions Precedent to the Closing.
10. The Plan of Reorganization.
11. Brokerage.
12. General Provisions.

Note, however, that the above simplified contract does not contain a brokerage clause included as item 11, above. The difficulties which may arise as a result of claims for brokerage commissions are discussed in Chapter 3. As a result of the possibility of such difficulties adversely affecting a transaction, the parties should insert a brokerage provision in the contract indemnifying each other from brokerage claims asserted by alleged finders, brokers, or providing which party is to pay the broker.

The next chapter contains additional suggested forms of acquisition contract clauses, grouped under the above 12 categories of clauses for convenience of analysis.

CHAPTER 13

The Acquisition Contract—
Additional Clauses

Each acquisition contract should reflect the details of the transaction as these details are developed in the course of the negotiation and, to the extent possible, the investigation. No acquisition agreement can or should contain only "boilerplate" provisions. However, this chapter contains suggested forms of additional contract provisions which may be useful in drafting the acquisition contract, if these forms are revised to meet specific situations. A general (but not fixed) pattern has evolved from the thousands of acquisition contracts which buyers and sellers have signed in past years, and in this chapter clauses which may be utilized in contracts for the acquisition of stock or assets of sellers, or statutory mergers, are printed under headings which follow a loosely established contract pattern.

The simplified form of contract printed in the preceding chapter is a stock-for-stock contract, containing many of the provisions required in a stock-for-stock transaction. Many of the clauses printed below relate to transactions where assets are acquired or a statutory merger is contemplated, but may also be used in stock-for-stock or cash-for-stock acquisitions. Where comment is deemed helpful, for example if a buyer's use of cash rather than stock to make an acquisition would have an effect on a particular suggested clause, comment is made. Hopefully, these clauses will be helpful in drafting acquisition contracts; they should not be used verbatim without consideration of the details of the specific acquisition. Following the format of Chapter 12, all contract clauses and forms are printed in italics and explanatory text or comments are printed in roman type.

The general pattern under which these clauses are printed is as follows:

1. General Statement of Agreement.
2. Representations and Warranties of Seller.

235

GENERAL STATEMENT OF AGREEMENT

Many acquisitions contracts begin with a general statement of the transaction, often in the form of a whereas clause.

(a) Stock for Assets.

Whereas, buyer and seller desire to enter into this agreement and plan of reorganization (herein sometimes called "agreement") with each other under the terms of which (i) seller will, in exchange solely for voting $3.80 cumulative convertible preferred stock, without par value, (herein called "convertible perferred stock"), of buyer, convey and transfer to buyer, and buyer will acquire from seller, all of seller's right, title and interest in and to all of the properties and assets of seller, including, but not limited to, cash, moneys on deposit, all the goodwill of the business carried on by seller, the right to the use of its name, trade names, and trade-marks, all of its customers' lists, credit and sales records, and all other interests to which seller has any right by ownership, use or otherwise, and (ii) buyer will assume all the liabilities of seller, all as hereinafter provided.

In the above stock-for-assets provision, the buyer has agreed to assume all of the liabilities of the seller. If the buyer were assuming only specified liabilities, clause (ii) might read "Buyer will assume certain liabilities of the Seller, all as hereinafter provided."

(b) Stock For Assets—Section 368(a)(1)(C) Reorganization.

AGREEMENT AND PLAN OF REORGANIZATION ("Agreement"), made as of the   day of November, 1970, by and between BUYER, a New Jersey corporation, having a place of business at 000 Madison Avenue, New York, New York 10019 ("Buyer"), and SELLER, a Wisconsin corporation, having a place of business at 8000 Main Street, Milwaukee, Wisconsin 53502 ("Seller").

WITNESSETH:

The Reorganization, pursuant to the provisions of Section 368(a)(1)(C) of the Internal Revenue Code of 1954, as amended, will comprise the acquisition by Buyer of substantially all of the property, assets, goodwill, and business as a going concern of Seller subject to certain liabilities of Seller as hereinafter provided, in exchange solely for a part of Buyer's voting stock and the prompt dissolution of Seller and the distribution of said stock to the shareholders of Seller according to their respective interests, all upon and subject to the terms and conditions of the Agreement hereinafter set forth.

In order to consummate the Plan of Reorganization herein set forth and in consideration of the mutual benefits to be derived therefrom and of the mutual agreements hereinafter contained, the parties hereto do represent, warrant, covenant and agree as follows:

The foregoing general statement of agreement in a stock-for-assets acquisition sets forth at the outset that the acquisition is to comprise a "tax-free" reorganization under Section 368(a)(1)(C) of the Internal Revenue Code. Where a tax-free acquisition is contemplated, it has become customary to set forth in the first portion of the general statement of agreement the section of the Internal Revenue Code pursuant to which the parties contemplate carrying out the "tax-free" reorganization.

(c) Statutory Merger.

Agreement of merger dated this 29th day of July, 1971, by and between buyer, a Delaware corporation (hereinafter sometimes referred to as "buyer" or the "surviving corporation"), and the directors thereof or a majority of them, and seller, a Missouri corporation (hereinafter sometimes referred to as "seller"), and the directors thereof or a majority of them (said corporations being hereinafter sometimes collectively referred to as the "constituent corporations"),

WITNESSETH:

Whereas, buyer is a corporation duly organized and existing under the laws of the state of Delaware, having been incorporated on May 9, 1929, under the General Corporation Law of the state of Delaware, and has an authorized capital stock consisting of 500,000 shares of prior preference stock, without par value, none of which is now outstanding, 600,000 shares of 5% cumulative preferred stock, par value $50 per share, of which on the date hereof 586,213 shares were issued and outstanding, and 15,000,000 shares of common stock, of the par value of $1 per share, of which on the date hereof 10,001,218 shares were issued and outstanding: and

Whereas, seller is a corporation duly organized and existing under the laws of the state of Missouri, having been incorporated on November 7, 1914, under the General and Business Corporation Act of the state of Missouri, and has an authorized capital stock consisting of 100,000 shares of 4.80% cumulative preferred stock, par value $100 per share, of which on the date hereof 35,490 shares were issued and outstanding, and 6,000,000 shares of common stock, par value $5 per share, of which on the date hereof 3,005,472 shares were issued and outstanding; and

Whereas, a majority of the directors of each of the constituent corporations deems it advisable and for the best interests of said corporations that seller be merged into buyer as authorized by the statutes of the states of Delaware and Missouri under and pursuant to the terms and conditions hereinafter set forth;

Now, therefore, in consideration of the premises and the mutual agreements, covenants, and provisions herein contained, and for the purpose of prescribing the terms and conditions of said merger, the mode of carrying the same into effect, the manner of converting the shares of each of the constituent corporations into the shares of the surviving corporation, and such other details and provisions as are deemed necessary or proper, the parties hereto have agreed and do hereby agree, subject to the adoption of this agreement of merger and approval of the plan of merger set forth therein by the requisite statutory vote of the stockholders of each of the constituent corporations, and subject to the conditions hereinafter set forth, as follows:

Article 1.

Seller shall be merged with and into buyer, and buyer is hereby designated as the surviving corporation, and said surviving corporation shall continue to be governed by the laws of the state of Delaware.

The statutory merger provision is a general statement of a proposed merger between a Delaware and a Missouri corporation which follows the usual statutory pattern for mergers, in that (1) "a majority of the directors of each of the constituent corporations deems it advisable and for the best interests of said corporations that Seller be merged into Buyer" and (2) the seller shall be merged into the buyer "subject to the adoption of this agreement of merger and approval of the plan of merger set forth therein by the requisite statutory vote of the stockholders of each of the constituent corporations." In a statutory merger, it is required that a form of agreement of merger or certificate of merger to be filed with state authorities and the procedure follow the statutory provisions of the states involved to the letter.

The form of agreement of merger to be filed with the states involved, in the form prescribed by statute, will normally not contain most of the protective representations and warranties contained in asset or stock acquisition agreements. If the statutory form of agreement of merger is the only document to be executed between the parties, the buyer should have completed his investigation and the boards of directors of both parties should have satisfied themselves that all conditions which are normally protected against by representations and warranties have been fulfilled. To obtain the usual protection contained in an acquisition contract, the parties may execute an agreement containing full representations and conditions precedent to closing, to which a statutory agreement of merger (in form satisfactory for filing with state authorities) is attached—not to be filed until all the conditions contained in the acquisition agreement are met.

Since a statutory merger agreement may differ radically in form from an asset or stock acquisition contract, a complete form of statutory merger agreement is printed and discussed separately in the next chapter.

REPRESENTATIONS AND WARRANTIES OF SELLER

Through the seller's representations and warranties the buyer (1) obtains additional information and (2) legal protection should the facts represented and warranted prove false. Since the representations and warranties of the seller should concern all aspects of the seller's business, such representations and warranties will generally be the same, whether the seller acquires assets or stock of a seller. Some minor variations in the seller's representations and warranties may exist, however, where stock is acquired rather than assets. For example, the representation number 1(c) as to free and clear stock ownership printed in the stock-for-stock acquisition contract in Chapter 12, would normally not appear where a buyer is acquiring assets. In an assets transaction the buyer does not concern itself with specific stock ownership, but rather with corporate procedure in the sense that proper directors' and shareholders' action be taken to transfer legal title of the assets to the buyer.

Where a subsidiary or subsidiaries form an important part of the seller's business, all representations and warranties of the status of the seller's business should also be made concerning such subsidiaries. In this way the buyer will obtain the same information and legal protection with respect to the subsidiaries as it has with respect to the seller's business.

Printed below are forms of seller's representations and warranties which expand upon or are in addition to those printed in Chapter 12. These representations and warranties may generally be used in contracts for the acquisition of both stock and assets:

(a) Financial Statements.

At or prior to the date of this agreement, seller has delivered to buyer separate balance sheets of seller, seller-sub ABC and seller-sub Canada as of November 30, 1968, November 30, 1969, and November 30, 1970, respectively, and the separate profit and loss and surplus statements of such companies for the periods ended on said dates (said financial statements being certified by Messrs. Right, Right & Right, Certified Public Accountants, in the case of seller and seller-sub ABC, and by Messrs. Jones, Jones & Co., chartered accountants, in the case of seller-sub Canada), and said financial statements, including the related notes and explanatory notes, present fairly the financial position of said companies respectively at said dates and the results of their respective operations for said periods, in conformity with generally accepted accounting principles applied on a basis consistent in each case with that of the preceding year;

The above representation expands on the representation of financial position contained in paragraph 1(b) of the stock-for-stock contract in Chapter 12 by requiring the seller to represent not only one balance sheet, but balance sheets for three successive years, as well as profit and loss statements for the three periods involved. Such expanded representations as to financial statements obviously provide the buyer with more information than the simplified representation of the correctness of only one balance sheet contained in the preceding chapter.

Furthermore, the above clause illustrates a technique which should be utilized where a buyer is acquiring important subsidiaries with the seller's business. In such instances, as in the financial representation, above, the buyer should require the seller to make representations and warranties of the condition of each element of each subsidiary's business to the same extent as made with respect to seller's business itself.

(b) Qualification Status in Various States.

Seller and each of its subsidiaries is duly organized, validly existing and in good standing under the laws of the state of its incorporation, has full power to own all of its properties and to carry on its business as it is now being conducted, and is qualified to do business as a foreign corporation in the jurisdictions listed opposite its name in Exhibit B hereto, which are the only jurisdictions in which its ownership of property or the conduct of its business requires it to be so qualified.

The above clause expands on paragraph 1(d) of the contract printed in Chapter 12 in that it contains a representation that the seller is qualified in all jurisdictions in which qualification is legally required and provides for a listing of all such jurisdictions. Such a representation is possible where the seller is certain of the jurisdictions in which its activities are sufficient to require qualification. Where the seller cannot be certain, it may just represent the jurisdictions in which it is qualified as follows:

Seller represents, warrants, and agrees as follows:
    (a) Seller is a corporation duly organized, validly existing and in good standing under

the laws of the state of Delaware; it has the corporate power to own its properties and to carry on its business as now being conducted and is duly qualified as a foreign corporation to do business and is in good standing in the states of California, Illinois, New York, Pennsylvania, Texas, Virginia, and West Virginia.

(c) Income Tax Representation.

That all returns for income taxes, surtaxes, and excess profits taxes of seller for all prior periods up to and including April 30, 1970, have been duly prepared and filed in good faith and all taxes shown thereon have been paid or are accrued on the books of seller and seller's income tax liability has been finally determined by the Internal Revenue Service and satisfied for all fiscal years prior to and including the fiscal year ended April 30, 1968; all franchise, sales and use taxes and real and personal property taxes due and payable by seller for all periods ending at or prior to the close of business April 30, 1970, have been paid or accrued on the books of the seller;

The above representation concerning the seller's income tax status expands on 1(i) of the contract at page 225 in the preceding chapter by requiring the seller to list its income tax returns which have been audited by the Internal Revenue Service. The use of the language that the seller's "income tax liability has been *finally* determined by the Internal Revenue Service" may be inaccurate. Even after an audit by the Internal Revenue Service, unless a closing agreement has been signed or the statute of limitations has run, additional changes in income tax liabilities may occur.

(d) Renegotiation Status.

Where government contracts are concerned, the status of renegotiation proceedings may often be more important than the tax situation:

All renegotiation proceedings in connection with sales through December 31, 1969, made under government contracts, have been concluded and no further amounts are refundable by seller in connection with any such sales; with respect to sales made since December 31, 1969, and to and including December 31, 1970, under government contracts which are subject to price redetermination or renegotiation, the aggregate amount refundable will not exceed $100,000 net after credit for tax savings resulting from such refunds; to the extent that the aggregate amount so refundable with respect to sales made since December 31, 1969, and to and including December 31, 1970, exceeds $100,000, after such credit for tax savings, seller shall forthwith upon buyer's request pay the full amount of such excess.

(e) Accounts Receivable.

None of the accounts and notes receivable of seller or its subsidiaries, is subject to counterclaims or setoffs, and all of such accounts and notes receivable are good and collectible at the aggregate recorded amounts thereof, less the amounts of the applicable reserves for doubtful accounts and for allowances and discounts.

(f) Insurance.

Seller maintains insurance in responsible companies in such amounts and against such risks, as, in its opinion, prudent business management would deem advisable.

(g) Inventions and Disclosures.

Copies of all invention or improvement disclosures which have been made by em-

ployees of seller on behalf of seller are in the possession of Messrs. Ward, Ward & Ward, of New York, New York, and seller is the sole owner of such invention or improvement disclosures. The stockholders have no ownership rights, except indirectly as stockholders, in any of the domestic or foreign patents, patent applications or invention or improvement disclosures relating to the business of seller.

The above clause was used in a situation where the seller's major asset was a great number of patents protecting its processes. This patent structure was constantly being reinforced by inventions conceived by the seller's engineering division. Since the seller did not wish to disclose such inventions prior to the closing, the parties agreed to the above representation and the inventions and disclosures were delivered to Messrs. Ward, Ward & Ward, well-known patent attorneys.

(*h*) **Permits, Licenses and Franchises.**

Seller and each subsidiary has all permits, licenses, franchises and other authorizations necessary to, and has complied with all laws applicable to, the conduct of its business in the manner and in the areas in which such business is presently being conducted, and all such permits, licenses, franchises and authorizations are valid and in full force and effect. Neither Seller nor any subsidiary has engaged in any activity which would cause revocation or suspension of any such permits, licenses, franchises or authorizations, and no action or proceeding looking to or contemplating the revocation or suspension of any thereof is pending or threatened. No approvals or authorizations will be required to permit Seller or any subsidiary to continue its business as presently conducted after transfer of the capital stock of the seller pursuant to this Agreement.

A clause similar to the above may be of importance in acquiring a business in which licenses are material—such as a television business, busline, or a brewery.

(*i*) **Conflict of Interests.**

No officer or director or Stockholder of Seller or any subsidiary has any interest in any property, real or personal or tangible or intangible, including inventions, patents, trademarks, or trade names used in or pertaining to the business of either Seller or any subsidiary.

(*j*) **Condition of Business.**

There have been no material adverse changes since December 31, 1970, in the business, properties, financial condition, or earnings of seller, whether or not arising from transactions in the ordinary course of business.

The above representation by the seller of its financial condition and its earnings is a much stronger financial representation than the representation concerning the condition of the seller's business printed as paragraph 1(1) of the form contract in Chapter 12 at page 226.

REPRESENTATIONS AND WARRANTIES OF BUYER

The representations of the buyer will often not go beyond those contained in paragraphs 2(a), 2(b) and 2(c) of the simplified form of contract discussed at page 227. As long as a seller receives assurance that the stock paid by the buyer is properly authorized, fully paid, and non-assessable, issued and delivered to the seller, the seller will normally be satisfied. Where the buyer pays the seller in cash, the seller will generally want no assurances or representations from the buyer except that the transaction has been properly authorized. On the other hand, where the buyer pays the seller in stock and the seller signs an "investment" letter, the seller may properly seek representations and warranties from the buyer concerning the condition of the buyer's business.

Furthermore, the buyer may be required to warrant that the acquisition does not violate loan agreements:

> *Buyer is not subject to any charter, by-law, mortgage, lien, lease, agreement, instrument, order, judgment or decree, or any other restriction of any kind or character, which would prevent consummation of the transaction contemplated by this agreement, provided that the holders of its capital stock approve the creation of the convertible preferred stock issuable in accordance with the terms hereof.*

and:

> *The consummation of the transactions contemplated by this agreement will not result in the breach of any term or provision of, or constitute a default under, any indenture, mortgage, deed of trust or other agreement or instrument to which buyer or any of its subsidiaries is a party or by which it is bound.*

ASSETS ACQUIRED BY BUYER

Where the buyer acquires stock, the definition of the assets to be acquired is generally simple. However, where the buyer acquires assets, particularly if the assets do not constitute all of the assets of a seller but only a portion of such assets, the definition of the property being acquired may be complicated.

(a) Division's Assets for Cash.

Article I

Agreement to Sell and Purchase

Subject to the terms and conditions contained in this agreement, seller agrees to sell to buyer, and buyer agrees to purchase from the seller the assets and property described in Article II hereof, consisting of all of the assets and property of seller's XYZ Division ("division") other than cash, accounts receivable and certain incidental items herein noted. As used herein, the terms "assets and property of division" shall mean property in the possession of division on seller's or division's books and recorded or standing in the name of division.

Article II

Assets and Price

The said assets and property and the purchase price of the said assets and property shall be as follows:

1. Land listed on Exhibit A, attached hereto	$ 75,000.00
2. Buildings and plant known as 1000 West Clinton Street, Chicago 22, Illinois	263,000.00

3. *Machinery, equipment tools, jigs, office furniture and fixtures, major items of which are listed on Exhibit B attached hereto* 729,000.00

4. *Non-expendable dies* 100,000.00

5. *Inventories* (Book Value)

6. *Prepaid items other than insurance and prepaid royalty* 16,000.00

7. *Patents and patent applications listed on Exhibit C attached hereto and all other miscellaneous assets of division being sold hereunder* 5,000.00

Total

The above clauses illustrate an attempt to define assets of a division of a seller bought by a buyer for cash. As is often done in a cash transaction, the purchase price is allocated to the separate assets by the parties in an attempt to fix the tax consequences of the acquisition. Sometimes in such instances, the purchase price is stated as a lump sum and the parties rely upon their own allocation, outside appraisals, and their persuasive powers to convince the Internal Revenue Service of the correctness of the allocation. The inventory value was left blank, to be filled in after the taking of a physical inventory and the pricing of the inventory under a complicated formulae printed below in section 5.

(b) All of Sellers Assets.

Assets To Be Acquired by Buyer

On the closing date hereinafter provided, and upon the terms and conditions herein provided, buyer shall acquire all of seller's assets, business, and properties, including without limitation upon the generality of the foregoing, all of seller's right, title and interest in and to its real estate, plants, structures, fixtures, processes, equipment, machinery, tools, dies, jigs, appliances, cash, notes, and accounts receivable, executory contracts and purchase orders for the furnishing of goods or the rendition of services to seller; its inventories, materials, and supplies, (including raw materials, work in process and manufactured products and prototype models); its patents, inventions, licenses, trademarks, and trade names of every sort and kind; its books of account and records which in any way relate to the conduct of its business; the name "XYZ" as a trademark and trade name, together with the goodwill symbolized by said name and by the business, and all other franchises or other privileges used, or of use in, or acquired for use by or in connection with the business, including gas, power, light, water and other tributory and utility properties being and intended to be all of the assets, business, and properties of every kind and nature, and wherever situated, of seller.

(c) Seller's Tax Refund Claims Excluded.

Excluded from this sale are: claims for, and the proceeds (including interest) of, refunds of federal income taxes paid in respect of income of seller for any of the three calendar years next preceding the year in which the closing date shall occur, whether or not in being or known at the closing date and including, but not by way of limitation, any claims for refund founded upon or arising by reason of a loss realized by seller in respect of the transactions contemplated by this agreement. Seller hereby indemnifies and agrees to save buyer harmless in respect of federal income tax deficiencies for any of such three calendar years, but only up to the aggregate amount of refunds of such taxes received in respect of such years and hereby reserved to seller. All proceeds (including interest) of claims for refund of federal income taxes paid in respect of income of seller for the fourth year prior to the year in which the closing date shall occur and preceding years, whether or not in being or known at the closing date, shall pass to buyer; and seller undertakes diligently to file and press any such refund claims, under the direction and at the expense of buyer, and to pay to buyer the proceeds realized therefrom.

PAYMENT OF PURCHASE PRICE

Sometimes the purchase price is a fixed number of dollars or a fixed number of shares of stock of the buyer. On other occasions, however, formulae are utilized to define the amount of cash or stock the buyer will pay; sometimes these formulae are based upon future earnings of the seller's business.

(a) A Definition of the Price of Inventory.

The purchase price of the inventories shall be the value of the inventories as at the closing date at the lower of cost or replacement market value in accordance with good accounting practice consistently followed by seller at seller's division ("division"), subject to the modifications set forth below. The inventory valuation shall be based on a physical count conducted at the plant of division immediately following the closing date pursuant to procedures satisfactory to Right, Right, Right & Co., buyer's independent auditors. As soon as practicable after the physical count, buyer shall cause the inventories to be valued in accordance with the principles set forth herein. The expense of taking and pricing inventories shall be borne equally by buyer and seller, except that seller will pay in any event the amount accrued at the closing date by division for auditing purposes.

In determining the value of the inventories, Exhibit I attached hereto, which describes inventory valuation methods of division, shall be deemed in accordance with good accounting practice.

The above clause providing a method of valuing inventory permits the attachment of an Exhibit to include the detail with which the value of inventory must sometimes be defined.

(b) A Formula Price Based on Market Value of Buyer's Stock:

The stock to be delivered by buyer pursuant to this agreement and plan of reorganization shall be the voting common stock of buyer, approved for listing on official notice of issuance, of the same class of voting common stock which is at present issued and outstanding, and which shares buyer shall have full and lawful authority to deliver, and which, when so delivered, shall have full and equal voting rights and shall be fully paid and nonassessable.

The number of shares of such stock to be delivered shall be determined by the method of computation as provided in (a) below, but subject to the limitations provided in (b) and (c) below, and then subject to adjustment as provided in (d) below.

(a) Initial computation: In making the initial computation the parties shall determine a number of full shares which has a total value as nearly equal to $6,370,000.00 as is practicable, by dividing into $6,370,000.00 the average of the closing quotations of buyer's voting common stock on the New York Stock Exchange for a period beginning on and including December 20, 1970, and ending on and including January 20, 1971.

(b) High limitation: If the number of shares as computed in (a) above exceeds 79,494 shares, such number of shares computed shall be deemed to be 79,494 shares.

(c) Low limitation: If the number of shares as computed in (a) above is less than

70,876 shares, such number of shares computed shall be deemed to be 70,876 shares.

(d) Adjustment: The total number of shares of stock to be delivered as computed in accordance with (a) above, and subjected to the limitations in (b) and (c) above, ("Total Shares") shall then be subject to downward adjustment as follows:

For each share of seller's Class A or Class B common stock "dissenting" the Total Shares shall be reduced by that fraction of the Total Shares which has as its numerator the number one, and as its denominator, the number 192,816.

The term "dissenting" as used herein means the action of any shareholder of seller in respect of holdings of seller's shares, or a portion thereof, in demanding payment therefor as provided in Section 180.72 of Chapter 180, Title XVII of the Wisconsin Business Corporation Law.

In no event shall the Total Shares exceed 79,494 shares nor be less than 70,876 shares (except in the case of stock splits or combinations of shares requiring proportionate adjustment of the number of shares to carry out the intent of this agreement and plan of reorganization).

The above clause illustrates one method for a buyer and seller to agree on a dollar purchase price and convert it into shares. The averaging of closing prices is an attempt to relate the number of shares delivered at the closing to the agreed upon dollar price on a realistic basis; the upper and lower limits of shares to be delivered results from an attempt on the part of the buyer to protect the earnings per share from the seller's business on the shares delivered by the buyer; and the reduction in shares delivered by the buyer as a result of dissenting shareholders of the seller is required where the seller's shareholders have a right to dissent in a merger or assets transaction.

(c) A Formula Price Based on Future Earnings of Seller's Business:

The clause below provides for the payment of additional purchase price by the buyer based upon earnings of the seller's business, after allowing a pre-tax return to buyer of 20% of buyer's aggregate investment in the seller's business:

The balance of the purchase price for seller's assets shall be determined in accordance with the following procedures:

(a) For each of the calendar years 1963 through 1969, the pre-tax profit of the business acquired by buyer hereunder shall be determined in accordance with the usual accounting practice of buyer as of the end of such years.

(b) For each of the calendar years 1963 through 1969, the aforesaid pre-tax profit shall be applied as follows:

(i) That portion of the pre-tax- profit equal to 20% of the total of the initial purchase price determined in accordance with paragraph 1 above when added to the "average additional investment" in the operation of the business acquired by buyer hereunder in the form of working capital or contribution of assets or cash to capital made by buyer from the closing date to the end of the year in question (such total hereinafter referred to as the "aggregate buyer investment"), shall be retained by buyer.

The "average additional investment" shall be determined for any period by averaging the monthly totals of such additional investment as reflected on the monthly balance sheets during such period, and multiplying such monthly average by the number of months in the period in question.

(ii) The remainder of the pre-tax profit for such years, after the setting aside of the amount noted in (i) above for the account of buyer, will be divided between buyer and seller in the following proportions:

Buyer	*60%*
Seller	*40%*

Seller's proportion will be paid within three months following the year for which it was determined as additional purchase price for the assets noted in paragraph 1(a) above;

(iii) If the pre-tax profit for any of the calendar years 1963 through 1969 is less than 20% of the aggregate buyer investment determined in accordance with paragraph (b)(i) above, the pre-tax profit for subsequent years will be retained by buyer to the extent necessary to make up past deficiencies.

(c) In no event will be aggregate of all payments to seller under this agreement exceed a maximum sum of $1,250,000.

A clause such as the above, where a buyer pays a seller a greater purchase price if the seller's future earnings justify such greater price, may bring a buyer and seller to agree on price where their estimates of the present value of a business are far apart. The buyer may say, "All right if you think your business will earn that much in the future, I'll pay your price, provided your estimate of future earnings is realized." In such provisions for determining the price on the basis of earnings, the definition of future net earnings of the seller's business must be drafted with great care to avoid future disputes between the parties.

(d) A Formula Price—Detailed Definition of Future Earnings:

The clause below illustrates the detail with which future earnings of a seller are often defined to determine an installment price based upon the seller's projected earnings. The more carefully the accounting principles to determine future earnings are set forth, the less likelihood that disputes will arise in the future as to items of income to be included and expenses to be subtracted:

Determination of Shares to be Delivered on the Closing Date.

The number of shares to be delivered by Buyer to Seller on the closing date shall be determined by dividing the average closing price of Buyer's common shares on the New York Stock Exchange for each of the days for which a closing price is quoted during the period (Valuation Period) commencing with the date of execution of this Agreement and Plan of Reorganization and ending on December 13, 1970, into Seven Million Dollars ($7,000,000.00). Any fractional share produced by such computation shall be rounded to the next full share. For purposes of this Article, the first business day following the expiration of the Valuation Period, i.e., December 14, 1970, shall be deemed the Valuation Date.

Determination of Contingent Shares to be Delivered by Buyer.

In addition to the shares of the common stock of Buyer to be delivered to Seller on the closing date, Buyer shall issue and deliver to Seller, or the designees of Seller at the times hereinafter set forth such number if shares, of any (hereinafter called Contingent Shares), as shall be determined in accordance with, and subject to the limitations set forth in Sections   and   , below.

For purposes of Section   below, the following definitions shall apply:

a. PAT: shall mean consolidated after tax earnings of Seller, for any period under consideration computed in accordance with the accounting principles set forth in Appendix II.

b. BASE: shall mean $550,000.

c. PAT INCREMENT: shall mean the increase in PAT over BASE for the fiscal year ending September 30, 1971; for each of the fiscal years ending September 30, 1972 through 1974 inclusive, it shall mean the increase in PAT over BASE or over highest preceding Contingent Year PAT, if any such preceding Contingent Year PAT is higher than BASE, but not exceeding Two Hundred Thousand Dollars ($200,000.00) with respect to any Contingent Year except the fiscal year ending September 30, 1974.

d. PAT DECREMENT: shall mean the decrease in PAT below BASE for the fiscal year ending September 30, 1971; for each of the fiscal years ending September 30, 1972 through 1974 inclusive, it shall mean the decrease in PAT below BASE, or below the highest preceding Contingent Year PAT, if any such preceding Contingent Year PAT is higher than BASE.

e. EXCESS PAT INCREMENT: shall mean that portion of PAT INCREMENT with respect to any Contingent Year, which exceeds Two Hundred Thousand Dollars ($200,000.00) after giving effect to EXCESS PAT INCREMENTS and PAT DECREMENTS, if any, for preceding Contingent Years.

f. Contingent Year: shall mean each of the fiscal years ending September 30, 1971 through September 30, 1974, inclusive.

Contingent shares, if any, to be issued hereunder shall be determined on the basis of the after-tax consolidated earnings of Seller for each Contingent Year, computed in accordance with the accounting principles set forth in Appendix II or any amendment thereof. Such determination shall be made as promptly as possible following the close of each Contingent Year under consideration, and in any event within sixty (60) days of the close of such Contingent Year.

The number of Contingent shares to be issued with respect to any Contingent Year shall be determined by dividing the average of the closing prices for each of the days for which a closing price is quoted for the month of October following the close of such Contingent Year into the product of five (5) multiplied by the PAT INCREMENT for such year, after giving effect to carry forwards of EXCESS PAT INCREMENTS and PAT DECREMENTS for prior Contingent Years.

Special Provisions Regarding Contingent Shares.

The obligation of Buyer to issue Contingent Shares and the right of Seller to receive Contingent Shares shall be subject to the following limitations: (i) Except with respect to the last Contingent Year ending September 30, 1974, the total value of Contingent Shares, (computed with respect to each Contingent Year by multiplying the number of Contingent Shares issued for such Contingent Year by the average price determined pursuant to Section   above with respect to such Contingent Year) to be issued and delivered by Buyer with respect to any one Contingent Year shall not exceed one million dollars ($1,000,000.00); (ii) the cumulative total value of all Contingent Shares to be *issued and delivered by Buyer, computed as aforesaid, shall not exceed four million dollars ($4,000,000); (iii) the cumulative total number of Contingent Shares to be issued and delivered with respect to all Contingent Years shall not exceed one hundred ten thousand (110,000) shares.*

Buyer shall have the right to set-off against the total value of shares otherwise required to be issued and delivered with respect to any Contingent Year or Contingent Years, the amount of any liability of Seller or Seller's Stockholders pursuant to their indemnity obligations under the provisions of the indemnity agreement of Seller and Seller's Stockholders delivered at the closing.

The total value of the Contingent Shares to be issued with respect to each Contingent Year shall include interest, computed at the date of determination of the amount of Contingent Shares payable, by application of Column (a) of Table I—PRESENT VALUE OF DEFERRED PAYMENT—of Treasury Department Regulation 1.483–1(g)(2). The number of shares designated as being in payment of interest shall be determined by dividing the total interest computed as above by the per share value of the Contingent Shares determined pursuant to Section   above. Separate stock certificates shall be issued for the portion of the Contingent Shares deemed to be in payment of principal and the portion deemed to be in payment of interest. Fractional shares resulting from such computation shall not be issued, but shall be rounded to the next full share subject to the maximum limitation set forth in Section

In the event, prior to distribution of Contingent Shares with respect to any Contingent Year, the number of the one dollar ($1.00) par value common shares of Buyer outstanding, shall be increased or decreased as the result of any stock split or recapitalization, or the shares of the common stock of Buyer shall be changed into or exchanged for a different number or kind of shares or securities of Buyer then an appropriate and proportionate adjustment shall be made in the number or kind of shares, or both, of Buyer thereafter to be delivered with respect to Contingent Years, including an appropriate and proportionate increase or decrease in the maximum number of shares which may be received under this Agreement and Plan of Reorganization but in no event shall Seller or its designees receive other than voting stock of Buyer. No adjustment shall be made hereunder with respect to stock dividends not exceeding three percentum (3%) of Buyer's outstanding stock, per year.

The above clauses relating to the determination of contingent shares to be paid by the buyer make reference to accounting principles set forth in Appendix II of the acquisition contract. Appendix II is set forth below:

APPENDIX II

Accounting Principles for the Preparation of Financial Statements For the Determination of Contingent Share Payments

For the Fiscal Year Ending September 30, 1970:

1. *Unless otherwise stated hereafter, the accounting principles employed shall be the same as those applied on a consistent basis in preceding years.*

2. *In the preparation of a pro forma combined balance sheet and income statement covering the five corporations and the partnership required under the agreement,*

these statements should reflect the elimination of all intercompany transactions, including intercompany profits in inventories, and the provision for full U.S. corporate income taxes on the profits of foreign subsidiaries as though earnings were repatriated on a current basis.

3. *In the determination of net income for Seller Subsidiary of Canada, Limited, provision will be made for the following extraordinary charges.*

   a. *Write down to the lower of cost or market value (at September 30, 1970) those securities held as an investment at that date.*

   b. *Provision for a 15% designated surplus tax which after the acquisition will be levied under Section 105B of the Canadian Income Tax Act upon the distribution of existing earnings and profits of the Canadian Company.*

4. *Any significant inconsistencies in accounting principles and practices, as between the various corporations, will be spelled out by the audit of the Seller's certified public accountants in appropriate notes to the audited pro forma combined statements and covering transmittal letter.*

5. *Extraordinary charges for write-down of securities and provision for 15% designated surplus tax with respect to Seller's Subsidiary of Canada, Limited, provided for in Item 3 above shall be excluded from the determination of "minimum" pro forma combined after-tax earnings for the year ended September 30, 1970, provided for in Section 9.08 of the Reorganization Agreement.*

For Fiscal Years—September 30, 1971 through September 30, 1974:

1. *Depreciation will be computed on a basis consistent with that used for the fiscal year ended September 30, 1970 for all plant, property, and equipment. These depreciation policies are as follows:*

   a. *Book and tax depreciation are the same.*

   b. *Additional first year depreciation of 20% is taken for both book and tax purposes on qualified assets.*

   c. *Depreciation methods are as follows:*

      (1) Items with a useful life of 3 years or less are depreciated straight-line.

      (2) Generally, items over 3 years, declining balance.

      (3) One-half year's depreciation is taken in the year acquired and also in the last year of useful life.

      (4) Molds, patterns, and tools are usually 3 years straight-line.

      (5) Most office furniture and equipment is 10 years double-declining balance.

      (6) Paved parking lot—15 years straight-line.

      (7) Most buildings and additions—20 years straight-line.

      (8) Most plant machinery—10 years double-declining balance.

      (9) Items costing under $400 but with lives over 3 years—double-declining balance (this is usually a 5-year life).

2. *Prior period adjustments and extraordinary items, as defined by Accounting Principles Board Opinion #9 of the American Institute of Certified Public Accountants, will be excluded from the determination of after-tax consolidated earnings for the then-current year.*

3. *Inventories will be costed on the basis consistently employed by the Seller in prior years, i.e., at standard cost using the first-in, first-out method of costing and providing for a write-down market value where cost exceeds market at balance sheet dates.*

4. *Comprehensive U.S. income taxes will be provided for and deducted in determining after-tax consolidated earnings based upon the consolidated taxable income shown by the books of account for the Seller, excluding as a tax reduction any amortization of capitalized patent or other costs arising upon dissolution of the partnership. Full U.S. income taxes will also be provided on the profits of foreign subsidiaries.*

5. *Sales of finished goods of their manufacture by Seller to Buyer and Buyer's subsidiaries will be on a "most favored distributor" basis.*

6. *Sales of finished goods of their manufacture by Buyer and Buyer's subsidiaries to the Seller will be on a "most favored distributor" basis.*

7. *All cash in excess of normal working capital needs will be remitted to Buyer weekly. In recognition of the need for funds for capital investment, Buyer will provide funds up to $250,000 each year for approved capital projects, or $1,000,000 for the four years, plus any additional amounts generated as a result of the liquidation of assets not in the normal course of business, without a charge for interest. Seller will be charged interest at a rate equal to 1/2 of 1% over the prime bank rate for funds provided by Buyer in excess of expenditures for capital projects and will be credited with interest at the same rate for funds remitted to Buyer in excess of such capital expenditures, provided that such credit for interest shall not exceed $7,000 per year.*

8. *Specific service requests by Seller to Buyer for technical aid, special research programs, advertising etc., will be charged to Seller on the basis of cost.*

9. *General services, such as auditing, tax, legal, etc., provided or paid for by Buyer for the Seller in lieu of obtaining such services from other sources will be charged to Seller on a basis consistent with Buyer's current accounting practices. However, charges for such services shall be limited to services provided and shall not exceed costs at which Seller could reasonably expect to obtain similar services from other sources. Arbitrary charges by Buyer for management or administrative services or similar charges which are neither controllable by Seller nor properly chargeable against the operations of Seller will be excluded from the determination of after-tax consolidated earnings.*

10. *Consolidated income for the Seller shall exclude any amortization of capitalized royalty rights or other costs arising upon the dissolution of the partnership.*

11. *Except as indicated above, the accounting principles currently followed by the Seller are to be consistently applied throughout the periods upon which payment of the contingent shares are based.*

The foregoing clauses contain provisions to determine the number of contingent shares payable to a seller under a formula based upon future earnings of the seller, as well as detailed accounting principles to be applied in computing those earnings. The "seller" in the particular situation, included a combination of three corporations (one a foreign corporation) and two partnerships. The detailed provisions in the acquisition contract and in the appendix of accounting principles illustrate some fundamentals which should be considered in drafting clauses to provide for future installment payments of a buyer's stock based upon a seller's future earnings.

Two fundamental determinations are involved.

First, the acquisition contract should contain a formula under which the future earnings of a seller are to be converted into shares of stock of the buyer. Such a formula may involve:

(1) Definitions of the seller's fiscal years to be utilized in determining future earnings—the buyout period.

(2) The amount of future earnings for each fiscal year in the buyout period which will result in payment of additional stock.

(3) A determination whether the earnings of the seller during the contingency payment period are to be considered on a cumulative basis.

(4) A choice of stock price averaging periods or formulae for converting the seller's future earnings into additional shares of stock, and

(5) Dates for delivery of the buyer's stock.

Second, the acquisition contract or a related document should contain a detailed accounting definition of the accounting principles to be applied in computing the earnings of the seller during the buyout period. The accounting definitions should include resolution of matters such as those listed below to make the determination of earnings:

(1) Whether the basic accounting principles to be employed should be those used in the past by either the buyer or the seller.

(2) Inconsistencies from such accounting principles in determining future earnings of the seller during the buyout period should be set forth in detail.

(3) Unique circumstances involving the seller's business, such as treatment of intercompany transactions where subsidiaries are involved or foreign taxes where foreign subsidiaries are involved, should be provided for.

(4) The depreciation policies should be provided for in detail, including consideration of the following:

  (a) Relationship of book and tax depreciation;

  (b) The extent to which determination of depreciation is made on other than a straight-line basis.

  (c) Detailed depreciation methods involving such aspects as (i) Items with useful life of 3 years or less, (ii) Items of useful life in excess of 3 years; (iii) Whether one/half year's depreciation is taken in year of acquisition of the asset; (iv) Depreciation on molds, patterns and tools; (v) Depreciation on furniture and fixtures; (vi) Depreciation on unique assets such as parking facilities; (vii) Depreciation on real estate; and (viii) Depreciation on plant and machinery.

(5) Treatment of prior period adjustments and extraordinary items.

(6) Treatment of inventories.

(7) Computation of taxes where foreign jurisdictions and different entities are involved.

(8) Determination of prices where future sales of products and supplies between buyer and seller and their subsidiaries may be involved.

(9) Working capital to be made available to seller and treatment of interest charges between buyer and seller with respect to funds respectively made available to each other.

(10) Charges for special services such as accounting, legal and other general and administrative services to be made available to seller.

BUYER'S ASSUMPTION OF LIABILITIES

When the buyer acquires stock of a seller the liabilities of the corporate business continue,

since no change in the corporate entity has occurred. On the other hand, where a buyer acquires assets for cash, the buyer generally assumes only liabilities specifically assumed by the
buyer in the contract (subject only to bulk sales or similar laws). Clauses defining what
liabilities, if any, are assumed by the buyer must often form part of the acquisition contract:

Assumption of Liabilities

*1. Subject to the provisions of this agreement and plan of reorganization, buyer will
assume as of the closing date and pay or discharge the following obligations and liabilities of seller:*

*(a) Disclosed on its balance sheet as of April 30, 1970, attached hereto as Exhibit
A in the amounts recorded on the books as of closing date;*

(b) In connection with the suits numbered 1, 2 and 3 Exhibit C;

(c) Under contracts and agreements listed in Exhibit D; and

*(d) Under leases and agreements listed in Exhibit F, and under commitments for
the purchase of raw materials and sales of merchandise and under contracts, agreements,
and commitments, all as made in the ordinary course and conduct of business since
April 30, 1970, down to the closing date.*

SELLER'S INDEMNIFICATION OF BUYER

Where the buyer does not assume all of the seller's liabilities, the seller often agrees to
indemnify the buyer against unassumed liabilities, contingent or otherwise. Sometimes this indemnification includes a pledge of stock or other collateral. The indemnity clause printed below is a continuation of the above clauses which fix the obligations which the buyer agrees to
assume, and this indemnity clause indemnifies the buyer against all other obligations. The
parties of the second part referred to in the clause were the two principal shareholders of the
seller:

*2. The parties of the second part each jointly and severally will indemnify and hold
harmless the buyer from any and all liabilities of seller and/or affecting the business of
seller incurred by buyer by reason of the transactions contemplated by this agreement
and plan of reorganization, except as to any obligations or liabilities specifically assumed
by buyer pursuant to paragraph 1 of this Article IV [printed above]. To that end 800
shares of the total number of shares noted in Article III (in such registered names as
the parties of the second part shall select) shall be endorsed in blank by the registered
owners thereof and redelivered to buyer under pledge agreement entered into on the
closing date, with instructions to hold the same until the third anniversary of the closing
date, or until the ultimate determination of the litigation listed in the attached Exhibit C
as number 4, whichever last occurs. All dividends on such shares shall be paid to the
record holders thereof who so endorsed them in blank. After the satisfaction of any claim
by buyer under this paragraph 2, buyer shall pay the balance of shares to such record
holders. Any expenses, including reasonable attorneys' fees in connection with the conduct of any suit or claim against seller not noted in paragraph 1 of this Article IV, or in
connection with any other liabilities not so assumed by buyer, shall not be borne by
buyer, directly or indirectly.*

The foregoing clause, in addition to providing an indemnification for the buyer against
unassumed liabilities, provides that 800 shares of the buyer's stock will be pledged by the seller

to secure the seller's indemnification. Ordinarily, the form of pledge agreement is attached to the acquisition contract. A form of pledge agreement is set forth in the next chapter.

CONDUCT OF BUSINESS PENDING CLOSING

Pending the closing, the contract usually restricts the seller from certain action during the period from the contract signing to the closing date, and in addition often requires the seller to conduct the business only in the ordinary course. Paragraph 3 and 4 beginning at page 227 of the contract printed in Chapter 12 contain usual restrictive and affirmative covenants on the part of the seller or the selling stockholders. Such covenants will be similar whether the buyer is acquiring stock or assets of the seller, but must, of course, be modified to fit the particular situation. For example, exceptions may be made in the restrictive convenants permitting the seller to pay its next regular dividend (specifying the date and amount) or to make sizable capital expenditure known to be required at the time of signing the contract.

CONDITIONS PRECEDENT TO THE CLOSING

Both the buyer and seller may require the insertion of specified conditions precedent in the contract. If a condition precedent is not fulfilled, the party affected may refuse to carry out its obligations under the acquisition contract, and not suffer any legal liability as a result of its refusal. The stock-for-stock contract printed in Chapter 12 contains many of the usual conditions precedent to a buyer's obligation to close, in paragraph 7 beginning at page 229. That contract contains no conditions precedent to the seller's obligation to close—an unusual situation. Normally a seller will insist on at least some conditions precedent such as an opinion of buyer's counsel as to the validity of buyer's representations and warranties or a ruling of the Commissioner of Internal Revenue that the transaction is tax free. Printed below are conditions precedent which buyers or sellers may wish to insert in acquisition contracts in addition to those printed in Chapter 12.

(a) "Pooling of Interests" Ruling—A Buyer's Condition Precedent.

That buyer shall receive an opinion from the Securities and Exchange Commission to the effect that the transactions contemplated by this agreement and plan of reorganization may be treated, for accounting purposes, as a "pooling of interests."

(b) Tax-Free Reorganization Ruling—A Seller's or Sometimes Seller's and Buyer's Condition Precedent.

The obligations of seller hereunder are subject to seller's receiving prior to the closing of title a ruling from the Commissioner of Internal Revenue that the proposed transactions will constitute tax-free reorganizations within the purview of Sections 368 and 354 of the Internal Revenue Code of 1954 and the regulations thereunder.

(c) Correctness of Buyer's Representations—A Seller's Condition Precedent.

That the representations and warranties of buyer contained in Section 2 of Article 1 of this agreement and plan of reorganization are true and correct when made and as of the closing date hereinafter provided.

(d) Opinion of Buyer's Counsel—A Seller's Condition Precedent.

That seller shall have received the opinion of Jones & Jones, counsel for buyer, dated on said closing date, to the effect that:

(a) Buyer is a corporation duly organized, validly existing and in good standing under the laws of the state of New Jersey.

(b) Buyer has been duly authorized by its board of directors to execute and perform this agreement and plan of reorganization, and all corporate action required by its charter, by its by-laws and by the laws of the state of New Jersey, necessary to perform such agreement and plan of reorganization has been duly taken.

(c) That the shares of common stock of buyer to be delivered to seller are duly and legally issued, fully paid and non-assessable, free and clear of all liens and encumbrances, and will be approved for listing on official notice of issuance on the New York Stock Exchange and are equal in all respects, (including, but not by way of limitation, voting rights), to every other share of the common stock of buyer, issued and outstanding, excepting only that the shares of common stock to be delivered to seller will not have been registered with the Securities and Exchange Commission.

(e) A Group of Miscellaneous Conditions Precedent.

(i) A tax ruling involving "Section 306 stock":

Seller shall have received from the Internal Revenue Service a ruling satisfactory to its counsel (i) that the reorganization herein contemplated will not result in the recognition of gain or loss to seller, or to its stockholders upon the subsequent distribution of shares of convertible preferred stock to such stockholders upon the dissolution and liquidation of seller; and (ii) that such convertible preferred stock will not constitute "Section 306 stock" within the meaning of the Internal Revenue Code.

(ii) That dissenting shareholders do not exceed a specified percentage:

In the event that this agreement and plan of reorganization is authorized by the holders of at least two-thirds of the shares entitled to vote thereon, that no more than a total of 3% of the total outstanding shares of seller's common stock are dissenting shares.

(iii) Delivery of certified documents.

The obligation of buyer to purchase the assets and properties to be conveyed and transferred hereunder is subject to the satisfaction on or prior to the closing date of the following conditions:

(a) Seller shall have furnished buyer with (i) certified copies of resolutions duly adopted by the holders of at least a majority of all of the outstanding shares of capital stock of seller, approving the execution and delivery to buyer of this agreement and authorizing and consenting to the conveyance and transfer of the assets and properties to be conveyed and transferred hereunder in accordance with the terms hereof, (ii) certified copies of resolutions duly adopted by the board of directors of seller with respect to both of the aforesaid matters, and (iii) all other documents, certificates and other instruments required to be furnished to buyer by seller pursuant to the terms of this agreement.

PLAN OF REORGANIZATION

Where the transaction is to be treated as tax-free, the acquisition contract will often contain a Plan of Reorganization tailored to the specific Internal Revenue Code provisions under which tax-free treatment is sought. The plan of reorganization in paragraph 6. of the contract printed in Chapter 12 beginning at page 228, is a stock-for-stock plan of reorganization under Section 368(a)(1)(B) of the Internal Revenue Code. The plan printed below is for an acquisition contract under which a buyer acquires substantially all of the assets of a seller in exchange for buyer's voting stock, a reorganization pursuant to Section 368(a)(1)(C) of the Internal Revenue Code:

Plan of Reorganization

Subject to the terms and conditions of this agreement and plan of reorganization the parties have adopted and agreed to the following plan of reorganization to be performed on the closing date hereby designated as April 30, 1971, at 11:00 a.m. E.S.T., at the offices of Peck & Peck, 500 East 42nd Street, New York, New York 10047.

1. Seller shall exchange, assign, convey, transfer and deliver unto buyer by appropriate documents of transfer satisfactory to counsel for buyer, all of the properties and assets of seller as an entirety (except such as are retained pursuant to paragraph 3 of this article), being the same and all the properties and assets described in Article II, free and clear of all liens, restrictions and encumbrances, except taxes not delinquent and except such liens, restrictions and encumbrances as have heretofore been disclosed by seller to buyer in writing.

Seller will deliver to buyer a certificate of amendment of its articles of incorporation, in executed form suitable for filing with the secretary of the state of Wisconsin, or such other public official with whom such documents are customarily filed, changing the name of seller to another, dissimilar name.

2. Buyer will deliver to seller certificates of stock of buyer representing full shares of voting common stock of buyer in the amount as adjusted in accordance with Article III, being the shares noted in Article III. In the event there is any change in the voting common stock of buyer through the declaration of stock dividends or through recapitalizations resulting in stock splitups or combinations of shares of voting common stock of buyer prior to the closing date, the number of shares deliverable hereunder shall be adjusted proportionately. Such certificates shall be issued in such names and denominations as seller shall have requested of buyer in writing not later than 10 business days prior to the closing date. Buyer shall not be required to issue or deliver any certificates for fractional shares.

3. Seller shall retain such sums as are necessary to pay the holders of dissenting shares, and to pay reasonable and proper expenses and costs incurred in connection with the transactions contemplated by this agreement and plan of reorganization, including costs and fees for filing and recording instruments of conveyance or assignment, costs of dissolution and liquidation, costs of distribution to its shareholders of certificates of stock of buyer (including federal and state transfer taxes and fees and disbursements of any agent appointed to conduct such distribution), reasonable counsel and accounting fees and other costs and fees customarily incident to transactions of the kind contemplated by this agreement and plan of reorganization. Such sums retained shall be in cash if on hand at the closing date, or, if not on hand, then in such cash as is on hand together with accounts receivable, and if necessary, other assets having a fair value equal to the balance. After the payment of such holders of dissenting shares in settlement of their rights as dissenting shareholders and payment of the other costs and fees noted, any balance remaining shall be forthwith paid to buyer.

4. Seller shall, immediately after the closing date, deposit the voting common stock of buyer received hereunder with City Amalgamated Bank ("bank") as agent for the share-

holders of seller who did not dissent to this agreement and plan of reorganization, and who, upon delivery of their shares of seller, duly endorsed with signatures appropriately guaranteed and accompanied by any evidence required by seller's transfer agent, Trust & Co., shall be entitled to receive voting common stock of buyer in exchange for their shares of seller, in the ratio of one full buyer share for each 2.3 shares of seller's common stock (Class A or B), except that no fractional shares of buyer's voting common stock will be distributed. For a period of 90 days after such deposit of buyer's stock deliverable hereunder with the bank, each seller's shareholder shall be given an opportunity to sell any fractional interest through the bank or to round out such fractional interest into a whole share of buyer's voting common stock by purchasing an additional fraction through the bank. As soon as practicable after the expiration of said period, all buyer's voting common stock held to cover fractional interests for which buy or sell orders shall not have been received by that time will be sold for the account of the persons entitled to such fractional interests and the proceeds distributed to such persons when they shall have surrendered their seller's shares as above provided. The costs and expenses of the bank (exclusive of the cost of any fraction of a share of buyer's voting common stock purchased to round out a fractional share into a whole share, or costs of any transfer taxes on the purchase or sale of fractional interests, which costs shall be paid to the bank by the seller's shareholder desiring to round out his share) shall be assumed and paid by seller. The bank shall be entitled to rely on any instructions received from seller and on any certificate of seller. Seller shall furnish the bank as soon as practicable after the closing date with a certified list of the shares voted in favor of the transfer and dissolution contemplated by this agreement and plan of reorganization and instructions as to the bank's procedure in distributing buyer's voting common stock to the seller's shareholders entitled thereto.

5. Buyer will assume the liabilities of seller as provided in paragraph 1 of Article IV, but buyer shall not assume or pay any expenses or charges incurred by seller in connection with the transactions contemplated by this agreement and plan of reorganization.

6. Seller, immediately after the closing date, will discontinue and not renew the business which it is now conducting, will initiate proceedings or continue previously initiated proceedings to dissolve its corporate existence and liquidate its affairs, and will take all corporate actions requisite to make available to buyer for its exclusive use the corporate and trade name "XYZ Electric Company" and the name "XYZ."

The above plan of reorganization is somewhat unusual in that the buyer may be required to deliver more than one certificate to the seller for its assets. Quite often the plan will provide for the delivery of a single certificate issued in the name of the seller for the total number of shares included in the purchase price. This certificate is then deposited and drawn against to issue separate certificates to the seller's stockholders as they deliver their certificates for shares of the seller. Note also that seller's stockholders rather than the seller pay for transfer taxes in rounding out shares.

BROKERAGE

Each acquisition contract should contain a clear brokerage provision indicating which of the parties, if any, is to pay brokerage commission and providing that each party indemnifies the other from payment of commissions where the indemnifying party has caused the commissions to become due and payable. Brokerage might also be considered under the last group of contract provisions, General Provisions printed below, but because of the importance of brokerage it is treated as a separate category:

Buyer and seller each represents and warrants that all negotiations relative to this agreement and the transactions contemplated hereby have been carried on by each directly with the other without intervention of any persons other than their respective employees, agents and consultants, (except for the services of John Jones & Associates, of St. Croix, Arizona, whose fee if any, seller agrees to pay), and each indemnifies the other to hold it harmless against and in respect of any claim against the other for brokerage or other commissions relative to this agreement and the transactions contemplated hereby by the indemnifying party's employees, agents or consultants.

GENERAL PROVISIONS

In addition to formal provisions, such as clauses restricting the assignment of the contract, and clauses detailing the mechanics of giving notices under the contract printed in Chapter 12 beginning at page 232, an acquisition contract may contain other general provisions of considerably more substance. Printed below are additional general provisions found in acquisition contracts where circumstances warrant, both of a substantive and mechanical nature:

(*a*) A Clause Requiring Buyer to Keep the Results of His Investigation Confidential.

The clause printed below indicates the lengths to which buyers and sellers will go when the seller's business, investigated by the buyer, involves trade secrets and many patent applications:

Seller grants to buyer and its representatives and attorneys complete access to seller's respective premises, books, records and accounts and will cooperate with buyer to the end that buyer may satisfy itself as to the corporate authority and structure of seller, the accuracy of the balance sheet, the amount of seller's income for the 6 months ended June 30, 1970, the fulfillment by seller of all of the terms and conditions hereof and seller's compliance with all of its obligations hereunder and so that buyer may become fully acquainted with seller's plants, customers, suppliers, tangible and intangible assets, rights and liabilities, and all other matters and things pertaining to the operation of the business of seller, but nothing contained in this agreement shall be deemed to obligate seller to reveal to buyer or permit buyer to examine any invention or improvement disclosure of any of them or to permit buyer to examine any patent application of seller otherwise than upon a confidential basis and upon written request of buyer. In the event that the transactions contemplated by this agreement shall not be consummated, (1) all information received by buyer from seller with respect to any of the business of seller shall not at any time or in any way or manner be utilized by buyer for its advantage, or disclosed by buyer to others to the detriment of seller, (2) buyer will take no action to prevent, delay or otherwise interfere with the issuance to seller or their assigns of letters patent based on any patent application of any of them revealed to buyer at its written request or which buyer is permitted to examine at its written request and (3) buyer will not, on the basis of information with respect to any such patent application or invention or improvement disclosure revealed by seller to buyer at its written request, question the validity of or otherwise contest, affirmatively or by way of defense, any such patent

or patent application of seller, or attempt to patent any process or other invention con-
tained in or based on any such patent application. Notwithstanding the foregoing, the
obligation of buyer contained in clause (1) of this subsection shall not apply to written
information supplied by seller to buyer prior to July 3, 1970, or to information which
is a matter of public knowledge or which has heretofore been or may hereafter be printed
in any publication. In the event that the transactions contemplated by this agreement
shall not be consummated, buyer shall furnish to seller copies of the financial statements
of seller and all reports relating to seller prepared by buyer's certified public accountants.
In the event that the transactions contemplated by this agreement shall not be consum-
mated, all information received by seller from buyer with respect to the business of
buyer (other than written information supplied by buyer to seller prior to July 3, 1970,
and information supplied which is a matter of public knowledge or which has hereto-
fore been or may hereafter be printed in any publication) shall not at any time or in any
way or manner be utilized by seller for its advantage or disclosed by seller to others to
the detriment of buyer.

(b) Anti-Trust Escape Clauses.

Where the parties fear that private or governmental action may be taken to block a proposed acquisition, they may provide for such contingencies in the acquisition contract. The
first clause printed below gives either party a right to terminate where such party is informed
and believes that litigation may be instituted:

Any party may terminate its obligations under this agreement prior to the closing of
title if the transactions contemplated hereby would be in violation of any judgment, order
or degree of any courts or any order, notice or regulation of any United States govern-
mental agency having jurisdiction with respect thereto or if such party is informed and
in good faith believes that litigation may be instituted by a governmental agency, which,
if successful, would preclude such transactions.

The next clause printed below, in which the parties provided for an original closing date
of April 30, 1970, permits a postponement of the closing date only if the closing would be in
violation of a judgment, order or decree of a court:

In the event that on April 30, 1970, or on any other date set as the closing date, the
transactions herein contemplated have not been submitted for the approval of stock-
holders of seller, or the consummation of the transactions herein contemplated would
be in violation of any judgment, order or degree of any court, the closing date shall be
postponed to the same time and place on the last business day of the first or second fol-
lowing month agreeable to the parties (with, if necessary, successive postponements
to the last business day of succeeding months); provided, however, that if for any reason
the closing has not been consummated on or before September 30, 1970, this agreement
shall terminate without liability or obligation of either party to the other except pursuant
to sub-paragraph 4(a) hereof. Unless there is a judgment, order or decree of any court
outstanding which would be violated by the transactions herein contemplated, seller
will promptly submit the transactions herein contemplated for approval of its stock-
holders, but the calling of the meeting for such submission, if deemed advisable by seller,
need not be made before March 22, 1970. Such meeting shall be held within sixty days
of the calling thereof.

The above clause is also an example of the parties providing for possible postponements of the closing in the acquisition contract. Such provisions are customary where the closing is contingent upon receipt of rulings from governmental agencies, but every acquisition contract should contain a realistic termination date setting forth the liabilities and obligations, if any, of the parties to one another if the closing has not occurred by that date.

(c) A Bulk-Sales Law Provision.

As indicated in Chapter 7, state bulk sales laws should not be ignored in an assets acquisition. Such laws need only be considered where a buyer is acquiring assets, and in such instances the contract may provide that the law will be complied with or, where compliance would be burdensome or disadvantageous, that the seller will indemnify the buyer against the effect of non-compliance. The clause below is an indemnification clause in which the "parties of the second part" are the principal shareholders of the seller:

> *Buyer waives compliance with the provisions of any applicable bulk sales law and the parties of the second part agree to indemnify and hold harmless buyer from any liability incurred as a result of the failure to so comply. The pledge of shares noted in paragraph 2 above shall be to secure this indemnity as well as those therein noted.*

(d) A Sales and Use Tax Clause.

Although casual or one-time sales are often exempt from sales taxes, in some states a sales tax may be payable with respect to some of the tangible assets transferred in an assets acquisition. Signing contract and closing outside such states may not avoid liability for the tax where the states impose a compensating use tax. Under the circumstances, the parties should provide in the contract whether the buyer or seller will pay the tax. Below is a clause in which the buyer agreed to pay the tax:

> *Buyer will pay all recording fees and all sales and use taxes payable in connection with the sale, transfer, deliveries and assignments to be made to buyer hereunder.*

(e) Clauses Dealing with Employees.

(i) Employment Contracts.

Where a buyer wants seller's key employees to remain with the business, he may require the seller to deliver signed employment contracts at the closing, and also may make receipt of such contracts a condition precedent to closing:

At the closing of title:
A. Seller shall deliver to buyer:
Employment agreements substantially in the form annexed hereto as Exhibit C signed by each of the persons listed in said Exhibit C.

If the parties do not wish the terms of the employment contracts to become known, the form of employment contracts may be agreed upon in advance, executed and separately delivered at the closing, not attached to the contract.

(ii) **Employee Benefit Plans.**

Where the buyer is acquiring substantially all of the assets and business of the seller:

On the closing date, buyer shall be substituted for seller as the employer under seller's retirement plan and all other employee benefit plans of seller and assume all of seller's obligations thereunder as of the closing date. All of seller's right, title and interest in and to such plans shall be vested in buyer. From and after the closing date, said plans shall be continued in full force and effect for employees of the XYZ division of buyer, provided, however, that nothing contained herein shall in any way limit the right of buyer to amend or terminate any of said plans at any time to the same extent that seller had a right to do so on the closing date, or thereafter might have secured a right to do so.

Where the buyer is acquiring a division of the seller:

(a) All employees of division as of the closing date will be transferred from the seller's payroll to the payroll of buyer.

(b) The parties will take all steps necessary and use their best efforts to amend and segregate the respective retirement plans covering salaried and commission-paid employees, and hourly-paid employees, and the supplemental benefit plan which constitutes appendix A of the hourly plan to provide for the continuation of the accrual of benefit rights, and for the continuity of service credits, and for the change of name of these plans, insofar as the employees of division will be affected.

(c) The parties will take all steps necessary and use their best efforts to amend the applicable trust agreements under which the pension plan for hourly-paid employees of the division, the supplemental benefit plan and the retirement annuity plan for salaried and commission-paid employees of division are, respectively, funded. Such amendments shall make provision for the segregation of assets arising in respect of the employees of division who will continue as employees of buyer. It is contemplated that such segregated assets will be held by the existing trustees under separate trust agreements but may be subsequently transferred or consolidated into other retirement funds of buyer.

Where pensions are payable to previously retired employees of seller:

The liabilities of seller assumed by buyer hereunder shall include seller's obligations as of the closing date to make pension payments directly to former employees of seller who have theretofore retired from active service. As to all employees of seller who continue after the closing date in the employ of buyer, and who otherwise qualify for participation in buyer's pension plan, buyer will give credit under that plan for the past service of such employees with seller or its predecessor companies. As to employees of seller who are actively in its service on the closing date, and who do not continue in the employ of buyer thereafter, buyer shall have no obligation of any kind with respect to pension allowances. Promptly after the execution hereof and in any event prior to the closing date, buyer and seller will make such arrangements as may be appropriate under the circumstances for the disposition or administration of the existing pension fund of seller under its pension trust agreement for eligible salaried employees, dated August 21, 1970.

(iii) **Employee Stock Options.**

In some instances a buyer will refuse to assume any liability for previously outstanding stock options of seller's employees. In others, the buyer will agree to substitute options on his stock for the options held on the seller's stock. Such substitution may be made without tax consequence to the employees of the seller, provided the substitution complies with the requirements of Section 425(a) of the Internal Revenue Code of 1954. Generally, under these requirements the substituted option may not place the employee in a better financial position than under the old option.

Where the buyer assumes no liability for outstanding options:

The liabilities assumed by buyer hereunder shall not include any obligation on the part of buyer with respect to the stock options outstanding on the date of this agreement for employees of seller. To the extent that seller shall settle or satisfy its obligations under such options after the date of this agreement by either buying shares in the open market for such purpose or by making cash payments, such expenditures shall be for its own account and shall be credited on the closing date against the purchase price to be paid by buyer hereunder. The purchase of its shares by seller for this purpose shall not constitute a violation of the covenant by seller contained in Section 3(e) of Article IV.

Where the buyer will substitute buyer's options:

Buyer shall substitute for the stock options granted under seller's qualified option plan, to the extent that such options have not become exercisable prior to the closing date, options to purchase shares of buyer's common stock in lieu of shares of capital stock of seller, on a basis which will comply with Section 425(a) of the Internal Revenue Code of 1954, as amended, and which, subject to compliance with said section, will on the closing date be as favorable to the holders of such options as their options with respect to seller's capital stock.

(iv) A Collective Bargaining Agreement.

Buyer will assume all obligations for hourly-paid employees under the agreement between division and International Union of Electrical, Radio and Machine Workers, A.F.L.—C.I.O., Local 204, with respect to all employees transferred to buyer as provided in paragraph (a) above. The parties will take all steps necessary and use their best efforts to amend the said agreement in such fashion as to provide two separate agreements, one covering the employees to be transferred to buyer and the other covering employees retained on the seller's payroll located at the Los Angeles plant.

(v) Employee Security Clearances.

With respect to the employees of division taken over by buyer as of the closing date, seller will retain all personnel security clearance records and will, to the extent permitted by government regulations, make such records available to buyer as required from time to time.

(f) Books, Records and Classified Documents.

A sale of a division where classified documents are not involved:

With the exception of division's books of account, income tax returns and correspondence relating thereto, and any documents of over-all company significance, such as corporate procedure manual, corporate organization manual, policy manual, controller's manual, engineering and manufacturing standards manual and the like, seller will deliver, on the closing date, division's correspondence, files, drawings, data and other records, papers and documents.

Buyer agrees to preserve such records for a period of six years after the closing date or for such longer period or periods as may be required under contract relating to such documents and entered into prior to the closing date, and during such period or periods, make the same available for examination (or for the making of copies or extracts), if necessary, by seller at reasonable times so as not to interfere with buyer's business.

Seller agrees that the books of account of division retained by seller shall be made available for examination, if necessary, by buyer, at reasonable times so as not to interfere with seller's business.

In the case of any request for examination of documents by either party, the party having possession of the desired records may, at its option, deliver the appropriate records to the requesting party in lieu of allowing visits onto its premises. Such documents so delivered shall not be retained for an unreasonable amount of time. The cost of delivery and return shall be borne by the party requesting examination.

A sale of a division where classified documents are involved:

Books and Records.

(a) With the exception of division's (1) books of account, income tax returns and correspondence and documents relating thereto, (2) document log recording incoming and outgoing transmission of classified documents, (3) record of reproduction of classified documents, (4) certification of distribution of classified documents, (5) accounting for all secret security information, and (6) visitors register, on the closing date seller will deliver to buyer all of division's correspondence, files, drawings, data and other records, papers and documents and manuals or portions thereof relating specifically to, or used by, division.

Custody and Responsibility for Classified Documents.

With respect to those classified documents which are to be transferred to buyer hereunder, seller and buyer will take all steps necessary to obtain the consent for the transfer of such documents from the governmental authorities respectively involved or for other disposition of such documents. Pending transfer, responsibility for and custody of such classified documents will rest in seller.

(g) Avoiding Double Dividend to Seller's Stockholders.

Should the record date for the payment of the next quarterly dividend on buyer's common stock (buyer's date) occur subsequent to the record date for the payment of the next quarterly dividend on seller's common or preferred stock (seller's record date) then, the closing date shall not, in any event, occur on any date subsequent to the seller's record date and before the buyer's record date. It is the intention of the parties that the shareholders of seller not receive both the next regular buyer's dividend and the next regular seller's dividend.

(h) Transfer of Seller's Assets to Buyer's Subsidiary Rather Than to Buyer.

This may be accomplished tax free under the Internal Revenue Code of 1954:

On the Closing Date the Stockholder will transfer to Buyer or the Buyer's Subsidiary, as Buyer may elect, the number of shares of Common Stock of each Corporation set forth on Exhibit A hereto as issued and outstanding, such shares to constitute all of the outstanding capital stock of each Corporation. All certificates representing shares of such stock shall be in form for transfer by delivery and all transfer taxes payable on transfer thereof shall be paid by the Stockholder.

(*i*) Bank Accounts.

Where numerous bank accounts are involved, a buyer may want knowledge of the details:

Seller 15 days prior to the closing date will deliver to buyer a true and complete list as of the date of this agreement certified by its treasurer showing (i) the name of each bank in which seller and its subsidiary have an account or safe deposit box and the names of all persons authorized to draw thereon or to have access thereto and (ii) the names of all persons, if any, holding powers of attorney from seller or its subsidiary and a summary statement of the terms thereof.

(*j*) Retention of Cash by Seller in Stock-for-Assets Transaction.

Where a buyer acquires substantially all of the assets of a seller for the buyer's stock, to avoid possibly upsetting the tax-free nature of such a transaction, a seller will often retain cash to pay incidental expenses, rather than have the buyer pay them:

Anything in this agreement contained to the contrary notwithstanding, seller, at any time prior to the completion of the transaction contemplated hereby may pay in whole or in part such of its liabilities as mature in the ordinary course of seller's business, and shall on and after the closing date retain from the assets deliverable hereunder an amount of cash sufficient to pay, and shall pay therefrom as promptly as possible, all reasonable expenses incurred by seller, in making this agreement or in carrying it into effect or which are otherwise incidental thereto including, without limitation of the foregoing (i) all reasonable compensation and expenses of its counsel and independent accountants, (ii) any and all stamp taxes, federal or state, required on the transfer by seller to its stockholders of shares of convertible preferred stock, including the expenses of the exchange agent for the seller's stockholders incident to such transfer, (iii) any and all taxes, federal or state, required to be paid by seller in respect of the conveyances, assignments or transfers to buyer of the properties and assets of seller and the filing and recording thereof, (iv) any and all fees, taxes and charges required to be paid by seller in connection with its withdrawal from the states in which it is qualified to do business, (v) the amount required to be paid to stockholders of seller who have demanded payment for the value of their shares pursuant to the provisions of section 271.415 of the Kentucky revised statutes and (vi) an amount not to exceed $20,000 for the liquidation of seller, it being understood that buyer shall bear no part of the liquidation expenses in excess of this amount. Upon the payment of such expenses from the cash so retained, any balance so remaining of such cash shall be paid to buyer.

Note the comment after the Plan of Reorganization printed in item 10, above, beginning at page 256.

(*k*) Novation of Customer Contracts.

Often, particularly where government contracts are involved, the question of whether the buyer or seller should be responsible for performance becomes of importance. Sometimes, where contracts are not novated, the buyer agrees to perform for the seller's account, but on other occasions the buyer agrees to perform for its own account—as in the clause below:

It is agreed by the parties hereto that the contracts listed on Schedule B are contracts which are to be the subject of novation agreements between buyer, seller, and the third parties to the contracts. Seller and buyer agree that they will use their best efforts to effect such novations. The work called for under such contracts from and after such novations, which shall date as of the closing date, shall be performed by buyer for the account of buyer and buyer shall hold seller free from any loss arising from any claim or litigation arising from such work. From and after the closing date, buyer shall assume all losses and retain all profits arising from such contracts.

In the event that novation agreements are not entered into through factors beyond the control of either party hereto, then buyer shall, nevertheless, perform such work as is required for the account of buyer and profits or losses therefrom shall be treated the same as if such contracts were novated.

With respect to any cost-plus-fixed-fee contract or field service contract listed in Schedule B, if additional funding of any contract appears necessary prior to transfer, buyer and seller will coordinate in a request, as may be mutually considered appropriate and timely, for such additional funding.

Where the buyer agrees to perform non-novated contracts for the account of the seller:

Buyer and seller agree to use their best efforts to effect novations of the aforesaid obligations and liabilities assumed by buyer hereunder. If any customer contracts to be assumed by buyer hereunder are not assignable by their terms and the parties are unable to effect novations of them, buyer will nevertheless perform the work thereunder for the account of seller at the price and in accordance with the other terms and conditions provided in such customer contracts. Except as just noted, the work under all sales contracts and commitments assumed by buyer hereunder will be performed by buyer for its account and buyer will indemnify and hold seller harmless from and against any loss or liability arising from any claim or litigation relating to work performed by buyer.

(l) A Covenant Not to Compete.

From a business point of view a buyer may want a seller not to compete in the business which the buyer is acquiring. This is particularly true where a buyer is acquiring a division or product line of the seller, rather than the whole of the seller's business and the employees intend to remain with the seller. From the buyer's point of view, if the buyer is at all vulnerable under the anti-trust laws, it should weigh the economic value of the covenant not to compete against the legal implications. Furthermore, the buyer should keep the covenant not to compete within legal bounds or it will not be enforceable. If the seller is a diversified company, it must be careful to define the non-compete area as narrowly as possible to avoid restriction on normal future growth. A clause to reconcile these viewpoints, where a division was sold, follows:

Covenant Not to Compete

A. Subject to the exceptions herein provided, seller agrees that for a period of two (2) years after the closing date, seller will not, directly or indirectly, engage in the United

States in the manufacture, distribution, or contract development of the following division products:

1. An electronic data display system which internally generates alpha-numeric characters and geometric symbols and displays them on the face of a cathode ray tube in response to external signals;

2. Simulators for training of crews of manned aircraft in operation of the following airborne equipment: radar, electronic countermeasures, gunnery and bombing systems;

3. Radar transponder beacons designed to assist in the radar tracking of drones, missiles and aircraft; and

4. General purpose automatic test equipment employing the concept of standard modular units of the general type described in that certain brochure captioned "Soldier, Series 500" published by seller (division) or the specific modular units described therein as an end product for use in such equipment.

Provided, however, that seller may develop, manufacture or distribute any of the above products as and only as a part of a system or major sub-system of substantially larger scope.

B. Seller further agrees that for a period of two (2) years from closing date, seller will not directly or indirectly within the United States (1) solicit or accept work which is a direct follow-on to work under contracts performed or being performed by division prior to closing date except as a second source to buyer, or (2) represent, in connection with seller proposals for new business, that it retains the specific group of technical talent through which seller performed on division contracts prior to the closing date or through which seller performed on contracts at the Electronics Division, El Paso, California, on the products defined in paragraph A above. This restriction does not extend under any circumstances and in any manner to a description of the qualifications and experience of individuals within seller.

C. Buyer agrees that the foregoing covenants not to compete and restrictions imposed upon seller shall become nonoperable in their entirety in the event of a declared national defense emergency or a state of war and shall become nonoperable with respect to any product or system defined above, the marketing of which buyer ceases to actively pursue or which the United States government strongly urges seller to supply.

D. Nothing contained in the foregoing paragraphs shall be construed as restricting seller from the manufacture, distribution or contract development of any of the foregoing products through a business acquired by seller after the closing date which business is partly but not primarily engaged in the manufacture, distribution or contract development of any of the foregoing products.

E. Seller agrees that it will not during the above mentioned two (2) year period, directly or indirectly endeavor to recruit any employees of buyer, including but not limited to division employees whom buyer elects to retain.

(m) Non-Infringement and Invention Assignment.

Particularly where a seller's business involves technical know-how or trade secrets, a buyer may wish to receive assurances that the seller's processes or products do not infringe any other inventions, that seller is not improperly utilizing another's trade secrets, and that the seller's employees have properly assigned all inventions and know-how to seller. The representation set forth below treats these areas in one clause, although, often, the two areas are treated in separate clauses in acquisition contracts:

Except as may be set forth in the Schedule referred to in Section 5.5, Seller has never been charged with infringement or violation of any adversely held patent, trademark, trade name, or copyright and there are no unexpired patents, except patents under which Seller is licensed, with claims reading on products of seller or on apparatus or methods employed by Seller in manufacturing or producing the same, or any patented invention or application therefor which would materially and adversely affect any product or operation of Seller, nor is Seller using or in any way making use of any patentable or unpatentable inventions, or any confidential information or trade secrets, of any former employer of any present or past employee of Seller except as a result of the acquisition by either of them of the business of such former employer. All engineering and technical employees of the Seller engaged in research and development work are obliged by the terms of their employment to assign to Seller any improvements in their respective products or in new products in their respective fields of activity, or in methods or machines for making any such products, which they have devised or invented, either solely or jointly with others.

(n) SEC Registration of Buyer's Stock.

(i) No SEC Registration—Stock Legend.

Where a buyer delivers stock in payment of an acquisition and the stock is not to be registered with the SEC, the contract often provides that the buyer may imprint a legend on its stock certificates, as follows:

All certificates representing shares of Buyer's Common Stock issued to the Stockholders of the merger of Seller into Buyer shall bear the following legend:

The shares represented by this Certificate have not been registered under the Securities Act of 1933, as amended. The shares have been acquired for investment and may not be sold, offered for sale, or transferred in the absence of an effective registration statement for the shares under the Securities Act of 1933, as amended, or an opinion of counsel to the Company that registration is not required under said Act.

(ii) Agreement to Register in Future.

Sometimes a seller's stockholders will only accept unregistered stock, where a buyer will contract to register its stock in the future. The clause below sets forth in some detail the elements which should be contained in an agreement by a buyer to register its stock in the future:

(i) Buyer agrees that if at any time two years after the closing, either Stockholder so requests in writing, it will, within 90 days after receipt of such request, file a registration statement with the Securities and Exchange Commission relating to all or part of the Buyer's Common Stock delivered to the Stockholders on the merger of Seller into Buyer, subject to the limitations hereinafter set forth, and will thereafter use its best efforts to cause such registration statement to become effective, (ii) Buyer agrees that, if at any time after the Closing and on or before the second anniversary thereof, it determines to register for sale, for its account, any of its common stock under the Securities Act of 1933, as amended, on Form S-1 or any form replacing such form, it will give written notice thereof to the Stockholders, and if so requested, in writing, by a Stockholder within 10 days after the date of the giving of such written notice, Buyer will, subject to the

limitations hereinafter set forth, include among the shares which it shall then register, all or part of the Buyer's common stock delivered to the Stockholders on the merger of Seller into Buyer as the Stockholder shall request, and (iii) the rights granted to the Stockholders under sub-sections (i) and (ii) of this section shall be subject to all of the following limitations:

(1) Such rights shall relate only to shares of buyer's Common Stock delivered to the Stockholders upon the merger of Seller into Buyer;

(2) Any notice by Stockholder to Buyer pursuant to sub-sections (i) and (ii) of this section must specify the number of shares which the Stockholder wishes to have registered and shall include a statement that it is the Stockholder's then present intention of selling the number of shares which he requests to be registered upon the date of the registration statement relating thereto;

(3) Any registration under sub-section (i) or (ii) of this section above shall be at Buyer's expense, except that the Stockholder shall pay any underwriter's discounts and commissions and all stock transfer taxes relating to the shares which he sells;

(4) The Stockholders shall be entitled to demand registration under sub-section (i) above only one time;

(5) The Stockholders shall not be entitled to register any shares of Buyer's Common Stock pursuant to sub-section (i) or (ii) of this section, (a) if counsel to Buyer is of the opinion that the Stockholders may sell the shares of Buyer's Common Stock received by them on the merger of Seller into Buyer, without registration under the Securities Act of 1933, as amended, or (b) if the Stockholders are then permitted to sell the shares under any rule adopted by the Securities and Exchange Commission pursuant to the Securities Act of 1933, as amended, permitting sales in a manner and with quantitative limitations similar to those contained in Rules 133 and Rule 154 adopted by said Commission as presently in effect.

(o) Filing Statutory Merger Agreement.

Where an acquisition is to be made in the form of a statutory merger, a detailed acquisition contract may provide for the filing of the statutory form of merger agreement after the conditions precedent in the detailed acquisition contract have been met:

If Seller and the Seller's Stockholders shall have complied with the conditions precedent to Buyer's obligations hereunder, and if Buyer shall have complied with the conditions precedent to the Seller and the Seller's Stockholders' obligations and performance hereunder, the Closing of the transactions contemplated by this Agreement shall take place on August 10, 1971, at 11:00 a.m., New York time, at the offices of Jones & Jones, 123 Seventh Avenue, New York, New York, and the Merger Agreement shall be filed with the Secretary of State of the State of Delaware as soon as practicable thereafter; provided, however, that at the written request of either Buyer or Seller, the Closing may be adjourned, but not beyond October 10, 1971.

(p) Publicity.

As a practical matter, plans for publicity should have been coordinated before a contract is signed, but the first draft of a contract containing a publicity clause may act as a reminder and an understanding of approach to suppliers and customers:

Buyer and seller agree that all notices to third parties and all other publicity concerning the transactions contemplated by this agreement shall be jointly planned and coordinated by both parties, and neither party shall act unilaterally in this regard without the prior approval of the other, such approval not to be unreasonably withheld.

(q) Specific Performance.

The following clause is addressed to the legal remedies available upon breach of an acquisition contract and constitutes an attempt to provide for specific performance of an acquisition or recision of the contract:

The parties mutually acknowledge and agree that in the event of any default by either party under this agreement and plan of reorganization the injury to the aggrieved party will be irreparable and damages will be inadequate, and that in addition to any other remedy provided by law the aggrieved party shall, at its option, be entitled to either specific performance of all covenants provided in this agreement and plan of reorganization or to recision thereof.

(r) Survival of Representations and Warranties.

Whether or not representations and warranties should survive the closing, and the length of time after the closing during which they may be actionable, may become a major issue of substance:

Unless otherwise expressly provided herein, the representations, warranties, covenants, indemnities and other agreements herein contained shall be deemed to be continuing and shall survive the consummation of the transactions contemplated by this agreement provided that any claim in respect to any thereof must be asserted on or before April 1, 197_.

(s) Additional General Provisions which Might be Looked upon as Form Provisions.

(i) Diligence to Close.

Buyer and seller agree that each shall with reasonable diligence proceed to take all action as may be required to consummate the transaction herein contemplated.

(ii) Right to Waive Failures of Other Party.

This clause may grant unilateral rights to either party to waive failures of compliance by the other party:

Each party hereto may:
(a) Extend the time for the performance of any of the obligations of the other party,
(b) Waive in writing any inaccuracies in the representations and warranties made to them contained in this agreement and plan of reorganization or any exhibit hereto or any certificate or certificates delivered by the other party pursuant to this agreement and plan of reorganization,
(c) Waive in writing the failure of performance of any of the conditions herein expressed, or alternatively, rescind for such failure, and
(d) Waive in writing compliance with any of the covenants herein contained by the other party and so waive performance of any of the obligations of the other party hereto.

(iii) **Further Assurances:**

Each party hereto agrees to execute such further documents or instruments, requested by the other party, as may be necessary or desirable to effect the purposes of this agreement and plan of reorganization and carry out its provisions.

(iv) **Entire Agreement Contained in Contract.**

The entire agreement between the parties should be contained in the acquisition contract particularly where a memorandum of intent forms a part of the transaction:

It is understood and agreed that all understandings and agreements heretofore had between the parties hereto, including, but not limited to, a certain memorandum of intent dated April 12, 1971, addressed to buyer by seller, signed for seller by Mr. R. J. Boy, and accepted for buyer by Mr. W. A. Jones, are merged in this agreement and plan of reorganization, which alone fully and completely expresses their agreement.

(v) **Applicable State Law.**

Where the laws of a number of states are involved, the choice of the law of a particular state, ignoring for the moment conflicts-of-laws problems, may decide whether provisions such as non-compete clauses are legal and enforceable:

This agreement and plan of reorganization shall be construed according to the laws of the state of California.

As a conclusion to this chapter, it should again be mentioned that form clauses should not be used verbatim unless careful consideration has been given to their effect upon the particular acquisition.

CHAPTER 14

The Acquisition Contract— Continued

A STATUTORY MERGER

In some respects a merger resembles an acquisition of assets. In both types of acquisition the former separate businesses (unless a new subsidiary is formed to conduct the seller's business) are conducted within one surviving corporation. In spite of this superficial resemblance, major differences exist between asset acquisitions and statutory mergers. In a purchase of assets, a buyer may generally make the acquisition without seeking approval of its stockholders, but in a merger the buyer generally must submit the merger plan to its stockholders for their approval. Furthermore, in an assets transaction, title to the seller's property may pass to the buyer only through delivery of title documents such as deeds to real property, bills of sale personalty, assignments of contracts and leases, and patent assignments. On the other hand, in a statutory merger, the merger agreement acts as a single instrument to transfer to the buyer, the surviving corporation, all right, title and interest in the seller's assets and business. This transfer of title by operation of law normally takes place when the merger agreement has been properly adopted and filed with the state authorities involved, and no further title documents are required to vest legal title in the buyer.

In addition to these distinctions between an assets acquisition and a statutory merger, where the parties plan a tax-free acquisition the statutory merger route allows greater freedom in the type of securities which may be utilized to make the acquisition and still qualify the transaction as tax-free. This tax aspect is discussed in greater detail in Chapter 10.

Chapter 12 and Chapter 13 contain a general form of acquisition contract, as well as numerous additional clauses applicable to many specific situations which may arise in acquisitions. The form of contract developed is structured upon a stock-for-stock form of acquisition contract, and provides precedents to develop a form of contract for the acquisition of assets through miscellaneous clauses (in Chapter 13) useful in both stock and asset acquisitions.

The form of acquisition contract developed in the preceding chapters, may, and often is, also utilized for acquisitions structured as statutory mergers. In a statutory merger, the basic form of acquisition agreement may be similar to a form of acquisition agreement used in a transaction involving the sale of a seller's assets for a buyer's stock. Such an acquisition contract may contain all of the representations and warranties a seller would normally make, as well as all of the various covenants and conditions contained in acquisition contracts, whether involving acquisitions of stock or assets. In addition, however, where the acquisition contract contemplates closing of the acquisition as a statutory merger, the contract should provide for the execution and filing of a statutory form of agreement and plan of merger—after the conditions in the detailed acquisition contract have been fulfilled. A form of clause which provides for the filing of a statutory merger agreement or merger certificate is printed in Section 12 of Chapter 13, at paragraph (o) appearing at page 267. This clause provides that after the conditions precedent in the acquisition contract have been met, the statutory form of merger agreement or merger certificate may be filed with the state authorities involved as the final step to consummate the statutory merger.

The form of statutory agreement and plan of merger or merger certificate for filing with state authorities, must meet each of the requirements contained in the corporation statutes of the particular states involved. In preparing such statutory merger agreements or certificates, the objective should be to meet the statutory requirements in as simplified a form as practicable, although state statutes normally permit the inclusion of miscellaneous items in a merger agreement which are deemed pertinent by the Boards of Directors involved. Since, as mentioned above, in a statutory merger, the transfer of titles to assets from the seller to the buyer takes place by operation of law upon the filing of the merger agreement with the Secretary of State (or upon the effective date provided in the agreement of merger), a formal closing involving transfers of title documents, as in acquisitions of assets or of stock, is not necessary. In a statutory merger, the filing of the agreement and plan of merger or the merger certificate with the Secretary of State constitutes the closing.

Printed below is a form of agreement and plan of merger between a Delaware corporation and a Missouri corporation, for filing with the Secretary of State of Delaware—the state of incorporation of the continuing corporation. The form of agreement illustrates the comparative brevity of such statutory agreements prepared for filing with secretaries of state. Also note that the merger agreement provides an opportunity for the continuing corporation to amend its charter and by-laws. It is not at all unusual for a continuing corporation to adopt a modern streamlined certificate of incorporation in connection with a statutory merger, particularly where the continuing corporation has been in existence for many years and its charter has undergone numerous amendments.

Agreement and Plan of Merger

This agreement and plan of merger dated as of the 16th day of April, 1971, made by and between buyer and a majority of the directors thereof, parties of the first part, and seller and a majority of the directors thereof, parties of the second part, said two corporations, parties hereto, being together hereinafter sometimes referred to as the constituent corporations.

Whereas, buyer is a corporation organized and existing under the laws of the state of Delaware with its principal office in the state of Delaware, being located at 100 West Tenth Street in the city of Wilmington, county of New Castle, and the name of its registered agent at such office is the Corporation Trust Company; and

Whereas, buyer has a capitalization consisting of (i) 20,505 1/4 authorized shares of $5 preferred stock, without par value, of which 20,505 1/4 shares (including 1,036 shares held in its treasury) are issued and outstanding and (ii) 3,000,000 authorized shares of common stock, without par value (which authorized number of shares will be increased to 5,000,000 shares prior to the effective date of the merger) of which 2,187,567 shares are issued and outstanding, 182,303 shares are reserved for issuance upon conversion of buyer's 4 3/4% convertible subordinated debentures, due April 1, 1973, and 71,300 shares are reserved for issuance upon exercise of outstanding options; and

Whereas, seller is a corporation organized and existing under the laws of the state of Missouri with its principal office in the state of Missouri, located at 4,100 Olive Street, St. Louis, Missouri, and the name of its registered agent of such office is John Jones, and

Whereas, seller has an authorized capitalization of 250,000 shares of common stock, $5 par value, of which 169,555 shares are issued and outstanding and 35,625 shares are reserved for issuance upon conversion of seller's outstanding 4 3/4% convertible subordinated debentures, due March 15, 1974; and

Whereas, the respective boards of directors of the constituent corporations have determined that it is advisable that seller be merged into buyer, on the terms and conditions hereinafter set forth, in accordance with the applicable provisions of the laws of the state of Delaware and of the state of Missouri, which laws permit such merger;

Now, therefore, in consideration of the premises and of the mutual agreements, covenants, and provisions hereinafter contained, the parties hereto agree that seller be merged into buyer, and that the terms and conditions of such merger, the mode of carrying the same into effect, and the manner and basis of converting the shares of seller into shares of buyer shall be as follows:

I.

Seller and buyer shall be merged into a single corporation, in accordance with the applicable provisions of the laws of the state of Delaware and of the state of Missouri, by seller merging into buyer, which shall be the surviving corporation. The separate existence of seller shall cease and the existence of buyer shall continue unaffected and unimpaired by the merger with all the rights, privileges, immunities and powers, and subject to all the duties and liabilities of a corporation organized under the General Corporation Law of the state of Delaware.

II.

The certificate of incorporation of buyer shall continue to be its certificate of incorporation following the effective date of the merger, until the same shall be altered or amended, except that, upon the effective date of the merger, a new paragraph, to precede the present last paragraph of article four shall be added to the certificate of incorporation, to read as follows:

"No holder of stock of any class of the company now or hereafter authorized, shall have any preemptive right to subscribe to shares of the stock of the company issued upon conversion of 4 3/4% convertible subordinate debentures due March 15, 1974 of seller subsequent to the merger of that corporation into the company."

The by-laws of buyer shall be and remain the by-laws of buyer until altered, amended or repealed, except that, upon the effective date of the merger, Section 1 of Article III of the by-laws shall be as follows:

"Section 1. The number of directors shall be fifteen but the number of directors may, from time to time, be altered by amendment of these by-laws. The directors shall be elected at the annual meeting of the stockholders, except as provided in Section 2 of this article, and each director elected shall hold office until his successor is elected and qualified. Directors need not be stockholders."

The directors and officers of buyer in office on the effective date of the merger shall continue in office as, and be and constitute, the directors and officers of buyer for the term elected until their respective successors shall be elected or appointed and qualified, except that John Jones of St. Louis, Missouri, shall, on the effective date of the merger, be and become a director and a vice-president of buyer to serve until the next annual meeting of stockholders or until a successor to him is elected.

III.

On the effective date of the merger:

1. Buyer shall possess all the rights, privileges, immunities, powers, and franchises, as well of a public as of a private nature, and shall be subject to all of the restrictions, disabilities and duties of each of the constituent corporations; and all property, real, personal and mixed, including all patents, applications for patents, trademarks, trademark registrations and applications for registration of trademarks, together with the goodwill of the business in connection with which said patents and marks are used, and all debts due on whatever account, including subscriptions to shares of capital stock, and all other choices in action and all and every other interest of or belonging to or due to each of the constituent corporations shall be deemed to be transferred to and vested in buyer without further act or deed, and the title to any real estate, or any interest therein, vested in either of the constituent corporations shall not revert or be in any way impaired by reason of the merger.

2. Buyer shall be responsible and liable for all the liabilities and obligations of each of the constituent corporations; and any claim existing or action or proceeding pending by or against either of the constituent corporations may be prosecuted to judgment as if the merger had not taken place, or buyer may be substituted in its place and neither the rights of creditors nor any liens upon the property of either of the constituent corporations shall be impaired by the merger. Buyer shall execute and deliver any and all documents which may be required for it to assume or otherwise comply with outstanding obligations of seller.

3. The aggregate amount of the net assets of the constituent corporations which is available for payments of dividends immediately prior to the merger, to the extent that the value thereof is not transferred to stated capital by issuance of shares of stock or otherwise, shall continue to be available for the payment of dividends by buyer.

IV.

The manner and basis of converting the shares of stock of each of the constituent corporations into shares of stock of buyer are as follows:

1. The shares of $5 preferred stock and common stock of the buyer, whether authorized or issued on the effective date of the merger shall not be converted or exchanged as a result of the merger, but upon said date, all shares of $5 preferred stock and all common stock of buyer therefore authorized (whether issued or unissued) shall be *deemed to be shares of $5 preferred stock and common stock, respectively, of buyer and all such shares of stock of buyer outstanding on the effective date of the merger (including shares held in the treasury of buyer) shall remain outstanding, shall be and be deemed fully-paid and non-assessable and shall retain all rights to accrued and unpaid dividends, if any.*

2. Each share of common stock of seller issued and outstanding on the effective date of the merger and all rights in respect thereof, shall on said date, be converted into and exchanged for ninety-five one hundredths (.95) of a share of presently authorized and unissued common stock of buyer; provided that no fractional share of common stock of buyer shall be issued in connection with the exchange of shares of seller.

3. As soon as practicable after the effective date of the merger, each holder of an outstanding certificate or certificates theretofore representing shares of common stock of seller shall surrender the same to buyer, and such holder shall be entitled, upon such surrender, to receive in exchange therefor a certificate or certificates representing the number of whole shares of common stock of buyer into which the shares of common stock of seller theretofore represented by the surrendered certificate or certificates shall have been converted as aforesaid. No fractional shares of common stock of buyer will be issued in connection with the exchange and no certificate therefor will be issued, but in lieu thereof, arrangements will be made to issue to an agent for the holders otherwise entitled to a fractional share interest, a certificate or certificates for the number of whole shares representing the aggregate of such fractional share interests. The agent will sell such whole shares and distribute the proceeds of sale to the stockholders entitled thereto in proportion to their fractional share interests. Until so surrendered for exchange, each outstanding certificate which, prior to the effective date of the merger, represented shares of common stock of seller shall be deemed for all corporate purposes to evidence the ownership of the number of whole shares of common stock of buyer which the holder of the certificate for shares of common stock of seller would be entitled to receive upon surrender thereof for exchange as aforesaid.

4. The restricted stock option plan of buyer as in effect on the effective date of the merger and all options theretofore granted thereunder shall continue without impairment or alteration by the merger.

5. All shares of common stock of buyer into which shares of common stock of seller are converted, as above provided, shall be fully-paid and non-assessable.

V.

Buyer shall pay all expenses of accomplishing the merger.

VI.

If at any time buyer shall consider or be advised that any further assignment or assurances in law are necessary or desirable to vest or to perfect or confirm of record in buyer the title to any property or rights of seller, or to otherwise carry out the provisions hereof, the proper officers and directors of seller as of the effective date of the merger shall execute and deliver any and all proper deeds, assignments and assurances in law, and do all things necessary or proper to vest, perfect, or confirm title to such property or rights in buyer, and otherwise to carry out the provisions hereof.

VII.

Each of the constituent corporations shall take, or cause to be taken, all action or do or cause to be done, all things necessary, proper, or advisable under the laws of the state of Delaware and of the state of Missouri, or either of such states, to consummate and make effective the merger, subject, however, to the appropriate vote or consent of the stockholders of each of the constituent corporations in accordance with the requirements of the applicable provisions of the laws of the state of Delaware and of the state of Missouri.

VIII.

The effective date of the merger shall be at the close of business on June 28, 1971, provided that upon such date, all acts and things shall have been done as shall be required for accomplishing the merger under the applicable provisions of the laws of the state of Delaware and of the state of Missouri.

IX.

Anything herein or elsewhere to the contrary notwithstanding, this agreement and plan of merger may be abandoned by action of the board of directors of either buyer or seller at any time prior to the effective date of the merger, whether before or after submission to their respective stockholders, upon the happening of any one of the following events:

1. If the merger fails to obtain the requisite vote of stockholders of buyer or of stockholders of seller not later than June 28, 1971; or

2. If, in the judgment of the board of directors of buyer or of seller, the merger would be impractical because of the number of stockholders of either thereof who assert their right to have their stock appraised and to receive payment therefor as provided in the General Corporation Law of the state of Delaware or in the General and Business Corporation Law of the state of Missouri.

Buyer and seller each represents and warrants that between the date hereof and the time when the merger becomes effective they will not enter into any employment contracts, grant any stock options, or issue any stock or securities except upon the exercise of presently outstanding restricted stock options or upon the exercise of conversion rights appertaining to their respective outstanding issues of debentures, or declare or pay any dividends in stock or cash or make any other distribution on or with respect to their outstanding stock except (i) the regular quarterly cash dividend upon the $5 preferred stock of buyer; (ii) a cash dividend not to exceed 37 1/2¢ per share payable on June 14, 1971, to holders of common stock of buyer and (iii) a cash dividend of 25¢ per share payable on June 3, 1971, to holders of common stock of seller.

In witness whereof, the corporate parties hereto, pursuant to authority given by their respective board of directors, have caused this agreement and plan of merger to be entered into and signed by their respective directors, or a majority of them, and in their respective corporate names by their respective presidents or vice presidents, and their corporate seals to be hereunto affixed, and to be attested by their respective secretaries or assistant secretaries, all as of the date and year first above written.

Buyer

By /s/ L. A. Johnson
Vice President

Attest:

/s/ G. H. Peck
Secretary

(Corporate Seal)

/s/ *A. J. Swan*
/s/ *L. A. Johnson*
/s/ *Robert F. Jones*
/s/ *Tom P. Black*
*Being a majority of the board
of directors of buyer.*

Seller

By /s/ *Fred G. White*
Vice President

Attest:

/s/ *Tom Jones*
Secretary

(Corporate Seal)

/s/ *A. A. Rich*
/s/ *A. F. Thompson*
/s/ *J .T. Judge*
/s/ *Fred G. White*
/s/ *H. A. Jackson*
*Being a majority of the
board of directors of seller.*

SCHEDULES AND EXHIBITS

In addition to the basic text, acquisition contracts often include as attachments, or provide for separate prior delivery, of schedules and exhibits which describe in detail selected aspects of the seller's business. Normally, the sellers are required to represent or warrant the correctness of the schedules and exhibits which are delivered with the contract. The contract clauses set forth in Chapters 12 and 13 contain many forms of sellers' representations and warranties of schedules and exhibits describing a seller's business.

Where the schedules and exhibits would be unusually bulky to attach to an acquisition contract, or include confidential information, the contract may provide for the delivery of such schedules and exhibits prior to the execution of the contract, identified by initials or signature on each page of the seller's officer responsible for delivery of such schedule or exhibit. A description of some customary forms of schedules or exhibits follows.

Seller's capitalization and subsidiary and affiliated companies. A buyer often requests a seller to deliver a complete description of ownership of seller's outstanding stock (where seller is closely held) and of seller's subsidiaries and affiliated companies. Such a description may take the form of a schedule annexed to the acquisition agreement containing information of the names of seller's stockholders, of subsidiaries, jurisdictions of incorporation, types of stock outstanding, and the ownership of the stock. For an example of such a form see Schedule A.

SCHEDULE A

Seller and Subsidiary and Affiliated Companies or Entities of Seller
Capital Structure and Jurisdictions in Which Qualified to Do Business

Name of Entity	Jurisdiction of Incorporation	Jurisdictions in Which Qualified	Type of Stock	Par Value	Capital Stock Authorized	Capital Stock Outstanding	Identity of Owner	No. of Shares

Outstanding warrants or options affecting seller's and subsidiary's stock. As part of the description of the seller's capitalization, the buyer may request a description of outstanding warrants, options or outstanding subscriptions to the capital stock of the seller or any of the seller's subsidiaries or affiliated companies. Where the seller's capital structure is at all complicated, or where the seller has outstanding employee stock options, the information required with respect to such options may be valuable in determining the extent of possible dilution of the seller's equity. A form of such a schedule making reference to the form of Schedule A, printed above, is presented as Schedule B.

SCHEDULE B

Outstanding Warrants, Options or Subscriptions to Capital Stock of Seller and
Entities Listed in Schedule A

Real estate owned by seller. An acquisition contract normally provides for a complete list and description of all of the real estate owned by a seller and its subsidiaries and affiliated companies. Such a listing of real estate should include a legal description of the properties involved, the street address, a brief description of the improvements on the real estate, including the use made of the premises, and the owner of the premises. In addition, a buyer may often request the seller to describe the zoning or other restrictions which may apply to the use of the property. A form of real estate schedule is printed as Schedule C.

SCHEDULE C

Real Estate Owned by Entities Listed in Schedule A

Parcel No.	Legal Description	Situs State, County, Municipality	Owner	Use

Properties leased by seller. In addition to real estate owned by the seller and related companies, an acquisition contract should specify in detail the properties which the seller leases from other owners. Such leased property may include a description of the leases involved, as well as any renewal or purchase options exercisable upon the termination of a lease. With such a description, the buyer may incorporate the date of the renewal or purchase option in the buyer's files to avoid the possibility of overlooking the right to renew the lease or to purchase the property in the future.

Occasionally, where the personal property owned by the seller consists of valuable major items of machinery or equipment, such as multi-colored printing presses, the acquisition contract may provide for a schedule listing and describing such machinery in detail, including, where available, serial numbers. A form of schedule listing seller's leased properties is presented as Schedule D.

SCHEDULE D

Leased Properties

(1) Real Estate Leased by Entities Listed in Schedule A

Lessor Lessee	Location and Description	Term Original Expiration	Rent	Renewal or Purchase Options

(2) Personal Property Leased by Entities Listed in Schedule A

Lessor Lessee	Type of Equipment	Acquisition Date	Term	Expiration Date	Balance Due	Purchase or Renewal Option

Patents and trademarks of seller. Acquisition contracts normally make provision for a list of the seller's patents, trademarks and similar intangible properties. Not only should all of such properties be listed, but the seller should provide information of license agreements effecting patents and trademarks to which the seller is a party, either as licensor or as licensee. A form of schedule requiring such information of the seller and the seller's related companies is illustrated as Schedule E.

SCHEDULE E

Patent Rights, Trademarks, Licenses and Royalty Agreements owned or to which Entities Listed on Schedule A are Parties.

(1) Patents Owned

(2) Patent Applications Owned

(3) License Agreements as Licensor

(4) License Agreements as Licensee

(5) Immunities from Suit Granted or Received

(6) Trademarks and Trademark Applications Owned

(7) Royalty Agreements not Otherwise Listed

General contracts of seller. Sellers are normally parties to contracts under which they have certain rights and obligations, whether such contracts be oral or written. To obtain a complete description of a seller's business, a buyer should require a description of all of the major contracts to which the seller is a party. Such contracts may include employment contracts and related employee plans, contracts affecting the purchase or sale of real estate or substantial personal property, financial arrangements including mortgages or pledges, leases, collective bargaining agreements, contracts for purchases of materials or supplies, distributorship or salesmen contracts, contracts with subcontractors or manufacturers' representatives, guarantees or other material contracts which involve substantial sums, or will remain executory for a substantial period of time. A form of schedule listing the details of the type of contracts a buyer may request a seller to describe is illustrated in Schedule F.

SCHEDULE F

Contracts to Which Entities Listed on Schedule A are Parties

(1) Employment contracts; pension, profit-sharing, bonus, retirement, stock option, or similar incentive or deferred compensation plan or arrangement with any officer, director, employee or other; employee benefit plans, hospitalization, insurance, etc.

(2) Contracts for the acquisition or disposition of real estate or fixed assets in an aggregate amount exceeding $5,000.

(3) Financial arrangements involving mortgaging, pledging, or other hypothecation of assets or any borrowing which cannot be repaid in full or in part on not more than 30 days notice with refund of unearned or unamortized discount and without premium or penalty.

(4) Leases, contracts, or other instruments not assignable without consent or not cancellable without penalty on not more than sixty days notice.

(5) Collective bargaining agreements.

(6) Continuing contracts for the future purchase of materials or supplies in excess of its requirements for normal operating inventory for business currently booked.

(7) Distributor, sales agency, or re-seller agreements having an unexpired term of more than, or not subject to termination without penalty within a period of, sixty days.

(8) Contracts with any subcontractor, commission agent, or manufacturers representative.

(9) Contracts under which any entity listed in Schedule A has assumed, guaranteed, endorsed, or otherwise become liable in connection with the obligation of any other person, firm, or corporation.

(10) Any contracts not included in the foregoing which are material and were not made in the ordinary and usual course of business.

Major suppliers and customers of seller. A list of the major suppliers and customers of a seller and its subsidiaries may be helpful to a buyer in determining the strengths or weaknesses of a seller's business. If the seller's business is disproportionately dependent upon either one or a number of major suppliers, or one or a number of major customers, information of this fact may be valuable to the buyer. The criteria for determining which suppliers or which customers of a seller and its subsidiaries should be included in a list will differ with the differing natures of seller's businesses. Presumably, a list of customers of a retail business would have little value and could be impracticable to supply, whereas a list of customers could be of major importance if the seller is a manufacturer of components for computers. Schedule G is a form for listing major suppliers and customers.

SCHEDULE G

Major Suppliers and Customers of
Entities Listed on Schedule A

Suppliers

Name & Address of Supplied	Type of Goods Supplied	Description of Supply Contract	Annual $ Volume	%age of Supply

Customers

Name & Address of Customer	Type of Goods Bought	Description of Purchase Contract	Annual $ Volume Bought	%age of Seller's Gross Sales

Description of litigation. A buyer should require a seller to supply a description of all of the litigation in which a seller is engaged, or which is threatened against a seller. Where litigation is voluminous, the description may be restricted to major litigation. The litigation may be described on a schedule such as Schedule H which requests information of litigation affecting not only the seller, but also all of the seller's subsidiaries and affiliated companies.

SCHEDULE H

Litigation Pending or Threatened Against Entities Listed in Schedule A or their Shareholders

---

Lists of significant stockholders. Occasionally, lists of special stockholders are important in fixing the legal obligations under acquisition contracts. For example, major stockholders may be required to sign investment letters, or named stockholders may be required to indemnify the buyer. Where certain stockholders are of particular significance, they may be listed on a schedule attached to the acquisition contract.

SUPPLEMENTARY DOCUMENTS AND AGREEMENTS

Often, acquisition contracts, in addition to schedules and exhibits, provide for the delivery of supplementary documents and agreements.

Financial statements. Among such supplementary documents are the financial statements of the seller. In acquisitions, it is almost universal practice that a seller represent and warrant the financial position of its business, as well as results of its operations for specified past periods. The financial statements upon which the representations and warranties of the seller are based may be attached to the contract as an additional exhibit or may be delivered separately, either before or after execution of the contract. Since financial statements may be bulky, it has become the practice in many acquisitions for the seller to deliver such statements to the buyer separately, rather than attach the statements to the acquisition contract.

Indemnity agreement. Where an acquisition contract does not contain detailed provisions indemnifying a buyer against loss or damage resulting from misrepresentations of a seller, the indemnity may be provided in a separate agreement to be delivered at the closing. Such an indemnity agreement would normally contain a reaffirmation of the truth of the representations and warranties contained in the acquisition contract, the covenant of the seller to hold the buyer harmless for any loss or damage incurred as a result of any misrepresentation or breach of warranty, and the terms for the seller to assume or participate in the defense of any claims against the buyer for which the seller would be required to indemnify the buyer. A form of indemnity agreement is printed below.

INDEMNITY AGREEMENT

> *THIS AGREEMENT made as of the   day of   , 197_, by and among SELLER COMPANY, an Ohio Corporation (hereinafter called "Seller Ohio") and*

SELLER COMPANY, a Washington corporation (hereinafter called "Seller Washington"), TOM SMITH, JOHN JONES and RICHARD ROE (hereinafter called individually "Shareholder" and collectively "Shareholders"), parties of the First Part;

and

BUYER, a Delaware corporation (hereinafter called "Buyer"), and SUBSIDIARY COMPANY, a Delaware corporation and a wholly owned subsidiary of Buyer (hereinafter caller "Subsidiary"), parties of the Second Part;

WITNESSETH:

WHEREAS, Seller Ohio and Seller Washington entered into a certain Agreement and Plan of Reorganization with Buyer dated as of   , 197   (hereinafter called the "Reorganization Agreement"); and

WHEREAS, Seller Ohio and Seller Washington, as part of said Reorganization Agreement have made certain representations and warranties to Buyer and Subsidiary; and

WHEREAS, said Reorganization Agreement requires as a condition precedent to closing the delivery of an Indemnity Agreement executed by Seller Ohio, Seller Washington and Shareholders;

NOW, THEREFORE, in consideration of the foregoing and of the benefits to be derived from said Reorganization Agreement, and in order to induce Buyer and Subsidiary to proceed with the closing of the transactions contemplated by said Reorganization Agreement, Parties of the First Part covenant and agree as follows:

1. Parties of the First Part jointly and severally agree, represent and warrant to Parties of the Second Part that the representations and warranties contained in Sections 2.01 and 2.13, inclusive are true and correct as of this   day of   197_, (the Closing Date) with the same force and effect as if made on this date.

2. Parties of the First Part jointly and severally agree to indemnify and hold harmless the Parties of the Second Part and their officers and directors from and against all loss, liability, damage, or expense incurred by Parties of the Second Part, or either of them, attributable to any misrepresentations or breach of warranty made by Parties of the First Part pursuant to Paragraph 1, above, or which would not have been incurred by Parties of the Second Part, or either of them if such representations and warranties had been true and correct, and against any and all loss, liability, damage, or expense arising out of any claims, demands, suits or actions brought by any person whomsoever under any retirement, profit-sharing, bonus, stock options or similar compensation plan or agreement at any time in effect or entered into by Parties of the First Part, or any of them, and which has not been expressly assumed by Buyer and Subsidiary by an instrument making specific reference to such plan or agreement.

3. The obligations of Parties of the First Part under this Indemnity Agreement shall terminate as of September 30, 197_, with respect to any matters arising or becoming known after such date.

4. Upon request by Shareholders and at Shareholders' expense, Buyer will tender to Shareholders and their designated counsel the right to defend against any claim by third parties which would give rise to an obligation or liability on the part of Shareholders under this Agreement whereupon Shareholders will assume the defense of such claim. Buyer will cooperate with and give assistance to Shareholders and their designated counsel in their defense against any such claims. The conduct of such defense will be within the complete discretion of Shareholders who may either settle, compromise, or litigate any claims as they deem proper; provided, however, Shareholders shall not settle or compromise any such claim without the consent of Buyer, if the settlement or compromise would oblige Buyer to make any payment or part with any property, to assume any obligation or grant any licenses or other rights, or to be subject to any injunction by reason of such settlement or compromise.

WITNESS the due execution hereof as of the day and year first above written.

ATTEST: *SELLER COMPANY, an Ohio corporation*

                                             By _____
_____
Secretary   *President*

ATTEST: *SELLER COMPANY, a Washington corporation*

                                             By _____
_____
Secretary   *President*

WITNESS:

_____

_____   _____
                                                          Tom Smith

_____   _____
                                                          John Jones

_____   _____
                                                          Richard Roe

                                             PARTIES OF THE FIRST PART

ATTEST:
                                             BUYER

                                             By _____
_____
Assistant Secretary   *Vice President*

ATTEST: *SUBSIDIARY COMPANY, a Delaware corporation*

                                             By _____
_____
Assistant Secretary   *Vice President*

                           PARTIES OF THE SECOND PART

Escrow agreement. Not only is a seller often required to indemnify a buyer against loss from misrepresentation or breach of warranty, but the seller is also often required to place a portion of the consideration received for its business in escrow, to secure such indemnify. Such an escrow agreement may become a lengthy document. Among other things, it should set forth:

(1) The amount of funds or stock to be escrowed;

(2) The name of the escrow agent;

(3) The disposition of dividends paid on stock held in escrow, as well as voting rights;

(4) Provisions for delivery of the escrowed stock or cash upon realization of losses or alleged losses by the buyer;

(5) Mechanics for participation of both the buyer and seller in defending against claims affecting representations or warranties;

(6) Fees to be paid to escrow agent, and how paid;

(7) The termination date of the escrow agreement; and

(8) Mechanical provisions such as notice provisions.

A form of escrow agreement is printed below:

ESCROW AGREEMENT

THIS AGREEMENT, made this   day of   , 19   , by and between: SELLER COMPANY, an Ohio corporation (hereinafter called "Seller Ohio"), SELLER COMPANY, a Washington corporation (hereinafter called "Seller Washington"; and Seller Ohio and Seller Washington hereinafter being sometimes called collectively "Seller Corporations"); TOM SMITH, JOHN JONES and RICHARD ROE (hereinafter collectively called "Shareholders" and individually "Shareholder"), parties of the first part;

and

BUYER, INC., a Delaware corporation (hereinafter called "Buyer"), party of the second part;

and

a national association organized under the laws of the United States of America and qualified to carry on a banking and trust business in the Commonwealth of Pennsylvania (hereinafter caller "Bank"), party of the third part;

WITNESSETH THAT:

WHEREAS, Seller Corporations have entered into a certain Agreement and Plan of Reorganization with Buyer dated as of the   day of   , 19   (hereinafter called the "agreement"), pursuant to which Seller Corporations undertake to transfer substantially all of their assets and business to a subsidiary of Buyer (hereinafter called "Subsidiary") in exchange solely for shares of the one dollar ($1.00) par value common stock of Buyer and the assumption by Subsidiary of certain of the liabilities of Seller Corporations, all as is more particularly provided in said Agreement; and

WHEREAS, said Agreement requires the deposit by Seller Corporations of certain of the shares of the stock of Buyer to be delivered to them with an escrow agent, such shares be held as security for the indemnity obligations of Seller Corporations and Shareholders as provided for in said Agreement or the closing documents; and

WHEREAS, Seller Corporations, Shareholders and Buyer desire Bank to serve as escrow agent, and Bank is willing to do so, all upon the terms and conditions hereinafter set forth.

NOW, THEREFORE, it is agreed:

ARTICLE I. Escrow

1.1 Seller Corporations and Shareholders agree that upon the closing of the transactions contemplated in said Agreement, and the delivery to Seller Ohio and Seller Washington by Buyer of the shares of Buyer's common stock therein provided for, Seller Corporations shall forthwith deliver to Bank as Escrow Agent, a certificate or certificates for a total of   shares of said Buyer's stock, with separate stock powers endorsed in blank, attached.

1.2 Bank agrees to accept and hold such shares as escrow agent hereunder, and to promptly cause the same to be registered in its name or that of its nominee.

1.3 Bank shall also hold, as part of said escrow, all shares of stock received by it with respect to said shares on account of any stock dividend or stock split. Cash dividends received by Bank on account of any stock held by it hereunder shall be distributed to Seller Corporations or Shareholders.

ARTICLE II. Distribution and Voting

2.1 Bank agrees that it shall make distribution of the shares of stock held by it only in such number of shares and at such times as shall be authorized by Buyer in writing, or as is otherwise hereinafter provided in Section 3.4.

2.2 Bank shall distribute shares authorized to be distributed either to Seller Corporations, to the Shareholders, or to Buyer as such authorization shall direct.

2.3 Bank shall vote any shares of stock held by it in accordance with the written instructions of Seller Corporations, or if Seller Corporations or either of them be dissolved, in accordance with the written instructions of the Shareholders beneficially interested therein, determined in accordance with Section 4.6.

ARTICLE III. Indemnity Security

3.1 The shares of the common stock of Buyer deposited hereunder shall stand as security for the faithful performance of the indemnity obligations of Seller Corporations and Shareholders under the Indemnity Agreement delivered to Buyer and Subsidiary until the expiration of two (2) years from the Closing Date, and thereafter, with respect to such number of shares, if any, as Buyer shall reasonably require to be held to satisfy indemnification obligations of Seller Corporations or the Shareholders with respect to matters not absolute as to liability or not liquidated as to amount of such date. Such shares shall be held by Bank until such time as Buyer shall demand the return thereof or authorize their distribution to Seller Corporations or the Shareholders.

3.2 In the event that on or prior to the expiration of two (2) years from the Closing Date, Seller Corporations or Shareholders shall default on any of their indemnification obligations, Buyer shall notify Bank and each of the Shareholders of such default or matter in writing, setting forth the nature of such default or matter in reasonable detail, and make demand upon Bank that it retain for future return to Buyer, or return, such number of shares as Buyer shall direct.

3.3 Promptly after the expiration of two (2) years from the Closing Date, and in any event, within ten (10) days thereafter Buyer shall deliver to Bank and each of the Shareholders written notifications of the number of shares required by Buyer to be retained on account of matters for which Seller Corporations and Shareholders would be liable under the Indemnity Agreement but which were not, at the expiration of two (2) years from the closing date absolute as to liability or liquidated as to amount, and additional shares, if any, to be retained or returned pursuant to Section 3.2 above, setting forth the nature of each of such items in reasonable detail.

3.4 Upon the expiration of fifteen (15) days following the expiration of two (2) years from the Closing Date, all shares not required by Buyer to be retained for return or returned by notice given pursuant to Section 3.2 and 3.3 hereof, shall be released from the provisions of this Escrow Agreement, and shall be distributed by Bank to Seller Corporations or Shareholders in accordance with Section 4.6. Failure of Buyer to give Bank notice as aforesaid shall operate as an automatic authorization to Bank to distribute escrow shares.

3.5 Bank agrees that upon receipt of instructions pursuant to Section 3.2 or 3.3 hereof, to retain shares for future return, it shall hold such shares until directed by Buyer to deliver the same to Buyer or to distribute such shares to Seller Corporations or Share-holders.

ARTICLE IV. General Provisions

4.1 This Agreement shall become effective as of the date hereof, and shall continue in force until the final distribution of all shares held by Bank hereunder, or until termi-nated by an instrument in writing signed by Buyer, Seller Corporations, and sharehold-ers, or if Seller Corporations be then dissolved, by Buyer and the Shareholders.

4.2 Bank shall be entitled to a fee of ($) per year for its services hereunder, one-half to be paid by Buyer and one-half to be paid by Shareholders in advance. Bank shall also be entitled to compensation for all out-of-pocket expenses it shall incur with respect to any distribution of stock required to be made hereunder. Expenses incur-red with respect to any distribution shall be borne by the distributee of the stock and shall be reimbursed to Bank at or before the delivery of the stock certificates by Bank.

4.3 Bank shall have no responsibility to Buyer, Seller Corporations, or Shareholders except those specifically provided herein and shall not be responsible for anything done or omitted to be done by it, except for its own gross negligence or wilful default. Buyer, Seller Corporations, and Shareholders covenant that they will not commence any action against Bank, at law, in equity, or otherwise as a result of any action taken or thing done by Bank pursuant to this Escrow Agreement, or pursuant to any written de-mand or authorization of Buyer as herein provided for, or for any distribution made as authorized herein upon failure of Buyer to give notice or make any demand within the times herein prescribed. Bank shall be entitled to rely conclusively on any notice, author-ization, or other document delivered to it hereunder bearing the signature of any execu-tive officer of Buyer.

4.4 All distributions required to be made by Bank to Buyer, Seller Corporations, or Shareholders hereunder shall be made in accordance with written instructions furnished to Bank by Buyer, except as otherwise provided in Paragraph 3.4 hereof, and all distri-butions so made shall be valid and effectual to discharge the liability to Bank with respect thereto. Bank shall have no liability under any circumstances with respect to the appli-cation of the proceeds of any distribution made by it.

4.5 Bank agrees that Buyer and Seller Corporations or Shareholders, if Seller Corpo-rations be dissolved, may, by mutual agreement at any time, remove Bank as escrow agent hereunder, and substitute an individual or a bank or trust company therefor, in which event Bank, upon receipt of written notice thereof, shall account for and deliver to such substituted escrow agent all shares of stock and cash held by it, less any amounts then due and unpaid to it for expenses as herein provided for, and Bank shall there-after be discharged of all liability hereunder.

4.6 It is contemplated by the parties hereto that Seller Corporations will wind up their affairs, liquidate, and dissolve within one year from the date hereof. Upon completion of the dissolution of Seller Corporations, Shareholders shall cause to be delivered to Buyer and Bank a certified copy of the Certificate of Dissolution of Seller Ohio and Seller Washington, whereupon Shareholders shall succeed, in proportion to their stock interests, to all of the rights and obligations of Seller Ohio and Seller Washington here-under.

4.7 Any notice, authorization, request, or demand required or permitted to be given hereunder shall be in writing and shall be deemed to have been duly given when mailed by registered or certified mail, postage prepaid addressed as follows:

To Seller Ohio and Seller Washington:

> Mr. Frank Perkins
> Seller Company
> P.O. Box 1
> Maine, Ohio 43120

To Shareholders:

> Mr. Tom Smith
> N. Main Street
> Maine, Ohio 43120
>
> Mr. John Jones
> S. Green Street
> Maine, Ohio 43120
>
> Mr. Richard Roe
> E. North Street
> New York, Washington 98310

To Buyer:

> Buyer Corporation
> P.O. Box 10000
> Marketplace, Pennsylvania 18105
> > Attention: Fred Martin, President

To Bank:

A United States Post Office registered or certified mail receipt showing delivery as aforesaid, shall be conclusive evidence of the date and fact of delivery. Any notice given hereunder shall be deemed delivered at the time of deposit in the United States Post Office.

Any party hereto may change the address to which notices are to be delivered by giving to the other parties not less than 10 days' prior written notice thereof.

4.8 This Agreement shall inure to the benefit of, and be binding upon the parties hereto and their respective heirs, executors, administrators, personal representatives, successors, and assigns.

WITNESS the due execution hereof as of the day and year first above written.

ATTEST: SELLER COMPANY, an Ohio corporation

_____   By_____
        Secretary   President

ATTEST: SELLER COMPANY, a Washington corporation

_____   By_____
        Secretary   President

WITNESS: SHAREHOLDERS:

_____   _____
                                         Tom Smith

_____   _____
                                         John Jones

_____   _____
                                                Richard Roe

                                   PARTIES OF THE FIRST PART

ATTEST: *BUYER, INC.*

                                   By _____
_____
        Secretary   *President*

ATTEST: *PARTY OF THE SECOND PART*

                                   By _____
_____

                                   PARTY OF THE THIRD PART

Investment letter. Where a buyer delivers stock to a seller's stockholders, and relies upon the non-public offering exemption contained in Section 4(2) of the 1933 Act to avoid filing a registration statement with the Securities and Exchange Commission, the buyer should have the seller's stockholders confirm their investment intentions by executing a form of investment letter. Such a form of letter may also be requested by the buyer's accountants to obtain added assurance of a continued equity interest on the part of the seller's stockholders, in rendering a "pooling of interests" accounting opinion. The request for an investment undertaking from a seller's stockholders may require serious consideration on the part of counsel for both the buyer and seller. From a seller's viewpoint, an investment undertaking may materially reduce the value of the consideration; the buyer's stock, which the seller's stockholders receive in exchange for the business they are selling. A form of investment letter is printed below.

Buyer, Inc.
P.O. Box 1000
Marketplace, Pennsylvania 18105

Gentlemen:

This letter is delivered to you pursuant to Section 9.05 of the Agreement and Plan of Reorganization dated as of   19   , to which agreement Buyer, Inc. (Buyer), Seller Company, an Ohio corporation (Seller-Ohio) and Seller Company, a Washington corporation (Seller-Washington) are parties.

In connection with the delivery to me by Seller-Ohio and Seller-Washington, in liquidation and dissolution of Seller-Ohio and Seller-Washington, of presently authorized by unissued shares of Common Stock of Buyer as contemplated by the provisions of said Reorganization Agreement, I hereby represent and agree that I will not take any of such shares of Common Stock of Buyer with a view to distribution of any thereof (as defined in the Securities Act of 1933, as amended, and the Rules and Regulations of the Securities and Exchange Commission thereunder) except to the extent permitted by and within the limits of paragraph (d) of Rule 133 of the Securities and Exchange Commission.

I agree that I will not transfer any of such shares of Common Stock of Buyer unless, in each such instance, a "no action" letter from the Securities and Exchange Commission or an opinion of counsel acceptable to you covering such transfer shall be obtained and if such opinion of counsel or "no action" letter so requires, the transferee of such shares shall furnish in writing to you an appropriate letter to the effect that such shares are being taken for investment and not with a view to distribution and agreeing further to the provisions of this paragraph and to the placing of appropriate legends upon the certificates for such shares.

I understand that if for some reason I am unable to obtain such a "no action" letter or opinion from counsel acceptable to you, and if I still desire to transfer or sell any of such shares of Common Stock under circumstances which would constitute a sale or distribution within the provisions of Section 5 of the Securities Act, Buyer will register under the Securities Act, such shares of Common Stock that are to be offered for sale on the following terms and conditions:

(a) I and the other shareholders of Seller-Ohio and Seller-Washington as a group shall have the right to call upon Buyer to file one registration statement covering a proposed public offering by giving written notice to Buyer on or before November 1st of any year of our intention to sell and the number of shares to be offered for sale, in which event Buyer will on or before January 31st of the year following the year in which such notice is given, file a registration statement on the suitable form covering such shares of Common Stock.

(b) In addition to the right given under (a) above, I shall have the privilege to call upon Buyer to register any of such shares of Common Stock whenever Buyer shall file a registration statement in connection with any secondary offering of its Common Stock, and Buyer shall give reasonable notice to me of any such intention to file.

(c) I shall bear and pay my fair proportion of all costs and expenses relating to the preparation and filing of the registration statement under (a) and (b) above, and all costs and expenses relating to the sale, consisting of transfer taxes, brokerage charges or commissions if the offering is non-underwritten, and underwriting commissions, spreads and fees if it is underwritten, and all other expenses (such as fees and disbursements of special counsel retained by me).

I agree that appropriate legends may be placed upon the certificates for any of such shares of Common Stock to give notice of the transfer restrictions set forth in this letter, and that I will indemnify Buyer and its directors and officers, and each person who may be deemed to control Buyer, with respect to all liabilities and expenses in connection with any distribution of any such shares.

I also understand that Buyer desires to treat, for accounting purposes, the acquisition of the business and assets contemplated by the Agreement and Plan of Reorganization as a pooling of interests. Accordingly, in addition to, and within the limitations of the representations and agreements made above, I also represent that I have no present intention of distributing or disposing of in any way during the first year after the closing of the transaction more than 25% of the shares of Common Stock of Buyer received by me nor during the first and second years after the closing of the transaction more than 50% of said shares in the aggregate. It should be understood that a change in circumstances may require me to change my position but I do not foresee any such change in circumstances at this time and I will advise you if any such change of circumstances occurs.

Very truly yours,

_____

To be signed by:
Tom Smith
John Jones
Richard Roe

Employment contract. Often as a condition precedent to closing, a buyer will require key employees of the seller to enter into employment contracts, either with the seller prior to acquisition or with the buyer simultaneously with the acquisition. Rather than annex such employment contracts to the acquisition contract, the parties may prefer to have the form of agreements prepared before the closing, and have executed copies exchanged at the closing.

ACQUISITION CONTRACT CHECK LIST

Printed below is a check list of acquisition contract provisions, organized to follow the format and headings developed in Chapters 12 and 13. Not every item in the check list will be included in a particular acquisition agreement. For example, where a buyer acquires assets the contract will normally not contain a representation or warranty of title to the seller's stock, and conversely, where the buyer acquires stock, the contract will normally not contain a "bulk-sales" act provision. The check list should prove helpful in determining whether any particular item may have been omitted from a proposed form of acquisition contract before the contract is executed.

A CHECK LIST FOR ACQUISITION CONTRACTS

General Statement of Agreement.

1. Are assets being acquired?
2. Is stock being acquired?
3. Will payment be made in stock?
4. Will payment be made in cash?
5. Is the transaction tax-free?
6. Is the transaction taxable?
7. Is the transaction a statutory merger?

ARTICLE I—Representations and Warranties of Seller.
(Where a seller owns stock in subsidiary corporations, the seller's representations and warranties should also be made with respect to the subsidiaries.)

    1.1   Seller's corporate status.
        (a) Proper organization of seller.
        (b) Capital structure of seller.

1.2 Seller's shareholders unencumbered title to their stock, and description of stock ownership.

1.3 Authority of seller's officers to act.

1.4 Seller's financial statements.

    (a) How many balance sheets are warranted?

    (b) Are profit and loss statements and statements of retained earnings warranted?

    (c) Are financial statements recent?

1.5 Necessary qualifications of seller to do business in foreign states.

1.6 Description of and title to property and assets.

1.7 Description of and condition of machinery and equipment.

1.8 Listing of patents, trademarks, tradenames and copyrights and infringement warranties.

1.9 Listing of contracts and suppliers.

1.10 Litigation.

1.11 Representations as to actions not taken since latest financials:

    (a) No issuance of securities.

    (b) No distributions on stock.

    (c) No mortgages or encumbrances.

    (d) No sale of assets.

    (e) No extraordinary losses or obligations.

    (f) No catastrophes.

    (g) No salary increases.

1.12 Tax returns and accruals.

1.13 Tax withholdings.

1.14 Government contracts renegotiation status.

1.15 Accounts Receivable.

    (a) Do any offsets exist?

1.16 Insurance.

    (a) Sufficient in amount?

1.17 Inventions and Improvement Disclosures.

    (a) Do they belong to seller?

    (b) Where are they located?

    (c) Will patent applications be executed?

1.18 No defaults under contracts.

1.19 Compliance with federal and local laws.

1.20 No liabilities except as stated in contract.

1.21 Non-declaration of dividends.

1.22 Buyer's stock taken for investment purposes only.

1.23 Truth of representations and warranties and no omission of material facts.

ARTICLE II—Representations and Warranties of Buyer.

2.1 Buyer's corporate status.

    (a) Proper organization of buyer.

    (b) Buyer's capitalization.

2.2   Status of Buyer's stock.
   (a) Classes.
   (b) Properly issued.
   (c) Listed on stock exchange.
   (d) Registered
2.3   Authority of Buyer's officers to act.
2.4   Seller's stock taken for "investment purposes" only.
2.5   Buyer's financial condition.
2.6   Non-violation of buyer's loan agreements.
2.7   Truth of representations and warranties and no omission of material facts.

ARTICLE III—Assets to be Acquired by Buyer.

3.1   All of seller's stock.
3.2   Substantially all of seller's assets.
3.3   Selected assets.
   (a) Clear definition of assets.
   (b) Exclusion of tax refunds.

ARTICLE IV—Payment of Purchase Price.

4.1   Tax-free acquisition
   (a) Payment in solely voting stock.
   (b) Assumption of liabilities.
   (c) Types of securities in statutory merger.
   (d) Formula price based on market value of stock.
   (e) Formula price based on future earnings.
   (f) Imputed interest.
   (g) Effect on price of dissenting shareholders.
   (h) Limitations on numbers of shares.
4.2   Taxable acquisition.
   (a) Allocation of purchase price.
   (b) Internal Revenue Code Section 1245 assets.
   (c) Internal Revenue Code Section 1250 assets.
   (d) Investment credit recapture.
   (e) Price stated as one lump sum.
   (f) Pricing of inventory.
   (g) Formula price based on future earnings.
   (h) Imputed interest.
   (i) Effect on price of dissenting shareholders.

ARTICLE V—Buyer's Assumption of Liabilities.

5.1   Assumption of all liabilities, unknown, contingent or otherwise.
5.2   Assumption of specified liabilities only.
   (a) Those disclosed in seller's balance sheet.
   (b) Disclosed litigation.

(c) Obligations under listed contracts and agreements.

(d) Obligations incurred in ordinary course of business since balance sheet.

(e) Other obligations specifically listed.

ARTICLE IV—Seller's Indemnification of the Buyer.

6.1 Indemnification against all but assumed obligations.

6.2 If seller is to be liquidated, indemnification by seller's principal shareholders.

6.3 Stock or cash placed in escrow to satisfy indemnification.

(a) Amount of escrow.

(b) Length of time of escrow.

(c) Gradual reduction of escrow.

ARTICLE VII—Seller's Conduct of the Business Pending the Closing.

7.1 Positive covenant to conduct business only in ordinary course.

7.2 Negative covenants not to:

(a) Issue securities.

(b) Make distributions to shareholders.

(c) Subject property to liens.

(d) Sell capital assets.

(e) Make substantial capital expenditures.

(f) Increase compensation.

(g) Incur any liabilities, except current liabilities in ordinary course.

ARTICLE VIII—Conditions Precedent to the Closing.

8.1 Buyer's conditions precedent:

(a) Seller's warranties and representations true at closing.

(b) Opinion of seller's counsel as to corporate organization, titles, etc.

(c) Certificate of seller's officer re: conduct of business since contract signing.

(d) Report of buyer's auditors.

(e) Seller's business not materially adversely affected by storm, etc.

(f) Seller's performance of all covenants.

(g) Tenders of resignation of seller's directors and officers.

(h) Delivery of secret processes.

(i) Delivery of invention and improvement disclosures.

(j) Employment contracts with key employees.

(k) Securities and Exchange Commission favorable opinion on "pooling of interest."

(l) Securities and Exchange Commission "No Action Letter."

(m) Investment letters from principal stockholders.

(n) Delivery of escrowed shares.

(o) Limitation on percentage of dissenting shareholders.

(p) Internal Revenue Service Ruling.

(q) Justice Department Ruling.

(r) Certified resolutions of seller's directors and shareholders.

8.2 Seller's conditions precedent:
(a) Internal Revenue Service Rulings.
(b) Opinion of buyer's counsel as to buyer's corporate status, officers' authority, validity of stock delivery, etc.
(c) Truth of buyer's representations and warranties at closing.
(d) Certified resolutions of buyer.
(e) Certificate of officer of buyer that all action properly taken.
(f) Buyer's business not materially, adversely affected by storm, etc.

ARTICLE IX—*The Plan of Reorganization.*

9.1 Stock for stock:
(a) Delivery of seller's stock properly endorsed.
(b) Minimum percentage of seller's stock acceptable to buyer.
(c) Payment of stamp taxes.
(d) Delivery of buyer's stock—no fractional shares.

9.2 Stock for assets:
(a) Documents delivering title to seller's assets.
(b) Certificate of amendment changing seller's name.
(c) Delivery by buyer of his stock.
(d) Retention of funds by seller to defray acquisition and liquidation expenses.
(e) Deposit of buyer's shares with agent for seller's shareholders—to match fractional rights.
(f) Assumption of liabilities by buyer.
(g) Liquidation and dissolution of seller.

9.3 The Statutory merger:
(a) Literal compliance with requirements of the state statutes involved.

ARTICLE X—*Brokerage.*

10.1 Payment of brokerage commissions.
(a) Parties indemnification of each other against brokerage claims.
(b) If broker involved, provision for party liable to pay.
(c) Terms of any written brokerage agreement.
(d) If broker involved, agreement should be reduced to writing.

ARTICLE XI—*General Provisions.*

11.1 Non-registration of shares of buyer's stock—or closing or post-closing registration of buyer's stock.
11.2 Access to investigate seller's business—buyer to keep information confidential.
11.3 Anti-trust escape clause.
11.4 Bulk sales clause.
11.5 Sales and use tax clause.
11.6 Employment contracts.
11.7 Pension and profit-sharing plans.
11.8 Pensions of previously retired employees.

11.9 Employee stock options.

11.10 Other employee benefit plans.

11.11 Collective bargaining agreement.

11.12 Employee security clearances.

11.13 Delivery and retention of books, records and classified documents.

11.14 Avoidance of selling shareholders receiving double dividend.

11.15 Transfer of assets to buyer's subsidiary.

11.16 Bank accounts—information as to amounts and signatories.

11.17 Novation of customer contracts.

11.18 Covenant not to compete.

11.19 State "blue sky" laws.

11.20 Publicity.

11.21 Specific performance—a legal remedy.

11.22 Survival of representations and warranties.

11.23 Due diligence of parties.

11.24 Right to waive failures of other party and conditions.

11.25 Further assurances of execution of additional documents.

11.26 Entire agreement in contract.

11.27 Governing state law.

11.28 Third parties.

11.29 Transactions and documents subject to approval of counsel.

11.30 Assignability of contract.

11.31 Execution of additional counterparts.

11.32 Date, time, and place of closing.

11.33 Notices.

In addition to many of the clauses check-listed in Articles I through IX, above, most acquisition contracts will have miscellaneous exhibits or schedules attached. What exhibits or schedules are to be attached must be determined from the agreement itself. For example, if patents form an important part of a seller's business, the contract may have attached to it a complete list of seller's patents and patent applications. Finally, the acquisition contract may provide for the execution by the parties of forms of supplementray agreements which are normally delivered at the closing.

A list of some usual exhibits or schedules as well as supplementary agreements follows:

Exhibits or Schedules

A. Financial Statements.

B. Seller and Subsidiary and Affiliated Companies or Entities of Seller—Capital Structure and Jurisdictions in Which Qualified to Do Business.

C. Outstanding Warrants, Options, or Subscription to Capital Stock of Seller and Entities.

D. Real Estate Owned by Seller.

E. Properties Leased by Seller.

F. Patents and Trademarks of Seller.

G. General Contracts of Seller.

H. Major Suppliers and Customers of Seller.
I. Description of Litigation.
J. Lists of Significant Stockholders.

Supplementary Documents

A. Indemnity Agreement.
B. Escrow Agreement.
C. Investment Letter.
D. Employment Contract.

CHAPTER 15

Closing and Post-Closing

The closing of an acquisition means the actual transfer of the legal title of property from the seller to the buyer which is contemplated in the acquisition contract. The execution and delivery of the acquisition contract fixes the rights and obligations of the buyer and seller to one another, and fixes the time and circumstances under which the acquisition is to be closed.

In closing a stock acquisition, title to the seller's stock, evidenced by stock certificates, is transferred to the buyer by endorsement and delivery of the certificates by the seller's stockholders. In closing an asset acquisition, titles to the seller's property is transferred to the buyer by proper bills of sale, deeds, or other documents of transfer. In closing a statutory merger, title to a seller's assets is transferred to the buyer by operation of law by filing a merger agreement or certificate of merger with the secretary of state of the state involved. In each type of acquisition, the closing means the time at which the actual transfer of legal titles from the seller to the buyer takes place.

The simultaneous closing. Sometimes the buyer and seller may sign the acquisition contract and close the deal all in the same day. Such a transaction is possible, and sometimes preferable, where the contract does not contain conditions precedent to the closing such as obtaining tax rulings or Securities and Exchange Commission opinions as to "pooling of interests" accounting treatment. For example, if the buyer is buying selected assets of the seller for cash, the execution of the contract and the closing of the deal at the same time may be preferable. This is especially true if inventories are a part of such a transaction, and the price of the inventories depends upon a physical count. The buyer and seller may agree upon the language of the acquisition contract in its entirety in advance (as well as upon the form of all of the closing documents), and the contract may contain a blank for the insertion of the price of the inventory. The buyer and seller may, then, jointly take a physical inventory of the seller's assets and fix the price to be inserted in the contract. The insertion of the price in the contract, and the signing and delivery of the contract, closing documents, and payment of the purchase price complete the transaction.

Fulfilling closing conditions. In many acquisitions, however, the closing is contingent upon obtaining rulings from governmental authorities or approval of stockholders, or listing or registering stock with a stock exchange or the Securities and Exchange Commission. For example, the acquisition contract may contain a condition precedent to the buyer's requirement to close that the Securities and Exchange Commission approve a "pooling of interest" accounting treatment of the transaction, or that the United States Department of Justice clear the deal from an anti-trust point of view. The seller may have conditioned its requirement to close upon obtaining a ruling from the Internal Revenue Service that the transaction be treated as a tax-free acquisition. Also, the contract may require the buyer to register its shares with the Securities and Exchange Commission or list newly issued shares on a stock exchange. In order either to obtain rulings or fulfill the mechanical requirements of registration or stock listing, circumstances may require the parties to sign an acquisition contract in advance, and provide, in the contract, sufficient time prior to the actual closing to permit the contract conditions to be met. In such instances the contract is signed, and then the closing takes place some time later—often as long as two, three, or four months later.

Closing—a mechanical process. Chapter 12 sets forth reasons why the acquisition contract is the most important document in any acquisition. The result of the investigation of the seller's business and all of the negotiations between the buyer and seller should be reflected in this contract; the signing of the contract fixes the rights and obligations of the parties to one another. Once the contract is signed, what follows, the fulfillment of the conditions contained in the contract and the formal closing follow the requirements and procedure set forth in the contract. In this sense everything that occurs after the contract is signed is purely mechanical, whether the steps taken are required by state laws, Securities and Exchange Commission Regulations, Internal Revenue Service Regulations, stock exchange regulations, or the conditions fixed in the contract—although these mechanical steps often require skill and and know-how for their proper execution.

Meeting regulatory requirements. Regardless of the conditions contained in the acquisition contract, federal laws, state laws, and requirements of other regulatory authorities may require the buyer and seller to take certain steps to pass title from the seller to the buyer, and conversely, to pass title from the buyer to the seller of the consideration paid. Since this book is limited to a discussion of acquisitions of industrial companies, specialized requirements imposed by governmental authorities such as the Interstate Commerce Commission, Federal Communications Commission, Civil Aeronautics Board, Federal Power Commission, Federal Reserve Board, or state utility or banking commissions are not discussed, and the discussion is limited to such governmental regulations as may affect industrial corporations generally.

SEC registration. Chapter 8 outlines the rules under which stock used in acquiring a seller must be registered with the Securities and Exchange Commission and the circumstances under which such stock is exempt from registration. If registration is necessary, the preparation of a registration statement on Form S-1 (including financial statements meeting requirements of the Securities and Exchange Commission) may consume a considerable period of time, and, after preparation and filing, more time will pass before it becomes effective. Therefore, as soon as the acquisition contract is signed, the buyer should immediately begin preparation of the registration statement to make it effective within the period specified in the contract.

To be realistic, the buyer and seller should generally allow a period of 90 days or more after signing the acquisition contract for the registration statement to become effective.

It is beyond the scope of this book to discuss all the details of the registration statement and what is required to be done. However, speaking generally, the full registration statement, referred to as Form S-1 provides for the inclusion of a mass of detailed information.

The prospectus, which forms Part I of the S-1 Registration Statement provides for the inclusion of the following information:

Part I

INFORMATION REQUIRED IN PROSPECTUS

Item

1. Distribution Spread.
2. Plan of Distribution.
3. Use of Proceeds to Registrant.
4. Sales Otherwise than for Cash.
5. Capital Structure.
6. Summary of Earnings.
7. Organization of Registrant.
8. Patents of Registrant.
9. Description of Business.
10. Description of Property.
11. Organization within 5 Years.
12. Pending Legal Proceedings.
13. Capital Stock Being Registered.
14. Long-Term Debt Being Registered.
15. Other Securities Being Registered.
16. Directors and Executive Officers.
17. Remuneration of Directors and Officers.
18. Options to Purchase Securities.
19. Principal Holders of Securities.
20. Interest of Management and others in Certain Transactions.
21. Financial Statements.

The above list of information required in an S-1 prospectus indicates the detail of information which must be gathered. In addition to the information required in the prospectus, Part II of the S-1 Registration Statement requires submission of the following:

Part II

INFORMATION NOT REQUIRED IN PROSPECTUS

22. Marketing Arrangements.
23. Other Expenses of Issuance and Distribution.
24. Relationship with Registrant of Experts Named in Registration Statement.

25. Sales to Special Parties.
26. Recent Sales of Unregistered Securities.
27. Subsidiaries of Registrant.
28. Franchises and Concessions.
29. Indemnification of Directors and Officers.
30. Treatment of Proceeds from Stock Being Registered.
31. Financial Statements and Exhibits.
Undertakings
Signatures

The financial statements submitted with the other information must comply with requirements set forth in Regulation S-X. Due to the detailed requirements for the form in which financial statements are to be set forth, it is wise to retain an accounting firm for preparation of the financial statements, which has experience with the requirements of the Securities and Exchange Commission.

The table of contents for Form S-1 provides as follows with respect to contents of financial statements:

Part III

Instructions as to Financial Statements

A. The Registrant:
    1. Balance Sheets of the Registrant.
    2. Profit and Loss Statements of the Registrant.
    3. Omission of Registrant's Statements in Certain Cases.
B. Consolidated Statements:
    4. Consolidated Balance Sheets.
    5. Consolidated Profit and Loss Statements.
C. Unconsolidated Subsidiaries and Other Persons:
    6. Unconsolidated Subsidiaries.
    7. Fifty-Percent-Owned Persons.
    8. Omission of Statements in Certain Cases.
    9. Affiliates Whose Securities Secure an Issue Being Registered.
D. Special Provisions:
    10. Reorganization of Registrant.
    11. Succession of Other Businesses.
    12. Acquisition of Other Businesses.
    13. Filing of Other Statements in Certain Cases.
E. Historical Financial Information:
    14. Scope of Part E.
    15. Revaluation of Property.
    16. Capital Shares.
    17. Debt Discount and Expense Written Off.
    18. Premiums and Discount and Expense on Securities Retired.

19. Other Changes in Surplus.
20. Predecessors.
21. Omission of Certain Information.

State "blue sky" laws. Chapter 6 summarizes briefly the effect of so-called state blue sky laws on acquisitions where securities form a part of the purchase price, and the effect of such laws should have been provided for in the acquisition contract. In some instances, notwithstanding that registration of securities is not required with the Securities and Exchange Commission under the Securities Act of 1933, a state will require registration with or notice to a state securities commission. Since state blue sky laws may void a buyer's delivery of its stock and give a seller the right to monetary recovery after receipt of a buyer's stock issued without compliance with such laws, before closing the transaction, the buyer should assure itself of compliance. Consider California law, since the California Corporation Code is probably as restrictive as the laws of any other state. To indicate the completeness of the information a buyer must reveal in its application for the qualification of its securities under the California Corporations Code, a standard form of facing page of an application is printed below:

Form No. 3
STANDARD FACING PAGE FOR APPLICATIONS
FOR QUALIFICATION OF ISSUER TRANSACTIONS

DEPARTMENT OF CORPORATIONS
FILE NO.
*(Insert file number of previous filings before
the Department, if any.)*

FEE: _____

*(To be completed by Applicant.
See instructions on reverse side.)*

Date of Application: _____

DEPARTMENT OF CORPORATIONS
STATE OF CALIFORNIA
FACING PAGE
*NOTE: INDICATE THE TYPE OF FILING BY CHECKING THE APPROPRIATE ORIGINAL
OR AMENDMENT APPLICATION HEADING SHOWN BELOW.*
APPLICATION FOR QUALIFICATION OF SECURITIES BY (CHECK ONLY ONE):
☐ *COORDINATION, SECTION 25111;*
☐ *NOTIFICATION, SECTION 25112;*
☐ *PERMIT, SECTION 25113;*
☐ *PERMIT, SECTION 25121;*
☐ *NEGOTIATING PERMIT, SECTION 25102 (c)*
OF THE CORPORATE SECURITIES LAW OF 1968.
☐ *Amendment number_____ to application filed under Section_____
dated_____(Check and complete if applicable)*

1. Name of Applicant _____
*2. State whether applicant is a corporation, partnership, trust or other entity, and the
State of incorporation or jurisdiction under which organized.*

_____
3. Address of principal executive office of applicant

Number and Street	*City*	*State*	*Zip Code*

4. *Name and address of person to whom correspondence regarding this application should be addressed.*

5. (*a*) (*b*) (*c*)

Title of each class of securities being qualified (e.g., "$10 par value common stock")	*Total number of shares or units of each class of securities being qualified in California (e.g., "20,000")*	*Proposed maximum offering price per unit (e.g., "$10")*	*Proposed maximum aggregate offering price for securities being qualified in California (e.g., "$200,000") Note: Fee calculated on total of this column*

(*d*) *Consideration to be paid for securities if other than cash and the value thereof, e.g., "Real Property, $100,000"; "Assets of a going business, $50,000."*

(*e*) *There is no adverse order, judgment or decree entered in connection with the offering by any State regulatory authority, any court or the Securities and Exchange Commission, except as follows: (if none, so state)*

6. *State whether this application is for a(n) open or limited offering qualification (check as applicable).*

☐ *Open*   ☐ *Limited*

7. *Applicant, if a corporation, is in good standing in the State of its incorporation.*

State corporation laws, the corporate charter and by-laws. In addition, the parties must comply with the corporation laws of the states involved. Chapter 7 outlines the requirement of various state laws that the shareholders of a seller approve a sale of assets by a required favorable percentage. Therefore, in an assets transaction, for the seller legally to convey assets to the buyer necessary shareholder approval must be obtained. The required approval may generally be obtained at an annual shareholders meeting or a special shareholders meeting called for the specific purpose of considering the sale of the assets of the seller. Not only the laws of the state of incorporation, but also the corporate charter or the by-laws of the seller, will fix the period of time which must elapse from sending notice of a meeting to the seller's shareholders and holding the meeting. Such period of time must, of course, be taken into account in establishing the timetable for the closing, and should have been taken into account in drafting the acquisition agreement.

Stock exchange rules. As noted in Chapter 6, under the Rules of the New York Stock Exchange a buyer must obtain the approval of its stockholders before the Exchange will list stock where directors or officers have an interest in the seller, or where an increase of 20 per cent in the outstanding stock of the buyer will result from the acquisition, or where the size of the buyer will increase by 20 per cent. Where the circumstances of an acquisition involve any of these three situations, the buyer must obtain approval of its shareholders although state law or its charter does not require such approval.

Disregarding the need to hold special meetings as a result of stock exchange rules, where a buyer is listed on an exchange and intends to utilize newly issued shares of stock to make an acquisition, it must generally list the stock on the particular exchange. Such listing involves the preparation of a listing application, normally not difficult, but nevertheless another item involving passage of time which must be prepared before the closing. For example, where the buyer will list stock on the New York Stock Exchange, the acquisition contract should provide for a period of approximately three weeks to prepare the application and obtain the approval of the application by the Committee on Stock Listings of the Exchange—although, when necessary, approval has been obtained in a shorter period of time.

Printed below is a form of application for listing on the New York Stock Exchange:

LISTING APPLICATION TO
NEW YORK STOCK EXCHANGE   *June 17, 197_*

BUYER

12,592 ADDITIONAL SHARES OF COMMON STOCK
IN EXCHANGE FOR THE ASSETS OF SELLER

Number of Shares of Common Stock issued and outstanding as of May 31, 197_: 5,553,610 (including 47,956 shares in the treasury)	*Number of Holders of Common Stock at May 31, 197_: 29,295*

DESCRIPTION OF TRANSACTION

The Buyer will acquire substantially all the property, assets, goodwill, and business, subject to stated liabilities of the seller in exchange for 12,592 shares of its Common Stock. No officer or director of the Buyer or any of its subsidiaries has any interest, direct or indirect, in the Seller.

The Seller manufactures and sells bicycles, wagons, and hobby toy items. This acquisition will afford the Buyer entry into that segment of the toy industry as an addition to its present products for the recreation and leisure-time field.

Reference is made to Exhibit A hereto for a description of the history and business and for the financial statements of the Seller.

The acquisition of the Seller will be treated as a "pooling of interests" for accounting purposes. Peck & Peck, independent public accountants of the Buyer, have reviewed the proposed accounting treatment and approve it as being in accordance with generally accepted accounting practice.

It is the present intention of the Buyer that the Seller will operate as a subsidiary in the recreational segment of its business.

RECENT DEVELOPMENTS

The buyer has released publicly notice of all important developments relating to its business.

AUTHORITY FOR ISSUE

On May 3, 197_, the Board of Directors authorized management to negotiate and acquire the Seller and on June 7, 197_, the Board of Directors approved the Agreement and Plan of Reorganization dated June 6th, 197_, and authorized the issuance and list-

ing of the 12,592 shares of the Buyer's Common Stock. No further corporate authorization is required for the issuance of the Buyer's Common Stock.

OPINION OF COUNSEL

There has been filed in support of the Application, the Opinion dated June 10, 197_, of Jones, Jones & Jones, New York, New York, stating that all proceedings necessary to authorize the issue of the shares of Common Stock covered by this Application in connection with said acquisition of the Seller, have been duly taken and the issue and delivery of certificates representing such shares of Common Stock of the Buyer have been duly authorized; that said shares when issued in the manner now contemplated will be validly issued and outstanding, fully-paid, and non-assessable with no personal liability attaching to the holders thereof under the laws of the State of Delaware, the State of incorporation of the Buyer, or under the laws of the State of New York, the State in which the Buyer has an executive office; and registration of said shares under the Securities Act of 1933 is not required since the issuance and delivery of such shares to the Seller for distribution to its shareholders (who have represented that they are acquiring the Buyer's Common Stock strictly for investment with no intention of selling or distributing any thereof in any manner which would render the issuance of such shares subject to the registration requirements of said Act) will not involve a "public offering" within the meaning of Section 4(2) of said Act.

BUYER

By   John Johnson
President

In addition to the above, the listing application includes a balance sheet, a statement of income and retained earnings, a description of the history and business of the seller, an accountant's report and an officer's certificate as to the accuracy of the financials, which have here been omitted. Also, the Exchange may require other supporting documents such as an opinion of the counsel as to the need to register the buyer's shares, an accountant's opinion as to "pooling of interests" accounting treatment, an undertaking to advise the Exchange when the shares have been delivered for the purpose described in the listing application, and other documents which may be pertinent to the particular listing of the stock. The above form of listing application, upon approval, is subject to receiving "official notice of issuance," since stock may not be listed unless it has actually been issued. Where the buyer's transfer agent does not attend the closing, the transfer agent will officially notify the Exchange of the issuance of the stock after it gives the certificates to the custodian (normally an officer of the buyer) for delivery at the closing. Upon receipt of notice from the transfer agent, the stock is listed by the Exchange. Then after the stock has been delivered at the closing in exchange for the seller's assets or stock the custodian should send a notice to the Stock Exchange that the transaction has been completed. A form of such notice is printed below in this chapter. On the other hand, where the transfer agent attends the closing, the agent normally will not give official notice of issuance until the transaction has been closed.

Meeting requirements imposed by the contract. In preparing for the closing, in addition to compliance with the requirements of federal and state authorities and other public bodies, such as stock exchanges, the parties must comply with all of the conditions and covenants contained in the acquisition agreement. In addition to requiring delivery of title documents such as deeds and opinions of counsel, many acquisition contracts contain conditions precedent to the closing, i.e., conditions which must be fulfilled before the closing may take place. The remainder of this chapter contains discussion of some major contract conditions precedent and what should be done to fulfill them.

Tax rulings. One condition precedent frequently present in the contract is the prior receipt by one or both parties of a tax ruling from the Commissioner of Internal Revenue that the acquisition will be a tax-free acquisition. The application for such a ruling should be made to the Commissioner of Internal Revenue, Rulings and Corporate Reorganization Division, Washington, D.C. No standard form of ruling application exists. However, as a suggested basic approach to the ruling application, the applicant should reveal all facts and circumstances of the proposed transaction in the application. The ruling should, of course, also set forth the applicant's contentions and the sections of the Internal Revenue Code under which it believes the acquisition should be treated as tax-free. If a favorable ruling is obtained, a copy of the ruling will be required to be attached to the income tax return of the applicant filed for the fiscal year in which the acquisition takes place.

Normally, a revenue agent examining the tax return will accept the tax effect of the transaction as expressed in the copy of the ruling attached to the return. However, if there is a deviation in the form of the transaction as it actually took place from the form of transaction as proposed in the ruling application and repeated in the ruling itself, the examining agent, may, if circumstances warrant, take the position that the acquisition is taxable, in spite of the ruling.

Anti-trust clearance. The United States Justice Department is willing to consider proposed acquisitions to determine whether they would violate the anti-trust laws. Experts in the field, however, often advise the parties not to avail themselves of this opportunity to obtain an informal ruling from the Justice Department. In those instances where the parties fear that the acquisition may result in a violation of the anti-trust laws, particularly Section 7 of the Clayton Act discussed in Chapter 6, the acquisition is such a borderline case that the consent of the Justice Department will probably not be forthcoming. Therefore, in borderline situations it is often advised that the parties make their own determination and act accordingly.

However, in those instances where the contract provides for prior clearance of the acquisition with the Justice Department, the parties may approach the Justice Department on an informal basis. Either the buyer or seller may make an appointment with the Justice Department and then describe the details of the proposed acquisition. In coming to its conclusion, the Justice Department will naturally request material such as the form of the proposed acquisition agreement, financial and distribution data of the industry involved, the relationship between the buyer and seller and other miscellaneous items such as major supplier and customer contracts and distributorship agreements. Should the parties be fortunate and obtain Justice Department clearance, they still, however, have no binding assurance that the Federal Trade Commission may not institute a proceeding to upset the acquisition on its own initiative.

The S.E.C. "no action" letter. Where the contract provides that the buyer will not register its shares with the Securities and Exchange Commission, the seller, or in some instances the buyer, may wish to obtain assurance from the Securities and Exchange Commission that registration of the buyer's stock will not be required. The method of obtaining such assurance is through the issuance by the Securities and Exchange Commission of a so-called "no action" letter. Application is made in writing to Chief Counsel, Division of Corporate Finance, Securities and Exchange Commission, Washington 25, D.C. Pertinent details of the transaction are laid before the Commission. If the Commission has any problems in issuing its "no action" letter, it will generally make this known to the parties and an informal conference may be arranged to delve deeper into the transaction.

Miscellaneous preparations. In preparing for the closing, in addition to obtaining opinions or rulings mentioned above, the lawyers for the buyer and seller must carefully study the acquisition contract to determine the additional documents required under its terms for closing the transaction. For instance, the contract will probably require an opinion of the seller's lawyer that the seller is duly qualified and in good standing in named states in which it does business. If so, the seller's lawyer should obtain certificates of good standing of the seller from the Secretary of State or other state authority of such states before he renders his opinion. If the contract requires warranties on the part of the seller or an opinion of the seller's lawyer of status of the seller's real estate, title companies or local counsel should be engaged to search titles, and either provide a title search, title insurance or render an opinion of the status of the titles. In an assets transaction, where employment contracts or other contracts may be non-assignable by their terms, consents to the assignments of these contracts should be obtained. In addition, lawyers for both parties should commence preparing closing documents such as bills of sale, deeds to real estate, legal opinions, and miscellaneous certificates of officers of the buyer and seller required by the contract. Procedurally, the preparation for closing requires a detailed study, listing and preparation of all documents required for the closing, plus agreement by the lawyers for the buyer and seller, prior to the closing, that the documents are in proper form. In this connection, the lawyers for both the buyer and seller should prepare drafts of the necessary documents and exchange the drafts well in advance of the closing to assure that both counsel are satisfied and that no unexpected difficulties with forms of documents will arise at the closing.

Conducting the closing. As well as preparing for the closing, the lawyers should carry the burden of conducting the closing. Purely as a matter of client relationship, the attorneys for both parties should prepare for the closing as carefully as possible. Clients will become impatient if, at the closing, necessary documents have not been prepared in advance and the closing is delayed to amend or prepare such documents. Where stock is exchanged for stock, often the closing may be quite simple. On the other hand, where assets are being acquired closing the transaction may require many title documents to be exchanged, and unless careful preparations have been made, the closing may become emotional and tedious. In those instances where numerous documents must be exchanged, the lawyers may arrange a pre-closing exchange of executed documents, to be held in escrow, making the actual closing as painless as possible.

The closing check list. By the time the day of the closing arrives, the lawyers should have prepared and agreed upon a closing check list. The check list should list all documents which must be exchanged, indicating which party is to deliver specified documents and which party is to receive them. As a further means of expediting the closing, the check list should contain appropriate columns for the buyer and seller to acknowledge delivery or receipt of closing documents. The lawyers should determine in advance the parties expected to attend the closing and include their names and relationship to the transaction at the beginning of the closing check list. Each check list must, of course, be tailored to the provisions of the particular acquisition contract involved; however, as a possible aid in preparing future check lists printed below is a form of closing check list utilized in an acquisition where the buyer's stock was exchanged for the seller's assets, where the seller consisted of two separate corporations, one an Ohio corporation, and the other a Washington corporation, and the assets of both corporations were being acquired by a subsidiary of the buyer in exchange for common stock of the buyer. In this transaction, the selling Ohio corporation owned the stock of a number of subsidiaries, including a Canadian company and a Mexican company.

The form of check list follows:

ACQUISITION

OF THE ASSETS OF

SELLER COMPANY, an Ohio corporation

and

SELLER COMPANY, a Washington corporation

by

BUYER SUBSIDIARY

a Delaware corporation and
wholly owned subsidiary

of

BUYER

MEMORANDUM OF CLOSING

*January 14, 197_*

A closing with respect to the transactions contemplated by that certain Agreement and Plan of Reorganization ("Agreement") dated as of November 15, 197_, by and among Buyer Corporation ("Buyer"), Seller Company, an Ohio corporation ("Seller Ohio"), and Seller Company, a Washington corporation ("Seller Washington"), was held at the offices of Buyer in Marketplace, Pennsylvania, on January 14, 197_.

I. Persons present.

Attending the closing were the following:

On behalf of Buyer:

D. F. Jones—Executive Vice President
M. C. Roberts, Jr.—Vice President and General Counsel
J. F. Smith—Assistant Secretary

On behalf of Seller Ohio:

D. Johnson—President
John J. Right—Secretary

On behalf of Seller Washington:

> *John J. Right—President*
> *D. Johnson—Secretary*

On behalf of Buyer Subsidiary, a Delaware Corporation:
> *F. Jones—Vice President*
> *J. F. Smith—Assistant Secretary*

On behalf of First National Bank of Marketplace, Pennsylvania:

> *William Roe, Vice President and Trust Officer*

On his own behalf as a Shareholder:

> *John J. Right*
> *A. Olsen*
> *D. Johnson*

II. The Closing.

The following documents were delivered on the closing date, or included in the closing documents as of such date. All transactions at the closing were deemed to have taken place simultaneously and no transaction was deemed to have been completed and no document was deemed to have been delivered until all transactions were completed and all documents delivered. For convenience of reference, Buyer Subsidiary, a Delaware corporation, is referred to herein as "Subsidiary."

AS TO THE REORGANIZATIONS

1. *Agreement and Plan of Reorganization dated as of the 15th day of November, 197_, among Buyer, Seller Ohio, and Seller Washington.*
2. *Schedules A through G to the Agreement.*
3. *Appendix I to the Agreement—"Allocation of Consideration."*
4. *Appendix II to the Agreement—"Accounting Principles for the Preparation of Financial Statements for the Determination of Contingent Share Payments."*
5. *Appendix III—form of "Escrow Agreement."*
6. *Appendix IV—form of "Investment Letter."*
7. *Form of "Agreement of Employment" for:*
   a. *D. Johnson*
   b. *John J. Right*
8. *Form of "Indemnity Agreement" to be executed by Messrs. Johnson, Right and Olsen, as Shareholders of Seller Ohio and Seller Washington.*
9. *Letter Agreement dated November 15, 197_, among Buyer, Seller Ohio, and Seller Washington concerning submission of certified financial statements.*
10. *Indenture transferring all property and rights to Subsidiary by:*
    a. *Seller Ohio*
    b. *Seller Washington*
11. *Assignment of Intangible Assets to Subsidiary by:*
    a. *Seller Ohio*
    b. *Seller Washington*
12. *General Warranty Deeds and Title Insurance Binders for Real Property listed on Schedule D, Item a.*
13. *Deposit records for transfer of all bank accounts of Seller Ohio and Seller Washington. (omitted)*
14. *Endorsements of all insurance policies of Seller Ohio and Seller Washington to Subsidiary.*

15. *Assignments in form for recording of all patents, patent applications, trademarks, and license agreements listed on Schedule F to Subsidiary.*

16. *Receipt for payment and bill of sale for equipment acquired from equipment Lessor by Seller Ohio.*

17. *Receipt and Satisfaction Piece for Real Estate mortgage executed by Jamestown National Bank.*

18. *Certificates of stock of subsidiaries of Seller Ohio endorsed as follows:*

Entity	No. of Shares	Endorsed to
Seller of Canada, Limited	21,000	Subsidiary
Seller Interamerica Corp.	300	Subsidiary
Seller Europa	994	Subsidiary
	1	Buyer
	1	M. C. Roberts, Jr.
	1	D. F. Jones
	1	E. J. Townley
	1	L. P. Lista
	1	J. E. Mann
Seller de Mexico, S.A. de C.V.	246	Aviles*
	1	Bananera*
	1	Romeo*
	1	Rodriguez*
	1	Milo*

* Held under declaration of trust for Subsidiary.

19. *Certificates of Title to Motor Vehicles, endorsed in blank:*
    a. *Seller Ohio*
    b. *Seller Washington*

20. *Certificate of Chief Executive Officers of Seller Ohio and Seller Washington pursuant to Section 9.01 of the Agreement.*

21. *Opinion of Seller's attorney, John Jay, Esquire, pursuant to Section 9.02 of the Agreement.*

22. *Investment Letters executed by:*
    a. *John J. Right*
    b. *A. Olsen*
    c. *D. Johnson*

23. *Certificate of Treasurer of Seller pursuant to Section 10.03.*

24. *Opinion of counsel for Seller pursuant to Section 10.02 of the Agreement.*

25. *Employment Agreements between Subsidiary and*
    a. *John J. Right*
    b. *D. Johnson*

26. *Receipts for certificates for a total of 155,556 shares of the One Dollar par value Common Stock of Buyer as follows:*

	No. of Certificates	No. of Shares
a. Seller Ohio	7	128,023
b. Seller Washington	2	27,533

27. *Assumption of certain liabilities of Seller Ohio and Seller Washington by Subsidiary.*

28. *Escrow Agreement among Seller Ohio, Seller Washington and Shareholders and Buyer and The First National Bank of Marketplace, Pennsylvania, Escrow Agent.*

29. *Receipt of Escrow Agent for 15,555 shares of Common Stock of Buyer with executed Stock powers attached, received from:*
    a. *Seller Ohio*   *12,802 shares*
    b. *Seller Washington*   *2,753 shares*
30. *Indemnity Agreement executed by Shareholders.*

SUPPORTING DOCUMENTS

As to Seller Ohio:

31. *Certified copy of Resolutions of the Board of Directors, approving the Agreement and calling a special meeting of the stockholders.*
32. *Certified copy of resolutions of the stockholders approving the Agreement, authorizing the liquidation and dissolution of Seller Ohio and authorizing the change of Seller Ohio's name to X.Y.Z. Liquidating Corporation.*
33. *General release by officers and directors of Seller Ohio for all liability except for compensation due and unpaid at the closing date, rights under pension and profit-sharing plans, and distributive rights on dissolution.*
34. *Certificate of Incumbency of Officers of Seller Ohio.*
35. *Certificates of Good Standing for Seller Ohio and its subsidiaries in the jurisdictions of their organization.*
36. *Amendment to Articles of Incorporation to change name in form for filing.*

As to Seller Washington:

37. *Certified copy of Resolutions of the Board of Directors, approving the Agreement and calling a special meeting of the stockholders.*
38. *Certified copy of resolutions of the Stockholders approving the Agreement, authorizing the liquidation and dissolution of Seller Washington and authorizing the change of Seller Washington's name to X.Y.Z. Liquidating Inc.*
39. *General release by officers and directors of Seller Washington for all liability except for compensation due and unpaid at the closing date, rights under pension and profit-sharing plans and distributive rights on dissolution.*
40. *Certificate of Incumbency of Officers of the Seller Washington.*
41. *Certificate of Good Standing in the State of Washington.*
42. *Amendment to Articles of Incorporation to change name in form for filing.*

As to Buyer:

43. *Certified copy of Resolutions of the Board of Directors adopted November 22, 197_, ratifying the execution of the Agreement and authorizing the issuance of a total of not to exceed 310,000 shares of the Common Stock of Buyer, the filing of a Listing Application with the New York Stock Exchange, the incorporation of Subsidiary and extending the appointment of Buyer's Transfer Agent and Registrar to the Common Stock authorized to be listed.*
44. *Certificate of Incumbency of certain officer of Buyer.*
45. *Listing Application to New York Stock Exchange and related supporting documents.*
46. *Instructions to Transfer Agent and Registrar and related supporting documents not elsewhere included.*
47. *Custodial Letter to New York Stock Exchange.*

As to Subsidiary:

48. *Copy of Certificate of Incorporation and By-Laws, Minutes of Incorporators Meeting and First Meeting of Board of Directors.*

49. *Certified copy of Minutes of the Board of Directors meeting held January 2, 197_, authorizing receipt of assets of Seller Ohio and Seller Washington and execution of agreements assuming certain of the liabilities of Seller Ohio and Seller Washington and the filing of applications of Subsidiary for qualification as a foreign corporation in the states of Ohio, Washington, and California.*
50. *Certificate of Incumbency of certain officers of Subsidiary.*

POST CLOSING DOCUMENTS

As to Buyer:

51. *Telegraphic notice of issuance of stock to New York Stock Exchange with copies to Transfer Agent and Registrar.*

As to Seller Ohio:

52. *Certified copy of Amendment to Articles of Incorporation.*

As to Seller Washington:

53. *Certified copy of Amendment to Articles of Incorporation.*

As to Subsidiary:

54. *Telegraphic notice of filing of qualification papers in Ohio and Washington.*
55. *Certified copy of Minutes of Special Meeting of Shareholders held January 14, 197_.*
56. *Certified copy of Minutes of Special Meeting of Board of Directors held January 14, 197_.*

Publicity and Notices. The buyer and seller should agree, in advance of the closing, the publicity, if any, which should be ready for release on the closing day. In many instances, the buyer and seller may have issued a press release at the time of signing the acquisition contract, or before that time. Whether or not the parties have previously issued press releases, they should consider what further information they may wish to make public at the time of closing, and if they decide that any further announcements would be advantageous, a press release satisfactory to both the buyer and seller should be prepared, and be ready for release as soon as the closing has taken place. In addition, the parties should prepare, in advance, all notices which they deem desirable to persons with whom the seller has been doing business, such as customers, suppliers, service organizations, lessors and banks, and to the seller's employees. As previously indicated in this chapter, where a buyer is listed on a stock exchange and uses stock to make an acquisition, if the stock is newly issued it must be listed on the particular exchange involved. The form of listing application filed with the New York Stock Exchange is normally approved subject to a notice of issuance to be given by the buyer's transfer agent either after delivering the stock certificates to the custodian, or after the closing where the transfer agent attends the closing. In addition, if the transfer agent does not attend the closing, as soon as the closing has taken place a notice of closing, generally in the form of a telegram, should be addressed to the stock exchange involved. Printed below is a form of notice of closing in the form of a telegram addressed to the New York Stock Exchange:

MR. JOHN SMITH
NEW YORK STOCK EXCHANGE
DEPARTMENT OF STOCK LIST
11 WALL STREET, NEW YORK 10005

THE 42,911 SHARES OF COMMON STOCK OF BUYER WERE DELIVERED TO-
DAY TO THE SELLER IN EXCHANGE FOR ITS NET ASSETS.

FRANK JONES

Each company listed on the Exchange has a particular person in the Department of Stock List who handles the company's listing and is the person to whom the notice is generally addressed.

Notice to seller's stockholders. Where a buyer has acquired the assets of a seller, the seller is left with the consideration paid by the buyer, whether cash or stock. In winding up its affairs, the seller normally distributes the cash or stock it holds to its stockholders in exchange for the stockholders' certificates of stock in the seller. Printed below is a form of notice to a seller's stockholders of a distribution of a buyer's stock together with a transmittal form for the seller's stock, as well as instructions for transmittal of the seller's stock certificate:

TRANSMITTAL AND ORDER FORM

(To accompany certificates for Common Shares of the former Seller, Incorporated)

Dated: _____

UNION TRUST COMPANY, Exchange Agent
1102 Green Street
St. Louis, Missouri 63101

Gentlemen:

Pursuant to the Plan and Agreement of Reorganization between the former Seller, Incorporated (now ABC, Inc.) and Buyer Company, the undersigned herewith surrenders for extinguishment the following certificate(s) for Common Shares of the former Seller, Incorporated (now ABC, Inc.) in exchange for certificate(s) for shares of Common Stock of Buyer Company:

Certificate Number _____   *Number of Common Shares*

_____   _____

              _____

Total Common Shares Surrendered   _____

Please deliver certificate(s) for Common Stock of Buyer Company in the name and to the address shown below in the stencil impression, unless other instructions are indicated below.

In connection with any fractional share interest in Common Stock of Buyer Company to which the undersigned is entitled, you are authorized to buy or sell a fractional share interest as indicated below. You are authorized to sell such fractional share interest if no instruction is indicated.

☐   *BUY for my account the fractional share interest in Common Stock of Buyer Company which, when added to the fractional share interest to which I am entitled, will equal a full share. I will pay you for the cost of purchase upon receipt of your bill.*

☐   *SELL for my account and send me a check for the proceeds of the fractional share interest to which I am entitled.*

Note: Use ONLY if the name in which the new stock certificate(s) and check (if any) are to be issued or the address for record is different from that shown in the stencil impression below.	Use ONLY for special mailing or delivery instructions. Mail ( ) Deliver ( ) to: ......at......

PLEASE NOTE CAREFULLY THE INSTRUCTIONS ON THE OTHER SIDE

100-10-1000

Sign here......

Please sign exactly as your name or names appear at the left.

Please insert Social Security or other identifying number.

JOHN A. JONES
00 PARK AVENUE
NEW YORK, N.Y. 10017

Zip Code—

DO NOT WRITE IN SPACE BELOW

Number of Shares Surrendered	Entitled to Receive	Fractional Share to Be Purchased	Fractional Share to Be Sold	Full Shares to Be Issued
				$ Amount of Check or Bill

INSTRUCTIONS FOR SURRENDERING CERTIFICATES

Upon surrender of certificates for Common Shares of the former Seller, Incorporated (now ABC, Inc.) the holders thereof are entitled to receive certificates for full shares of Common Stock of Buyer Company at the rate of .76 of a share of Buyer Company Common Stock for each such Common Share surrendered. Such Common Share certificates should be surrendered promptly in accordance with the following instructions:

1. This Transmittal and Order Form must be properly signed and there must be enclosed the certificates to be surrendered. If you send in your certificates by mail, it is recommended that you use registered mail for your protection.

2. If the Buyer certificates are to be issued in the name of the registered holder of the surrendered certificates, the surrendered certificates need not be endorsed and no stock transfer taxes will be payable.

3. If the Buyer certificates are to be issued in a different name from that in which the surrendered certificates are registered, the surrendered certificates must be endorsed

or accompanied by appropriate stock powers and the signature in the endorsement guaranteed by a bank or trust company having a New York City or St. Louis office or correspondent, or by a member firm of the New York, American, or Midwest Stock Exchange. Endorsements by trustees, executors, administrators, guardians, officers of corporations, attorneys-in-fact, or others acting in a fiduciary capacity must be accompanied by proper evidence of the signer's authority to act.

4. No Fractional Shares of Buyer Company Common Stock Will be Issued. Prior to the close of business on March 28, 197_, a holder surrendering his Common Shares who would otherwise be entitled to a fraction of a share of Buyer Common Stock, may elect either to purchase an additional fractional share interest or to sell the fractional share interest to which he is entitled. Such election must be indicated on this Transmittal and Order Form at the time certificates are surrendered. Each shareholder electing to purchase a fractional share interest will receive a bill therefor from St. Louis Union Trust Company, the Exchange Agent. Each shareholder electing to sell a fractional share interest will receive a check for the proceeds as promptly as practicable.

Promptly after the close of business on March 28, 197_, the Exchange Agent will sell, for the account of the holders thereof, the number of full shares of Buyer Common Stock equivalent to the sum of any fractional share interests, as indicated by certificates for Common Shares which have not yet been surrendered. Thereafter, the Exchange Agent will hold and will pay to such holders or their duly authorized transferees upon surrender of their Common Share certificates the pro rata proceeds of such sale.

To the extent possible, the Exchange Agent will offset orders for purchases and sales of fractional share interests and will make purchases and sales of the Common Stock of Buyer as necessary to settle the balance of orders not offset. Such purchases and sales will be effected on the New York Stock Exchange at current prices prevailing on such Exchange. In the case of matching transactions, purchases and sales will be settled on the basis of the closing price of the Common Stock of Buyer on such Exchange on the last day preceding such matching on which the Common Stock of Buyer was traded on such Exchange. Purchases and sales of fractional share interests will be charged with any applicable service charges, brokerage commissions, or transfer taxes.

Integrating the seller's employees. A major element in every business consists of the employees, the people who keep the organization functioning efficiently. Preparing these people for the take-over of the seller's business by the buyer should be one of the important considerations of both the buyer and seller as the closing date approaches. If the buyer maintains pension, profit-sharing, hospitalization, group life insurance, or other fringe benefit plans, the status of the buyer's new employees under such plans should be explained to the employees by the personnel department of the buyer. A careful and thoughtful approach to the new employees will help achieve an orderly transition, causing the change in status from employee of the seller to employee of the buyer to be less fearsome to the seller's employees.

However, in spite of all the care taken prior to the closing, additional effort on the day of the closing or immediately thereafter will further help to allay the fears of the seller's employees. Many approaches are available. Should the closing take place at the seller's place of business, an informal meeting of the seller's employees at which an officer of the buyer presents the buyer's plan for the continued success of the seller's business and the continued employment of the employees, together with descriptions of fringe benefits which the buyer will make available, may be most effective. If a personal statement is not practical, the chief executive officer of the buyer may send a letter welcoming each new employee and describing the buyer's business in general terms as well as the employee's status in the new organization. In approaching its new employees, the buyer should bear in mind that the seller's business consists to a large extent of individuals, each of whom, due to human nature, will have fears and worries concerning the effect the acquisition will have on him individually.

Integrating the seller's business. Finally, in the process of integration, the seller's business procedures should be altered to coincide with the procedures of the buyer. The process should commence as soon as possible and in this connection meetings between personnel from the buyer's and seller's buying, manufacturing, selling, advertising, accounting, insurance, and personnel departments should be held promptly after the closing to plan an orderly transition. In general, a form of notice to each department involved should be distributed by the buyer. From a mechanical point of view such a notice should concern itself with accounting procedures, insurance coverage, bank accounts, authorized signatures on such accounts, forms of notice, the type of letterhead to be utilized, automobile registrations, and other details involved in the everyday conduct of a business.

Index of Forms

Index

Q

R

S